perry boys
ABROAD

perry boys
ABROAD

THE ONES WHO GOT AWAY

IAN HOUGH

Pennant Books

First published in paperback 2009
by Pennant Books

Text © Ian Hough 2009

Foreword © Andy Mitten 2009

The moral right of the author has been asserted.

British Library Cataloguing-in-Publication Data:
A catalogue record for this book is available from
The British Library

ISBN 978-1-906015-38-1

Design & Typeset by Envy Design Ltd

Printed and bound in Great Britain by Clays Ltd, St Ives plc

*Every reasonable effort has been made to acknowledge the ownership of copyright
material included in this book. Any errors that have inadvertently occurred will be
corrected in subsequent editions provided notification is sent to the publisher.*

Pennant Books
PO Box 5675
London W1A 3FB
www.pennantbooks.com

Ian Hough can be found online at http://thenamelessthing.com and http://perryboys.com

For Mark Stephen James Kelly

CONTENTS

One day your life will flash before your eyes. Make sure it's worth watching.
— Unknown

ACKNOWLEDGEMENTS

Kim – for being here always. I love you.

Cass – for contributing and publishing.

Colin Blaney – cheers for all the stuff, mate.

Carl H. Spiers – for his bit, and for Ged's story.

Rob W – for a better and truer Manchester.

CCR – thanks a million, mate, for keeping the faith.

Robin Peters – for your story and co-operation.

Mellow Yellow – don't go mental.

Dominic Lavin – for humour in the heart of darkness.

Jeff Marsh – your steamer's/smuggler's accounts were much appreciated.

Johnno – for tales of Down Under and latter-day decadence in Blighty.

Scally Jeff – for making me laugh myself silly on many a night, in many a bar, right up till yesterday.

Pete – for putting some red Ancoats sausage into the late 80s.

Killer, Jock, Bungle, Rob, Manc, Scouse – if you ever buy/nick this and read it, let me know what you think.

Kenny Lewis – for introducing me to some major heads and being my mate since 1977.

Pete Lewis – for the cover picture.

The 'Unknown Scouser'.

All other contributors – Dave-D-, Spanish Dave, Cockney John, Oxford Gary, Roger et al.

Anyone I've ever travelled and gone bananas with.

Dave Hewitson – you are The Man.

Mum and Dad – for having me.

Zara – for forcing me to type this with one hand while bawling in my earhole . . .

INTRODUCTION

By Andy Mitten – founder of
United We Stand fanzine

It wasn't always so easy to get to European away games. Before 1996 and the subsequent boom in budget airlines, air travel was for a wealthier minority. When stories were recounted from trips in the 70s and 80s, you were as likely to hear of a week-long trans-Europe trek by train and ferry. The sight of the white cliffs of Dover meant that Manchester was only half a day away. Ports like Harwich, Ostend and the Hook of Holland were regular drinking venues, as were the train hubs, Aachen, Brussels or Köln. Not any longer.

My first Euro away was as a callow 17-year-old on a Scandinavian pre-season tour in 1991. Around 20 of us travelled, most funding the trip by selling swag to wedged 'Scandis'. Most of the lads journeyed in an ageing, suffocating mini-bus from Manchester via seedy dens of iniquity in Amsterdam and Hamburg. We cheated though, considering a £180 flight to Copenhagen a bargain, and booked through the Student Travel Association. From Denmark we caught a train and ferry to Sweden, then another rattler north to Gothenburg. Accommodation was a spartan campsite in the woods. Sir Alex Ferguson encouraged travelling fans to mingle with the team back then when United's best-paid player, Bryan Robson, was on £3,000 a week.

Football was only part of the package. Wine, women and song – make that beer, getting blown out by the local honeys and chanting – were the other attractions on these voyages of discovery. If there was a local scam to be worked out, the lads were onto it within minutes – whether it was a ten-pence piece being worth five times as much in a vending machine or the use of shining Volvo estate hire cars for free. Their endeavours were not always successful and two lads were briefly jailed. They returned to the campsite raving about the quality of Swedish prisons, their beds, bathrooms and prison-issue pyjamas. It beat camping, apparently.

Euro-travel changed irreconcilably with budget airlines. Where once the wily had planned routes to Budapest on travel tickets which had to be acquired through a knowing contact or fan-organised charter, now a £20 flight to Bergamo was a few mouse clicks away and accessible to all. We used Easy Jet's only plane for the first time to Juventus away in '96, a circuitous route via Luton to Nice. It was an eye opener. Wasn't air travel supposed to be luxurious? Deprived of free peanuts and Heineken, blinded by the orange uniforms and even more orange fake tans, one Red stood up as the plane taxied us to our destination and said he'd never use such a 'peasant airline' again. (He did.)

And so did many, many more. Some say it was too many, as aways then became a free-for-all. But such was the elixir of travel that some lads continued to journey the globe, even when United weren't playing. And even when they were, what was the point in going to Turin for the fourth time when you could visit Krakow or Prague for a score? Some are still on the road, or permanently settled in Thailand or Spain, a Mancunian diaspora to rival the Lebanese, Irish or Galicians.

Football took provincial working-class lads to see United in Istanbul, Russia or America. As United took their football to the world, so that world opened up to those who ventured out to see them.

Andy Mitten
April 2009

PROLOGUE

British football supporters love to drink and love to fight. We also love to travel, to sing and to hear music. This combination has made football the national pastime in Britain's cities and towns. It's also created armies of drunken drug-fiends in foreign designer gear who live for their weekly fix of fun.

Much of the thrill comes from simply being on foreign ground; running amok in your home town is *good*, but doing it in someone else's is *better*. Doing it in another country is best of all, especially when the locals are considered dangerous. The Golden Age of all this was the 70s and 80s, but the 90s and 00s have seen foreign travel become an end in itself, with or without a game to go to. In short, there's more than football out there.

As a friend put it recently, 'I grew up eating chips on Blackpool Prom, but these days it's bird's nest soup and tigers' balls in fuckin' Thailand!'

The British are given to contradictory attitudes that confuse foreigners; politeness and loud obscenities go hand in hand. We gladly explore this great, stinking, sexy planet whenever the opportunity presents itself. Even when we love our football team back home, the temptations of distant places are many: the unfamiliar squelch of alien mud, the strange aroma of exotic women and drunken sunsets over tropical hinterlands. Run-ins with moody natives and policemen in strange uniforms are common. And it matters not if we're skint or wadded. The have-nots of yesteryear now have much, but class awareness remains strong.

'Class' has a blurred meaning today. Football's Disney-like makeover is forcing the working-class elements out, even those wealthy enough to go abroad regularly for football or recreation. The legacy of terrace song passed from father to son has been rudely interrupted. Traditional three o'clock Saturday KOs are extinct. The atmosphere at once-intimidating football grounds like Old Trafford is mocked by visiting away fans. There's something missing.

Exotic or high-pressure away matches now appeal more than home games to the original 70s and 80s hardcore. This generally means games against the so-called Big Four, or 'European nights'. The British travel well, like India Pale Ale. They're generally found in much higher numbers than their foreign counterparts, sleeping rough, cramming into cheap hotel rooms and boozing in public squares. The Germans and French, on the other hand, do not travel well (like expensive wines), and are mocked by us for this failing. Travelling Brits are a social phenomenon of recent years; a 1970s groom-to-be would relish a major piss-up with his mates down the town, but today stag parties in New York, Amsterdam and Bangkok have become the norm. A Ricky Hatton fight at the MGM Grand attracts thousands for a long weekend in Las Vegas. When I was a kid, Vegas may as well have been the dwarf planet Pluto.

As the menu has changed from chips to tigers' testicles, so the latter quarter of the 20th century is as distant from us as the Stone Age. And what an age: men in flares wreaking havoc and daubing graffiti on walls with paint and brush. Despite general poverty, supporters of teams like Manchester United and Leeds travelled in vast numbers through the wind and rain. Football grounds resonated with regional accents across the length and breadth of Britain, an exhilarating soundtrack or prelude to violence of mass proportions. But behind the scenes, a trickle of supporters was escaping beyond the confines of Europe.

Brits had been flying the nest since the 50s, and it was a purely one-way affair; Australians certainly weren't clamouring to live in the UK. The modern exodus started in the football grounds of the 1970s, where songs and booze were the antidotes to gales and drizzle.

Many of those old terrace chants were based on popular music or traditional songs; Man United's 'Down where the lights are flashing / we're goin' City bashing' was sung to the tune of 'Scotland the Brave'. 'We had joy, we had fun / we had scousers on the run' was United's version of 'Seasons in the Sun'. And our FA Cup anthem, 'Que sera sera' is taken from – of all things – a Doris Day song. Music brings football fans together, but it cleaves the tribes elsewhere.

In mid-70s Manchester, the northern soul crowd in narrow pants, polo shirts and boat-pumps had been labelled 'Perry boys' after the polo shirt named for tennis star Fred Perry. These trendsetters were possibly the first to dictate the direction of brand marketing, but not the last. They were more clubland than football crowd, but in time a crossover occurred which spawned designer hooligans and paved the way for Madchester. Music had driven youth trends into many factions over the past few decades, but it was the Sex Pistols who stole the day. Notwithstanding Lennon's 'Working Class Hero', punk rock preserved the words 'fuck' and 'cunt' officially on virgin vinyl. This was important; as the older generation threw the towel in, the media became youth's oyster.

But punk died. Brand marketing and football filled the '78-'79 fashion vacuum in England's Northwest, with the help of a lively underground/overground scene featuring bands like Buzzcocks, Magazine and, in our Prestwich neighbourhood, the Fall; Mark E. Smith lived in the area, and the band's name was spray-painted in four-foot-high letters along a wall we passed daily on our way to school. Buzzcock Steve Garvey had also attended our school, the notorious Heys Road Secondary Modern, a few years earlier. The retrospectively-fabled Joy Division hadn't quite the same appeal for 'normal' football lads back then, but today the story has been twisted; increased access to information via a maturing media and the internet means everyone now knows the history of coolness in Manchester, or thinks they do. Unfortunately (for them) the past is solidified and congealed. It cannot be changed.

Manchester was always a queer place and difficult to pin down. It abhorred pop culture, favouring mass humility over the arrogant punk planet surrounding it. Clubs like the Factory in Hulme functioned as a dark stop-gap between Manchester and England. The Factory was a brooding bunker manned by those bored by the Carnaby Street postcard that punk had become. It reflected an energised city whose music sounded like youthful insecurity and machinery.

Late-70s Liverpool adopted a spikier post-punk look, John Cooper Clarke-style: mohair jumpers, drainpipe pants and jelly sandals composed a uniform quickly usurped by more sophisticated attire among football supporters. Scouse taste in music differed from Manchester's, too; the rough-arsed footy lads packing Eric's nightclub to see Deaf School were completely unlike the Factory's Oxfam-clad intelligentsia. Scousers were also the first to mesh street/club/football terrace fashion en masse. Additionally to small collars and narrow trousers they sported a hairstyle known as the wedge, a girlishly-layered side-parting, both retro-mod and futuristic. It had long been the hairstyle of soul boys, its androgyny typically English. The Manc version of this phenomenon was slower to propagate than the scouse one. But they got there in the end, courtesy of an attitude-injection by David Bowie that propelled soul style into the future. These second-generation Perries were now going to football as much as nightclubs. When they encountered the scouse style, Mancs were impressed. Scousers proudly held up their carrot to what they believed to be a Manc donkey, but they were mistaken. It was a zebra. These untameable pioneers fed on adrenalin and lived for the moment it 'went off'. But violence wasn't the problem; it was just symptomatic of an imprisoned ape gone mad, the means to an end.

Grafters worked markets, food-stalls and pubs in the 1970s. They sold flags, t-shirts and scarves to fans at Britain's major football grounds. As with all trades, over-exposure to their commodity created a derogatory attitude towards it. They undermined the football scarf as a symbol of allegiance, creating a vacancy which needed filling. The bland post-punk canvas enabled the composite acquisition of previously unrelated ski-wear, jeans and tennis shoes. Tight-knit grafting 'firms' hit Europe, cherry-picking Lacoste and Adidas from under the noses of naïve shopkeepers and the broken glass of smashed façades. This thing was about travel, but travel was only one part of it; journeys can occur within as much as without.

Many who attended the Factory in the late 70s were students, not hooligans. A decade later it happened again, only this time it was the Hacienda providing the spills, chills and Eccles cakes. By then, those of the casual persuasion had completely replaced the student crowd. Manchester finally arrived, having lagged behind Liverpool and London in the national imagination for decades. Both the hooligans and the bands of Manchester appeared to have suffered a form of cultural amnesia in the interim. The hooligans insisted they were always bang into artsy underground music, while the musicians insisted they'd always been huge footy supporters. The truth lies somewhere in between.

By the mid-80s travel, drugs, music, fashion and football provided a DIY recipe for thrills. When electronica hit Ibiza, psychedelics were its biochemical chaperone. For some though, Europe wasn't far enough away; trips to Greece and Spain were superseded by the Americas, Australia and the Far East. East Asian prostitutes and forgers captured westerners' imaginations with their ingenious fakery, be it sexual or simply an ability to manufacture identical replicas of all and any western commodities, from digital watches and sunglasses to designer clothing. Orlando and Sydney may have replaced Majorca and Ios, but any of those cultures could be instantly forgotten or counterfeited on the swarming streets of Bangkok.

Snide goods had always been sold on old-fashioned British markets but, in the 1990s, the internet would open new doors as cyber-grafting went mainstream. Two distinct travelling populations now existed: the Mad Dogs, who'd disappeared off the radar to distant outposts, and those who settled in England but frequently hit the continent for football or partying. Just as punk rock had rode in on rare winds from New York a decade earlier, the rave culture rode out on holiday jets to the islands of Tenerife and Ibiza and to mainland Spain in the late 80s. In the early 90s the formation of the European Champions League also reintroduced football to the cultural blender; the hooligans were finally invited to the party, with mixed results. It was to be expected. When full of lager and ecstasy many people wouldn't have known Balearic beat from the Miami Sound Machine, but who gives a fuck when it's *fun*?

European football, the concert swag game and German construction had already sent thousands onto the continent to wreak havoc. Beyond this, Israel's kibbutz system, the famous 'Magic Bus' to Greece and fruit-picking opportunities elsewhere caused the number of British youngsters hitting the trail to slowly multiply. New York, Miami, Sydney and Bangkok provided destinations for lads who were grafting, or growing and smuggling marijuana. Some bought snide merchandise and sold it on eBay to designer sportswear fetishists back home. Some travelled great distances to buy the genuine article for much the same reason. The opportunity to live a sun-blasted desert existence with only huge spiders and snakes for company was grasped by others with both hands. Los Angeles, Morocco and tropical Mexico were all given a good going over by those little sharks that never seemed to stop moving. Some returned triumphant, others were reduced to shells by drugs or imprisoned for smuggling. A few barely made it back at all, or only in body but not in mind.

England is noted for its ability to merge the vintage with the futuristic, as the co-existence of Saxon artefacts, British cars and London's finest architecture testifies. The transition from traditional to techno was a comfortably easy one for us to make. Football hooligans in labelled sportswear devolved into hippie-like creatures in flares. The numbers involved in organised violence shrunk to a fraction of what they'd been in the early 80s. Madchester was a hybrid beast, a modern classic. The media of the time appropriated our secret dictionary of slang, albeit in a half-arsed form. Scally pop bands and warehouse parties reunited football and music like the soul-mates they truly were. Suddenly everything was 'sound' and the appearance of pop groups grew distinctively casual. The long-swarming nests of grafters and hooligans burst from their underground lair and were welcomed by a culture hungry for realism. And what could be more real than bands of veteran Manc monkeys, swinging to the beat and proclaiming their love of drugs and Manchester United? Unfortunately the high water mark would break and recede, leaving an anti-social brood in its wake, allegedly an entire generation of post-ecstasy hoodies or chavs.

And so we find ourselves in a new millennium. The lads who laid the foundations for the travelling football fan today find themselves rejected. Others who settled and paid off their homes now own them outright, spending their extra money on several foreign holidays per year. Those who created the appetite for travel to football matches are priced out of the domestic market while this nouveau middle-class displaces them and buys up season tickets. The lads still provide support at Euro aways though, because travel is *cool*.

But the story is more complex than that. Many of those who introduced foreign culture to Britain remain stubbornly entrenched in modern stadiums, a shrinking but always loud voice of dissent. Others left Britain behind and began new lives far away, homesick for the sense of humour and the sport, but content to bask in hot weather, drink cold beer and view the growing cable and satellite networks which beam in live English Premier League games. Mad dogs eat mad dogfish and chips in the noonday sun wherever you may wander, the British influence cast far and wide.

Like my first book, *Perry Boys*, this story isn't just about our culture's leaders and its famous criminals. It's about the average scallywag, the ones who truly *made it* a culture or a mass movement. Embark on this journey with us. These are the tales of the ones who got away. Maybe you're one, too. If so, I hope this book brings back memories. If not, welcome to our world.

PART ONE
SWAG

I

A WORLD LIT BY FIRE

Try the House of Fun … it's quicker if you run
— Madness

We never went abroad when I was a kid. We couldn't afford it. As a result many questions would surface from my mind about 'foreign countries'. I devoured facts and figures about these places and Manchester's relative position to them. The fact that the sun set over America fascinated me. I lived in a terraced street not far from Trafford Park and its adjoining Salford Docks. A place of many chimneys and coal fires. The dusky southwest sky was a sea of black and red. The distant sounds of monstrous industrial processes pulsed through the air like the roar of a gargantuan robot. Somewhere beyond all that industry lurched a vast bowl of tranquil blue water. There were other countries, other people and wild animals there. I wanted to see them in the flesh.

We left that satanic place when the high-rise towers of Salford appeared and the old streets were depersonalised and demolished. We moved to a new house close to a colliery and power station. One day my dad pointed at the grey, top-heavy housings of the lifts that carried miners deep underground. He said, 'Yer ancestors were dinosaurs. The forests they once lived in 'ave turned to coal now. We're usin' that coal to keep ourselves warm in winter. When the dinosaurs lived 'ere it was tropical. The sunshine that helped the trees grow comes out when we burn the coal. Our 'ouse is heated by sunshine from millions of years ago.'

This seemed strange because our new house had central heating. It was amazingly clean, like living in the future. Needless to say, my questions and my confusion grew exponentially. This planet was fucking insane (and so was my dad).

3

In 1973 industrial action plunged Britain into darkness. The robot Gargantua was dead and fire was our only friend. Homes were lit by candles. The flickering shadows were a chaotic, primeval substitute for black and white television. I quite liked it myself. The days were short and dim and you didn't have to be an Apollo rocket scientist to work out that cold temperatures were *not recommended*.

But a chink of light began to penetrate the grey. Rob W of Salford, still in secondary school in late 1975-76, remembers a sight he saw walking through the centre of Manchester one day while 'wagging' school.

'I often think back to a day immediately before punk came in,' Rob says. 'I saw a woman walking past the Royal Exchange Theatre. She was dressed very smartly, like a secretary: sensible shoes, pencil skirt, nice hair and a pillbox hat. Everything about her was meticulous, apart from one thing: her entire ensemble was magenta, including the hair. I later discovered that this woman was Bette Bright from the Liverpool band Deaf School. The funny thing is, if this had happened just a few months later I'd never have remembered her, because things had changed so much by then.'

Rob W will provide further glimpses, into the primeval rock-pool of Manchester's Factory era later. Through it all, football and fashion melded so tightly to the music that it was difficult to tell where one ended and the other began. As a young kid I was agog at Old Trafford, like an ape-child in the face of a space-age marvel. It took several attempts before I finally breached those hallowed turnstiles, but then I was reborn; crush barriers and terraces, a sea of red seats, the cantilever roof, the executive boxes and the smoked glass of the Grill Room, all were fixed in that unearthly radiance cast down by the giant floodlights. They magically illuminated the green pitch on a winter's afternoon like surreal stars.

Replica football kits were a new fetish item back then. Being poor in 1977, Christmas was my one hope of ever owning one. I remember nervously scrutinising the only red home shirt I ever had like it was a lunar astronaut suit. As the crackers and glasses of sherry made the rounds, I couldn't believe I'd finally managed it. Mentally obsessed by that stadium and feeling unworthy of the colours, I made my trembling way into the world of Manchester United. I was branded for life, penned in behind those red railings with the other animals, my heart held aloft on a roasting rod, sacrificed to the immortals who stroked that white leather pill about the park. United were an integral part of Salford culture, and back then the craze for wearing team colours was at its height. It wasn't until I was much older that it occurred to me I might never have supported United at all – though quite how that could have happened, I'm not sure. United are bigger than anything to most kids growing up in Manchester. The claims by other clubs that we're all cockneys and out-of-towners are ridiculous.

And there were oddities; Cousin Trevor supported City even though he came from Ordsall but his scarf was kept well invisible. Years later he sampled the fizz of Old Trafford and was soon coming to games every week. At one game against Norwich, Trev announced, 'If we score, I'm gonna slap that bald cunt in front of us right on the top of the head.' United scored and his hand came down in a cupping arc. The thunderclap was even louder than the roar in the Scoreboard End and Kezz, who was also there, loved it.

It was Kezz's first ever United match (he'd passionately supported City before) and he was hooked on the craic from that day forth. City were a top club back then though. Their true strongholds were across the city in Manchester proper, or at least the portion of it that lay to the east and south of the centre. The general perception I had was that Salford was red and Manchester was blue. Perhaps because of the team's colours, City cast a cold vibe, like an institution. United, on the other hand, felt warmer, more like a family. A dim awareness was developing in my mind that United was more than just a football club; it was a religion.

Football was the opium that distracted us from society's fashion quagmire; flared trousers, big collars and assorted hippie Americana more befitting the buffoonish look of a Burt Reynolds movie. The 60s mod phase was a high watermark on the British sartorial seawall, but what came after represented stagnation in thought and being. We toiled for years, fighting bad goonery until travel opened that magic door. The flickering candles of the 70s were both literal and metaphorical; a world hit by power cuts, lit by fire and populated by cavemen.

Music, bizarre fashion, adventure and football riots were four cardinal points on a straining compass that was searching for something, but never quite found it. But we were curious. The adventurous point on the compass grew like an inquisitive tendril. Cheap jet fuel and a room in a newly-constructed concrete jungle on the Med began a stuttering stream which quickly became a river. Package holidays to Spain were a status symbol as the great unwashed flocked off on airliners to enjoy a fortnight of English breakfasts, Sunday roasts, *Daily Mirror*s and British pubs, the whole length of the Costas. Some bold groups immediately began to explore the possibilities, often staying on the move and stealing all they needed on a daily basis. Blackpool, Tenby, Morecombe, Brighton, Margate and Scarborough were all exposed for their failings back home. People reached for those faraway lagoons instead.

In 1977 young kids like us were running rampant at home, oblivious to the dawn of the grafters already travelling around Europe. The lads I grew up with were many in number and they were insane, all of them. Our street was alive with football and chatter. Adults in our world were poor people. Most hadn't travelled unless they'd been in the armed forces or sailed from Salford Docks on Manchester Liners. My Uncle Norman had been a merchant seaman and his favourite country was New Zealand. Several other family friends and acquaintances had sailed from our city. My mum's side of the family was a collection of dockers and sailors from Salford and Liverpool. (My middle name, Bernard, came from a great uncle who'd been the captain of a merchant ship.) The Northwest was a place full of nomads.

35 miles up the road, scouser Robin Peters had an early exposure to travel via his father's time in the service. It fuelled a desire to do one, to go out and see the world. Peters was to become a grafter as a young man, working Europe's stadiums, robbing shops and whatever else he could. He recalls the tales from childhood that first set his mind-a-reeling:

'Me ol' feller often sat me on his knee and told me stories of his seafaring and Second World War days. He spoke about places like Rio de Janeiro, Hong Kong, Fremantle and Manhattan in the 30s. He gave me the bug to travel, and since then I've been lucky. I've travelled to those places, more often than not living on my wits. I also heard about the time a German fighter pilot gave him a walk over after the fall of France in 1940. He must have thought me da was a Frenchman and decided not to shoot him on a fly past. Me ol' feller always said he didn't like to talk about the war, except on Sunday afternoons when he'd come in bevvied from the Half Way House pub.'

We'll be seeing a bit of Peters' grafting and thieving expeditions on the continent later.

Kenny Lewis was a mate whose dad had been in the forces in Korea. Kenny himself was to embark on long-distance travel when he grew older and I'll be telling you about some of it here. Kenny ended up living in Australia, but Ken Senior died in January 2009. He was a great man and he turned out two brilliant lads in the twins, Pete and Kenny, both of whom appear on the cover of this book.

Kezz was another case altogether. He wasn't much for travelling. He was more for sticking the nut on people and cracking razor-sharp jokes at everyone's expense. Athletically catlike from an early age, he earned a reputation for explosive viciousness and merciless humour. The neighbourhood was tagged with all our names, painted and magic-markered on many surfaces, but somehow Kezz's name always managed to stand out. He had an answer for everything and led us on loads of mad expeditions into enemy territory.

The six-week holidays seemed to last an age in the 70s. Summer-holiday mornings meant American animation or the European Children's Film Foundation. We looked forward to *The Banana Splits*, *Spiderman*, *White Horses* and *Belle and Sebastian*, an intoxicating blend of zany New World swagger and quieter continental sensibility. But Kezz and I spent most of dawn-till-dusk exploring unknown neighbourhoods and parks. His dad had been a seaman in the Royal Navy and this was a source of great pride to him.

Back then the RAF based an air show in Heaton Park. Planes thundered overhead while we played in the local woods, pretending we were deep in the jungles of foreign countries we'd never seen. The air show coincided with a large construction project in Prestwich Clough. Diggers and dumper trucks gouged out entire hillsides to insert large concrete and steel pipes. Our dens and hiding places were obliterated. Lancashire was becoming Greater Manchester and they made sure we knew it. The earth-movers and the incessant rush of low-flying triangular objects wheeling above created a wild, alien sense of change. As a small child I'd witnessed high-rise towers replacing ancient streets in the inner city. The same thing was happening here in a different way. It was obvious that humans had experienced a sudden acceleration in their development, and it involved the appearance of big, scary machines that flew about and built things very fast.

*   *   *

Inner-city Manchester always had a reputation for poverty and crime, but back in the 70s the nature of that crime was somehow saner and more justified. The network of terraced streets and high-rise flats surrounding central Salford and Manchester was a forbidding world to outsiders. Its denizens spoke with a rare accent, unbroken from Moss Side to Salford to Collyhurst, to the frightful precincts of Newton Heath and Ardwick. Gorton's Belle Vue Zoo was a recreational marvel among council estates. Not far away was a massive indoor bus depot, steaming dark and cavernous, full of diesel fumes: Hyde Road.

This zone of aural distinction, whose voice was utterly absent from all media of the time, was like a secret we shared. There was a sense of belonging that only we were qualified to recognise. The accent altered slightly from place to place, but only true natives could detect the differences. It would take many years for this animal to see the light of day in British broadcasting. Kezz, originally from Moss Side, was one such specimen, a lad whose words flew off his tongue like spearmint, direct and colourless. This was proper 'Manc', the rainwater-clear, streamlined jazz lingo that sounded more black than white. Saturated in intimidating vibes, it caused the instincts to bristle in genetic response.

At night, the entire area was a sodium-lit puzzle best left to those who hailed from the brickish holes and entries. Millions of smooth, rounded cobblestones reflected the yellow streetlights like rivers of shaved heads. In time, the cobbles were ripped up and replaced by asphalt and tarmac, and the character of the natives was similarly changed. Back in the old days it was a macabre trip to walk through the inner city at night – as my family did often, not owning a car – but in later years it became outright dangerous; outsiders accidentally caught there were picked off in seconds and stripped clean, like cumbersome beasts gripped by a vicious tropical stream. The piranhas have grown in number over time and it no longer matters if it is day or night. It is the way of the world, unfortunately.

Ancoats is a fabled area in north Manchester. Right off Piccadilly, it has inspired tales of gangsters and Victorian 'Scuttlers' for generations. CCR was an old-school Ancoats lad who in time moved away. He remembers the area well:

'In the beginning there was Ancoats. Postcode M4. How it missed being M1 always bugged me; was anywhere else closer to town? Ancoats in the 60s was loads of red brick dilapidated mills, empty warehouses and small streets. You'd be content to live in M4 with a garden of cobbles and broken glass. The streets throbbed with life. Every fucker knew every fucker else, and their business. Nothing went unnoticed. Nothing went unpunished.

'A huge Italian influx to the area showed in the quality of cloth on Saturday-evening display when pubs and spielers filled up. Italian names dominated the school registers, local barbershops and ice cream merchants. The area had style; sharp suits, razor-cut hair, knitted wool ties passed right down to the 16-year-old up-and-comers. Impregnate a young girl on our estate and your lifestyle choices became limited to two: Get out of Dodge *completely*; move towns. Better still, move counties . . . Or marry her – with a collective of bent-nosed uncles acting as best men.

'Those streets spawned the mighty Bengal Tigers back in the 1890s. The mills and streets hadn't changed a bit. The worst of the slums were now on the deck but the local tendency towards parochial gang violence remained untouched nearly 100 years since the Scuttlers ruled. The lads were still at it: Salford, Miles Platting, Collyhurst, Harpurhey. Crews met in battle and were summarily dispatched to Manchester Royal Infirmary. In the absence of anything tastier on the menu Ancoats fought itself. Street versus street, school versus school, pub versus pub.

'The last great unifying influence on the whole area was when the "gypos" pitched up on the croft. Middle-aged blokes strutted down streets, knocking on doors, asking if yer dad was back from work yet. The dads of the manor were massing up to take on the colourful Romany invaders. Impressive sight: 20-odd old fellers marchin' off to war. Shirt sleeves being rolled up en route. Watches wrapped in hankies. Woe be-fuckin'-tide your family if yer ol' feller gave this one a swerve. We watched the scrap from the coarse gorse surrounding the croft. Ten wagons had arrived. They may as well have put them in a circle, because this was no joke. Huge fistfight, no tools, *mano a mano*, great crack altogether. Invaders vanquished, defending heroes off to toast victory in the Cob'o Coal pub – first round on the house, complimentary alibis all round.

'The soundtrack of the street was Piccadilly Radio 261; happy-clappy 60s pop beats with cheese-flavoured DJ's. Towards the end of the decade Motown was the new rooster in the henhouse. To chat up inner-city Manc birds you had to know yer Detroit Spinners from yer Emeralds. The Temptations' 1969 monster, "I Can't Get Next to You", played on the hour every hour from the bedroom window next door; Julie, flighty-looking, bottle-black hair, plucked eyebrows, short leather mini-coat, white boots, tight sweater packed into it. First crush? Oh yeah, baby. I've had a thing for black eyeliner and candy-pink lips ever since.'

There were indeed alien species that prospered here, and not just Romany folk; men who'd made a small adjustment to their position on the globe by a couple of degrees of latitude. They'd moved into the area from Glasgow, or Eire, and had quickly found rich, unexploited avenues along the shadier side of the street. These individuals extended their tendrils into the local broth. Their gang came to be named after a brand of chocolates made by Mackintosh, called Quality Street, an alternative to Cadbury's Roses. Manchester was heading for distinction as a Metropolitan County and within a decade would sever all ties with Lancashire. A Quality Street advert appeared during the first ever screening of the soap opera *Coronation Street*, with the 'Quality Street Gang' alighting from a black vintage car in the form of a succession of naughty-looking blokes. The Scots' fast-growing organisation had found its brand amid the clashing ironies that framed the modern era.

A code of silence ruled the area with an iron fist, and mothers, daughters, fathers and sons shared a sense of place that is rare in an industrialised country like England. Manchester and Salford contained numerous indoor and outdoor clothing and food markets, street vendors and freelance wheeler-dealers more befitting Africa or Asia than northern Europe, whose vestiges remain today. Indeed, the Far East was the source of much of the counterfeit or 'Jekyll' (Jekyll and Hyde = 'snide') clothing sold on Manchester market stalls, often imported by Asians but sometimes by whites with the right connections. The poorer neighbourhoods were a riot of snide clothing. Places like Salford Precinct and Collyhurst oozed an almost tragic air of sartorial forgery; towels, shirts, jumpers, rags and trousers flapped in the wind that whipped about the balconies and courtyards of the terraced streets and estates, while within a young army was being prepared for a new dawn in organised crime.

The red roses and the soap opera were both hopelessly outdated, even then. The game was all about quality, and the name of the game was grafting. Grafting encompassed both selling and thieving, though not necessarily in that order. The selling was done at markets, street corners and stadiums, and the thieving was done everywhere. The commodity ranged from football scarves and flags to digital watches and kids' toys. From the petty shoplifter to the jewel fence to the barrow boys on the fruit 'n' veg stalls in town and souvenir sellers at Old Trafford, everyone played according to underworld protocol. Like any code it was fairly manageable until it hit foreign soil, then it was a case of who dares wins.

As the culture expanded into the continent, guided by clever innovators, horizons swelled and expectations created a hierarchy of grafting excellence. Young grafters working the Manchester streets were serving an apprenticeship for bigger things abroad. Colin Blaney was a young man who grew up in this ecosystem, in the flats of Collyhurst. Blaney's dynamic autobiography, *Grafters*, is an intense story of how young men in north Manchester easily made the transition from young scallywags on the streets to enlisted foot-soldiers for those who ruled these labyrinths. Blaney's book is a unique glimpse of a world ill-represented even in the currently fashionable body of 'thug' literature. Blaney remembers his baptism as a traveller well, and relates it here:

'I had been to Europe the first time back in 1966 on a school holiday to Blankenberge, not far from Oostende,' he remembers. 'The very first day see us all on the rob with me getting nicked and then bringing it right on top, as the lads all got pointed out by the women staff whose shop we'd robbed blind as they was opening up. What a start to my travelling life! Then in 1975 I had gone over to France working the grape and apple picking season, with a scouser who was not really up for the hot day's work in the fields. Scouse tried his best to get a strike going; "Typical Mickey," I thought to myself. Anyway, after a few weeks we robbed a till which felt at that time as though we'd done the crime of the century. We only got £300! Those two times, when I got back into Blighty, the mind was full of erotic thoughts; the style of the wonderful women and their classiness and panache, the aromas of the food which was so special at that time period, like garlic and coffee and the strong cigarettes they smoked over there. It was all so foreign yet so superior to what we were used to, if I'm gonna be honest. The cafés were too good to be true, the décor and the general layout of it all. Gorgeous outdoor tables, with big open fronts, long stainless steel and glass counters with loads of dead strong beer on tap all along them. You could stroll in a café and find cheese butties that tasted like angels had made 'em. There was rabbit meat in garlic sauce, aubergines and courgettes. Never seen anythin' like it in me life. We'd drink coffee from bowls for breakfast, and dip croissants in it, like the French did, but fighting back our hangovers just to get something down our Gregory Pecks. The boutiques were loaded with top-notch stock, the Frogs being experts at puttin' on the Ritz. The easy pickings when it came to cash and clobber would always flood my brain, and we thought it was just a phase in the beginning, but it proved to be more than that. We acted like we'd discovered it back in the 70s, but to the Frogs it was just a way of life. So I suppose there was no way that stuff would ever go away, yet in a way I thought it was just me getting carried away. It was a certain trip to France with Manchester United in 1977 that was to seal my fate for life.'

Blaney's escapades in France will be revisited later as a key moment in an era which recruited hundreds, if not thousands, of young English lads, all willing to jump on the bandwagon and do a bit of grafting abroad.

This was the Premier League of British skulduggery, and competition for a place on the lowest rung of the Manchester crime ladder was fierce for Blaney and his crew, as he describes:

'After I finished *Grafters*, it got me thinking what I should write about next. I was bangin' me head on the wall, rememberin' the hard times, how even when we was the wide awake-ist fuckin' boys in town there was still plenty of other cunts waitin' in the wings ready to knock us out. It wasn't like we was swannin' round Manchester an' every cunt was lappin' us up. We had to fight for every bit of recognition we got. There was always the older blokes in the QS, the Scottish-Irish fellers who ran it all, and other lads from Ancoats and Collyhurst who had our numbers from when we were little kids. I couldn't put a number on how many crews were operating round the area, never mind the number of individual lads sharp as fuck and ready to pounce on every opportunity like fuckin' sharks. You had to be on top of your game every minute of every day, and it was a jungle. I wondered where I'd go and live after I'd travelled for a bit, after *Grafters* came out and all that. It soon dawned on me that the best place had to be Collyhurst, simple. It's a common fact. In our day there was a local saying people would use: "If you need a top footballer or boxer, go to the Bradford Coal Pit (where my old man worked)," they'd say, "put yer hand down and take your pick, every one's a winner."

'Nowadays you could add actors, writers, musicians, the list is endless. I went back there to sample the latest talent, for material for my new book. Every day I took time out on the tram, or at bus stops, to tune into the local chit-chat. Corner shops, then libraries, all became nests of endless sources of material for my next venture, which will be photos of the changing face of Collyhurst with local folks' stories. I've travelled all over the world grafting, doing the t-shirts, the tickets and what-have-you. It used to feel like the energy would never run out, but even a rocket to the moon has to splash down someday. I hope my day never comes, or when it does it's in an ocean of joy, right here on these streets. Believe me, I've seen the stars, from all angles and at top speed.'

* * *

Blaney typifies the mood of the area; a high-octane matrix of encrypted slang, illicit trade and a desire to travel to foreign parts, preferably while watching Manchester United in Europe. The so-called Red Army were rampant when in transit. They took thousands to their Euro away-games, an unruly crew that vowed to always return to Manchester well in the black thanks to spontaneous crime blitzes. They were always after free continental designer sportswear or a night in a deluxe suite at someone else's expense, and sometimes they found it.

Ancoats lad CCR takes up the story again from the late 60s, when mod began its long, strange trip towards skinhead. CCR had at this time relocated to Prestwich – the supposed suburbs. The Ancoats refugee was soon to learn that the area had already been fully infected by earlier overspills from Salford; the geographic suburb hid many sins more appropriate to the crannies of the diesel and grime-saturated inner city. He adds his own recollections of the time:

'On a bright white June Saturday morning, 1969, we packed up and moved three miles north. The destination: Prestwich, or "somewhere in the country with the nutters," as our soon-to-be ex-neighbours called it. Streets were being reduced to hardcore; Ancoats' urban development masterplan was being implemented by a council who believed that the Arndale Centre was the shiny new post-industrial future . . . gorra love 'em. We moved next door to the biggest mental hospital in England –

"Home for the Feeble-Minded of the Northern Counties" being a previous title. There was a village vibe; pubs, antiquey second-hand furniture shops and a bandstand in the park. I got hay fever.

'Not an Italian in sight.

'In many ways the area was not without charm. But when you scratch the surface of this antiquey, hanging-baskety society – this rotary club in a leafy village – you find that the whole fucking area is tinged with madness. In the words of local boy John Cooper Clarke, "People turn to poison quick as lager turns to piss."

'The estate we found ourselves on soon gave up its little secrets. Short kecks turned to Oxford bags and tank tops turned starry. Post-school activity centred on mind-numbing, pointless gang violence; thrills and machismo aplenty for testosterone-fuelled 14-year-olds. In a paradox which I have yet to see explained by any sociologist alive, Prestwich had a taste for "scuttling" which flawlessly mirrored that of the inner city. Indeed, the Carr Clough estate was a universal factory outlet producing as fine a crop, year after year, of "scuttling" chaps anywhere outside Salford. Mind you, most of the families on the estate claimed Salfordian heritage. We stayed well clear; there were three of us, after all, with Ancoats accents. The Ancoats accent was clearly different to the local. It must have stirred deep feelings of apprehension in those with Salford DNA. This went deep, back to the primeval tear-ups of Greengate versus Angel Meadow. We were given a wide berth until we decided we wanted in.

'The 70s dragged on. Miners and binmen out on strike, power cuts and feather cuts. The bastardised version of the school uniform included Barathea blazers with a Lancashire red rose and silver-buttoned cuff. Match days at Maine Road. Man City providing their usual brand of haphazard genius and comedy gold on the Moss Side acre. Saturday nights at Wigan Casino. Oxford bag trousers and black brogues (first by Timpson, later, when earning and wadded-up, by Loake) complete with segued heel. This was a decade of soul. Prestwich had it. North Manchester kept the faith. The 70s turned; trousers became faded jeans, Crombies, Ben Sherman shirts, Wrangler jackets. Brogues morphed into DM's (an eight-hole minimum) in cherry red. Hair was cropped. We became an updated version of the classic late-60s skinhead look. No one had the Number One crop though; this was a step too far. Unless you had a "borstal spot" (one inky blue dot just below the left eye, or teardrops falling heroically down the cheek, a badge of honour that proved you had somehow survived gladiator school and didn't give a fuck about the possibility of gainful, regular employment – ever) it looked faintly ridiculous on lads who were still growing into their ears.'

CCR remembers the connection between northern soul, drugs and football. It was the melding of mod styles with the cold terraces of that bygone era.

'You went to the match. You "stood" with your estate crew in the face of foes from London and the street half a mile away alike. You indulged in increasingly bigger toots of whiz on your way to Wigan for the all-nighter. You spun on the floor on your talc. You tried to cop off. You noted tunes, release dates and record labels. You never went anywhere without a little plastic triangular record "middle". You took yer lumps, you never ran. (Well, hardly, unless it was Millwall at Bury, and that was allowed – for fuck's sake, 14-year-olds versus Sarf Landan dockers in their 40s . . .)

'Coming to the end of the 70s the pseudo-skin look has gone. The soul-boy style has returned in a big way. Most of the mid-decade soul boys had worn mod gear. I'm not talking the Lambrettas/Secret Affair two-tone suits, narrow ties, parkas and porkpie hats crap from the 80s revival. I'm talking original mod gear: Levi Sta-Prest and Farrah trousers. Good quality cotton pique polo shirts, frequently by Fred Perry. Penny loafers and haircuts by Don (yup, an Italian) on Great Ancoats Street Saturday mornings.

'Wigan Casino closed, amid rumblings from the cognoscenti that popular hit-parade tunes were impinging on the dance-floor play lists. The embarrassment of "Wigan" bands releasing covers of obscure northern classics . . . and finally, the arrival of punk. Ho, ho, punk; same clothes, same drugs, same three-minute max dance tunes. Get in. The zippy, chainy, mohawky London punk didn't exist in Manchester. Not until Marks and Spencer started stocking tartan bondage strides. And when things get to that stage you know they're dead.'

This was an era when the skinheads had enjoyed years of domination. They were a large body of youth who had managed to assemble a frightening uniform of big boots, short jeans, braces and shaved hair. The mere sight of it sent other groups scattering, terrified of receiving a beating, and the skinheads lived on Easy Street for years.

I thought they looked daft but there are many who disagree. Ex-skinhead Carl Spiers is one such example:

'I was calling myself a mod at the beginning of 1978,' he remembers, 'but I'd been a skinhead for a few years. I was forever attracting trouble but was more into the clobber than the aggro. That sounds hypocritical because I was a football hooligan. I was a boy skinhead at 13, impressed by the original skins in their Crombies, cherry-red Docs and Ben Sherman shirts. They looked so cool. I based myself on them. When punk became big in '77 there was a backlash against it. Many youths became skins and attacked the punks. Ironically, most of them were into punk music and sniffing glue, certainly not my idea of a skinhead!'

Punk rockers were a different kettle. They weren't quite as challenging as the skinheads, choosing to rely on their bizarre clothes and hairstyles to bewilder their adversaries. But punks would spit, posture and bully whenever they had the chance. In Manchester it quickly became evident that if you were a punk you'd better be able to use your fists. If not, the Perry boys would leave you undone like straw dogs.

The Perries sported that weird haircut, an extraordinarily long fringe lobed across one eye, the length and thickness of which extended horizontally back across the ear to a piled wedge of layers at the back of the head. From the rear, these hairstyles resembled spinning tops, top-heavy and tapering to a perky, breast-like point at the nape. When combined with Fred Perry polo shirts, baggy trousers with narrow bottoms and boat pumps, the ensemble struck fear into all. From its soul-boy roots, Perry had suddenly evolved in a lunge towards punctuated equilibrium; David Bowie had assumed the look during his Philadelphian *Young Americans* period and Manchester's youthful soul crowd reciprocated by deferring to his sartorial lead. Both Manchester and Philadelphia were cites of soul (and speed) in the mid-70s. Philly, soul, speed, Bowie – and a famous blade – formed a web of not-quite-coincidence that was enacted around 1975; according to American lore, a Philadelphia knife-maker had been the first to manufacture explorer Jim Bowie's notorious knife in the 1830s, after Bowie used a homemade version to slay a Mexican general during a battle. The distinctive curved blade-tip was to live on in a 70s popularisation known as a 'sheath-knife', sharpened on both edges for slashing. The Bowie association lent this dangerous edge to the Perries, who adopted a knife culture and jarring flamboyance via baggy dress-shirts, casual 'peg' trousers and an addiction to speed, soul and Bowie's music. These were a form of hooligan mod who lived and breathed soul and embraced the lifestyle described by CCR. Some attended football matches and even more of their younger brothers and their friends did. These younger cohorts would be the ones who changed everything, as we shall see, when they discovered an untapped wealth of continental designer logos.

Lads like Colin Blaney were the advance expeditionary force, sewing the seeds for the likes of Scouse Robin Peters and others too young to do it in the 70s. Once the 80s dawned, a whole new rampaging peer group inherited the legacy of those who'd gone before. The continental styles had by then been embraced and assimilated into everything we did and thought, and coming and going to foreign lands had become a regular occurrence.

The allure of the continent began in the dark midst of the Industrial Revolution. Britain's culture represented a discontinuity from that of Europe, hooked on the machinations of mass production, capitalism and exploitation. Life was horrifically cheapened. While the soot-stained hell-broth of our industrial jungles simmered and coughed poisonous smoke, continental craftsmen were busy fashioning life's implements with great care, building arcades, boulevards and clever alleyways, always with aesthetics in mind as much as utility. Britain's forbidding gothic canyons, blackened and boxy, symbolised strength and resilience. Europeans quietly recognised this recipe for cultural and environmental disaster. They kept things small and simple. Even Germany, that future industrial powerhouse, was treading gently on the earth, in the form of artisan colonies. In fact, Manchester Corporation sent a special committee to Germany, in 1897, to "discover the cause of England's industrial decadence". Alderman Crossfield, one of the delegation, remarked, "The English workers are half-savages when compared with the intelligent artisans of Germany." Little did he know, it wouldn't be the last time the English were labelled as savages when compared to the continentals – even by their own people. At the time, it was supposed that Germany's industrial rise would be similar in nature to what had happened in England, but the word 'industrial' in Germany pertained more to thoughtful mechanics than it did to the innumerably replicated inanities of mass production.

One of the few distractions for the English, apart from pub games, was football. Football kept men young and gave them hope and happiness. In a sea of grey sheets, cold beds and hunger, football was a beacon that radiated warmth and belongingness to all. Even the continentals loved football; like a pleasant virus disseminated by travelling Britons, football functioned as a rivet, an industrial-strength fastener which in time would take all of the world in its exhilarating embrace. But along with that virus came the 'English disease', the subject of this book . . .

The continental version of football was a more refined affair than in Britain. Where England's future great football clubs were forged with anvils on rainy Sheffield Wednesday afternoons, the clubs of Europe were voted into being by relaxed groups of educated businessmen, Oxbridge transplants, high-society types and all-round athletes proficient in a variety of sporting activities.

There's no question that a class system existed in Europe similar to that of Britain, but continental artists, scientists and aristocrats were welcomed by sporting institutions. In Britain they were kept off-limits until very recently. When the prosperous classes finally made it through the turnstiles, they were met with the furious Roy Keane – who labelled them the 'prawn sandwich brigade' – and promptly blamed for the decline of football's atmosphere.

The English Premiership's Number One spot in world football leagues is beside the point; the days of shit football and swaying terraces thundering with song, when an FA Cup Final felt like a World Cup Final, are gone. And it's all the prawn-sandwich brigade's fault. The expression is used nowadays to mock Manchester United supporters, but the intrusion of the middle classes is a nationwide phenomenon and not limited to Old Trafford.

It is obvious that something was lacking in English culture or present in continental culture which facilitated this blend of athletics, education and style. That something was all-roundedness. Those early continental *sports clubs* were precisely that – not rag-tag organisations of scruffy, lunchtime-bound miners and steelworkers. Any variety of professional and amateur sports was contained therein, such as football, polo, tennis, rugby, boxing, rowing and gymnastics. The teams belonging to such clubs all wore the same kit, club logo and colours, and the seeds of brand marketing and designer sportswear were sown here. Ironically, the travelling British were often instrumental in forming these continental sports clubs; Italy's oldest football club began as Genoa Cricket and Athletic Club, founded in 1893 by Englishmen. Associazione Calcio Cricket and Football Club (AC) Milan was also founded in 1899 by British expatriates Alfred Edwards and Herbert Kilpin, firstly as a cricket club. AC have kept the English spelling of their city's name to honour those who founded it.

British football inserted its tendrils into Spain, too; in 1895, Real Madrid's original founders included several Oxbridge graduates. Valencian citrus-fruit exporters also witnessed British sailors regularly kicking a ball around that city's ports, and by 1908 Valencia boasted several football teams.

Contrast this citrus sunshine with the grimy coal-heaps of England, the black-and-white world populated by men in flat caps, living in terraced slums. Back then only the aristocracy enjoyed access to the secret continental wonderland, the clean air of Swiss lakes and Italian villas. The working-class English shovelled coal into the furnaces of the Industrial Revolution, working themselves into early graves, while their wealthy fellow countrymen slid off to play in the sun, to bed Europe's fittest females and escape the ugliness of the smoking cities.

But there are important exceptions. In France, A.S. Saint-Étienne was created in 1919 by members of the employees' Union of the Casino grocery chain. Since green was the colour of the chain, green jerseys were also adopted. It was working-class Saint Etienne (situated in a coal-mining area) who, 57 years later, were to stage a couple of hugely significant football matches against an English opposition, matches that forever revolutionised British fashions and attitudes. That green shirt and its logos would figure quite heavily.

It was Liverpool and Manchester United, England's biggest clubs, who were to discover this world – or at least adopt its styles – before the rest of Britain, and Colin Blaney was right in the thick of it. But before we hear Blaney's outrageous story about the culture shock that followed a mini-riot in which several people were arrested for disorderly conduct, chiefly because they just wanted to sample the continent's marvels for themselves, we must hear another.

The subculture known as 'casual' is well documented, said to have been kick-started by Liverpool fans who became transfixed by continental goodies. One famous quote about the very dawn of the casual movement describes the scousers' first exposure to continental sensibilities during a European Cup run, played on March 2 1977. Saint Etienne was the team and the place which would play a pivotal role in forming the attitude and mindset of two entire generations:

'The year turned over into 1977, and the next round was Saint Etienne, some say the greatest two legs of football in the history of the club and who am I to argue? Saint Etienne's tree-lined boulevards, with the trendy café-bars and chic shops, were a whole new experience for the European red man.

'Liverpool was in the depths of winter when we left. Saint Etienne was not that far from the South of France and by contrast was mild and had turned the corner into spring. We all sat about in the numerous pavement bars watching the world go by, and were treated to an exclusive premier fashion parade that was about to change the face of the football supporter in England for the next 30 years.

'The girls, of course, caught most of our roving eyes: skin-tight designer jeans and trainers. The first time I ever saw a pair of crossover-strap trainers was on a girl who was riding pillion on the back of her female friend's trails motorbike – you know, the ones in Europe at that time with those huge wide wheels. She was sat side-saddle, and had this most unusual hair that was wedged at the back but with the wildest long fringe, flapping in the warm breeze.

'As the day wore on and the kick-off got closer the local fans started to pour onto the streets. Although it is not mentioned much, Saint Etienne had a firm. A couple of Reds came badly unstuck when they bumped into them that night. They were the smartest, coolest-looking bunch we had come across on our travels up until then, and the whole of this little town was starting to make us look like we had been locked in the Stone Age. Kickers, Pods, you name it, we saw the lot on both the males and females that day.

'Believe me when I say I'm not one for team shirts, in fact I wouldn't be seen dead wearing one, but even the Saint Etienne team shirt of the day was a step up from anything we had seen at home. It was more like one of those cycle shirts they have in the Tour de France. I have to admit, like most who were in France for that game, I had to have one.

'The French football magazine *Once* was pure class, even though we couldn't understand a word on its pages; the photography alone put our own *Shoot* to shame and we drooled over the girls in the adverts.

'After the heroics of that great night at Anfield we were handed a dream draw, FC Zurich. Zurich was like an open invitation, the designer shops might just as well have put up signs in the windows saying, "Special offer; next two days only, help yourselves, it's free!" And so the seeds were sown.

'Now, I'm not saying the lads at home didn't add their own take to this European look, far from it. The music scene at the time gave it another twist. But what Liverpool fans mostly brought to this new era was attitude, and buckets of it. The sulky look, the one-word "Woa!" answer to everything, even the blue-hooded Parka that became the must-have item was regulation waist-length and worn slung right back off the shoulders. With a new look, a fresh attitude and a top football team the whole of England was put on notice.'

That quote comes from a Liverpool online forum. Attempts to identify its originator proved fruitless. After enquiring among internet scholars of casual culture, I have to assume it's either the work of a wishful author masquerading as an anonymous scally or a genuine person. Either way, it tells a tale about a specific time and place. There's no question that the scousers sparked a new look in the dark realms of English football hooliganism. The current was also flowing 35 miles up the road in Manchester. Colin Blaney, lad-about-Europa, remembers how his Saint Etienne odyssey began on September 14, 1977:

'That first ever trip with the Red Devils abroad came about when I made the acquaintance of my first grafting partner, Rabbi, or Rab, from the London Flats on Eccles New Road in Salford, which were the spit of Collyhurst Flats. Rab was the perfect partner for blaggin' and running riot, 'cos neither of us gave a fuck about the rulebook of civilisation. Both of us were covered with Cash Cooper tattoos and we were both pisshead thugs and thieves, so no wonder we clicked. It was a case of the whole being bigger than the sum o' the parts, an' me an' Rab put our heads together an' started some proper schemes on that trip. At that time I was working for my old man's sandblasting company, Clean Walls. Right before that week in Europe I was informed that the three years' graft I'd done for the company meant they were now willing to let me run my own sandblasting crew on a job in Lincoln.

'The meet with the sandblasting lads was at Piccadilly Station, then off to get our lodgings sorted in Lincoln. I was just intending to sink a few jars on Oldham Strasse (as we later called it) beforehand, when all of a sudden in comes Rab, singing United songs. United had their biggest game for years in France that very week, in the '77-'78 Cup Winners Cup at Saint Etienne. Saint Etienne really were a mega team in 1977, undefeated at home with a crowd that backed them to the hilt, and everyone and his ferret was signed up for the mission.

'Within five minutes Rab had blagged my head to sack Lincoln and to fund our trip across the Channel instead. Automatically we hit Top Shop, who sold top-of-the range Van Gil suits, hand-stitched lapels, the works. We had a result, earning a McGarrett for 'em (AKA 50 quid, named after the copper on *Hawaii 5-0*) when we sold them to two Quality Street blokes who loved their clobber. A McGarrett was a decent start to that trip, courtesy of two lads who'd run the graft in years to come, ironically enough. North Manchester really was gangland then and the QS were rum as. If you ever had anything you were shit-scared about trying to fence, they'd laugh at you and have it right off you. They ruled the roost everywhere, a collection of mad Glaswegians, local boxers, bouncers and barrow boys. They were a crew of heavies no one could touch. Once they knew they had a major crew of Mancs in hand to send across Europe with the swag, they went to town.

'United had all planned to stay in Lyons on the Tuesday night, and what a sight at night that city is. Even the fucking car parks looked like museums with strobe lights and marble columns. It was another world, and our crew had penetrated it. Finally we made it right into the heart of their territory. The first head we see in the square is Coco; he's got all his new clobber packed away in the lockers at the station. Tricky Dicky had been over days earlier, taking the easy pickings very seriously and emptying the boutiques of the rarer tackle, the clever bastard. Coco took full advantage of the culture, carrying those purses for men, silk cravat scarf 'round his Gregory and other stuff to blend in. Being black was – and still is – a chink in yer armour, as France and other countries do look out for blacks, call it racist or whatever. But Coco never had a problem, with his flair-for-wear working for him. He was as stylish as they come and knew the proper way that the richest blokes carried themselves. Five minutes in France was more than enough for us. We took to it like ducks to water. All of us felt the call of those styles to different extents. It started a major fashion.'

It wasn't just the clothes either. European food grabbed the attention of the barbarians and they were determined to try different things. The futuristic public transport system was noted, and Blaney remembers how the United mob coveted a ride on the French 'Supertrain'. (The TGV 001, a prototype, had been built to counteract the effects of the '73 oil crisis a few years earlier, and by 1977 a succession of TGV-type trains were running in France.)

'We got off the boat for the Paris train and by then we'd picked up a right old crew,' Blaney says. 'Cockneys, Coventry and company. When we arrived, there was a crew of French dibble who wanted to escort us right onto the first shite train available, but we had other ambitions: We wanted to get on the Supertrain. They surrounded us, and there was a kick-off on the platform. The noise level went absolutely potty. It was a big run-off with unbelievable noise, and French people getting in the way copped for it. It was a top scene, proper Man United on the rampage.

'The race was on to jib the main Supertrain of Europe. I loved the name "Supertrain", it really was the dog's bollocks. No way were we gonna miss one of those top torpedoes. I'd never seen double-decker trains before. I remember how the restaurant had a waiting list. It opened my mind to the culture of the continent and why we were looked on as cavemen by the Frogs and the eye-ties. What a feeling, eating the best juicy steaks that the waiter burnt at the table with that scintillating sound. I can hear it to this day. We had to try it. I think that was the only thing we paid for, the full trip!'

Modern working-class England had finally penetrated this succulent world. They found luxurious substitutes for the cheap crimplenes and acrylics which had chafed them for so long. Like a tiger who sinks his teeth into human flesh after a lifetime gnawing on tough antelope and knobbly reptile, they wanted more. The expeditionary force pulled itself together and stormed the beaches – or, more accurately, the boutiques. Continental designer treasures were unleashed on Stone Age Blighty, creating the most violent sartorial revolution since suits of armour.

2

SAINT ETIENNE

A riot is the language of the unheard.
– Martin Luther King, Jr

The British media has for decades been an embarrassment to anyone under the age of 50. It has long struggled with a credibility lag which forced outdated, unrealistic representations of modern British subculture onto its audience, and it's this that needs to be addressed before we venture any further abroad.

This was partly because the people controlling the media were out-of-touch, middleclass college grads for whom a journey on a night bus in one of Britain's cities (where 'real people' lived) constituted a dangerous adventure, best avoided if at all possible. As a result, 'real people' never made it to the small screen, for example, and British television was an abysmal distraction barring the odd comedy. Eventually, through necessity, some depictions of working-class Brits found their way into the media. A predictably tiny cross-section began to monopolise what it meant to be poor, cool and shady in Middle England's consciousness. These were the cockney sparrers, the scouse wits and the scar-faced Glaswegians. Everyone else was a dildo-in-waiting; the geographically-anonymous working class was seen in much the same way as the US media saw the American Midwest, unwashed and unworthy of depiction.

By way of comparison, the most populous quadrant of the US is the northeast – where cities like Philadelphia, Washington DC, Baltimore, New York and Boston are sprawled across the landscape, their outermost tendrils entwining endless suburbs, freeways and satellite cities. The American media selected their chosen ones on the basis of profit, like everything else there. Historically, Europe has supplied huge numbers of Jews, Italians and Irish to the northeast, making up significant factions of the population, particularly in the Greater New York area. So it's no surprise that an inordinately high percentage of TV shows and movies have portrayed these ethnic groups more often than others; they became the original target audience, the safest income source, while other ethnic groups were marginalised. If a character was Jewish, Italian or Irish (in the '-American' sense), they stood a good chance of being portrayed as competent, stylish or lovably roguish. Southerners, Midwestern Scandinavians, Pennsylvanian Dutch and blacks were either seen as overly timid, backward, simplemindedly criminal or subservient. Today, we see this trend losing momentum as the media realises the need for diversity and other ethnic groups and regions become the focus.

Like America, Britain was always destined to have its media darlings. But unlike America, the reasons for this weren't strictly commercial; they were steeped in the British tendency to judge people by the fitness of their accents. The likes of Sunderland, Bristol, Carlisle and Sheffield were ignored in favour of those with more interesting slang, greater crime rates and – let's face it – cooler or more legible accents. The intra-class system worked to distinguish those who at least made an attempt at the Queen's English, particularly if their verbal atrocities were sufficiently dramatic to warrant attention from cameras, lights and microphones. While television stations in the USA stuck to the safe approach of targeting the highest represented demographic, Brits were forced to pay homage every week to this minute aural subset of the population.

In Britain over the past 15 years, a similar rethink to that of America has occurred; cities other than London, Liverpool and Glasgow have been recognised as centres of cool, one of which now completely dominates the hipper end of the media spectrum. That city is Manchester, the sleeping giant of British culture.

Despite being one of the largest urban zones in the UK, Manchester had always lagged behind the 'Chosen Three' in some important respects, namely commercialisation and marketing. Scousers discovered a way to package their accent and attitude for the rest of Britain long before Mancunians did. They arrived on the scene very late because they were utterly unaware that they were capable of taking the limelight. The reason? Manchester didn't practice bullshit-on-the-fly. While London, Liverpool and Glasgow enjoyed a collective media image of combined initiative, criminality and toughness, Mancunians recoiled in disgust at the incompleteness of that media stereotype, but had no clue as to how to change it.

They certainly weren't about to become actors; that was just too poofy. Even the Manchester police were drafted in from the outer edge, as proper Mancs always refused to participate in the control of their own, especially if locking people up was involved. You'd be hard pushed to find a policeman with a real Manchester accent even today. It was how things were then, and how they remain. People operated under terms of complete non-cooperation with official public mouthpieces. As a result they missed the opportunity to sell their 'language' to the public; but when they woke up, they woke up fast, fuelling a new race to monopolise how the media represented the black economy. The Chosen Three became the Chosen Four and, by tooth and nail, the Mancs muscled their way into the popular imagination.

An underground learning curve had been active in Manchester for years, knowing that media representation was a crucial benefit in the game of life. Somewhere among the punk rockers of 1977 a mutation was occurring. Rob W, still puzzling over that magenta vision he saw walking through central Manchester in early '76, concluded that there was trouble at t' mill – or, more accurately, at the Factory. Rob remembers how nights at Hulme's Russell Club (sometimes spelt 'Russel') were a precursor to the crossover with football and street fashions that came a year later, most notably at Pips nightclub in the city centre.

'To the then-unborn and the born-stupid,' Rob contemptuously snarls in his customary lingo, '"punk" is mohawks (aka "mohicans"), fast, dumb riffing and spitting. To Johnny-come-lately punks it was about food-dyed hair and bum-flapped bondage trousers bought from a classified ad in the back of *Sounds*; food dye because they could wash it out for work or more likely school the next day. To the marginally brighter it was about dole-queue rock and half-arsed leftwing or anarchist politics – these had the worst long-tem effect, and are almost entirely due to the influence of the Clash. The attraction of the Clash baffled me and my friends at the time and still does. The core bands of punk were the Sex Pistols, the Damned, the Clash and the Buzzcocks. The Damned were an entertaining and harmless Status Quo comedy band at heart. That leaves the other three, from which you could choose two bands that sounded like they had been beamed straight from the future, or some blokes who used to be in a pub band led by a public-school ex-hippie tosser with a phoney Lahndan accent. I'll leave you to figure out which was the Clash. But from the Clash, who had two or three OK songs, came the half-baked political wankpunks like Crass, the Anti-Nowhere League and all the other crap that led eventually to the crusties and travellers, deluded hippie parasites in late punk kit.

'Find yourself some early photos of punks, punks from late '75 to '77. You won't see a single bumflap or mohawk. The London punks, be they male or female, chose either a puritanical uniform of short, brightly-dyed hair, be it bleached blond(e) or electric blue or any unnatural-looking colour, deliberately overdone pissholes-in-snow eye makeup, drainpipe jeans, fluffy mohair pullovers and narrow-lapelled box jackets, or they dressed like they had lost their way to *The Rocky Horror Show*, like the much-mythologised Bromley Contingent.

'The Manchester Scene, the only UK punk scene independent of London, had a similar bifurcation of style, one tine of which was roundheads going out of their way to wear ordinary day clothes that weren't the flared, wide-lapelled abominations of tamed hippie that had become the default style of the day, and the other tine the cavaliers of the Roxy Room at Pips, who were essentially sixth-formers and art-student posers ripping off the look of Roxy Music and David Bowie. The roundhead tine were generally the ones with some musical ability, and the ones most likely to affect not to have heard of the prog- and hard-rock bands they had idolised only months earlier.'

Rob W approached it from a different angle to the football hooligans, but his dismissal of the mainstream was equally all-inclusive. Meanwhile, Colin Blaney was learning every trick in the book, way back before Manchester was Madchester. He and his United pals had it sussed, right down to the best way to affect entry through foreign customs, which they applied on that landmark trip to southeastern France. These kids were about to invent a new language to go with their new attitude and, as ever, it was all about grabbing something for nothing.

'We used to get snide one-year passports, which we called "passies",' Blaney recalls. 'Back then it was easy to do them on sleepy weekdays out, when you jibbed the rattler to Euston. On the way down to London for the Etienne game we robbed a full pack of Newkie Browns from the

27

offie, and soon met other devils who all had packs of ale. Next thing you knew we were singing away on the tube that not a one of us had paid for; one of the first slang words that came from our lot was "jib", which basically means, "to pay is to fail," so no surprise when around 30 of us all carried on the party with the ticket inspector coming nowhere near us.

'The word jib worked its way into our slang. Within a couple of years every kid that followed the Reds was talking about jibbing the train and jibbing in at the turnstiles when they got to the match. Jibbing was like dancin'. It was part of what we were all about. Punks pogo'd, we jibbed.'

Among the working classes in Britain there have always existed a body of persons in possession of oral rights and deeds, men long established as movers and shakers in the underworld. These men have their finger solidly on the pulse and are instinctively able to divine the next big thing in bent merchandise, much of it known as 'swag' by those who purvey it. In a stratified culture like that of Britain, the man at the top of the mountain remains shrouded in mystery. The black market in trendy or addictive contraband creates economies generations old. Those in the know enjoy life at a discount at the apex of the swag curve. It is no different than anything else in life; those who first colonise a place won't easily give it up to successive waves of immigrants and in time they become the established elite. Elites communicate their status via symbols and gestures, later emulated by those who wish to be the same. Being at the top means property, power, language, clothing, sex, jewellery and brute force. These symbols and energies remain unchanged since before humans were human, and they're not about to change anytime soon.

The expression 'learning curve' is an oft-used one. It's a steep line progressing from bottom left to top right on a graph. It describes a well-adapted phenomenon entering a high-pressure phase that tends towards success and prosperity. This prosperity is checked only when carrying capacity is exceeded and the line flattens out. Whether you're graphing the sale of mobile phones or the growth of English gangs, the curves are the same.

Same applies here. The learning curve these kids followed was a steep one. There was resistance every inch of the way, as Blaney describes it. But persistence paid off in time.

Think of it as a natural relationship that occurs spontaneously. The lofty mountain stream feeds its silt load to the sluggish river meandering aimlessly below. This is where the dildo-in-waiting waits. Meanwhile, upland, the stream rushes cold and direct. The fish living up there require a certain concentration of oxygen to survive. They fight the current every minute of every day and burn huge amounts of energy just to remain at that fixed altitude. Cold, rushing water contains more oxygen than warmer, slower water, but water runs downhill and life upstream is arduous. Animals are selected to occupy specific ecological niches and the expression 'horses for courses' applies totally here. It is survival of the fittest.

Whenever a group emerges which harnesses a superior means of manipulating its environment for its own benefit, a form of colonisation occurs whereby the group's language (often slang words), its sense of style and even its choice of weapons (say a Stanley knife, which evolved into a Magnum Rayrider with laser sights) come to dominate the landscape of that world. There are regions richly populated by such groups, indicating a genetic basis for their existence. And when they travel, they take their tendencies with them. In the late 1970s London's monopolisation of this world was forced to accommodate the northwest pretenders, as they received an injection of credibility and energy which enabled them to muscle in on the graft.

Some Londoners claim they were part of a burgeoning soul scene as early as 1975, featuring designer labels such as Gabicci and Lacoste. This is believable, as Manchester's second-generation (Bowie-influenced) Perries were up and running at that time, too. But it was during the late 70s when that fundamental shift in British fashion sensibilities really began, what one might think of as the third-generation Perries (or the first-generation scouse scallies), as the look filtered into the football terraces. The Perries' strange appearance clashed violently with the *de rigueur* terrace-wear of the time. In Liverpool, a city filled with the descendants of sailors, they began nurturing a form imported from abroad, one that focused on quality instead of the silly boots and green hair so proudly featured on London postcards.

Liverpudlians speak with an accent exceedingly rare. Their own sense of distinction and alienation from the rest of England is literally thrust upon them from without. An arrogant desire to advertise this difference emerged in the youth culture quite automatically.

Liverpudlians instinctively knew how to manipulate their 'Beatle-ish' media image to their greatest possible advantage. Mancunians, meanwhile, were imagined to be playing dominoes and drinking mild in the snug. They were unaware of what a goldmine of slang, music and style they had to themselves, and how unique a culture they'd built. But they escaped that sluggish river in the end and joined the hunt for clean water. They are no longer dildos-in-waiting.

* * *

In 1977, Robin Peters was a little scally learning how business often comes your way via fortunate geographic twists. Growing up in the shadow of Liverpool's football grounds solidified his wheeling and dealing at an age when most are quite unfamiliar with the coin of the realm. Long before he was a grafter, hitting the sweet spots of Europe, he saw at firsthand how business and pleasure are often rolled into one. Saint Etienne would play a part in yet another lad's enlightenment.

'I'd been minding cars since we lived on Everton Valley, when I was about five. "Mind yer car please, sir," would be the shout to punters on their way to the footy. All the out of towners, or scousers from outlying areas, would be parked as near to the ground as possible, and we lived just five minutes walk from the Kop. With easy access to the Mersey Tunnels, town, and areas like Bootle, Kirkby and so on, we had a prime patch. It sounds like part of an advertising campaign, but I'm actually describing the benefits of living on the wrong side of the tracks, not the right one. The streets of Everton Valley were tough corridors for a five-year-old car minder and I was finding it hard to earn a tanner with so much competition around. The main rule of thumb was, if you lived in the street where the cars parked, you owned the rights to that street. But around the terraced streets of Everton Valley there were so many kids on the make that it proved to be a cutthroat business.

'When I was seven, in 1973, we moved over the other side of Walton Road to a newer house which had been built in a street that had taken a direct hit during the May Blitz in 1941. Our house was one of about 12 newer ones and they stuck out like bright sore thumbs among endless drab rows of Victorian houses, from which people were starting to move to new houses with toilets inside. These were new towns and urban overspills, places like Kirkby, Croxteth, Skelmersdale and Runcorn. The community was slowly disintegrating and loads of kids went off to live in strange council estates, private houses and blocks of bizarre maisonettes in the country. But we were there to stay, like a Scouse Republican Guard; Liverpool was the place for us, not some weird concrete playland full of kids with funny accents. We arrived in our new street in the middle of one of the biggest slum-clearance projects in the UK, and it was carnage. Liverpool was getting torn to bits by machines. The Victorian streets around us were soon being flattened, and there was only one other kid in our street who had survived the slum clearance. His name was Colin Dixon and we soon became partners in the car-minding business.

'The demolition of the houses had left us with a huge expanse of land around our houses which the corpy had covered with some kind of black ash or coke. This left us young entrepreneurs with a huge car park which could take about 200 cars. This was about 1976, right at the beginning of Liverpool's glory years. Inflation had risen, and we were now receiving five pence or two bob [10p] a car, compared to the penny or tuppence I'd received on Everton Valley during my apprenticeship.

'Me and Colin were "smashing it", due to the rule of thumb that if Liverpool won you quite often got double. The redmen just kept on winning, and we had our regulars who always looked for us, as they knew they could trust us. One of them was a black Capri John Player Special, and on a European Cup game he would give us ten bob [50p]. I used to reserve a space for him right outside our front door, 'cos he was like a VIP to us. On a normal game he was a 20p punter.

'Saint Etienne played us on March 16 1977, and Liverpool were looking at a certain exit from the Big Cup. With the score in Etienne's favour and the clock running down, "Supersub" Davey Fairclough came on for Toshack, in the 82nd minute. Ray Kennedy sent that hopeful ball over the top for him to run on to, to score the goal that sent the Kop silly. Footage of the Liverpool supporters that night still makes the hair on yer neck stand up; flags, banners, the singing like a volcano erupting all 'round the streets. The red half of the city went mad and me and Colin were guaranteed a great payday. It was my birthday the next day, Paddy's Day, and when the Kopites started returning to their cars 20 minutes after the final whistle it was like all my birthdays had come at once. The Reds were coming back and just emptying the contents of their pockets into our hands. I'm certain we even ended up with a few pound notes that night. When all the cars had gone, me and Colin sat under the big street lamp outside our house and had a count up. We must have ended up with about 50 quid between us! What a result compared to the normal £5 each on a normal match day.

'I even appointed me own financial advisor – me ol' feller. He used to drink with Colin's dad, and was always saying to me, "Why don't you put your car money in a Post Office account like Colin Dixon does?" But I was having none of it, I wanted to spend, spend, spend. Posh and Becks had nothing on me; at the top of our street was a shop called Toyland, and I woke up on Saint Patrick's Day 1977 and headed straight there. An 11-year-old with a pony in his bin, there was no stopping me. First it was Hot Wheels, Scalectrix, Monopoly, Kerplunk and a Wembley Trophy football, then off to Clitheroe's sweet shop for gobstoppers, Kola Cubes and Strawberry Mivies. Next was comics, I grabbed *The Beano*, *Shoot* and *Whizzer and Chips*. I think I saw Colin heading to the William and Glyn's bank across the road but I can't be sure. He's done well for himself, Colin; he runs his own business and has a big house out in Crosby or somewhere. I think he's still got his Saint Etienne money as well!

'With all big businesses come problems, and mine and Colin's was no different. Our problem came in the shape of "Jimmy Swag the Boot" and "Macca GT", who were part of the Billogs gang from another part of Kirkdale. Kirkdale was near the docks and they were a lot older than us. Macca was a joyrider and Jimmy was a boot robber, and armed with scissors and FS keys they became a fucking nuisance. They'd sometimes turn up ten-, 15-handed, with younger kids who were schoolmates of mine. The general attitude was, "Sorry, lad, this isn't personal, this is business, it's not as though it's yer ol' feller's car, is it?" I had a few fights defending my turf but what could I do? I certainly wasn't going to the bizzies, I'd sometimes be able to blag them that I'd seen an RS 2000 parked a few streets away in Fountains Road, but that was only gonna work now and then.

'Truth was we needed a bit of back-up, and things came to a head one day when we sneaked off to the match instead of keeping an eye on our cars. When we returned to our patch we discovered that Jimmy and his firm had broken into our prized John Player Special. Naturally, the owner never parked with us again. We decided to get Colin's older cousin from Breck Road to join us on a three-way split, and it worked for a while, but to be fair the job was getting hard. Market traders who'd been evicted from Great Homer Street Market had started fly-pitching on our land on a Saturday. The council finally put up fencing to thwart them, thus fucking us up because cars no longer had access to the car park.

'I still giggle to myself nowadays when my 11-year-old nephew sneaks off from me at the match early to claim money from the ten or so cars he's minding, in the same street 30 years later.

'By 1978 I was getting a bit too old for minding cars. My balls were dropping and I wanted adventure. I was 12-13 years old, Liverpool were champions of England and Europe, and teams were starting to bring firms to Anfield 'cos we were the team they all wanted to beat. The city's urchins were forming two scally armies, with their own attitude, outlook and dress sense, and I wanted in.'

While Peters' generation graduated to the football mobs, the older lads were rampaging around Europe and a thousand ideas were being born. The British underground economy was stretching its tentacles across the dirty Channel, grasping for purchase at the possibilities. It found multitudes.

The parallels between northwest and southeast England's grafters and certain musical trends from those regions are interesting – just as the Rolling Stones appeared more raw and adventurous than the Beatles in the early 60s, so was the cockney spiv seemingly better equipped and represented than the Northwest in the early days of domestic grafting. For years, the popular image was of a cockney tout in requisite scruffy suit and trilby, spouting comical slang and taking over-the-odds cash in exchange for match tickets. Everyone loved to watch these colourful characters in action, be it in the flesh or in television programmes and films. The same might be said of the London-led mod culture, which certainly had huge parallels in the Northwest. But it was always Swingin' London that captured the popular imagination, not Liverpool (and certainly not Manchester). But just as the Beatles suddenly slid into fifth gear (and then interstellar overdrive) in the late 60s, so did the Northwest tune itself into a new wavelength of mischief and skulduggery in the early 80s, one that caused a revolutionary shift in the way people thought, planned and reacted to events.

The main distinction was the foreign travel. Saint Etienne represented the thin end of a wedge that, in time, would be crossed over by thousands of lads from northwest England. This lifestyle would completely infect Great Britain in the decades to come. Peters' cohorts were soon to follow, a constant feed from England to Europe of young grafters eager to exploit and experience the continent. But they had to have an excuse for being there; football and concerts provided that. Sports and concert tickets, t-shirts, flags and other memorabilia were to become the means and the smokescreen behind which the grafters would rampage, to their own end. In time these bands of English lads would strip the continent of its rare prizes, functioning as catalysts in the eventual maturing of Britain as a cultural presence in northern Europe. These young travellers regained ground on their continental peers, which might never have been made up if left to the straight members, the living-dead mortgage payers and other boredom merchants from the package-holiday realm.

But it wasn't all about football. Yet.

*　　*　　*

1977 was not a particularly busy year for transatlantic air travel, to say the least. But even then some very plucky individuals decided to go for it, and break into what was essentially a forbidden planet – the USA. One such person was John Allen, a musician, artist and all-round wild rover from Tideswell in Derbyshire. Allen is one of those characters for whom the art of storytelling was created. I took great delight recently upon learning that John was writing his autobiography, as his life makes for fascinating reading. I'll leave it to him to give you his unique, almost Pythonesque take on how he conquered the land of the free.

'I grew up in Tideswell, which we call "Tidza" locally. It's a little village, all made from stone, and not much going on. There's an ancient cathedral bang in the centre that's much too large for a small hamlet like Tidza, that goes back to the gold-trafficking days of the Celts. They brought the gold from Eire across England to northern Europe, to trade with the Vikings. Tidza was a major stop-off point and all the local priests took the piss by promising to look after the treasure and safeguard it against the dark forces. They hid it in sacred holes and caves and obviously nicked their share, which they used to build their oversized cathedral. There are stories everywhere in this world, right under your nose. You've just got to look for them, but they're there alright.

'I was never a massive football fan but I always followed the game.

My brother was into Derby County but I preferred the big teams like Liverpool and Man United. Derbyshire is the most partitioned county in Britain, kind of a mini North-South divide. The southern part of Derbyshire is all very so-so and Midlands, but the northern part is closer to Manchester, and cool as fuck.

'Because I was a good draughtsman, I won a scholarship to Liverpool College of Art – the very same one that John Lennon failed out of years before – and Lennon's mentor, Arthur Ballard, was still there. He'd booze with the students and tell bags of stories about how he used to hang out with Dylan Thomas and was some kind of fighting champion. Ballard is famous for telling Lennon, "John, you've got to stop this daft music business, or you'll get nowhere!" The funny thing was, there were lecture desks at the college still bearing John Lennon's name carved into them. Some of this graffiti was fresh, though, which was a bit of a joke. Lennon failed his finals and though he had the opportunity to return and finish, the music took him away. The rest is history. It was a great place, Liverpool, and I settled in right away, glad to be away from the stony nooks of Tideswell, but still missing certain favourite valleys and woods I'd grown up in. After all, they were *my* valleys. They were part of me.

'One day I was in the toilets there and I drew a crest, made to look like it was actually fastened physically to the shithouse wall, like a three-dimensional plaque. I wrote on a scroll under it, "California Dreamin' on such a smelly bog," as a skit on the lyrics to the Mamas 'n' Papas' classic song. I was already dreaming of going to America back then and it was only a matter of time till I managed it. Anyway, some famous artist was also engaged in that same cubicle at some point in his career at Liverpool, and he actually quoted the motto off my plaque. I was thrilled to bits!

'Anyway, to make a short story very long, when I graduated from art school I started to really think about getting away to the USA, as nobody I knew had ever been that way before, and it was just an amazingly tempting dream. I believed the art and music scene in New York had to be better than the shit in England, and I wanted in on it. I started to scavenge around my friends and family, distant relatives and all that, trying to establish links with people who knew people in New York, Florida, the Midwest, etc.

'It turned out that my mum knew an American curate in our village from years before. This bloke had been involved in the civil rights movement in the States, in Maryland, and when the shit hit the fan he'd been sent to England by the church. He was the village curate for a couple of years and he became friendly with my mum. We found out he had a lot of friends there, in New York and other places, and it was these that I targeted when I decided to hit the States. One of his old seminary friends lived right in Manhattan, and my mum arranged for me to stay there for a day or so when I flew into New York. I didn't really feel like meeting this holy man, to be honest, but at least it was a roof over my head and in 1977 New York was balls-out crazy territory.'

Allen's world resembles another planet relative to the escapades of the Manchester United mob. Where he went west in search of artistic experiences, the football thugs from Manchester went south in search of mayhem. Soon, others would make the transatlantic trek, also with music in mind. These guys weren't looking for the avant-garde though; they were looking for soul. CCR was among a small group whose thirst for music and adventure was growing by the day. We'll join CCR and his cronies on their New York trip shortly, but first let's take another look at the Red Army.

Back in England the ticket game dovetailed with other ventures, many of which involved the counterfeiting of designer clothing, watches, perfume and the tickets themselves. The gangsters of Liverpool established an early foothold in the market. They began churning their merchandise out like camouflaged wolves in a world full of sheep. The task of manufacturing the goods was outsourced to the Far East. In Liverpool this was old news; the port city had long forged illicit trade links with the Orient, and snide gear was merely a new twist. But any form of organised crime, even one as harmless as counterfeiting, requires a formidable army of people to produce, distribute and sell to the public.

The cities of Manchester and Liverpool have always been fertile ground for scallywags and creative lawbreakers, just as they've been a conduit for paradigm shifts in youth attitudes and popular music. The Northwest was the perfect location for an underground industry to emerge, whose grafters were already adapted to the task of hurtling long distances at short notice, sleeping rough and fighting to defend their swag, if need be.

An injection of continental fashions was about to infect the hooligan armies with its irreversible elixir. Speaking of which, Colin Blaney relates some more of United's exploits from that landmark trip to Saint Etienne:

'The next day, around 100 strong, we got an ordinary train into Saint Etienne and at every stop Reds boarded with funny heads and full bags of clobber. It was no surprise, once we got new clothes ourselves, that we went to graft full-time, loading up with Lois jeans, Kicker boots and shoes, Lacoste sweaters and cardigans worth a fortune. We knew the lads and the QS mob back home would be well into this clobber.

'Now, what's never been pointed out is the fact that, that night, the trouble was not only full on but was really like going back to the days when it was all about taking ends. After all the goings-on with a group of 500 all the way from the main square to that stadium, we arrived at the home supporters enclosure. It was a piece of piss to jib the turnstiles, hit the bars, then enter the top tier, packed with Union Jacks which the lads soon took the poles out of and used to steam into the Frogs.

'It wasn't a well-policed affair to start with, terrace-wise. It would have been a peaceful jib for the lads but there was a bread strike on in England at the time. The French had brought millions of loaves to chuck at us English, to mock us; they still had their staple food while we had to buy cornflakes and cake. The loaves were flying over the police segregation like you wouldn't believe, and it took United's lads a few minutes to realise what it signified. When it dawned, we went ballistic and steamed the Frogs, pinning them against the mesh fencing between the main mass of us and them. After ten minutes of fighting the French were scaling those huge mesh fences that only the Europeans have behind the goal. It was sickening when they got to the top, as there were so many trying to flee. The weight of them all started to cause a wobbling, flowing effect, which had many a body falling down onto the concrete or, if lucky, the grass. The ambulance service was in panic trying to stretcher away the injured, but the Red Army was intent on doing deathly harm like a swarm of agitated killer bees.

'By the time the riot dibble got together around 2,000 had taken their end. This was the only time a foreign club has taken another country's end, ever, in European competition. There was soon a price to pay as the French police in all the Robocop gear steamed into us, many ending up in hospital overnight. Me and Rab just jibbed into the VIP boxes. What got us in were our tracky tops, obtained via their souvenir shop, which had been ragged and wrecked the night before by the lads. They were beauties, green silk, made by French sportswear designers we'd never heard of. We'd traded some of our swag for these, as they looked fucking boss. It wasn't until three years later, in 1980, that the so-called casuals were wearing them en masse. The seeds were sown on that trip for the next decade, believe me. Amazingly, even today, on Sir Matt Busby Way, you'll see Saint Etienne tackle on sale. The game was goalless right till near the end, when the original King of All Cockneys, Gordon Hill, scored for us, but they got one back two minutes later. That game was a turning point. Even the song we made up on the way home – "Que sera, sera, whatever will be, will be, we're going to Wembley" – is still sung by every club on its way to the final. They'd played Liverpool in the European Cup earlier that year and there wasn't a peep out of the Mickies. When the Mancs arrived they must have wondered what the fuck had hit them. They didn't even have a souvenir shop left when we'd finished! When we got through customs at Dover all the press were snapping away. I would soon be away again to wherever the Reds would be in Europe. I suppose it's true to say we were all hooked on going to the Euro aways, like picking up an addiction. The life on the road really appealed to all us so-called Perry boys, as the rest of Manchester started to call us, after we adopted the French haircut and the European gear in proper numbers.'

The younger members on the mission were influenced by the styles. This modish continental look would completely makeover the complexion of British hooliganism over the next several years, as British football thugs suddenly became smarter, more organised and increasingly linked to organised crime. It was a symbiosis born of travel and necessity. Gangsters and entrepreneurs enlisted the football hooligans as their infantry, selling goods and services to punters on the front lines across Europe. The old-school Perries had terrified anyone young enough to be in the know around Manchester's clubs in the early to mid-70s, and these later football gangs bore an inevitable resemblance.

In my first book, *Perry Boys*, I described how this mistaken identity led to a general moodiness and quickness to violence among its proponents. The older Perries, with their mod and soul influences, had been sporting the wedge and high-end European clobber since the turn of the 70s at clubs like the Twisted Wheel in Manchester. The younger football mob exploded in number right at the end of that decade. At the time, the mod movement was experiencing its own 'plastic' revival, due to the release of the Who's 1979 film *Quadrophenia*. The old-school Perries looked on in disgust, as thousands of young kids began wearing mass-produced third-rate two-tone suits, patent-leather tasselled loafers, and, yes, the Fred Perry polo shirt. Carl Spiers from Oldham describes how modism grew and clashed with other youth cults:

'I became a mod because of the clothes ethic and the soul music of the 60s. Motown and reggae. As for the northern soul boys, I always classed them as mods; they were elitist but they were exclusively dancing to and behaving like the original mods from the 60s who discovered northern soul and all-nighters. And popping pills. And none more so than at the Twisted Wheel in Manchester, the ultimate mod club.

'But there were only half a dozen of us in Oldham in '78. Of course, you had the scooter boys who the press labelled as mods, but they were not mods. They were what we called "squares"; long-haired, Birmingham-bag-wearing twats! And yet they had the cheek to call us "plastic mods", the pricks! When the revival kicked in, in the summer of '79, all these scooter boys were wearing the two-tone suits and Ben Shermans. Half the teenagers in the country were, or so it seemed. I have yet to hear of or see a bigger cult in the UK. There were hundreds in Oldham and tens of thousands all over the country, all because of *Quadrophenia*. We early mod revivalists were always ahead of the new mods, who got their gear from Stolen from Ivor or off the peg. By '79 we were having our suits made to measure, buying classic English Loake loafers and Italian knitwear and shirts. I accept that in Manchester and Liverpool Perries and scallies were more fashionable, but in London, Brum, Leeds, Sheffield, Scotland, etc there were far more mods than anything else.'

The original Perries' mod-soul look had finally gone mainstream, but two different subgroups emerged from the melee in Manchester: plastic mods were rapidly extinct, while kids wearing sportswear and Adidas trainers managed to slip through the nets, hungry as they were for quality continental goods and a day out at the football. Blaney remembers how, as the trend took hold, these subgroups begin to pick up names for themselves:

'To be honest, we never tagged ourselves anything, but this name just grew and grew, 'cos people saw a lot of us wearing Fred Perries. The Fred Perry came to be worn by the lads who went to the footy and ragged the sports shops. But the fact was, we *never* called ourselves Perry boys, no way, as that was the name for the northern soul clubbers, not the footy lads. Even the name Man United's main boys picked up a couple of years later, the Inter City Jibbers, came from outsiders. We never got round to giving ourselves that name, yet we all agreed it was us to a tee. City's Kool Kats changed to the Governors and soon all the UK had casual gangs with calling cards. We never did bother with that kind of tagging. Our invented street sayings were plentiful, right up till the late 80s when the rave scene hit Madchester, with United's Men in Black running the show.

'One thing's for sure; we all put the travel bug down to supporting United at Etienne, and we had to play the return game in Plymouth as punishment for the hooliganism. We won that 2-0, with goals from Stuart Pearson and Stevie Coppell. Later, the FA arranged for us to play a friendly in Paris and around 500 of us went. The next round in the Cup Winners' Cup was Porto, which in that day was a long trek, and 1,000 was considered a good turnout. Years later United took around 15,000 to Porto for a second leg we knew we couldn't lose, but that 1,000 in '77 was a right turn-up. We got hammered 4-0, and beat them 5-2 at OT in the second leg. They were great days, when even a normal league match felt like a cup final, so you can imagine the drama at this one. The amazing thing is, 30 years after Saint Etienne, United did the exact same thing in Roma's ground. Only this time it was a fibreglass fence and the coppers were done up like Judge Dredd, a right nasty lot of fuckers who worked with Roma's Ultras. They broke heads in Rome in 2007, 'cos they'd deliberately set it up to happen like that. That's how times have changed for us in Europe.'

Since then, there's been more bother with United and Roma. Four United fans were jailed in Italy in December 2007 following disturbances in Rome. Italian Ultras actually smoothed the way for the United lads toward an easier passage when they were inside. This was facilitated partly by a Europe-wide communications network that has grown stronger over the past 20 years – manned by continental hooligans who emulate the English casual look by wearing designer clothing originally manufactured in their own countries, ironically enough. Friends and family of the jailed United fans travelled to Italy to offer support, while others behind the scenes utilised their connections there to emphasise solidarity against the authorities;

Italian football supporters are long-familiar with the heavy-handed tactics employed by Roman police, and were only too willing to guarantee peace for the incarcerated English. This must have been a huge relief for the families and friends of the four who were sentenced. The contrast between the 70s and the 00s is interesting. Back then, riots were dispersed, visiting supporters were complete strangers, and that was that. Today, the smallest infringement can provoke a brutal police response and ridiculous prison sentences. But the world is smaller, and thanks to improved attitudes and communication technology, innocent lads are afforded some degree of protection in otherwise hopeless circumstances.

But let's get back to '77. While the riot in Saint Etienne was underway, John Allen was hitting New York, eager to discover the blooming new-wave scene there and hoping to make his mark. Hoping to remain in the States indefinitely, he had to make it past the US Customs without a work permit, not an easy task back then:

'I had these letters that I'd been writing to people over there, and they'd replied, telling me I could work for them if I got over there. Stupidly, I packed these letters in my backpack, simply because I liked reading the fucking things, and they proved to be my downfall. As I was walking through customs at JFK, they randomly pulled me over for a search. They went right into the backpack and found those bloody letters. They gave me a summons, and agreed to let me go and stay with this vicar and his family. They lived an insane life in a rectory right in Manhattan, which is where I waited for my court date. They also took my passport and half of my money, so I was stuck.

'The rectory was a gigantic brownstone, right in the centre of one of the most alive cities on the planet. It was connected to the back of this massive church off Times Square. The corridors, halls and rooms were crammed with all sorts of peculiar oddities and trinkets. It was like a haunted house full of friendly ghosts, with the odd scary one thrown in for good measure. The vicar was fucking mental. His kids had this crazy long hair and his missus was a real earth mother. He was a gibbering conspiracy theorist, totally wacko, always ranting about government plots and evil forces. To cap it all off, they actually had a pet rooster living in the house. This thing would come to you if you whistled it, and it would sit on your knee and let you stroke it while you watched telly! The whole experience turned out to be even more stereotypically insane than I'd expected. I was anticipating *Kojak* crazy but I got *Monty Python* crazy instead. I thought it was ace.

'I had a pre-trial, trial and sentencing date lined up for court. When it came to the crunch they decided not to actually deport me, which was a blessing because if the Yanks deport you, you can't ever come back. Instead, they put this big purple stamp across the visa in my passport, stating Application Withdrawal. I was shipped home after one month.'

Allen offers no glimpse of America's streets, but the lad from Derbyshire must constitute a cultural Columbus among the travelling lads. His tale will resume later, as he returns to the USA for another crack, which sees him taking Greyhound buses cross-country and meeting all kinds of idiosyncratic characters.

Allen had tried something new purely because of an urge. But he wasn't the only one; people were becoming increasingly mobile. In Manchester, the music scene and the football hooligan gangs were overlapping more than ever; CCR, for instance, was doing Wigan Casino and Maine Road at the weekend, but soon he'd be doing the Big Apple instead. This was the stirring of a decade-long process that would propel Manchester into the media spotlight once and for all.

3

MIGHTY REAL

Of all that is written, I love only what a person has written with his own blood.
— Friedrich Nietzsche

What began as petty booty was about to be transformed into true swag. Musical genres, football and fashions reacted in a catalytic broth. Ideas in action monetised youth trends and movements. The economy was moving towards brand marketing. As the second-generation Perry boys and soul crowd matured they realised counterfeiting was a viable trick, as the hipsters and students fell into their trap. Small numbers of entrepreneurs began sourcing youth culture items en masse and the race to coin it was on.

Two contributors to this book, Rob W and Colin Blaney, present refreshingly different – from each other and from everybody else – perspectives regarding those Silver Jubilee days. Rob W lived on a council estate in Salford in 1977. He was a student at Manchester Polytechnic and graduated with a degree in fine art. He still lives on the same estate, in the same house. Colin Blaney, on the other hand, is made of somewhat different material. Neither of the two was content with Manchester's burgeoning music scene. Rob recoiled from the daftness of punk, while Blaney plotted ways to make money from it and hit the road, as others were doing.

Those who travelled with Manchester United were among the earliest to realise that money could be made from the underground tribes of the cities, by manufacturing fetish items for the worshippers. Manchester always had an appetite for the cooler music, be it soul or Roxy, but Blaney cites an unlikely contender for spawning the initial rise of duckers and divers in the Manchester grafting scene:

'Punk rock actually created a market for grafters in Manchester in the 70s. Around Crimbo 1976, going into '77, I was a school leaver. I was just starting a new job and my mates were too. Lads who were to become our firm were turning into young adults. Punks in the Jubilee period were at the crest of the wave, with the Sex Pistols at number one with "God Save the Queen" and the public outcry over it. The fashion in school was skinheads and safety pins through your earlobe, which you'd just put right in and keep in all day, no flaming the spike or fuck-all. It's a wonder half of us didn't joss it of tetanus. Not a one of us looked like punks, even though we were into the music, big time. We were all into plain t-shirts, training shoes and jeans that were getting narrower. A lot of the gear was wank compared to how it got a couple of years later, but the wheels were in motion. At night we'd be on the streets looking for action. We'd be at Collyhurst's Electric Circus, or Manhattan, waiting to see the Clash or some other band. Revelling in the changing scene and thinking about the history of the area. From the clogs of the 40s to the Scuttler gangs 100 years prior, it had all happened on that same Rochdale Road, right where these mad punks were now trying to rule the roost. After the gigs, the walk back into town for the punks could be hell. The Perry boys and others who hated punks were all over them like a bad rash. We were getting into the dressing race to improve and impress and punks were left eating our dust.

'Foo-Foo Lamarr, the drag queen, owned a club, next to another club called the Ranch, in the area at the time. The Ranch attracted all kinds of characters. The gay nature of the neighbourhood meant that new and socially-shunned acts like punk were welcome there. Foo-Foo was well in with some proper QS, and his bouncers were the hardest men in Manchester. They're famous for going into the Ranch one night and ordering the Buzzcocks to stop playing 'cos it was too loud for the drag-act punters next door.

'There's no doubt the grafting game was run by cockneys, but when punk hit Manchester things started to change. The fact was, punk came originally from the States. People will always say it was London, and that London and Liverpool sparked punk in the UK, but I disagree. The other spark that UK punk needed wasn't Liverpool. No way did that city have a venue to match the Electric Circus on Collyhurst Street. No other city had a punk movement at all, but we

had it going on, good style. The Buzzcocks, Sex Pistols, Angelic
Upstarts, Ruts, Stranglers, Stiff Little Fingers, Undertones, Clash, Ian
Dury, Siouxsie and the Banshees, you name it, we saw it and worked
it. Siouxsie Sioux even turned round once and said Manchester was a
cooler city than London, and all the bulldogs down there got the
hump massive. ['Bulldogs' are the more partisan Londoners.] A feller
called Vasie, who looked a ringer for Catweazle, started to give us a
bag of swag to sell before the shows. We'd knock out the swag, then
steam in and see the show. Then we'd all get positioned outside just in
time to sell posters when they were on their way home. The beauty
was it was all sale or return. Vasie later branched out with a stall on
Matt Busby Way and never looked back.

'At that time punk and heavy metal had loads in common when it
came to getting rid of our swag. They were interchangeable in terms
of what we could knock out to punters. The silk scarfs that punks
wore around their heads were worn by Quo fans around their wrists,
which they'd then use as air guitars. The leather wristbands, dog or
cat collars and tight black t-shirts, which normally they would rip the
sleeves off so as to have that cap-sleeve effect, we knocked all that
kind of stuff out by the vanload. Ultimately, this was just a bit of an
earner right on my doorstep, but I knew the bright lights of Europe
were there for the taking. It was like we were playing in the old
second division and we wanted to be in the first. But you had to work
your ticket if you lacked the ability to really graft. People like that
didn't last on the scene at all, so in time it ended up with a right load
of characters on it. It made us all of the same stock, comedians and
romancers who can have it night and day. That's why we're all such
smooth bastards with the ladies; we know how to talk to people
we've never met, and win their total confidence, and most of that
charm and happiness is genuine, that's the secret. I can sell anything
to anybody, and all the lads were like that. You've only got to cast
your minds back to how lads used to sound who were selling gear
anywhere; it was that proper Manc or scouse or cockney that you
knew in your guts was somewhere rough and poor. These days, half
the market stalls in town sound like they're from Northampton, for
some reason.'

Tony Wilson and others were coming into their own, and it was
Wilson who welcomed the Sex Pistols into the Granada studios long

before their infamous Bill Grundy incident down in the Smoke. My dad would point to the telly every night when *Granada Reports* was on and say, 'He's from Salford, that bloke, you know,' as if it were nigh on impossible that a Salfordian could have 'made it'. Maybe it was, but Wilson was right on time. While the famous Electric Circus epitomised the height of the Manchester punk scene, the Factory was waiting around the corner for the post-punk mutation to explode. The era between punk and Madchester hasn't been particularly well-documented, so I will let Rob W describe its beginnings in his home-grown quasi-mystical manner:

'We Factory-goers were like the Mandeans. The Mandeans came after the Old Prophets but before Jesus. We were a bridge. A foretelling.

'After the heavy metal idiots, the bacofoiled hod-carriers, the closet-queen showtunesmiths manqué, after the exciting abortion of punk, but before the perpetual now, we were.

'Yes, I'm a pretentious cunt, but my saving grace is that I know it. Through pretending we become.

'After the Electric Circus but before the Hacienda came the Factory Nights.

'The Factory was not a place like the Hacienda was a place. The Factory was a transformation, an occupying force, a portal.

'In the ulcerated colon of Hulme, on a bend in Royce Road slumped a characterless one-and-a-half-storey, council-built, cack-brick, 60s building. Lost amongst the limbo of crescents and vandalised rows of maisonettes, amid the confusion of planned tangle and narcotecture, driven past unnoticed by South Manchester's post-hippie dimtelligencia on their way to enjoy (read: doze through) a season of Yugoslavian agitprop animation at the Aaben Arthouse cinema a few hundred yards nearer to Trafford, and maybe "score" some "Leb Red" at a "shebeen" on their way home.

'What?

'Oh, just a social club. The Russell Club. AKA the PSV, the Public Service Vehicle Club, because it was opened as a club for Jamaican bus drivers and conductors. (Children, in those olden days a bus conductor conducted the sale of tickets and the behaviour of passengers on buses, and it was a Very Good Thing.)

'I don't think I ever saw a driver or conductor in the Russell, Jamaican or not. Black punks – yes, there were black punks; Alan

Erasmus, Tony Wilson's co-founder of the Factory Nights, was black, but he looked very early 70s, not punk at all; Rastamen, who sat crowded on the main stairs to the mezzanine, 'coz after all we were in their club, not they in ours; dealers; an impressively efficient bouncer. No Jamaican drivers or conductors. I think they must have been long bought out.

'You entered the Russell by a door down the side of the building that faced back along Royce Road toward south Manchester. Inside the narrow reception a ticket booth to your left, then through the door into the auditorium. The whole of the club was situated right of that door. There was a long bar immediately right, and facing the bar across the sticky floor of the audience space, a low, not very broad stage and the DJ's station. In between, in the early, quiet days, were tables where you could drink and talk before the DJ or the band came on. Our drugs of choice were beer, speed, cigs and ganja a distant fourth. Above the bar, looming into the auditorium was a mezzanine café that served fast food, mainly trays of chips in tomato sauce. That looming mezzanine provided a low ceiling to the downstairs bar which forced the tallest regular, a giant of about seven foot six, into an uncomfortable hunch. To either side of the bar were stairs to the mezzanine, the leftmost narrow and winding, the rightmost broader but crowded by those Rastas in their haze of sickly-sweet smoke, some of them very deftly dipping the dozier white boys and girls who climbed past them.

'And then Wilson. Posthumously "Mr Manchester".

'Half middleclass wanker-pseud. All genius.

'Professional Salfordian. Spent most of his childhood in the poverty-stricken Salford slum district of Marple, where gaunt and hungry accountants are worked all the late afternoons God sends, counting money. It's southeast of Salford Town Hall, just a 20-mile walk. His granddad sold me nana spuds, his other granddad pierced me mam's ears.

'In the earliest days of the Factory Tony would be on the door, taking your money.

'"Who's on tonight, Tony?"

'"Vini . . . the Durutti Column."

'Failing all else, Tony would have his mate Vini's band – a band in the very loosest of terms – on at the Factory. The Durutti Column was

– and is – nothing punk or post-punk. The Durutti Column was and is Vini Reilly and his melodic minimal ambient guitar.

'We had no enthusiasm for the Durutti Column, but the Durutti Column can stand for every reason why the Factory, why the Russell Club, was important, was great, was vital. As were the awful A Certain Ratio, who deserve a lot of credit for introducing funk to punk although their first musical babies were excruciatingly ugly, the poor little things.

'According to the New Testament, John the Baptist was the cousin and foreteller of Jesus. He was the bridge between Old Testament Judaism and the Christian and post-Christian world in which we have lived these last 2,000 years. He is almost forgotten, except by a small and endlessly persecuted minority in Iraq – every analogy eventually breaks down – who see him as the true messiah. They are the Mandeans.'

Rob W had witnessed big changes in young people during that bridging period, since a magenta Bette Bright had walked past him in Manchester in early '76. By late '77 Rob had tired of the hypocrisy and exaggeration of punk and he wasn't alone. A sudden shift in the type of footwear worn by hip young people occurred in a stepwise, almost enzymatic process as 1978 dawned. Outmoded and clumsy-looking 'bovver boots' were systematically excreted from the credibility chain. Royals, brogues and Gibsons – a totally plain leather shoe with an uncharacteristically hard sole, favoured by teeny hooligans like me for their superior kicking ability – all had their day, along with a daft denim/suede selection made by Levi's.

I well remember my mother ordering some Clark's Polyveldt for me from our catalogue, for which I spent weeks impatiently waiting. I wore them proudly to the local disco, sarcastically doing the kick to 'Ca Plane Pour Moi' by Plastic Bertrand, happy to be finally working my way into this nameless new fashion. Sarcasm was indeed a large part of it; take the piss out of everything. By mid-1978 Doc Martens and their various imitations were considered a joke. The tough-guy façade had been cast aside in favour of something much more fitting and final. The same could be said of football scarves; what had been a symbol of masculine territoriality had become an embarrassment overnight. The grafters' attitude towards souvenirs and memorabilia was taken up by the civilians and nutcases.

'I just got totally sick of the whole scene,' Rob continues. 'It was like, you'd go to the clubs that were meant to be top punk places, and they'd be playing stuff like Sylvester's "Mighty Real" all night, in between the music you were really there for. No one batted an eyelid. It was just the way things were. And the clothes and hairstyles were utter shit. I started backing off from it all, and began to wear very plain blazers, narrow jeans and shirts. I cut my hair in a short back and sides as a kind of rebellion. And I wasn't on my own in this boredom with the scene. The Roxy room at Pips was full of people in leather blazers ("Roxy jackets"), short back and sides and straight-leg jeans. Some of the kids who went to the match represented 1978's version of what you might call "street", and they definitely facilitated a crossover between the music, the clothes and the football. And God fucking help you if you ventured into the Roxy Room without being recognised by those in the know.

'All considered, the main fashion impact of punk was on male wear – it cleared out a decade of truly ugly shite. It allowed women to look more androgynous and wear tight trousers, but women's styles are rarely utterly contemptible, and there's a lot to be said even for a mid-70s Laura Ashley frock or a flared trouser suit. No, it was male fashion that punk revolutionised. Or more properly, reset back to the simplicity and purity of Beau Brummel.'

The look that came from the Roxy Room was somewhat separate from what was taking place in the Factory, but they were symptoms of the same dis-ease. In Liverpool club choices may not have been limited exclusively to Eric's, but the football-trendsetter hybrid was more quickly realised in that much-smaller pressure-cooker. Manchester's larger size created fractures in what would later become a singular fashion. The big collars, flares, bondage trousers and fluorescent socks were expunged by these trendsetters. But the caveman urge was not, and football was where this truth was manifest.

English football back then was a different business to what it is today. Stadiums were terraced; vast, stepped expanses open to the freezing wind and rain, packed weekly with tens of thousands of men, all of whom were working-class and full of mischief, beer and song. To the observer, the average football crowd resembled an ocean of heads, a swaying choir that gestured in unison. Thousands of raised forearms and critiques voiced in booming, obscene poetry. It was a form of organic calligraphy, steeped in local accents, exploding en masse when a goal was scored and taking a long time to settle down again. Supporters were penned in behind high railings which arched back over their heads. They assailed the players from their lairs along the touchlines like vicious caged animals hungry for blood. Just as different regions of the country used local accents to the most intimidating or humorous effect in song, different sections of football grounds projected various degrees of liveliness and evil. Millwall, West Ham, Newcastle, Chelsea, Tottenham, Leeds and Everton (to name but a few) were all notorious places to visit and few travelled to away games during this period who weren't at least partly looking for trouble. The various caged sections of these grounds attracted different personality types: the cheaper ends behind the goals became established lures for poorer people from the inner cities. The seated sections were more attractive to upper-working-class people and the terraced sections running along the wings were populated by a mixture of the decent, the half-decent and outright public menaces, depending on where it was and who the opposition were.

Manchester United's Stretford End was a notorious school of hooligan excellence, where innumerable young lads received tutelage in the ways of football violence. The art of covertly throwing a sharpened coin or a dart, or learning how to identify away fans by their (usually backward) fashion-sense, were all part of the hooligan skill-set, vital for young apprentices hoping to graduate to the frontlines as they matured. Those frontlines were the terraces of the Score-board End, and the United Road and Scoreboard Paddocks. From there they'd view the Stretford End in the same way a college boy would view his old school; fondly, but with a touch of condescension at the evident naïveté. Liverpool's Kop was a famous terraced end that was said to hold 26,000 people, twice as many as the Stretford End. The Kop has managed to retain an image of comedy and song, without being soiled by the shadow of violence so often associated with the Stretford End, despite the Liverpudlian tendency to use knives. This is probably because the knife-merchants jettisoned themselves from the Kop at a young age and chose to stand at the Anfield Road End instead, with that same sense of rank achieved. The Stretford End and the Kop are both dead and gone now, fossilised and buried amid the emotional debris of football history, drawing interest like the badlands where dinosaurs once left their footprints.

Behind the scenes and the hot dog stands, something more than just brutally battering visiting footy fans was taking place. Manchester soul seekers were going west. CCR remembers how the end of the 70s meant the beginning of a great relationship between a few Perry boys abroad and New York City:

'The decade spun and spun. Vinyl was king. Continental quilts became duvets. Aztec bars disappeared. Charlie replaced Billy. Druggy, soulful Prestwich was usurped by Manchester city centre. Punk lived and died within 18 months. And this boy was in a warehouse in Brooklyn, flipping through hundreds of deleted seven-inch soul singles. 1979. NYC via Manchester.

'Moving into Manchester was no big thing. I had a job on Princess Street as a junior draughtsman at an architect's. Jobs and apprenticeships weren't hard to come by in '78-'79. I kept fit at Moss Side Golden Gloves. Had a housing association flat above the Arndale. The city centre meant work, boxing and, ultimately, trawling ancient illegal Manchester gin palaces that had survived two world wars and a revanchist 60s council.'

The social scene of the time was a cool blend of grafters, up-and-coming piss-artists and other dropouts. The rest barely held down jobs Monday to Friday, just to pay for ale and turnstile. CCR was an obvious exception. Football grounds were very much the province of the male, but the Factory scene was more progressive. Rob W's take on it is a little different than most, and his sleights possibly considered blasphemous. What came out of this period was all about being you and *not* following the herd:

'Too many 70s music scenes were almost exclusively male and if you saw a girl, she was there because she was a girlfriend,' Rob explains. 'That was a large part of why going to gigs never appealed to me and my friends before punk. And obsessive pop fans were and usually are female. The Factory wasn't a club for boys. The Factory, like the whole punk thing, was a 50-50 male-female scene and as such fitted the forgotten rule of thumb: If something is usually of overwhelming interest to one sex only, it will likely be toss. If it appeals to both sexes equally it will likely be boss. Consequently people danced at the Factory Nights, both vertically and horizontally, though the horizontal dancing was perforce usually on the vertical as well, consummated in the biting ammoniac stench of the club toilets.

'Like any true scene, the movers and faces of the scene remained in the scene. Upstairs in the Mezzanine Chip Bar of the Russell on Factory Nights, the likes of the Buzzcocks and other bands would sit around comfortably enjoying their chip butties along with the ordinary punters, unhassled and uninterested in grandstanding. (Contrary to the claims of Buzzcocks and punk bores, nobody except Buzzcocks themselves ever called them Buzzcocks. They were always *the* Buzzcocks back then.)

'The Factory had punk bands on, but you were as likely to see Sheffield electroniks like Cabaret Voltaire, and the Human League before they were remodelled into BadABBA and had a couple of tolerable pop hits as a front band for Jo Callis and Ian Burden. And many of the faces from the Liverpool scene came to the Factory. Merging these two streams, people forget that almost-scouse electronikers Orchestral Manoeuvres in the Dark were originally a Factory band.

'The Factory wasn't a punk club. It was the First Club of the Lessons Learned.

'The lessons learned were these:

'1. Two minutes of inspiration should be packed into two minutes. Or less. Not stretched to half an hour.

'2. Doing the job earns the time. The point of dance music is to be danced to.

'3. There was nothing wrong with disco and funk at the Factory. If something can keep people dancing for ten minutes it deserves to be ten minutes long and it deserves to be played.

'4. Sing in your own voice, you aren't a black man from the Mississippi Delta and you aren't Jim Morrison; you're an electrician from Wigan and there's nothing wrong with your own accent.

'5. Punk is dead. Whatever the propaganda, punk wasn't going to change the world, start the revolution, politicise the poor misguided proles, or even kill the Dinosaurs of Rawk. It changed the cut of trousers and imposed the discipline of brevity, and that is enough. The Factory was the first public sign that Punk was, whatever the t-shirts said, Ded. This is a lesson that some still haven't learned three decades later, when many of the original learners of the lesson are grandparents or, on my council estate, great grandparents.

'So, with the Factory we had a club committed to chance-taking, a club for punks who had realised that punk wasn't the future and wasn't the end of Rawk, but had taught them useful lessons and a we-can-do-it attitude, a club with a deliberately-designed industrial look and a club that knew and didn't dismiss the pleasure of dance music. It did not wish death to disco.'

The music scene in the Northwest added that extra something to the styles coming in from Europe. Liverpool's post-punks converged in Eric's nightclub to eagerly explore their very own form of expression. The shit-stopper tight drainpipes, shetland wool jumpers and sandals had 'soul boy' written all over them. The wedge hairstyles told a tale all of their own. Bette Bright's band, Deaf School, with its unforgettably named vocalist Enrico Cadillac, sent Liverpool's proto-scallies silly. Deaf School's sound was polished and bizarre, a Zappa-esque vaudeville steeped in ironic dockside scouse sentiment, Manhattan Transfer twatted on acid in shameless rhinestone. Eric's is often cited as the place where the first football/post-punk crossover occurred. Manchester's Perries had also crossed from northern soul and jazz-funk into football songs, and off on an aimless search for form. For whatever reason it caught on like wildfire in Liverpool, but at least some of its roots were in Manchester. David Bowie and Roxy Music were ahead of their time with their own side-parted proto-wedge haircuts, small-collared shirts and narrow trousers and jeans. That their music was superlative was almost beside the point; they looked good, they had that same futuristic-yet-classic appeal, an English trait impossible to ignore.

The post-punk scallywags from Eric's and the Pips third-generation Perry crowd hybridised with football inside their own civic zones. Each spanned a growing radius like ink-blots on the landscape until the two formed one contiguous mass of peculiar fashion, unreported by the goons of Fleet Street. When those worlds collided, it was a chemical reaction gone very wrong; hatred was the product and the antidote couldn't be found. Only the grafters, the cosmopolitan pioneers, found common ground and that wasn't always an easy truce.

New wave was the music in the charts at this point, but the perennial soul and R&B were never far away. But like a tadpole whose rudimentary limbs are emerging as nodes in its flesh, another more melancholic but somehow intelligent form was finding its feet. I'd always believed the name 'Joy Division' to be a reference to bacterial reproduction – the pleasure of a primal sexuality that tore a thing apart – rather than the Nazi sex-slaves the band was actually named for. Rob W revisits this sooty transition, when the chimneys and industrial revolutions were finding a mechanised new voice that would inform much later strands of electronica. He also rubbishes my estimations of Ian Curtis's intelligence:

'Back to the Factory. The Factory wasn't a first-generation punk club. The first generation was the Electric Circus, Foo-Foo Lamarr's Ranch and perhaps the Squat, but these were just venues. They were rundown and/or small, and they became punk venues because they would let punk bands play, either because they were failing, or – like the Squat – they had a misplaced egalitarian commitment to allowing any old noise on. There were other venues like Rafters, and the various university auditoria, but these were incidental and could have been any club any time.

'The Factory was different. It was intended. It was deliberate. It was designed. It occupied the Russell Club but it wasn't the Russell Club. The Russell Club, with its brutal, ugly, barely functional, post-industrial Manchester architecture suited the Factory, it had the right ambience.

'But . . .

'The Factory was separate from the club it inhabited.

'The Factory/Factory Records had an ethos you probably know about, or have seen in *24 Hour Party People*, an ethos of being Magnetic North rather than Plughole London, of not binding its acts and workers to contracts, of taking a risk.

'The Factory had a consistent look provided by Peter Saville, and its records had a recognisable sound provided by Martin "Zero" Hannett, a curious blend of dub reggae mixing and string quartet attitude, where each instrument had the space to be heard on its own. This expansive open sound and the simple but memorable, melodic basslines of Peter Hook were the real genius behind Joy Division, not the maudlin self-pity and adolescent poetry of Ian Curtis. Curtis was a hollow-voiced Barron Knights Jim Morrison who couldn't hold a note, although he did have that vital thing – Stage Presence. Unlike most adolescent self-pitiers he had good reason to feel sorry for himself and it showed.

'The Hacienda was the venue in which punk attitude and Chicago house fused and then inflated into the dance universe that we inhabit in our perpetual now. But the seed of this universe was the Factory.'

Today many people bask in the refracted credibility of what the Factory and Tony Wilson were all about. But they do it from a distance of decades and from television documentaries and books that have informed them in the interim. I personally don't claim to know much about it but fortunately others do, as they were there.

*   *   *

In the Northwest, scousers and Mancs turned the tap on and let it run. To the tune of Viola Wills' 'Gonna Get Along Without You Now' and Buggles' 'Video Killed the Radio Star' we gave 1979's shite media vacuum a new twist. For two years the grafters watched droves of football supporters, punks, new wave freaks, heavy metal fans and others queue up to buy their wares. In turn they developed a derisory attitude towards those styles, as they began to chase their own desired look: the continental designer thug. Slowly, the French, German and Italian sportswear trickled into their hands, mingling with the domestic polo styles like Fred Perry and Peter Werth.

Bowie had catalysed the reaction by emulating the Perries several years earlier and adding to their look. A growing neighbourhood mob of eager lads were wearing their hair in the auburn-rinsed 'flick' style – the long fringe over one eye but lacking the more layered wedge at the back – often with black Fred Perry polos featuring yellow stripes on collar and cuff. Their taste in music was fluid and open, anything by Blondie, Roxy Music or Bowie plus the likes of Ian Dury, Elvis Costello and the Boomtown Rats.

It was this crew that dived onto the dance-floor of a local club when Madness' 'The Prince' was played there for the very first time. I jumped up with them, wondering what the hell this was, as they performed a cool dance to Suggs' bizarrely normal (for the times) cockney vocals – upper-arms by their sides but projecting forward below the elbow, fists raised up and out ahead like pivoting, twisting boxers, all the while bearing a hard expression, biceps straining against the black and yellow cuffs of the polo shirts.

The song electrified me; it totally lacked the bullshit of the new-wave scene, but contained keyboards and saxophones embedded into it like some ancient tradition. Feverish inquiry revealed the name of the band, which I mistook as 'Magnus', believing it to be a single bloke. I pictured Magnus wearing a fez, a Fred Perry and two-tone trousers, little realising how apt that was. I entered Wynd-Up Records, the local record store, the following day, and the Perry behind the counter sneered down at me when I asked for a copy of 'Orange Street' by Magnus. I wasn't even worth correcting; my money was rejected by the ultra-auburn employee in his burgundy chunky-knit jumper and white Perry polo shirt.

Fred Perry soon became Peter Werth became Lacoste. Me and my mates latched onto the styles quite early on, and people like Kezz quickly worked out where all the best shops in town could be found as we hunted down the rare and precious items. Some kids went for style while others went for labels, but Kezz, being a natural athlete, took a direct streamlined course that saw him unearth the most gleaming sportswear literally as it came off the production line.

1979 was a twilight zone, but by 1980 the Northwest's fashions were well-established, old hat even. Every day, before school, it was an exhilarating choice of what to wear: Kio's or Kickers? Slazenger or Second Image? French Connection or le Coq Sportif? One winter morning I remember my mother shouting me out of bed. It was dark and cold and she was very disturbed by something on the Piccadilly Radio newscast. When I went downstairs, she told me that John Lennon had been shot dead outside his apartment building in New York.

It was another brick in the wall of non-communication between ourselves and the scousers, guaranteed to ramp up the hatred when we played them on Boxing Day. It was something to look forward to; that sense of pure mutual alienation made the enemy so much more interesting. They would taunt us with songs about the Munich Air Disaster and we would laugh about Lennon – even as many of us practically worshipped the man and his talent, and many a football-loving Mickey was secretly in awe of the magic of the Babes.

The crowds were massive at those grudge games. Thousands of young lads in little crews of ten to 20 would converge into mobs hundreds strong. They would come on trains from early morning. Town was alive. Squads responding to rumours of locomotives arriving at specific stations combed the area. I remember lots of snowflakes but these were knitted into the ski jumpers the lads wore, not falling from the sky despite the bitter cold. The use of Stanley knives was commonplace, and every time two hooligan gangs collided there was always the possibility of serious slashings. The routine had become addictive; swaggering forward in one's best ski jumper or colourful corduroy jeans, imported Adidas tennis shoes or elaborate hiking coat. Hundreds would assume the formation; flicking the hair out of their eyes, striding along with arms going like the clappers, bouncing and pirouetting backwards to survey the size of the crew, the accents loud and offensive, raucous and game for violence. And then it would happen, that moment when the collective vehicle hit a patch of black ice. The inevitable collision of the two tribes.

You suddenly feel disoriented, frightened even, by the lack of recognition in the faces before you. It's a big mob wearing those same clothes, sending a wave of pure adrenalin physically into you. You can smell and taste it, that tactile flavour-burst on the bridge of the nose, the psychic taste of blood. That reeling sensation in the pit of the stomach, the twitching sphincter, quickly followed by the question: Fight or flight?

This was when the heroes were made. Mindful of the Stanley knives these bastards favoured, you would drift, numb on the feet, towards them, a contrived nonchalant smile on your face; anything to cause confusion in their ranks and make them believe we were unfazed. 'Casual' is a good way of describing it. And then the abuse, the goading and growling would start; no way were we ever gonna run from this lot. Each mob's disdain and viciousness resonated, forcing someone to make a move. Bigger lads would step up, their bigger lads would stand their ground. Then the nausea cleared and the cockiness returned. You became numb, drugged, game as fuck. That moment always happened collectively. The two sides would go mad, running into each other, shouting, kicking, punching, until the police and their dogs and horses converged at the interface, breaking up the melee before it was beyond recall. This was the dark winter's dawn of the Boxing Day casual era, when Manchester and Liverpool really did play for keeps and everyone else was a joke to look at.

* * *

The adult version of the children's TV show *Tiswas* was aired around this time. Called *Over the Top* (or *OTT*), it was hosted by Chris Tarrant and his assorted cronies. *OTT* came on around 11:00 pm every

Saturday night. It had a cast of characters perfect for the times: Lenny Henry with his taboo-yet-hilarious racial stereotypes, since mimicked but never equalled; Bob Carolgees, with his Spit the Dog puppet. Both of them had migrated to *OTT* from *Tiswas* with Tarrant. The show was hilarious but it wasn't the humour we craved, it was the music; each week, a three-minute slot was allotted to footage of 60s bands, beginning with the Honeycombs' 'Have I the Right?' in the very first show and followed by the likes of Manfred Mann's 'Doo Wah Diddy' and the Nashville Teens' 'Tobacco Road' on weeks two and three. Amazingly, we would cut our Saturday-night adventures short just to make it home in time to see these super-cool 60s stars strut their stuff, anxious that our parents didn't smell the alcohol on our breath. At the time there was simply nothing else like it. It was the music inspired by Merseybeat and the crazy Yanks from the peyote fields far away. It set the pace for the psychedelia we'd be bang into a year or three later.

Meanwhile, the likes of Colin Blaney were encountering the more vicious aspects of his cool new lifestyle. Blaney continues:

'By the time we hit the 80s the whole game was controlled by grafters who had worked and played the game on the roads of Europe. We'd hit everywhere, but one shady night sticks out, where we got justice a year or two later. Me and Rabbi were selling programmes around the Playhouse in Edinburgh, and we got chased by the local thugs who worked the security. They went over the top when they tried to slash Rab, even shouting they wanted to give him the Glasgow smile; Rab already had a huge razor scar on one side of his kipper, and one on the other makes it into that Glasgow smile, as when it's on the two sides it looks horrible. A bit like Jack Nicholson in *Batman*.

'When the big concerts were on at Maine Road, we'd blag the ice cream man to load up boxes of our programmes. We'd jib in later, grab a box each and hit the pitch, often selling out in five minutes. This one night, the security guards were getting their turnstiles ready to look after, and we spotted two of the Edinburgh goons who'd threatened to stripe Rab! I swear we had them crying for mercy. We just took over their turnstiles at certain times to jib in loads of punters for a score each. It was happy days. They never got a hiding, and while I sometimes feel that we should have kicked the shite out of them, you have to weigh up how many times in our life on the road we will come across divvies like these plonkers.'

Violence and blagging were never far from the obsession with fashion. Retail Manchester was excellent, but among the jumpers and training shoes cramming the sports shops there was plenty of unacceptable shite lurking. This is why only the discerning were able to survive and prosper. You had to go among the cotton, cashmere and leather and *know* what was what. So what if it had a Lacoste label? We didn't give a toss; it had to be styled correctly and that was that. This helped whittle down the Boys to a nice streamlined body whose sensibilities were One and who were as game as fuck.

The appearance of Mancs and scousers had been utterly transformed. The attitudes permanently pointed like a mocking finger towards convention. Going to the football was now a continental fashion show. The older lads in the neighbourhood were starting to notice that we were as with it as they were. They baptised us into the crew with a series of terrifying rites. One dark Friday night they took us in their car for a ride. They were giggling and winking at each other but we couldn't work out why. Goody, the driver, pulled the car down a narrow rat-run of a street stretching off to the vanishing point between the high walls of houses and gardens. His sidekick, Big Col, turned round to explain the drill.

'If you can handle this, you're one of the boys, alright?'

'Handle what?' we asked, puzzled.

'This,' Goody replied, laughing, suddenly giving the car a massive injection of petrol, sending us rocketing between the back walls and doorways on both sides of the passageway. Col turned again, an expression of wanton boredom on his face, a bizarre contrast to the sheer panic we were starting to feel.

'A main road goes right across the end of this little passage. We're gonna hit a little rise just before it, and jump right across the main road in the car. Alright?'

'*What*?!?'

Goody accelerated, and we could see the speedo moving up through the 60s and 70s, until the walls beside us were a blur. He gave a silent nod to Col, who did something truly horrific. Col deftly flicked off the headlights with a sausage-like finger, plunging the whole terrifying ordeal into total darkness. This was a practised move and the co-pilots braced themselves nonchalantly, like Wallace and Gromit in their space rocket.

The car was filled with the sound of our whimpering amusement. The walls were now completely invisible and the only discernible light was a small amber rectangle way up ahead; the streetlights on the main road. About 50 yards from the end, a car whizzed by from right to left and we gasped. Goody, instead of applying the brakes, accelerated some more and we let out a huge scream when we indeed hit a rise in the narrow ginnel and the entire car was airborne like something from *The Dukes of Hazzard*. We hit the ground on the other side of the road and skidded to a violent halt. All the doors flew open at once and we stumbled out, coughing, laughing, whooping, relieved to be alive. Goody gave my neck a few slaps and Col grabbed me in a headlock, scrubbing his immense knuckle against my scalp. Someone gave my arse a boot with an old, orange-dyed, flaking Stan Smith tennis shoe.

'Congratulations, dick'ead, yer one o' the lads now!'

As I lay in bed later that night, my scalp still tingling from Big Col's knuckle scrub, I thought about all the tales the lads had to tell. Stories about going to France and Germany, working on markets all over England, and going to away matches with United. I heaved a massive sigh before falling into a contented sleep; the next day we were going to Goodison Park to watch United play Everton, and by all accounts it was going to be a memorable trip. Everton were Merseyside's main firm and it was always a mad riot when we played them, even at Old Trafford. But you're probably tired of such things by now, so I'll move on.

In May 1981 I went to France, and even though the idea of finding exotic training shoes was an old one by then, France sowed a seed in me. I saw for the first time that entirely human-designed environments could be utterly beautiful (and very ugly, as testified by the unbroken mass of grey maisonettes which loomed from Calais all the way to Paris). As we drove through a multi-storey estate on the outskirts of Paris, I saw a gang of Liverpool supporters being corralled by French police, a mass of skinny kids in blue jeans, Adidas trainers and tracksuit tops; Liverpool were playing in Paris four days later, and this mob was easily 50-strong. They looked just like the French lads, with those tell-tale haircuts and designer labels.

Our trip took us all the way to Saint Tropez, Cannes, Nice and Monte Carlo. We spent days wallowing among the more expensive boutiques and cafés, scarcely able to believe the world could look and feel so good. I returned to Manchester ten days later wearing a pair of shoes never before seen in the city. I was more struck than ever by what these roving bands of grafters had created; every single clothes shop in Manchester had switched to selling designer gear in the space of two years. They had no choice, as fashion sensibilities had been irreversibly upgraded and the constant feed of new items from abroad meant there was no let-up. And, of course, the cockneys were on the case by now, adding their own grandiose slang and attitude. Things suddenly moved up a gear and moved roughly in the direction of the media. But it was too quick for them, even as the cockneys honed the styles right under their nose.

The road was long and winding, and increasing numbers of young people were shooting off in search of adventure. The economic downturn of the early 80s did much to propel these restless spirits off the map, away from the negative trend in working-class areas and across the sea to more positive climes. Nowhere was harder hit by Britain's early 80s recession than Liverpool's Toxteth community. Young men leaving school found themselves landing on the so-called scrap-heap before they even looked for their first job. Robin Peters was a young scouser growing up fast and weighing his options during the Thatcher years. What he saw developing on the streets of Liverpool comprised two worlds, and he knew full well which one he was going into. It wasn't a world that Margaret Thatcher dreamed existed, but she created most of the incentive for young lads to pursue it. Peters recalls this well:

'On the 3rd of July 1981, an 18-year-old black man by the name of Leroy Cooper was stopped by police on Selbourne Street in Toxteth, riding a stolen motorbike. A struggle started, triggering a series of events which led to the worst rioting ever witnessed on mainland Britain. It wasn't a race riot as some right-wing politicians would like you to believe. It was just the youth of Liverpool and the rest of the country, uprising. There are some in certain quarters that believe these riots facilitated the ease with which hard drugs such as heroin were able to enter the country. Maggie Thatcher's Tory government was under pressure around this time, and it is easily believed that the people in power were not really bothered about disaffected youth in inner-city ghettoes becoming addicted to smack.

'In the early 80s, you had to travel for a living or you were fucked.

There are fellers on estates in Liverpool in their mid-40s who've never done a legitimate day's work (cards in) in their life. They've seen five European Cups come to the city, three wars and four prime ministers, and they're still going strong. They're Maggie's Children.

'When I left school in May 1982 there were just 12 apprenticeships available in the building trade in Liverpool. The city was still hungover from the riots, and the television series *The Boys from the Blackstuff* was depicting the hopelessness felt by its inhabitants. Norman Tebbit had told us to "get on our bikes" to look for work. We went one better and chose Transalpino as our mode of transport. Liverpool being a port means that we've always had our large percentage of travellers returning home with stories from far-off shores, often laden with exotic goods not seen here before. The scallies of the early 80s were no different. It was partly due to what we called the "Transalpino rub-out".

'The 80s lads who weren't prepared to sit around were the kids that chose Transalpino. Transalpino was a magic word back then, like "Open Sesame!" and we were the thieves, only there were a lot more than fuckin' 40 of us. Basically, Transalpino was a student travel company set up in a portacabin in Myrtle Parade in Liverpool. The people who ran it must have been scratching their heads at the sudden surge in business in early May 1981 as hundreds of young "scholars" were booking trips to Calais and Oostende. Liverpool had just reached the European Cup Final in Paris, and Transalpino were unwittingly unleashing a crime wave on Western Europe. This crime wave probably made an impact on high-street fashion to this day. A mate of mine who's no longer with us was the original "Transalpino rub-out boy". He doctored Transalpino tickets so that you could book and pay for a trip to Calais, but then change it to Hamburg, Vienna, Zurich and the like with the use of a bit of brake fluid or an ink rubber. His bedroom was like a cross between a travel agent's and a sports shop. You had blank National Express tickets, Persil train tickets, stolen Austrian Inter-rails and doctored Transalpino tickets. These were joined in his room by Adidas training shoes like Forest Hills and Trimm Trabs, along with Fila Bjorn Borg tracksuits not yet seen on these shores. It was a right little cottage industry! The Inter-rail scam came to an end for us in Aachen, when we were awoken getting our heads down on a train in the sidings in 1983. The German police couldn't understand why four Austrian students couldn't extend their German vocabulary beyond the words "danke" and "bitte". I soon learnt three more words: "licht raus bitte" (turn the light out please), after four days in the local nick. Surprisingly, Transalpino later went bust.'

By neglecting the working classes for years, Thatcher created a monster with the imagination and stamina to outlast the decades and earn a crust by hook or crook. In northwest England necessity bore many children, and they were inventive little buggers.

As the trend grew, the tendency to travel simply to rob decent gear became a mainstream occupation in the two cities and in London and beyond. Much of this booty was brought back to England, where eagle-eyed fashion hawks considered its suitability for the boutique window. The fact is, many of the owners of Manchester clothes shops were begging for info on what might be the next big thing. The next big thing turned out to be simply the enhanced organisation of the entire grafting game, a development which attracted heavier attention and even larger numbers of boys eager to earn some beadage (cash). The Northwest probably has the largest organised crime culture outside of London, yet the Manchester underworld has remained relatively undiscovered by social commentators. True to form, Manchester's refusal to cooperate with media mouthpieces has created a huge amount of curiosity regarding the machinations of their secret structures and hierarchies. The buccaneering clan of Scots that evolved into the famous Quality Street gang matured into a mob able to control much of the organised crime in the Manchester area. The QS have been the subject of much speculation and there is no doubt that, from the 60s onward in Manchester, a reference from the QS meant doors would open and things could happen for you. Blaney continues his account of how things evolved, and why:

'New ideas always drove us on. Many a time we put our own money into posters and t-shirts. It was all about coming up with summat new. We were the first to print programmes, for instance. Back then the game was wide open, and if you had ideas you could fall out of bed and make money. When it came around November, we'd print a poster of Man United from that season, and at the bottom put the next year's calendar. They sold like hot cakes, a pound each outside Old Trafford. Over a few years we had our own stalls, but the new Premiership soon saw us and all the rest moved on, rapid. It's the same with all the concerts in town nowadays; it's all trading standards and masses of red tape, paraphernalia and fuckin' gobbledegook.

'When we went over to Europe on the rob with no football games to give us an excuse for being there, we really did start to pick up items of clothes that all the main workers in the best shops wanted to buy off us all. The Manchester lads have always had an eye for style, and this just took off like a lit match to a lake full of petrol. All the lads who were in borstal got visits off us and only then, on the visits, did we suss out all the scousers, weighing us up, asking loads about our clobber. We knew then we had sort of surprised them all as we'd done trips to Swissy, which they called the "Land of the Wad". We'd sell our Big Bens, which is what we called Rolexes, many a time to the main grafters who ran the concerts and sometimes even to the stars. Some performers would even chill out with us in bars, wearing a baseball cap so as not to be noticed. I suppose if I was a known artist I'd like to take time out with the street grafters and have a right old chinwag and a few scoops. The best thing about following the concerts round the world is it's a great excuse to be in the area, and even if you don't graft selling briefs [event tickets] you can always sell stolen clobber and drugs, which is all part of the extended entertainment business, as we like to say.

'There were a good few lads round town that had big notions of where all this could go, and it was only a matter of time before someone put the right formula together. The real big breakthrough was down to two brothers from Stretford called the Dinks, both United mad but not thugs. They recognised that us lot were needed to do the graft, 'cos who else is gonna fuckin' do it? And so the link between the grafters and the organisers came to pass. Their first deal was with Status Quo, which saw all the grafters staying at the same hotels and attending many parties with the band members and roadies. Around this time, I got my first ever deportation order from Rotterdam, for robbing the purser's [the bloke who works the money exchange] wallet; he fell asleep at the bar, so I dipped him clean as a whistle. I got nicked due to bad luck when the customs pulled us over at random and gave us a thorough going over. I was amazed how they took it so casual, as there were 3,000 guilders and bits of other cash. They just said, "Admit to it and we'll throw you back on the next boat," which was a blessing in disguise as I met a bloke called McKee and he got me in with the Dinks.

'We did the full Europe tour, then moved onto the heavy metal group Kiss. The Dinks by that time realised we were a danger to them, as we were too wide with the robbing. They jetted off to do a full Asian tour and now live the jolly life in Australia. This left a vacuum which was filled by the Kav brothers in Europe. Later, in the 1990s, a couple of other mobs moved in on the game. These were not people who you fucked with by any means, and though the game had gone bent by that time they were the main movers and shakers on the grafting front. Once the QS moved in on it, it was done and dusted.'

The Northwest and London enjoyed the chief spoils of this earner, but other regions were becoming involved too. Cardiff, long considered a wild and somewhat exotic place due to its tough docks area (nicknamed 'Tiger Bay'), spawned a roving mob. The Cardiff Soul Crew were fond of travel, especially if thieving could be incorporated into the usual football violence. The Northwest fashion influenced these Welsh seasiders, who eagerly threw themselves into the travel scene with no fear. Jeff Marsh, author of Cardiff hooligan tale *Soul Crew Seasiders*, was one who resisted the foreign styles at first but soon succumbed to the general challenge and sense of covert intelligence inherent in organised trips abroad.

'When I started out in the football hooligan game, everyone was skinheads,' Jeff remembers. 'The hassle from the police was unbelievable, taking your laces off you, or even confiscating your Doc Marten boots. As a direct result of this, some people started to grow their hair and tone down the out-and-out aggressive look of the skins. As time went by the bowl hairstyles were starting to appear, and tennis-style jumpers. This was sometime in 1982. I used to think they looked like a load of poofs, but I knew them and I knew they weren't. In fact they were just as violent, if not more, than we were, but they looked like the boys next door. I soon realised the police were targeting the skins and these new poofy-looking boys were getting away with murder. I remember I bought my first skiing jacket and had my hair shaped like a bowl. My girlfriend at the time laughed at me and said, "You look just like your trendy mates!" Pringle jumpers and Tachini tracksuits were coming in, and Adidas Gazelle trainers were all the go. We didn't have a lot of money so we had two options: nick them or buy them cheap from thieves. Many's the time we would smash-and-grab clothes shops at away games. If you had a load of gear from a shop, you'd fuck the game off and just get back in the van and go home.'

Despite the cockneys, Mancs and scousers controlling the 'official' situation in Europe, the wild Welsh and others like them weren't shy about venturing into the fray and grabbing whatever they could. The Soul Crew began to explore the continent themselves as the means of obtaining the prized labels grew both sophisticated and barbaric. Marsh participated in this free-for-all with mad abandon, all of his tribe eager to make money as well as to simply laugh at the establishment. While the Manc and scouse centurions were setting up their grafting fortresses, the Cardiff lads propelled themselves gleefully into robbing sprees and drunken raids on Britain and Europe's booty.

'The Cardiff Docks boys were famous for this, they'd drive up to towns where Cardiff were playing in a few vans, smash and grab or simply "steam" the shops, taking all the designer gear, then go straight home. The police would be looking for them, stopping people to see if they had more than one jumper on, but the thieves would be long gone. Stuff like Lacoste was gold dust, but places you could get it were few and far between. It was soon realised that this stuff was everywhere in France and a lot of the boys were over there all the time, with stolen cheque books, shoplifting or simply smashing the windows and helping themselves in the middle of the night.

'One time we went on a stag do to Brussels and in the middle of the night a paving slab went through a shop window, and all the boys ran in and helped themselves to all the clobber. We couldn't take it back to the hotel, so we hid it in the bushes on a canal bank, and sent one guy to get our van. How he drove it is anyone's guess, as we were all totally wrecked. He came back and we all piled in the back and drove back to the hotel. How we got away with it I'll never know, although there was no CCTV in those days. When we got back we sold all the stuff we didn't need and had some nice gear for ourselves. It was wicked as it was rare stuff no one else had.'

The Northwest project continued apace and faces from Liverpool and Manchester inevitably became acquainted. An unexpected friendship developed but this newfound peace wasn't always given a chance. The threat of serious violence lingered tantalisingly over camp. Sometimes there were fall-outs between the major crews and their uneasy world threatened to crumble. Only the fact that an intra-grafting war between different firms would destroy productivity stopped them going toe-to-toe. All the grafters wanted to be in on the big shows and their bosses were pressuring them to deliver the goods and earn. Those who represent the invisible force behind it all supply the momentum and the lads knocking out the swag are their battering ram. The big boys and the heavy mob wouldn't have wanted to back down in the event of a real conflict, so things would have deteriorated horribly. Blaney remembers such incidents with trepidation:

'The period from 1987 into '88 was the probably the best time to get on whatever tour, as they all went huge. Bowie's *Glass Spider*, U2's *Joshua Tree*, Jacko's *Bad* and many more were the golden age of grafting, money-wise. A big one that springs to mind was Villa Park, when the Boss was doing his two-shows-a-night tour, 1988. This was the night a very naughty kick-off nearly went on. The grafting game is forever changing and this causes conflict between touts. Touts were accusing other touts of nicking their punters, or charging too much or too little. It's a kind of price-fixing, but like in any business in the real world it has to be done. It's easy to fall out, as did Mickey Williams, who was Man City's top tout, after a barney with one of the top scousers. It was split up by the dibble or security before things got out of hand, but the entire swag game knew it wasn't sorted. The next biggie was Madonna at Wembley. All the Mickies had a meet in the Hilton nearby, while a crew of Moss Side came down tooled up. I'm glad to say it never kicked off, but it was the closest ever to a full-on riot as no doubt it would have spread wicked. Lots of people could have got hurt or nicked, with all the money wasted that each firm had invested in the venture. Even though the cockneys no doubt have always and always will run the show when it comes to touting, there was bad thunder in the air that frightened every fucker when these two firms went head-to-head. It was very much expected to kick off on Wembley Way that night, and no doubt if that call went up I would have been in like Flynn. But I'm glad it never, for my thoughts at that time were that the Mickies are still even today not mixers with the blacks. That gang fight would have turned into a race thing or war. It would have been worse than the Hillbillies versus Moss Side back home, a gang war that claimed many lives.'

The scouse grafter Robin Peters also has his take on the situation between Manc and scouse. He recalls an ambiguous relationship with the spivs and grafters of his neighbouring city:

'I still do the concerts and the swag and am very friendly with a lot of the Manc grafters. I well remember the mad adventures from the early 80s, before the scousers and Mancs were friendly. In fact the scouse lads were present at Mickey Williams' funeral a few years back. Our friendship went from strength to strength, little do the kids of today know. For instance, in the early 90s it came on top at a service station on the outskirts of Zurich. Me and two mates got nicked with a car full of video cameras and other stuff. I escaped, only to be rescued by five Mancs in a Fiat Panda who somehow fitted me in and took me 300 miles to Lausanne. I became great mates with one of the lads, Little Col from Wythenshawe, and travelled the world grafting with him until he died a year or two ago.'

Peters witnessed a number of clashes between Mancs and scousers on his travels, events which were long discussed in the world of grafters as rumour and friction travelled the grapevine, ramping up the tension.

'The two groups clashed again on another occasion, when four of the scousers were sitting on a train in Oostende, en route to Germany. They had to run for it when 40 Mancs boarded the train on their way to an England game. The four Mickies had to take cover in the bogs until border guards got on at Aachen and saved them. By then, the Mancs had actually battered a hole in the toilet door and were spraying fire extinguishers through it.'

Blaney and Peters dwelled in an alternative universe, as removed from the normal onionskin of the daily grind as the moon. The impulse to just fuck right off was always strong and this appears to be a genetic proclivity for a grafter. The nine-to-five is impossible for them. Blaney continues with his big-picture perspective:

'When it comes to the Brits abroad, we really run the show. Our bottle to go anywhere comes from our past: sailors on the rampage all over the world. It's in the blood. I suppose every country's grafters hate us yet we have to get along most times, for selling all the merchandise is better when it's passed around, with no sharks going through the slips with the dosh. A funny one is Scandinavia. Their street sellers are all Algerian, so at times when they step into the game it goes pear-shaped. Blade merchants. It's hard to say how many workers there were in total at the height, but I'd say from the mid-80s to the 90s, every country had concerts in halls, stadiums, parks, etc, going on three to five times a week. Around 250 grafters would cover that. Add to that the amount of countries and I work out that the swag game had at least 1,500 bulldogs, Mancs, Mickies and others covering them all. It's amazing.'

Jeff Marsh and the Cardiff crew somehow managed to make a living around the peripheries of this organisation, but the rigours of living on the wrong side of the law gradually wears people down, as Marsh discovered.

'The whole thing was a way of life for us, and although Cardiff don't often travel abroad we've gone abroad many times on missions. I can remember us breaking into an Armani shop in Greece while on holiday and getting back to the room only to find most of it was fake (although good quality fakes which still sold well back home). We really felt like the shopkeeper had "done" us. Cardiff lads went everywhere performing the same routine: smashing, grabbing, steaming, you name it. Some of our boys burgled a shop in Majorca and were selling the jeans and stuff on a street corner when they were nicked and deported. The fighting, the thieving, the clobber; it was as if we were born in that mould and we had no choice but to go with it. These days I've retired. I can't do the jail anymore, but I look back on all these adventures as the best times ever and I wouldn't change a thing.'

The young scousers and Mancs grafting at concerts and football games were overflowing into almost every town worth a five-minute scope for goods to steal. And there were plenty of humorous moments that have made their way into grafters' folklore:

'It was quite common to bump into other firms of scousers when walking out of train stations around Europe, even when there wasn't a game on, and instantly you knew you were wasting your time in that town, as the local sports shops had already been "ragged" and the local police would be looking for gangs of sportswear-clad urchins with girls' haircuts,' Peters remembers. 'Scousers and Mancs would often clash in Europe, and on one occasion at a Rolling Stones concert in Basle a group of Manc swaggies, who were also hooligans, clashed with a group of scouse thieves who were also hooligans. During the fighting Tony B was split up from the rest of the firm, and he ran through a park chased by the Mancs. When he thought he was out of sight he jumped into the bushes to hide. After a few seconds he heard rustling behind him and he started, thinking the Mancs had found him. Instead, it was two gays getting stuck up each other! They asked him if he wanted to have a bash, but he politely made his excuses and left. He decided to risk the wrath of the Mancs rather than engage the two batty boys enjoying a bit of al-fresco.

'But it wasn't just Mancs we had to watch out for on the continent. One time, a powder fire extinguisher was fired at Austria Vienna skinheads in '84, seconds before some of them were slashed by scouse grafters on a metro train in Vienna. They boarded wearing their purple and white colours but alighted wearing white powder with a mix of red claret. The travelling grafters had to disguise themselves in the ground with ski hats and bubble coats, while police accompanied by witnesses tried to identify certain scousers in the away end. The scousers were asking themselves: had the skinheads turned supergrass? They hadn't; it was the owners of jewellery shops and sports shops ransacked earlier in the day, trying to pinpoint the culprits.'

Blaney's realisation that weaponry was the order of the day didn't kill his sense of humour. His description of a typical scouse mob of dressed-up 'cutters' resounds with Manc provocation typical of the time. He urged me to include the following paragraph for the delight of winding up our friends to the west of Manchester:

'You could really tell the scousers back then,' he claims. 'They reckon it was 'cos they were wearing the proper styles earlier than us, but I swear the real reason was more to do with the stock they came from. If you saw a mob of young skinny Mickies it was unmistakable: fuckin' bobbing Adam's apples on long necks and big beaks for noses. Added to that were the ears, unreal flappin' jumbo jobs on the sides of their heads, and always flicking that hair like they did. They all came from some area of Ireland where everyone was a right ugly cunt and then they bred with each other in the 'Pool, making it worse. It was a gangling mass of apples, beaks and ears framed in wedge hairstyles, like Ringo cloned 200 times, going mad singing, "Twist and Shout". They'd be fuckin' twistin' and shoutin' alright when we got stuck into them and made a few dents in the fuckers' kites. We called it "flapping" when a mob got run, and these scousers looked like a gaggle of turkeys. There were all sorts of weapons going on back then, not just the Stanleys. It was war.'

The Glaswegian razor gangs of old seem to have transmitted their choice of weapon forward in time, where it was translated into a variety of implements. Sharpened combs were a good cover due to their being legitimate items to carry, but there were other improvised weapons which could be used and discarded once the fun was over. It was an evil way of defending oneself, but *in extremis* beggars could not be choosers; perpetrators would snap a car aerial off and wrap the skinny end around their two main fingers. It was easy to conceal when totally compressed up the sleeve, all wrapped and ready to deliver. A swiftly-moving platoon of lads could strip aerials from many cars rapidly and revert to 'lock and load' attitude, as they travelled at a steady pace through alien streets. Sometimes the aggressors, closing in on their prey, would find the tables suddenly reversed, the antenna unleashed like a cobra to its full four-foot length. The thing would telescope out in a split-second, ripping faces up with the jagged, snapped-off ends. Some claimed 'proper results' over time during this era of bloodletting. For every square foot of stitched Manc flesh there were cheeks and ears in Liverpool laced with scar tissue. The caveman boot-boy era of the 1970s had been left far behind. A new 'steel age' had been ushered in, thanks to the stainless tools of the trade. Going to the match took on a sinister edge, as did grafting around Europe. The possibility of receiving wounds that required hundreds of stitches in a flash was all too apparent. It was one thing when these grafters met on the continent in small numbers, but the real deal occurred when they were all back to reporting for duty to their respective clubs and those clubs clashed in pure hatred. Cockney Sam was a well-known member of United's hardcore firm. A large black lad belonging to United's London contingent, Sam was often in the thick of the action, as Blaney explains. Sadly Cockney Sam is no longer with us, having succumbed to an early death like many others who take the road less travelled.

'Other ways of defending ourselves were more simple, like always wrap a scarf or jumper around your hand which would be in action to stop the cuts. I knew lads who wore sheepskins even in the summer in Scouseville, as you tucked your hands in the cuffs when you steamed in if the Sheffield [steel] came at you. The thickness of your cuffs would catch the main part of the blade. At one time period when the scouse-Manc thing was at its peak, Man United had a firm which almost matched them for two or three years when it came to giving out the stitches. We had it so Cockney Sam had his own firm for which the younger crew carried all the blades, and Sam's orders were soon heard and carried out. The evil bladesmen were mainly Salford, and the firm of carriers were from our neck of the woods. They all ended up in Walton Prison in Liverpool, for a massive fight on the Blackpool Pleasure Beach, where they cut up the bouncers who thought they were kids to slap around. Around seven of them all got five to seven years each, and Walton's slashers were soon took back when they saw Billy Black and Co, as they'd been at each others' throats for years. The fact is, in the end they all got on like a house on fire! I've seen many a scouser scoring parcels of booty from these same lads when they'd finished their jail terms.

'True to say though, overall there's no city in Europe who have had the same amount of slashers as the scouse. They are the innovators if the truth be known. When you go back to the late 60s, when all the skinheads smashed the trains up to get a taste of aggro, they thought they'd invented it. But the Mickies were doing it in the 50s, wrecking trains and mobbing up proper.

'You felt sorry for them that got lifted and missed out on all the mobbin' an' a-robbin'. The scouse borstal kids would be looking at us with goldfish gobs, well open in despair, but their visitors, mainly the women, and even the screws, were gutted. Many a time they'd kick us off visits, jealous of all the scouse birds whispering to us that we looked mint, or for some old excuse, like passing a cigarette. We rocked the place when we turned up, looking brand new. The styles were bang on, a huge amount of thick hair, smoothed and layered in a mop or block wedge round the sides and back. We had the fucking things pampered fortnightly, and even had the tips coloured along the swinging fringe. We really were like pop stars and all had this one-eye look similar to the one the Scuttlers had in their day, a hundred years ago.

'There was a time for three or four years where every weekend all the grafters would visit others in Hindley, Stoke Heath and Weatherby, the main three borstals. There were people in Rochdale's Buckley Hall, Foston Hall and one near Boston. This was when even our haircuts were looked at with amazement, as we had our barnets cut every other week in airports round Europe. It was a pure buzz; the clothes and even our cars were checked out with confusion. At times we heard comments like, "Are they a new pop band?" The visits to Europe were a good excuse for being in the area: Augsburg, or along the lakes at Biel and Neuchâtel, with Austria, Swissy, Germany and French customs all in reach within an hour. Fucking magic playground for lads like me, that. We even had the odd bent caravan sorted so we wouldn't leave a paper trail with hotels on our case for dodgy passies.'

Cardiff's Jeff Marsh became ever more embroiled in his city's violence and crime, and forced himself to make a career change following a serious offence against supporters of my own football club, for which he was convicted – and which obviously has to be condemned. It is, however, a symptom of the period.

'In 1989 I was sentenced to two years inside for stabbing two Man United fans at Barry Island Butlins. When I came out I went back to the football, but I was a lot warier and less willing to take mad risks than before. That's when I took up smuggling booze. There was also a lucrative sideline in weapons, like CS gas, knuckledusters, etc, which cost peanuts in Calais and could be sold for up to £20 each. I daresay we had a bit of that.'

Marsh's smuggling adventures will be covered later. The unfortunate use of knives was common in Britain by the late 80s, and this age-old tendency in British men seems reluctant to ever go away completely. As time passes and the character of the youth changes, it continues to be a growing problem.

*   *   *

In the internet world of today, any commodity can be located and bought online in a matter of seconds, including events tickets and designer sportswear – much of which might be counterfeit. Sites like eBay have profited massively from people buying and selling at an inflated price, as well as providing bargains that one might not encounter elsewhere. The retro or vintage designer gear that people look for on websites – or the tickets and programmes to concerts and sporting events – have become a whole industry in themselves. The internet has become a feedback loop that supplies the world with designer clothing sought and gathered by collectors.

The current laws in Britain stipulate that any event ticket can be resold at a profit, except football tickets. It is imagined that this helps control football hooliganism by ensuring that the supporters of one team are kept segregated from the other. More recently, clubs like Manchester United and Chelsea have endorsed an official secondary web-based ticketing entity. They are responsible for selling unwanted match tickets for season-ticket holders online, charging the season-ticket holders a small fee and always selling the tickets at face value. There's been recent talk of creating a 'crown jewels' of British sports, which are to be protected from touts. It's very appropriate, given that many of the travelling grafters sometimes rifled hotel safes and jewellers' shops as a sideline to tickets or swag.

Today's online ticket industry is a booming juggernaut which has seen companies from the USA come into the European market and vice versa. Modern ticket companies employ dozens of people to man telephones and keep the register of events orderly and easy to access. There are many personality types involved in the upkeep of ticket resale websites, including web-developers, artists, programmers, HTML code writers, marketers, accountants and lawyers. Terms like 'search engine optimisation', 'pay-per-click' and 'point of sale technology' are bandied about as the multimillion-pound harvest keeps coming and punters flock to the arenas where their heroes strut their stuff.

Modern touts hold secret codes to access ticket resource banks. They have minions in possession of multiple IP and email addresses, phone numbers, aliases and family contacts of all ages that deliberately join fan clubs and web-based official sites in order to obtain tickets before the real fans. The array of services and the geographic scope of the transactions know no bounds. In truth, you're only as good as your last gig. When the touts buy up all the tickets the day they go on sale, they do the promoters and Ticketmaster a huge favour. Touts are investors and run the risk of misreading public demand for tickets. Sometimes they lose big, sometimes they make hay. You can find any ticket you desire in seconds with a simple internet query. If everyone chooses not to buy then the touts eat shit. If the world wants a ticket to a certain event, the touts become devils. They can't win, but they try. It is hard to believe today's multimillion-pound ticketing industry began with a handful of cockneys in long coats whispering to people outside football grounds. But it did.

*   *   *

The fish which climbs the mountain stream can sometimes find itself multiplying over-abundantly, and as the graft and touting caught on

IAN HOUGH

with other gangs around England, Blaney realised that they would soon outstrip their carrying capacity and a dieback was inevitable.

'A few other firms that were around at that time besides us, the cockneys and the Scousers were Southend, Stokies, Wilmslow and the Zulus from Brum,' he recounts. 'Today anyone can try their hand at it, 'cos it's all old hat. Even the ticket touting's been torn to pieces by the latter-day amateurs. The original ideas have been hijacked by cackheads from all over the gaff.'

The original grafters who maintained their dizzy heights at the top of the swag mountain had to assimilate newcomers, and what had been an adventure playground was reduced to old-fashioned business. The grafters had carved out a niche for others to follow, but oxygen was becoming scarce and it was time to move on, as some of these characters did. Some went into more serious crime. Some moved into more respectable avenues, which involved selling swag in its original rather than counterfeit form. The mid-80s saw those imported fashions go mainstream, setting up an appetite for designer-wear that was to become a serious addiction – or at least a fetish – for many British men. As they aged, many were sucked into the mortgage mangle, and needed their distractions.

Others had simply been infected by the travel bug.

4

THE STUFF THAT DID YER 'EAD IN

People don't take trips. Trips take people.
— John Steinbeck

982 was a funny year. It was the year Perry ran its course in Manchester. When Adidas issued their Korsika/Palermo shoe range – trainers that were actually shoes – we'd come full-circle from the Hush Puppy days of 1979. For some tribal elders, the whole Perry boy era had been just a latter-day pimple on the arse of something much more interesting. CCR was one such chap. By '82 he'd been around the block and found himself sitting on a stool in the corner of a boxing ring:

'It's 1982. Rotters club on Oxford Street, home of the disco divas. I'm bottom of the bill, opening bout. Facing a 35-fight perennial loser from some arsehole Derbyshire mining village. Hard as fuckin' nails this bloke; shoulders like a Hungarian grave digger.

'I'm sitting on my stool thinking, "It ain't no big thing to wait for the bell to ring . . . ain't no big thing, the toll of the bell."

'Easy enough for that suave twat Ferry to say, but then again he wasn't sat where I was sat.

'"Make sure he doesn't knock yer out," whispered corner man Jack, "yer mam's in the crowd."

'This was my second (and last) fight in the paid ranks. 250 bar straight in the back bin would go some way to sorting a deposit for a flat in Whalley Range, 11 grand in cold blood being the mortgage (yeah, I know, stop sniggering at the back). I had to virtually fellate the bank manager to part with the beadage. Three times yer income full fuckin' stop. That was the rule; miss one payment and we'll have yer guts for garters, Sonny Jim. It still put me way ahead of the pack.

'So I'm sweating like a blind lesbian in a fish shop, waiting for the bell to ring and cursing the lyrical talent of Ferry . . .

'Currently pitched up in a top Arndale housing association flat, 50 quid a week, unfurnished. Back in the 80s the tenants in these flats were just about the only residents in the city centre. There were a few poncey apartments down Liverpool Street generally reserved for *Coronation Street* thesps. Apart from that, gentrification of Manchester's core seemed impossible. But life was good. Well dug in work-wise at a city centre architect's. At uni burrowing through a degree which would take seven years out of my life.

'Good money, cheap rent, no travel expenses, occasional income supplements; never had it as good before or since. I had loads of time for nefarious recreational activities, which coincidentally involved minimum expense.

'Style-wise, the faith was kept. A few bad-influenced lapses had occurred, involving Adidas, Sergio Tacchini and Naf Naf. These were quickly eradicated. Faded Wrangler straight jeans with small frayed turn-ups lapped softly onto Loake brogues (tan) or loafers. Tops were still by Fred Perry (or Lacoste by this time). Expensive watches liberated by Man United's far-flung hordes from naïve Swiss airports abounded. The twin bullets of sheepskin and jumbo cord I neatly sidestepped. I was now clearly an old-school soulie, tinged with a little punk attitude . . . or so I thought. Madchester, E, the Hacienda, New Order, all that bollocks was swerved and left for the New Manc. I was all about doing something different, and New York was very different back then.'

CCR was about to launch himself off on more trips to New York, but others were heading in the opposite direction; sometime in 1983, my mate's sister Ruth and Lenny, another mate, went to Israel together to live on a kibbutz. When they returned, they had loads of great tales to tell, with plenty of photos to back them up. Pictures of Ruth and Lenny riding aerial runways into subtropical rivers and hiking across wild foreign terrain. It made me vow that I'd go and spend time on an Israeli kibbutz someday.

I was living in Salford during this time, but spending my weekends up in Prestwich or around town. The mainstream club scene comprised a preposterous tendency towards yuppie sounds such as Japan, Wham! and Forrest's reworking of the Hues Corporation's 'Rock the Boat'. Manchester was rearing its head like a great refreshed leviathan.

Switching from lukewarm Albert Tatlock bitter to cut-price Stella, served ice-cold to the chaps who mobbed pubs like Piccadilly's Portland Bars and the Auld Reekie on Market Street before heading to Old Trafford for the '82-'84 seasons. The huge numbers of Brits now spending an annual fortnight in Spain had sparked a market for continental-style lagers. Stella was *the* lager of 1983; strong, effervescent and, as the lads said, 'It did yer 'ead in.' It replaced '81-'82's Holsten Pils as the beverage of choice for Perries.

The youngest of those involved in the fashion shift of the late 70s were pub-qualified by now, the skinniness of adolescence replaced by a few extra pounds. Yesteryear's multicolour tracksuits had progressed to faded Levi's, brown Adidas shoes and plain sweaters. The youth bifurcated into two groups around this time, the tweedy hooligans rolling spliffs in the quieter corners and the 'parrotheads', who thronged impromptu pub dance-floors and shook their arses to 'Club Tropicana' and 'Give It Up', by KC and the Sunshine Band; parrotheads had no shame.

As ever, David Bowie positioned himself ambivalently between these two factions, as he had between the glam and soul crowds a decade earlier. His 'Let's Dance' was enjoyed by all, even if it did lack the edge of his earlier work. Bowie represented a musical equator, and the likes of Elvis Costello's 'Every Day I Write the Book' and Echo and the Bunnymen's 'The Cutter' were the tropics, shading out into exotic aural ecosystems. There was other stuff out there, like Toto's 'Africa', Irene Cara's 'Flashdance (What a Feeling)' and 'Buffalo Soldier' by Bob Marley and the Wailers. It all feels so long ago now. Between 1979's culture vacuum and 1983 we'd seen disco die and new romantics arrive. Now that was dead, too, and we were still looking to the 1960s for inspiration. Perries were reproducing across the country but still had no representation in the music world. The football biome was populated by artists like Public Image Ltd, the Style Council and New Order, whose 'Blue Monday' hit the charts like a grey Salford smog.

Increasing numbers became involved in grafting as the economy continued to insult anyone who wanted to earn money. Meanwhile, the parrotheads lapped up Lionel Richie, Paul Young, Culture Club and Michael Jackson's 'Billie Jean'. Many of them were swept up in the yuppie storm and went on to hideous careers, surrounded by O-level-pseud bullshitters in offices throughout the land. The stage was set for a schism in youth tastes, a branch of which evolved into a new club culture steeped in drug use with strong links to Amsterdam and Ibiza.

*   *   *

Sometime in 1981, the cockneys had jumped aboard the casual bandwagon and set about firming themselves up to outdo the Manchester and Liverpool crowd. Hordes of Londoners began to move to Spain, including some of the capital's worst criminals and hardcases. That accent, that attitude; it was hard for the rummest Mancs, scousers and others not to be intimidated, for cockney is the daddy tongue of British working-class crime. The holidays in Spain were a favourite of the British casual mobs by now, but West Ham United's notorious Inter City Firm began to lay proper claim to little pieces of the Spanish crust, starting in the hedonism hotspot of Majorca. Cass Pennant was a man in the eye of the cockney hurricane. His vivid memories tell a cautionary tale of how lawlessness can escalate out of control:

'The ICF and East End had a major say in all that is Tenerife and Playa de las Americas, particularly those beginning years of the early 80s. That was the true heyday of the notorious ICF, West Ham's violent football fan following. The opportunity to extend football-season fan rivalry and mix it abroad was really down to the football casual scene that had acquired the travel bug through following their clubs and England abroad. Full-scale England riots in Turin and Basle of '80 and '81, and the riots involving West Ham playing in Europe, would include a number of the same faces that first turned the sun-kissed isle of Spain's Magaluf into a virtual war zone for several football close-season summers. They next discovered Playa de las Americas after the inevitable clampdown in Magaluf. Magaluf had got so bad you had travel reps advising holidaymakers what bars to avoid if they wanted a peaceful holiday. The reps had even gone as far as to learn the names of the firms in order to be able to answer any bemused person who should innocently ask, "Why?" And in a couple of really short summers the ICF had made the island theirs to such a point it became a no-go zone for other firms, Arsenal's Gooners in particular.'

The bad blood between ICF soldiers and Arsenal's Gooners had escalated out of control. West Ham, along with Millwall, had enjoyed apex predator status in the London hooligan hierarchy for years, but things were changing. The casual phenomenon forced a reshuffling in the credibility rankings, and mobs were now judged as much for their fashion sense as their ability to fight. Tottenham had transformed their boys overnight, with a huge emphasis on sportswear like silk Sergio Tachini tracksuits and white leather Ellesse tennis shoes. Their neighbours Arsenal entered the casual scene from a different angle, and went straight to a semi-dressed-down look both smart and discreet. The Gooners shunned the flamboyance of multicoloured tracksuits, favouring high-end knitwear, stylish cords, casual shoes and expensive leather jackets. West Ham's ICF became embroiled in a tit-for-tat war with the Gooners that resulted in extracurricular incidents of personal violence; sometimes, members of the two gangs would seek each other out in their London neighbourhoods regardless of whether there was a match between the teams. When they encountered each other in Spain, the result was predictably bloody.

'The Gooners had emerged in the early 80s as a new, younger-than-average firm, with proper style and noted reputation,' Pennant remembers. 'Though really it was any club football lads that wanted to firm up on a close-season holiday that had to keep their heads down in those parts. In those early 80s, back at home it had been going off real bad with Gooners around the old East End borough postcodes. Things got so bad between these two firms, ages 15-25, there were a series of street tit-for-tat wars occurring even when no game was played. It came as no surprise that these vendettas continued beyond the football season right into the holiday season on the islands. The battlefield lines were never planned and really came down to who the types of characters were that were involved in all this, and the reputation of the firm they associated with. Result was Gooners found they were unable to take on the now-increasing West Ham numbers, so they just packed up and diverted their summers to the Balearic island of Ibiza. I would personally say that it was the Tenerife-escaping Gooners that made that island popular with the working-class masses in the very beginning, way before it become a Love Island for rave-seeking Brits.'

The football firms were starting to organise themselves in Europe, but they were just one piece in an expanding jigsaw comprising various criminal types from Britain. The drugs scene was about to take a serious turn, and this would influence the nature of some of the mobs who decided to use the continent as a source of inspiration. The way people lived was undergoing a full-scale revision, still in the early stages in

1983. As that summer strengthened its grip, many were availed of a deeper tool than football violence – psychedelia. Where we'd previously lived for the silly season and its magic mushroom harvest, we were now hot in pursuit of a more compact and discreet folly – one-centimetre-square pieces of blotting paper that had various cartoon images printed on them: Superman, Pink Panther, Smiley Mushrooms, Equinox, Black Star, Blue Asterix, Unicorn and California Sunshine. 1983 was the summer my generation embarked on the acid trek, and it wasn't long before a subculture every bit as intense as the football casual scene emerged. Again, travel was a chief component of this, as the market for this mind-expanding product was across the sea, in Amsterdam.

Dave-D- was a lad a couple of years older than me. He introduced me to many aspects of the acid scene, as did *Boxcall giganticus*:

'The best place to score acid at this point was the student bar at UMIST [University of Manchester Institute of Science and Technology],' remembers *Boxcall*. 'Every Saturday we flew down there on the bus, and copped for a couple of Superman each. There were two kinds of Superman circulating at the time; one had a little picture of Superman on each dose, and the other had a large picture of Superman on each sheet of 100 doses, with individual doses featuring an abstract dot-matrix of red, white and blue. This latter kind was the real McCoy.'

Indeed it was. Guaranteed to transport you to the Other World, as Aldous Huxley called it in *The Doors of Perception*. Acid was pretty scarce back then. Hippies, bikers and students controlled its availability. Dave-D- remembers what it was like being into a substance that hadn't been fashionable for at least ten, maybe 15 years.

'Acid was stuff you craved like fuck, but most dealers were doing draw and whiz,' says Dave. 'They'd occasionally get some as a kind of favour for the few who were into it. You'd go to UMIST, and there'd be hundreds of long-haired Led Zep freaks, Mott the Hoople blasting out of the speakers in the student union bar. You'd be excited as fuck when you managed to get past the security guards, who knew right away we weren't students, dressed as we were with smart haircuts and all that. There was one guy in UMIST called Drac, a freaky-looking geezer with big dreadlocks. He usually had some acid. Reeked of patchouli oil and full of hippie slang, but honest in his dealing – at least with the acid. When it came to the whiz, he had one good pocket and one shite pocket, and you had to remind him you knew about it. Some of the bikers in there warned us, and told us to tell him, "I want it out of the good pocket." People were like that back then; they looked out for others who they thought were decent. It might have been an illegal business, but they had their standards. Not like today, with all the scumbags.'

The scarcity of this fabulous chemical led many to resort to extreme measures in obtaining it. We were around 17 years of age for the most part, and back then you couldn't just walk around the different neighbourhoods in Manchester and expect not to be noticed. As *Boxcall* recalls:

'There'd be rumours of this or that dealer in this or that pub, who had some. They always seemed to be weird loners who dressed strange and were completely off it. I remember there was a pub in Eccles, which was a few miles from where we lived. We heard so much about there being acid available at the place, we decided to go there and see if our Golden Fleece was in the building. We walked most of the way, as we didn't even know which buses ran to Eccles, and it was pissing down. It was a Saturday afternoon. We're walking down the main street and every cunt was eyeballing us. When we get there, it's a pub right in the centre. We go in and the place is fucking deserted. We're asking a couple of old blokes if they knew such-and-such a guy, I forget what his name was, but he'd been blown up to legendary proportions in our minds by this time. No one had a clue who he was or what the fuck we were skulking about for. We necked a couple of pints in silence and left, dejected. We later discovered someone had been knifed in there the previous evening. It was a fiasco.'

This was a situation that had to be rectified. A few of the lads quickly saw the chance to make some money and they organised themselves into a tight little firm. Over the next several years they flitted across the Channel and the North Sea innumerable times, returning with LSD Sellotaped under their top lips, a bizarre thing to do but apparently undetectable in the event of a customs search or any other scrutiny. This crew, along with others from around Manchester, began to refer to themselves as the 'Dambusters' in reference to their ability to pop in and out of the Dutch city at will. Mellow Yellow was one of the original Dambusters. He loved Amsterdam.

'The first time I went to the 'Dam I just went mad,' Mellow says with a fond laugh. 'Going from one coffee shop to the next, trying the best herb they had for sale. I made a pig of myself and so did all my mates.

We couldn't believe it when they showed us bags of magic mushrooms from all over the world, different types and everything. The pubs and clubs were shady as fuck, with some very nasty characters hanging around. We used to stay at a youth hostel full of Arabs, Africans and Turks from Germany who were there to buy drugs and take them back across the border to sell. Once in a while there was a guy with a blade out. Once someone even got murdered, shot while we were there. But some of the characters were alright. They showed us the trick of Sellotaping the acid under their top lips, which we adopted once we saw that it could work. They would wipe the spot with ethanol or isopropanol to dry it out, which tasted fucking horrible, and the tape would stick tight. A sheet of acid is ten centimetres square, and you'd cut them into five strips, each two centimetres wide. This was a perfect size, as it fit in a curve around the upper lip. With three layers of tape insulating it from your saliva, the gear could be transported very easily. It wasn't exactly tons of the stuff but that's where it started.

'We were big Man United supporters and going to the match for a bit of a kick-off with the opposition had been our hobby for years. But as we got deeper into the trip we started to leave it out and chill instead. We loved our threads and kept up with the latest trends, but in 1983 we sort of decided to sack the bollocks with the clothes and dress down. I don't give a fuck what anyone tells you, it was drugs that changed things. The whole football mob was now old enough to experiment with pot and acid, and all of a sudden violence wasn't cool anymore.

'Travelling abroad to smuggle drugs led to travel for its own sake. I'll never forget the times I spent in Spain, wandering in the desert, tripping, looking at castles and churches that were a thousand years old. Meeting people from other countries who had the exact same outlook I had, even though I'd never met them before. I met lads living in Spain who let me in on the cigarette and telephone calling-card scams. Some of my mates ended up on Tenerife and down on the Costa del Sol. Some went to the Caribbean and Australia and never came back. Travel opened my mind as much as drugs did. It got me off the nine-to-five and into another reality. We were bringing gear back from our foreign trips for years before everyone started doing the acid in large numbers. Them days with the Dambusters was the best. We just talked nonsense and lived to laugh. We wished it could be like the 60s, and within a few years it fucking was!'

I had a full bench-set in my bedroom and would do weights five nights a week, then run wild at the weekend. The whole weights thing was an accoutrement to the football and fashions, but it also kept you fit. I well remember the uncertainty of what LSD did to us all back then; one night Dave-D-, Louis, *Boxcall giganticus* and myself were walking down the road tripping on Superman, a proper crew of enlightened scallies. I was rhyming names off of all the lads that do weights and can have a fight. Louis, his dreadlocks pulsing in indignation, freaking out on his first ever trip, suddenly shouts, 'What are we talking about *fightin'* for?' It woke me up and I altered course from that moment, realising I had been a bit of a dick for the past several years. Fortunately, I made few enemies compared to lads who were proper bang into the football.

Manchester's small acid population was buzzing every weekend and different heads started to make each other's acquaintance. People from distant parts of the city began to discuss forming bands, going on mad trips into the country and the festival circuit. The character of the acid dealers began to alter; where once there were freaks, loners and hippies, there were now young lads in Adidas training shoes and cashmere jumpers, not just selling but taking the stuff themselves and spreading the Good Word all the while.

Colin Blaney's crew made Amsterdam their base for years. Blaney is forever haunted by his personal journey and his story is a perfect example of how Manchester became one of Britain's coolest cities by the mid-80s, and has remained so ever since. His use of the obscure slang we all favoured is a reminder of how different Manchester was becoming from other cities:

'After a couple of years with the real casual look there, we got bored and wanted more thrills,' Blaney recounts. 'No doubt football travels with United was the path. We went to Luxembourg for an England game which saw our eyes popping at the sights. We also took in Amsterdam, nicknamed the Magnet 'cos of its tendency to keep pulling you back in. We were all hooked I suppose, really for the brass flutes and then to chill out with the weed. The brasses in the 'Dam were plentiful. You could always find a decent-looking piece that was new to the game, making it no less respectful than knobbing some bird from back home who'd never dream of being a working girl. But that's not to say we didn't do some right beasts once in a while. You have to understand that there were very few coffee shops at that point, and it wasn't really easy at all to score decent hash from the streets. The 'Dam wasn't packed with knobheads falling about on stag nights back then. It could be a dangerous place. Luckily I copped for a local gangster's daughter who loved all the rag-arsed lads. Soon her mates were all having a ball with the Wide Awake Firm. She was a fucking beauty. We got that name from the grafters who only worked selling swag at concerts, the reason being the states they used to see us in, pissed legless in the mid-mornings. Next thing they'd hear how at nine that morning we'd done the main gold shop in town. Our wired attitude to life caused that name, which summed us up best.'

The Wide Awake Firm patrolled Amsterdam and its regions, but Liverpool had its own contingent on the continent, who were eagerly raiding the cities as frequently as the Mancs were. Liverpudlian grafter Robin Peters tells a similar story to Blaney about the theft of serious fashion items, and the confusion the brand new grafter's slang caused, even among the sharpest lads:

'You may or may not know that slang for watches is "kettle". When we were grafting in Switzerland in the early 80s we bumped into an older heavy firm from Huyton. I only knew the Huyton Baddies from reputation, but my mates knew them personally. Anyway, we were having an afternoon bevvy with them near the Bahnhof, when one of them said to me and another mate, "Do you wanna see the kettles we copped for down in Lucerne?" I wasn't really interested, but me mate dragged me along to the car to have a peep. All the way to the car park I'm saying to me mate, "Let's fuck off from these knobheads. I thought they were big time, whatta they doin' coming all the way to Swissy to rob kitchen appliances?" Imagine my shock when they opened the boot and showed me ten of the finest diamond-encrusted Rolexes you've ever seen!'

From Scandinavia to Spain, the lads were on the march. There was something reckless yet intelligent about it, as if the finest of an entire generation had decided to go bananas and cast fortune to the winds. As the numbers of thieves, drug smugglers and outright hooligan mobs rose, the continentals lost patience. West Ham's stranglehold on Magaluf and Tenerife was attracting much attention from the Spanish police, especially as numerous serious assaults had been committed on holidaymakers. The nature of the cockney mob, violent and merciless to begin with, began to alter. Serious London criminals started moving in, many of whom knew the ICF personally. The stage was set for complete lawlessness to prevail. Arsenal's Gooners had fled to Ibiza, taking many others with them who were anxious to avoid being on the wrong side of the cockneys.

'Many other teams followed over to Ibiza because of Playa de las Americas being now labelled a known resort for trouble, just like Magaluf would become,' Cass Pennant says. 'At first people just rebooked themselves to the other resorts nearby, like Los Christianos. Los Christianos was a fishing village that was still being developed more for the holiday market and it was quiet – too quiet – until the London East End started to spread their wings. When I got out there part of the Playas Americas was being referred to by the locals as Little England. I innocently asked, "How come, Little England?" and the lads who'd become main faces there now simply said they'd taken over and the local Old Bill had nicknamed it that because of the frustration they felt in that they'd lost a certain control there. This was partly due to lack of manpower and partly the frightening level of violence from supposed holidaymakers that either didn't care about getting nicked or felt they were untouchable. In effort to reclaim the bars they started to call up the Spanish mainland police for reinforcements. I recall booking my plane seats and flying out at the invitation of a very well-known ICF character to have the craic with them. I flew out with a couple of my top security bouncers, as around that period of my life I was running doors for clubs and pubs. We had nothing sorted, only the flights, and we got a message from our east London host saying, "Sorry Cass, but I won't be able to meet you as I'm hiding in the mountains waiting for a boat to be arranged to smuggle me out. It's a bit on top, as the Old Bill from the mainland are now on the island looking for me. A lot has happened since we invited you over, Cass, been absolute murders, but you'll be okay for your little holiday stay because so-and-so will all look after you, mate."

'"Murders" is in reference to the fact that the rows have been pretty serious, but nobody actually killed – just. How bad is bad? Well, let's just say going on your yearly holidays and ending up on a drip-feed is not too good really for any lad, no matter whose firm they are linked with, so you get the picture. If you weren't West Ham or in with a certain group of faces there, you stayed low and tried to enjoy your holiday by carefully picking where you chose to dance and drink the night away. I remember one night walking into Bobby's Bar and I thought, "We've gotta be playing Millwall in a friendly out here!" It was pure firm but, most worrying of all, it was the ones who were often out of control even within the firm. But like I said, if your face fitted in during that particular time period on Tenerife it was best ever days. Pretty cool days to be honest, on one top holiday island, and true-to-word we were looked after by so-and-so and had a top stay. We had a few adventures of our own and weren't allowed to pay for anything, speedboats, booze, top fuckin' meals, you name it. Then you think at the time, the English could not do any business or work there without a work permit, the bars had to have a Spanish owner's name on the deeds and any business had to be with a resident partner. It was interesting that, a year or two later, when I went out there again, I saw certain faces that were more or less villains rather than lads who went to the football. All the same, mind, the football lads that I used to know even seemed to be moving into areas of proper villainy now themselves, rather than talking football bollocks.'

While the parrotheads embarked on their yuppie trip – with an annual fortnight in Spain as a treat away from the office – another group embarked on a voyage of discovery. This lot weren't mobbed up at all. They went in ones and twos, but collectively they numbered in the thousands. It was early days, but the natives of the Iberian Peninsula were beginning to see a change in the composition of its population. The fortnightly turnover of holidaymakers was leaving an increasingly noticeable residue in the form of British lads and girls who'd decided to make a summer of it. These youngsters created a subculture of nightclub bouncers, barmaids, hotel and construction workers and timeshare reps. Their numbers steadily grew; word of the good life spread back home and British youngsters began hitting Spain purely in search of work, bypassing the holiday phase altogether. Ex-skin/mod/football hooligan Carl Spiers from Oldham remembers his trip to the Costa Brava with mixed feelings, and a good deal of humour:

'In April 1984, life was great for me. I had a regular job paying decent dough. I was lodging with a mate who was hardly ever there and only wanted a score off me for rent and as much grub as I could eat. He stayed mostly at his bird's anyway, so I had the run of the gaff. I had a great wardrobe of decent clobber, and I was having an affair with a beautiful married woman. I'm not proud of the cheating bit, but she was top-drawer; gorgeous, five feet ten, long-flowing light-brown shiny hair, a great body, sexy, and game as fuck. She lavished me with gifts and affection. God knows why. I crumbled and we had a torrid affair for several months.

'So it would seem life really was going great, but I was always after adventures. I got bored very easily. One night I was chatting a barmaid up in the roughest nightclub in Oldham, as you do, and I mentioned to her I fancied working abroad for a couple of years. She gave me a number of a bloke she'd met in Lloret del Mar a few weeks previously who ran a chain of hotels. She reckoned he owed her a few favours, nudge nudge.

'Within a fortnight I was packing my bags and leaving my comfortable lifestyle back in Oldham. I got about £600 in cash, stuffed as many belongings as possible into a huge six-foot army canvas bag and bid farewell to my family and close friends. I never told the bird I was shooting though; she was too emotionally attached to me and would make things very difficult for me. It was a bit cowardly but definitely the right decision. (She never forgave me and never spoke to me again.) I got the midnight coach from Chorlton Street bus station to London Victoria train station, arriving at 6:30 am the next day. I had a full Monty English breakfast and caught the Dover train to catch the ferry to France.

'I love the cross-channel ferries; the wind howling all around, the freedom to walk about and take in everything. There's an atmosphere in the big, curved bar, all the people chattering, queuing up to buy snacks and beer. It's brilliant, especially at that time of year. April is when you've got it all ahead of you, and to spend it sailing away directly south feels fucking ace. Seeing the white cliffs of Dover disappear in the sea mist is as exciting as seeing the green fields of France emerge as you approach Calais.

'By mid-afternoon I was on the train to Paris from Calais; I was very impressed with the French train system, far superior to ours back in Blighty. I arrived in Paris at 6 o'clock, and my next train to Port Bou on the France/Spain border was not until midnight. I put my huge army bag into a locker and went for a mooch around Gay Paree. I didn't know where the fuck I was, because I ended up in a right fucking shithole, full of Africans and Arab-looking geezers. I went into what I thought was a restaurant and ordered some cake and Fanta. I asked for the toilet and was pointed down this long corridor. I found a room at the end with bundles of newspaper screwed up on a table next to a hole in the floor with a bucket of water next to it. "Oh no," I thought, "this is it, the primitive bastards." I really thought the French were a modern society; the trains were really sleek, but I was very uncomfortable with this hole in the floor nonsense. I still did the business, but I couldn't get away fast enough. I was very naïve, it would seem.

'I caught the midnight express train from Paris. It was a long train and took me well over half an hour to walk from one end to the other, with this big canvas bag slung over me shoulder. I had the cheapest ticket but I went looking for comfort and somewhere to get my head down for the long journey. I found myself a compartment with only one passenger, a young French girl, perhaps 18 years old. I put my bag at the base of the door to keep it locked. She giggled at that, I noticed. It was dark and the lights were very dim. I could see she was a bit tasty, with long dark hair and dark Latin features. I introduced myself. She told me her name was Helena and she was indeed 18. She was bound for Barcelona for the summer season. She was from Paris and had a lovely shy smile. I brought my bag across the floor and lay on top of that and soon fell asleep. Helena was stroking my hair – or was I dreaming? – which back then was long, shoulder-length curly. After what seemed ages and a lovely dreamy sleep, I was rudely awoken by a very aggressive train guard, who booted me in the guts and told me to get out. I had this massive urge to stick the nut on the French cunt, but on seeing three first-class-paying customers trying to get in, I thought the better of it. I glanced back at Helena and she just shrugged her shoulders and blew me a kiss.

'I ended up kipping amongst the luggage and fell asleep until the train pulled into Port Bou on the border. I then changed trains and got on board the Barcelona train. Lloret was only a few miles up the coast from Barcelona. I was hoping to find Helena, but no such luck. The train was packed and it was standing room only for the two-and-half-hour train journey to Barça. I was among loads of English, Dutch, Germans, Scandinavians and Aussies. The nearest person to me was a young Aussie girl who introduced herself as Morgan. She was 22 and was travelling around Europe. She'd just spent the last month in the UK, visiting her granny in South Wales and relatives in Yorkshire and

Nottinghamshire. She was very chatty and good looking, with that typical outdoor Aussie look, tanned, athletic and healthy, kind of like a perfect British dream-girl really, but from the other side of the planet. She could yap for England and was excited about seeing as much of Europe as possible. She was taking 12 months out to visit as many countries as possible, including Barcelona for a couple of days, before going to Majorca for a week. From there it was Greece for a couple of weeks, doing odd jobs as she went along in bars. "Wow, what a life!" I thought.

'We got on great and we spent a couple of hours at the harbour in Barcelona, where we had lunch and a few lagers. She insisted I come over to Majorca with her for a week, no strings attached, just as buddies. I was very tempted but declined, a decision that was to haunt me for years. In the space of a few hours I'd had two encounters with birds that could have made me a happy man for the rest of my life. We hugged as I boarded yet another train, up to Lloret. Morgan was a great girl with a great attitude and she was so excited about travelling around Europe. It was with serious regret that I bid Morgan farewell, another one that got away. My voyage was starting to sound like a fisherman's tall tale. In truth, it was exactly the kind of thing that happens to a young bloke when he covers some proper ground; there are some unbelievable birds out there, and you will meet them as you go. They're everywhere, and they can make or break your heart.

'By early evening I was in Lloret del Mar and had located the bloke, who was called Neil. He allegedly owned a chain of hotels and bars, but of course he did not. He managed this one hotel which was classy but fuck-all to do with him. He asked how much I had on me. I told him about £500 and he suggested I stay at "his" hotel for a fortnight until I found some work. He convinced me I would definitely get some graft, as I had timed it right, it being late April. I booked into the classy hotel which set me back £300 on the strength that I would soon be in graft. To tell you the truth, I just dossed about for the first week and had a holiday, but by the second week my dough was dwindling fast and I began my search for work. I ventured into bars, clubs, shops, restaurants and building sites, all to no avail. Everywhere it was nowt down. "Come back next week," many of them said, but I noticed that there were hundreds of fellow Brits looking for the same jobs, many of them kipping on the beaches and in caves.

'I got in with four scouse lads and a Wiganer, who we all called George Formby 'cos he sounded just like him. He kept saying, "Ee, it's bloody warm today, lads." The scousers were good fun though, and nicknamed me McEnroe because I looked like the mad tennis player with my long curly locks and high forehead. They were rum fuckers and would just go robbing every day, for grub and clothes. They all carried giant sports bags and would relentlessly go on the rob, especially leather jackets which they would sell on to British tourists. They looked after me for a few days, taking me for meals and drinks, but one day two of them got nicked and the other two told me they were going down to Benidorm. I never saw any of them again. The Wigan lad just got a flight back home to the land of pies.

'Neil, my so-called contact and fantasy hotel-chain owner, didn't want to know me once my two weeks of luxury were up. I ended up in a very cheap-and-nasty, rundown pension [boarding house]. It was horrendous, with just a bed-settee and a sink. I was down to my last few bob and under pressure. Finally I was skint, but had another week left in this doss-house. I actually went three whole days without anything to eat. I decided drastic action was required and I made the decision that I would go onto the beach and try and trap off with a bird in the vain hope she would carry me for a few days. I was a confident lad, never had any problems with birds, so the next day I was on the beach looking for likely suspects. Eventually I parked my bum next to these two hippie-looking chicks about my age, early 20s, with long hair and denim shorts. Not bad-looking actually, though that was not a priority. I lay down close to them and said good morning. They both giggled but were soon yapping away to me; they were from America – Florida – and were also travelling around various European hot spots. All I really wanted was some grub down me neck, but I chatted away and had them laughing. We were all relaxed, and they offered me some lemonade and an apple. After a while, one of them asked if I fancied coming back to their apartment for some "hash". Now by this time I am seriously hallucinating about grub, and when they mentioned hash I assumed they meant "tater hash", a very popular Lancashire stew, which was the main diet of many working-class families.

'I tried hard not to show my obvious glee at the offer of some hash and mumbled, "Uh, yeah, that would be lovely thanks," so we trundled off back to their nearby apartment. Upon entering, one of the girls went into the kitchen area. Me and the other one sat down in the lounge. After a few moments the girl in the kitchen shouted through, "Hey man, how much can you handle?" I replied, "Oh, a dishful will do, and have you any red cabbage?" Well, would you believe it, she went mad and started calling me an English jerk. She returned with a rolled-up fag the size of a *Daily Mirror*. I tried in vain to explain myself, but I was bundled out of the front door and abused further.

'After being thrown out of the Yankee birds' apartment, I humbly strolled back to my cheap-and-nasty gaff, feeling sorry for myself and cursing the fact I fucked it up with the Yanks. When I got back I collapsed onto the threadbare two-seat settee and drifted away. While sleeping, I thought back to my childhood days and the means of raising cash whenever I was skint. An old favourite of mine and my sister Karen was to put our hands down the back of the settee, where there was always loose change. It never failed; never too much, but always a few bob to keep us going. So I sprung up and then forced my hand down the back of the Spanish flea-ridden settee, and lo and behold I grasped a handful of change. Not much, probably 50p in Spanish coin in total, but it would at least get me a cup of coffee. I headed to the prom and spotted a café with tables and chairs on the pavement. I ordered a coffee, which I just had enough for. The mid-afternoon sun was blazing down and I was sweating cobs, but this little cup of coffee felt luxurious and I took my time to watch the world go by. A few moments later I was joined at my table by a big, fat, horrible, sweaty fucking German bastard. He looked as I imagined most 50-odd-year-old Germans looked: heavily built, in a fawn suit, sky-blue shirt and green kipper tie which was tied up tight to his neck, making it bulge. His thinning hair was swept over his napper, Bobby Charlton-style, and he had a permanent scowl on his fat face with several chins. He was an ugly fucker. He scowled and looked down his snobby German beak at me, as if I was the shit on his shoe. I took an instant dislike to him, especially when he ordered a steak, roast spuds, new potatoes and enough veg to feed a third-world country. I tried hard not to stare, but having not eaten for three days I couldn't help myself. He glared at me, as trickles of sweat cascaded down his fat face, then took a sharp steak knife and cut off a piece of fat from the huge piece of steak. He chewed it, then spat it out onto the floor, grunting like the pig he was.

'Amazingly, he then got up from his seat and fucked off. I could not believe my fucking luck. Instantly, I leapt onto the plate and shoved a few roast spuds into me gob, and chewed away for England. I grabbed hold of this huge steak and began to chew it like a caveman. Then a big dark shadow enveloped me; the fat Kraut had come back to the table. He'd only gone for a newspaper and on seeing me eating his steak he roared like a lion, calling me an English pig. How did he know I was English? (Then again, how did I know he was German?) I got up to scarper but he whacked me across my head, sending me flying across the pavement and onto my knees. All the while I hung onto this wonderful lump of best steak, as he kicked me up the arse, sending me another ten yards up the pavement. I got up and scurried away like a rat! I could hear much laughter in the background from locals enjoying this Tom and Jerry spat.

'I began to get into a serious trot towards the beach, heading towards a cave which I had used several times to shelter from the blazing sun. I spent the best part of an hour devouring this steak, bit by bit. It was tremendous. I even nipped back to the prom and nicked a salt pot to add to my feast. I felt like two Burt Lancasters after I ate it. I slept well that night, I can tell you – unlike the Kraut, who must have had fucking nightmares about the scavenging English cunt who robbed his steak!'

Spiers is a natural-born comedian and it's hard not to laugh at his tales. But things were quite serious in Spain. It was now officially a home from home (or at least a cave) for many Brits. While the little grafting firms and others made their way through Switzerland and Holland, Spain sucked in huge numbers of young people, all eager to soak up the sun and start a new life. But the cockney mob were still on the march. They'd destroyed the reputations of both Magaluf and then Playa de las Americas, but the infusion of hardened criminals would transform Tenerife yet further. The football territory and gangster territory were overlapping. It was a sign of things to come for cities like London and Manchester, where the rave culture hadn't yet begun to stir.

'The writing was on the wall for what this part of Tenerife had become,' Cass Pennant recalls. 'Going back to when they referred to Playa de las Americas as being a Little England – or at least an east London and Essex, with certain known members of the ICF – as so many football lads would come home and say who it was they had bumped into out there. If you looked at it closer there was a deeper situation unfolding. The real reason known ICF members could put out an intimidating statement like, "It's our manor now," to all their football rivals was that they now had a number of dangerous faces that were on the trot for non-football related stuff. Some of it was serious gangland offences, and now they were out there with them, forming alliances that would never have been made back in the East End due to their own serious local rivalry.'

*   *   *

CCR and his soul-boy crew had enjoyed their 1979 baptism in the Big Apple. In 1984 they were no longer debutantes on Atlantic flights, and they still wanted soul. They found more than deleted vinyl, thanks to certain larger-than-life Manchester gangsters with whom they'd made acquaintance. Hereby follows an epic tale of Manc lads at large in Manhattan.

'To my best recollection, and without recourse to notes or other participants, this was how it went down,' remembers CCR (barely). 'NYC-style . . . 1984. This wasn't our first or even second trip across the pond; '79 and '82's excursions had mainly involved scouring warehouses in Brooklyn for deleted soul vinyl and trying to catch the Ramones in their natural habitat at CBGB's. Freddie Laker had opened up cheap airline travel and, whilst most of the boys were content to mooch around Benidorm for a fortnight, a fair few north Mancunians became more than familiar with the delights of the big (gr)apple.

'For the '84 trip, however, Laker could shove his bargain seats. This was BA all the way. The cost of travel was neatly offset by some Manchester-based middle-aged gents; the kind with thick, gold-trimmed wrists, whom it could be assumed formed part of Manchester's better organised underground culture.

'The deal was this: Get to New York, visit a shop in the diamond district, pick up some krugerrands (already paid for), and bring 'em back . . . that's it . . . some sort of duty-free gold importation nobody thought to question the legality of.

'We were well up for it.

'So myself, Big Mick and Naïve Steve flew out from Ringway in style. BA at the time was all heart-attack-inducing MILF stewardesses. Smoking allowed and a free bar for the seven-hour hop. Happy days. We hit JFK around 12 midnight . . . nowhere to stay so we hit the bar in the airport and started on the draught American beers. An hour of

IAN HOUGH

this induced the barman to make a few calls and hook us up with a cheap room, Lower East Side Manhattan, the Pickwick Arms Hotel. We apologised for our 30-minute bitchfest about baseball and scored a yellow cab. All good in the hood. Checked in. Naïve Steve attempted to open the room window. Whole fuckin' frame came out in his hands. Caught in the twilight zone between jet lag and a nine-hour drinking sesh we decided to hit the town. We dug out threads considered sartorial enough to take the air. Me and the big fellow opted for Marc O'Polo t-shirts, dark Levi needle cords and Adidas trainers. As I recall I had a new light-brown pair with light-blue stripes. Lovely. Can't remember the name and don't care.

'Naïve Steve, however, was a bird of another feather. A natural Geordie, his brief stint in Manchester had failed to prise him from his north-eastern roots. Cardboard semi-flared Wranglers and a hideous cheesecloth shirt . . . God love 'im. A couple of liveners in McCann's bar and we were off looking for as much action as the Lower East Side could provide. No Studio 54, no Max's Kansas City, no CBGB's for the boys tonight. We were after loose women, loud soul and cheap beer. We found it.

'The gentleman hovering outside the gaff beckoned us over. The fact that he resembled a late-period George Melly, complete with fedora, chain around neck, three-piece suit and large, cheap-looking, ruby-coloured rock on finger didn't deter.

'"What's the story, mate?"

'"Whose is the finest club on the island, boys?" (He did a little soft-shoe dance.) "Where you from?"

'"England, mate."

'"New England? You got a long drive home!"

'"No, Old England . . . come further than you think."

'"Come in, first drink on da house."

'"Looks a bit dodgy to me, but hang, on they're playin' the Detroit Spinners."

'"Still, can't be any worse than Patty's, an' you're never outta there."

'"OK, we're in."

'As we slid through the timber-riveted door and the large black bouncer minding it, the room opened up before us . . .

'The Peppermint Lounge it wasn't. Strings of fairy lights adorning little semi-private bunkers presented itself. Looked like the sort of gaff where Joe Pesci would stick a biro in yer neck on a whim . . .

'Mine host Louie fronted up. "What's it ta be, fellaz . . . you like domestic?"

'"What's he say?"

'"He wants to know if yer inter Domestos, Mick."

'"Funny fucker, eh?"

'Lou slides three warmish, dusty bottles of Bud across the jump and indicates that he is willing to sport us a tab for the duration.

'"Righto," says I. "I'm gonna check the jukebox. This is Lower Manhat, boys, bound ta be a bit of black stuff."

'Off I popped to the corner machine, where presently I was joined by a rather hip-looking, be-afro'd disco chick, all lime-green halter-neck, long, rakish nails (same colour), eye-shadow and lippy to match. Wouldn't have carried it off in Manchester, where tutty only came in two shades of powder-blue back in the day. Her name was Gloria. I decided to call her "Glo".

'So, I'm grafting away on the lady and wowing her with an extensive knowledge of black disco tunes. "I Wanna Give You Tomorrow" by Benny Troy fires her and a few more punters from their booths and onto the dance-floor. Or the dance Formica in this case.

'"You dancin', honey?"

'"Uh, not yet, Gloria. Just poppin' to the jacks."

'The "jacks" is the toilet in north Manchester, but I'm not sure if she was that well-versed in the lingo. I needed pre-dance assurances from my travelling brothers that "Glo" was, in their estimation, not packing pecker. I mean with jet lag, full-on drinking and dim lights, mistakes can be made. I beckoned the fat lad over and we mooched off to the traps. A short piss and shorter conversation followed.

'"Whaddya think?"

'"Dump, mate, we shoulda gone up to Odyssey 2000."

'"Nah, not the gaff, the bird . . . pukka?"

'"Only one way to find out," he declared sagely with a shit-eating grin.

'Conversation was kept to a minimum in the gents, mainly 'cos the two trapdoors were both shut and occupied: Trap one contained some punter hoovering up a yard of the devil's dandruff. Trap two clearly contained a pair (at least) engaged in an act of fornication. As with "Glo", the genders of all khazi combatants remained a mystery. Upon exiting the bogs through a rusty steel door, we heard our Geordie companion from the bar . . .

'"I'll get these, Louie. Three more Domestoses or whatever the fuck you call 'em, bonny lad, and whatever the ladies are having."

'Exactly the sort of phrase that should never be uttered in Lower East Side clip joints. A good rule of thumb being that if you wouldn't do it in Patty's, then don't do it anywhere . . . there's experience for yer, boys.

'Naïve Steve, God love him, proceeded to drag up three creaky barstools and lay his newly-acquired Access card on the steel, beer-puddled bar top. A scene from *Macbeth* ensued. Our delightful hostesses included the lovely "Gloria", whom I was a little miffed to see transferring her attentions to a warm glass of bubble-less champers and Stevie's trouser frontage respectively.

'Big Mick looked a little disturbed, especially when Louie swiftly swiped the credit card and placed it beyond our reach. Negotiations to retrieve the fucker would no doubt be long and without charm. A fast round of Jameson's cut through the beer sludge and sharpened the combative instincts.

'Back then you had a sixth sense, you could feel an edge in a room, you just knew when a kick-off was on top. And so it came to pass.

'"Louie, for fuck sake give back the card, bro, play the white man will yer?"

'This being more in the way of a demand rather than a request from Big Mick at my immediate left.

'Eyebrows were raised. Bogs emptied. Hostesses disengaged themselves from rubbing rapidly-hardening Levi's crotches and floated away into distant memory.

'The extra-large, jet-black doorman appeared. "As if by magic, the shopkeeper appeared," I thought, recalling episodes of *Mister Ben*.

'Barstools scraped back and a hush descended upon the room. Our genial barkeep groped around under the bar for his blunt instrument of choice.

'The scene was now set. A brief glimpse around identified combatants and spectators alike. All became hushed.

'In a spectacular piece of choreography that Legs & Co would have died for, Margo and the Marvettes' classic "When Love Slips Away" struck up from the juker. Margo's cack-handed drummer pounded his first ill-timed cymbal smash as a size-12 Adidas Samba neatly parted the testicles of the by-now angry-looking doorman. Away we go.

'Not wishing to bore experienced readers, the details of the ensuing ruck are omitted here. Veterans of barroom brawls know how these things generally pan out. And why is there always one shifty-looking fucker (in this case clad in lime-green) who wants to pitch in despite offering nothing in the way of skill? "Glo" got her comeuppance after jumping on the back of the departing Steve and ripping a stripe in his "foookin' nar cheesecloth short, ya fucker!"

'"'Ave some of that, cunt!" An elbow swiftly dispatched backwards broke both grip and nose in the same instant.

'We emerged (again, experienced heads at this game will know the time vortex in play) after what seemed at least ten minutes' solid scrapping. Watches were unwrapped from pocket hankies and reinstalled upon wrists.

'"Fuck me!"

'"Wha – ?"

'"Done in a minute and a half."

'"Did we retrieve the card?"

'"Oh yeah," Steve brightened. "No real need for that, chaps. It's a snide. An' I've got three more just like it back in the room. We coulda took 'em for a full bar tab and the ladies."

'"Uh, why didn't yer say something?"

'"I thought I did."

'In the 80s no self-respecting travelling Manc (or minced-up Geordie) went anywhere without a cooked-up Access card. But the night was young . . .

'"Right, uptown top rankin', boys. Odyssey 2000 it is!"

'And off we popped.

'The guy we were doing the runs for was known as Big M. I'd first met Big M in the early 80s. He was part of a semi-mythical Irish-Mancunian clan, those chaps with Pierre Cardin suits, transparent socks, perma-tans and gold-trimmed extremities. We were introduced after they'd acquired a gym in Chinatown, some debt or other settled "out of court". Being a boxer meant I could smell a gym a mile away. I lived in town and it was inevitable I'd turn up there.

'The boys would hold forth Saturday afternoons in the gym bar, debating the topics of the day. The ongoing struggle to monitor shift changes within Greater Manchester's A-Division squad cars. Theoretical prices for swag Irish oil paintings liberated from country piles, in gravelly nicotine whispers. A select few gym rats would be invited for ale-swigging before taking the town air for evening tours of inspection. The chaps had interests in many dodgy drinking and gambling establishments within the city square mile. Most had been operating illegally since the 60s. Some had even received a lick of paint in the last 20-stretch. Smoky one-room card dens above pubs and tug 'n' rub shops supplied M with dubious-looking brown envelopes and Famous Grouse.

'Nights were spent in the Dickensian squalor of the Top Cat Tavern or Penny Farthing pub. Lovely auld Manc brasses poncing drinks. Trying to persuade this young boy that a good time was to be had in a Collyhurst ginnel for the price of 20 Regal King Size. Late nights drinking with no licensing inhibitions, usually ending up in the Auto Club or Brambles. ("Wanna see Bestie face down in his dinner?") Large ones, bottles of pink champers and Castellas all round.

'As Sir Freddie Laker's vision of cheap air travel for all gripped the nation, livewires like meself had got on board. Weekend trips on the batter to Dublin and New York meant fanatically scouring deleted vinyl warehouses. Of course, amongst the gym chaps – all Ancoats heads at heart – nothing went unnoticed; there were deals to be done. Fresh-faced, respectable (i.e. no criminal record) Mancunians with legal passports and unproven *cojones* would be enlisted to the cause.

'"You know New York?" Big M would ask.

"Yeah, been over and back a few times. Mainly buyin' deleted stocks of rare vinyl."

'"Whatever. You goin' over soon?"

'"Uhh, soon, yeah."

'"You could do me a favour next trip." Note: this was not a request.

'And so the great krugerrand runs began,' says CCR. 'Paid tickets were proffered. British Airways no less. Instructions given.

'"Get your arses over there, act like yer a tourist."

'"I am a fuckin' tourist!"

'"On the last day call in to see Louis at this address. Diamond district, midtown. Pick up a little velvet bag and get it back to Blighty. I wouldn't bother tryin' to stuff 'em up your arse, either. There's too many."

'"Hadn't even crossed me mind."

'This being the 80s, airport customs had yet to evolve into the fascist beastie that so enhances today's travelling experience. Large, genial, favourite uncle-type customs officers tousled our hair and offered sage advice:

'"If I were you I'd load up on the cigs in New York. They're cheaper than duty frees!"

'"Cheers, mate."

'No more effort was required than sticking the little velvet swag in the bottom of your head bag (kit item number one, 80s traveller) and drinking just enough pre-flight to forget you had the fucker. Trips were made, couple of mates recruited and a win-win situation resulted. Surely avoiding import tax and VAT is a victimless crime?

'New York trips generally occurred every second month, Dublin weekends every month. I'd meet my arse at the airport coming back from somewhere. You will note none of this is football-related. My boys at City failing to do the business for a couple of decades made me lose interest. Occasional derby day encounters on the pitch and the cobbles reignited the fires but these were few and far between. It would be '89 before the oppressed rose and put the red capitalist pigs to the sword, five-one. Great day, though my usual laddish enthusiasm was tempered by my being wedged in the Platt Lane with the invaders.'

*   *   *

By the mid-80s, the new British thug had found his feet and was busily working out where the money could be made and good times had. Some clever chaps had stumbled into schemes like CCR's. It went with the territory. But, for many, a dirtier route had to be taken; it was quickly established that money was in drugs. Drugs it was, then.

PART TWO
THE BUG DRUGS WON'T CURE

5

GIANT SAND

Sunshine all the time makes a desert.
— Arab proverb

985 was the year I took off to follow my own curiosity across the oceans and be forever changed by what I found. Barring a couple of minor sidebars, this was the first time I had travelled to somewhere truly foreign; my trip to France, aged 15 in May 1981, had served as a primer. The mesmerising sports cars, boutiques and women of the French Riviera were really something. A small pellet of desire had been deposited deep inside me. The pellet grew as time passed and, four and a half years later, I found myself sitting on a plane at Bradford Airport, bound for Tel-Aviv. I was wide awake that day, living in the Now, as they say.

My journey had its roots in proto-Madchester, a time of drugs, music and fun, fun, fun. It had started back in '83 at UMIST with Dave Dolan and *Boxcall giganticus*; drop some Superman acid or unbelievable speed, then off to the Hacienda to get knocked back at the door by the Neanderthal bouncers. We'd ask them, 'D'yer mind if I just run in quick to give me brother the backdoor key, mate? Me mam and dad 'ave gone away an' I'm stayin' at me bird's tonight, an' he won't be able to get in our 'ouse otherwise.'

Amazingly, it usually worked. Sometimes, one of us would distract them while another would steam into the club. In a way, the artsy types at the Hac were analogous to the punk crowd of '77 who bought Blaney's swag. Only now it was LSD for the hipsters. As far as we could see, there were no other 'lads' doing anything like that in there at that time. Little did the hipsters know, a two-minute walk to

UMIST could earn them the same chemical at one third of the price they paid in the Hacienda. They thought we were personally bringing the stuff in from Amsterdam because we had the hairstyle and clothes of bad lads, designer sportswear and expensive trainers. The truth was we were craving something more flavourful than casual hooliganism. It was too early for the world to know what was going on and we often had to make do with going back into the neighbourhoods, dancing it up for a laugh at a party somewhere, or in a pub packed with boys fresh from the football. All itching to jump aboard this strange biochemical vehicle we were riding and which we lovingly dispensed.

After the Dave-D-*Boxcall* tripod dissolved I'd started on it with Dave-B-, doing monster fat lines of sulphate for days on end. When it came time to crash I sometimes just lost the plot.

Dave-B and I had been mates for years and had been dragged to United games by the older lads for a whale of a time. He was a loveable rascal, a slightly-built lad who seemed to have no fear whatsoever. He would easily merge with the older lads and entertain them with his immense bag of tricks. He oozed the latest slang, a nonchalant coat-hanger for the top clothes that came in from mysterious sources external to England. Like Dave-D- he held an ongoing fascination with the glittering Manc underworld and its innumerable denizens. But we were bored with running with the United Boys and the symptoms were showing as clearly as a case of chickenpox, but in reverse.

The hooligan uniform had greyed out, from red Day-Glo Fila tracksuits to crew-neck jumpers from Marks and Sparks and Levi's. We were still conscious of a deliberate attempt at style but were jaded. By 1983-4 the inner colours and euphoria of acid and speed had us hooked. The only way to calm the nerves was a long pull on a Capstan Full Strength, or Woodbine and Park Drive if Capstans were unavailable. We were fear addicts, excitement addicts, and we always wanted more. We began wearing long, dark, blue-hooded coats for the rain-sodden all-nighters in Prestwich Clough or the reservoir, which we called 'trooping coats'. The familiar sight of Dave at my door will never leave me. A vision of insanity and rebelliousness, stood in a hawkish yet relaxed posture. The perfectly unkempt hair, which had once been a glossy, streaked wedge. One hand on his back hip, a leg stuck out in front of him, like Leonard Rossiter. A wicked, dazed, gargoyle smile on his thin face. The waterproof trooping coat buttoned and hanging like Batman's cape. Ready for action.

We spent our nights hurtling stoned up and down Bury New Road, the main drag into town, constantly diving into pubs, parks and petrol stations. Sometimes we'd stick our thumbs into the endless traffic and snag a lift. One time we were stood on an island at a junction. I just opened a car door and slid into the back seat. The bloke nearly jumped out of his skin, but I assured him in a polished radio voice we merely wanted a lift a mile or so down the road towards town. He silently obliged. When the traffic finally quietened we'd hit the woods, away from the eyes of the police, who we called the 'Macca'. There we'd continue those monumental conversations about centipedes, 'racing the sub-conny' (trying to avoid the wicked visions that persistently sprang from the corners of our ravaged minds) and shooting tigers with tranquiliser darts before shagging them. The usual stuff. We had a right fucking laugh. After a few rough comedowns, we discussed *lozzing* – stopping – the whiz, but we had to find a substitute first and then switch horses midstream. It was the only way.

The comedown waited like an evil presence at the end of every trip, and believe me speed was a trip in those days. If I didn't get straight to sleep I tended to go off the deep end with a vengeance. We got to the point where it was a half-gram straight up each nostril or it was nothing at all. But that kind of speeding carried a price called psychosis; seeing and hearing things, the Monty. Through '84 into '85 our appetites grew, as did the appetite of most lads we knew. We were still in our teens but already grizzled authorities on what drugs could do to your head.

One Saturday morning, coming down, I was trying for some kip and there were some kids playing and singing out in the street. Some busy cunt was cutting wood with a chainsaw. The chainsaw became an electric guitar and the kids singing became the vocals. The song was an in-depth psychoanalytical exposé of what a dickless twat I was and always had been. When I rushed to the window to catch them at it, they were nowhere to be seen. A fencepost behind a privet became a face and I thought the band were hiding there, taunting me. Then the insurance woman knocked on the door, making her Saturday rounds. I locked myself in the bathroom, terrified, holding my breath in silence. My mam and dad were out, Saturday-afternoon shopping. As I stood quaking noiselessly, I was amazed to realise she had come in the unlocked back door and was having a nosy. I listened as she slowly padded around all the bedrooms, taking it all in. She'd have got a right shock if she'd wanted a quick shit. I stayed in the toilet then, and when my folks came home from Sainsbury's I imagined they were burglars. I grasped a pipe on the wall with one hand and the toilet door handle with the other. When I heard my dad's voice I shouted, 'Quick! There's someone up here, a burglar!' I utterly failed to connect the two sets of sounds. My old feller come steaming up the stairs, thinking I was locked in the shitter with some lunatic, and he wrenched the door right open, tearing the handle off in my hand.

'*What the bleedin' hell's goin' on?*'

His face was like a beetroot, all ready for defending his home. I was a total radio-rental case, seeing frogs and lizards hopping about on the upstairs landing. I was trying to swat them off me, but they kept crawling on my body. My dad phoned the doctor who came out and administered a sedative. After the doc left, we were sitting around the dinner table and I was assuring them I was alright. As I said it, I was eyeing a troop of balaclava'd commandos in the trees behind the house, swinging from branch to branch, in black suits, rifles with telescopic sights slung over their backs on straps. I was totally shitting myself but daren't say a word to my family in case they were in on it. People were definitely out to get me; I could see it with my own eyes, sedative or no fucking sedative.

Another time in '85, I'd been at it all weekend with Dave-D-. We'd visited a Salford acid dealer and gone riding around on a motorcycle, out of my mind on four hits of Red Heart, visiting various faces and coming to rest back in the dealer's flat, which contained a six-foot python. I spent some time stroking the creature, trying to prevent myself from going over the edge. At one point I believed I was on a helter skelter, an impression which grew in magnitude until I felt as though I was literally sliding down the thread of a gigantic screw that was working its way into the earth. I knew if it continued the planet would explode, due to the immense pressure being released from its molten interior. I desperately tried to halt the dizzying twists, the entire room blurring into a kaleidoscopic swirl which completely engulfed me. When I came round I was snorting a mound of speed off an LP cover, but thankfully the lads made me stop.

When I tried to sleep the following night, I believed my dad had built an extensive network of shelves all over the walls of my bedroom, but these were just shadows. The tremors in my chest translated into movement and my bedroom suddenly became a long, moving railway carriage. Through the cracks around the edge of my bedroom door, I could see blue sky and big pine trees whizzing by. Somehow I was in North America. The door-catch morphed into the tiny head of a person silhouetted against the sky. His hair was blowing in the wind. He was shouting something to me but I couldn't hear. Slowly, I became aware of something moving at the end of my bed. In the light from the crack I saw that it was a giant black serpent, its glossy scales uncoiling as it towered up menacingly. The room was shaking and rolling along, and I let out a terrified shout as it poised to strike. My long-suffering father came bursting through the door and the whole scene disintegrated, replaced by the familiar (friendly, even) frogs and lizards. The next day, sitting in a city-centre pub with my graft-mates, an idea occurred; I made a spontaneous plan to run away to the Israeli desert, where all you could see was golden sand and sulphate couldn't fuck with your mind.

Things were filtering into all regions of Britain, with lads reaching their late-teens and early-20s, muscling up and wanting some extra beadage to pay the bills. By 1985 I'd been hammering the whiz and acid for a year or three, and had come some serious croppers with it. The time was ripe for me to *loz* it permanently – stop it forever. Many of the lads I was hanging around with were thieves or drug dealers, some on the fast track to criminal careers. Everyone was doing drugs constantly, listening to fantastic music, and most of the time life was good. In the months before my swift exit to the Israeli desert, many strange pigeons had come home to roost. A lifetime of being an oddball had fused with my genetic proclivity toward total mayhem. I went berserk like you read about, but you won't read about it here. My parents and extended family were salt-of-the-earth. They had mountains of amusing tales to tell from their upbringing and early working years, when they held massive parties for days on end and pilfered everything that moved in the Salford area (like everyone did back then). But my recent excursions into psychedelic landscapes and unbridled thievery had earned me a tag that said 'damaged goods'. It was time to either clean up or just *smishe* – get away.

I was found a job through a relative, as a way to get me on the straight and narrow. Unfortunately, it wasn't the sort of job a bloke on the straight and narrow gets. I didn't even know what I was going to be doing that first morning, as my dad drove me into the city centre to drop me off. It could have been carpet-cleaning or driving a forklift for all I knew. On the way in the car, the old feller cleared his throat and put his head down in the way he does when he's about to deliver a message.

'I'm tellin' yer right now, Ian, all this bleedin' palaver this last few months has got to stop. I don't know what the bleedin' 'ell's wrong with yer, ah mean yer like a bleedin' *wino*! *A junkie*!' His voice rose uncontrollably as he said those words, and I fought hard to stifle an embarrassed chuckle which threatened to escape my throat like a rat out of hell. 'You'd better not be talkin' a load of shite to these lads on this job, Ian, 'cos they won't 'ave it. These are good lads, so don't be showin' me and yer mother up by lettin' 'em know yer 'ead's full of crap, I'm warnin' yer. For Christ's sake, we're worried about you and you can't even see it!'

I felt that one, and the guilt crept over me like a delicate but lethal spider. The old man gritted his teeth as we hit town. Right before he dropped me off, we had a massive argument 'cos he knew I didn't want to work, the biggest crime of all. After my recent marathon shoplifting and looting extravaganza, the thought of having to get up early five days a week was frankly terrifying, and my chafing increased as we trundled between the office blocks. The old man noticed it and blew up, calling me a useless, lazy bastard and worse.

He dropped me off outside some office block, and there was a right motley crew stood on the steps outside. Then I realised they were my new mates and were actually waiting for me, like a fucking guard of honour or something. My nana's husband, the Whit Lane Warbler, emerged from the mob smiling, and explained what the script was for the morning.

'There's a big carpet comin' and we're gonna lift it in through the back window on the fifth floor usin' ropes. It'll be a doddle.' I nodded like a Marlboro Man, despite having no intention of involving myself in anything as ridiculous and difficult as what he'd just described. I wanted to give the impression I was with the programme.

Anyway, we managed it and after dinner we walked across town, way down Piccadilly. We spent the afternoon taking steel shelves apart in an immense, wavy glass building near the Mancunian Way. At one point I was laying down unscrewing some shelving and the Warbler's son, Bruiser, kept deliberately dropping screwdrivers, endways, onto the side of my face. After about four of these drops, I asked, 'What the fuck you doin', you cunt?' They both laughed, and I'd apparently passed my first test. Bruiser had a shaved head and a boxer's face bearing plenty of ancient troughs and craters, and he'd served his time around town long before I had, being over 15 years my senior. He was built like a machine and his voice was a deep bass, dripping with the dark, colourless tones of inner-city Salford. He rolled cigs from a big, silver Blackpool baccy tin that he carried everywhere. He made me feel at home. I still had no idea what the job description was by the end of the day.

The following day we were in some big tower off Piccadilly and Chorlton Street, moving furniture with trucks and dollies. We took a load of giant wooden racks apart. My Uncle Bill mysteriously appeared and drove away with it all in a trailer attached to the back of his Capri, apparently having done a deal with the Warbler. Just before lunch the foreman, an Irish bloke called Paddy, took me into a lift, saying he had a job for me. We visited several floors and he pointed out various empty filing cabinets positioned on the landings beside the lifts.

'Put them all on the wagon.'

I put them all on. Just as we were leaving he gestured to another filing cabinet, one which I'd literally just seen an office worker place a file in. It was part of a line of cabinets quite clearly in use. 'Get that one at the end, there, and throw it on the wagon,' he said.

'I think they're using that, aren't they?' I asked, confused.

'Just put it on. It'll be alright.'

I threw it on and then the two of us set off in the truck, with Billy Broughton driving. I was 19 years old and still hadn't learned to drive yet, as I couldn't afford lessons – or, more accurately, beer, drugs and music were more important. We ended up in Hulme, at a gypsy yard near the old Factory club. The guy was offering to buy scrap metal, tell your fortune, fix your car or fill you in. He was what we called 'all-inclusive'. He did the lot. Paddy had me unload the cabinets. A large wad changed hands. Then we went back to town and into a bar called Kicks, in Piccadilly. There was a blackboard outside advertising, 'Bitter, 50p a pint, till 4 every day.'

All the rest of the lads were in there, sat round a big empty table, waiting. Paddy took out the big wedge, placed it in the middle of the table and said to me, 'Right, you just keep 'em comin' all afternoon.' I kept 'em comin', and by half-three we were all pissed as arseholes. I wasn't prepared for this, but I certainly wasn't complaining. I slowly discovered that the true job description was, 'Hoisting furniture from office blocks, selling it and going on the piss for the rest of the day.' Apparently the first day had been an exception, but every day from then on proved to be a blur. And the best part was, every Friday Paddy gave me a bit extra to go round to Piccadilly Records and buy myself an album. They had a great psychedelic section there, and my record collection enjoyed a nice weekly boost from artists like the Seeds, the Beasts of Bourbon, Lipstick Killers and the Nomads. This was mid-1985. The first seismic psychedelic ripples were sent into the city's underground by the growing numbers that had been on the case for at least two years, fed by the subterraneous acid stream provided by firms like the Dambusters.

The company was a rum little outfit, based in Ancoats. Our crew were all either from Salford, north Manchester, Eire or Glasgow. Most of them were old school, untouched by the designer gear and the drugs. I was the youngest by at least a decade. They were all mad boozers and characters in their own right. Paddy was worth a fortune, and lived with a posh English wife in Cheshire somewhere. He chain-smoked Hamlet cigars from a five-pack, and wore a suit that announced his Irishness from a considerable distance. His greasy thick hair was wavy and miraculous in ways only a classical Irishman's hair can be. He was a very loveable and generous man. The only criticism I ever had of him was that he kept his Jack Russell terrier locked in his car all day 'cos his posh wife didn't like it in the house. Paddy often had us run scrap paper round to a place in Ancoats to weigh in, but, being Paddy, he couldn't resist putting a few bricks among the bales to add a few extra kilos. The place was said to be run by the heavy mob. It always amazed me how he continued to insert the bricks, even after being warned not to do it again. They knew Paddy and seemed to take it all in good stead. He was obsessed with ideas and schemes of any and every kind.

'Ian, you should start your own little game off,' he would say in his quiet, measured Dublin tone, "taking money from the day-trippers at

Heaton Park. You could say yer a car park attendant an' take money at the gates on a Sunday afternoon. Now can yerz run along an' get us foive Hamlets from the tobacconists up Piccadilly . . ."

I never did attempt that one; Sundays were for exploring lazy afternoon inner landscapes. It didn't stop Paddy from suggesting it on a daily basis though.

Billy Broughton was another Irishman, a wiry old feller with no belly whatsoever who could neck 20 pints of Holts' bitter and still get behind the wheel of a wagon and drive impeccably. He went to the bingo every week with his missus, and kept a strict log of the quantities he consumed for our titillation.

'20 pints of Holts and eight to ten whiskeys was not out of the question,' he'd say, a sparkle in his beady eye. The man was an alcoholic dynamo; he gleamed and fizzed with jokes, stories and general chatter from the Manchester jungle, delivered in that west Ireland accent with which Manchester is tightly stocked.

PG from Glasgow was a cracking bloke; he was one of the youngest, with a top head on him and a sense of humour to match. He'd come of age in the mid-70s, and he oozed that Rod Stewart-meets-Lou Macari-glamorousness we all know and love. His clothes always had a slight flair to them, like he cared about how he looked. He always made me feel like I was on holiday, a great quality in a person. He wore well-cut denim jackets that looked made-to-measure and even his jeans appeared tailor-made. He was sporting sleeveless black fleeces twenty years before they came in and even shades, which was scandalous in 1985. PG had been to Las Vegas, which was quite something back then, and it contributed to his general aura of extravagance and charm. Of course, he loved his ale. He had a cockiness that was marrow-deep, and a broad Glaswegian accent loaded with alien slang. It seemed like everyone he knew was somehow connected to Manchester's nightclub world, wheeler-dealers in tickets and swag. One night we ran into him with his mates, some blokes in jeans and t-shirts. PG was wearing an immaculate navy suit, a white shirt and a red and black tie, a streetwise version of Macari strolling into Wembley prior to kick-off like he owned it. The blokes with him cast the same aura. I was soon to discover the reason why.

But the star of the bunch was the Whit Lane Warbler, my nana's husband. He was an ageless, charismatic geezer, who loved nowt more than to get up in the boozer with a microphone and give them a tune by Dean Martin, Perry Como, Andy Williams and many more. He'd been in the navy, and used to tell me about sailing down the Saint Lawrence River through Quebec and into the ports of Lake Ontario and New York. It sounded fascinating. His face was framed by a mop of grey hair which he continually swept back from his brow with his hand. His shark-fin conk protruded and his eyes beamed like a magic elf's. Possibly due to boredom at being reduced to landlubber status since he'd left the service, the Warbler had invented a whole world of his own, populated by a cast of characters both beautiful and strange. He'd devised a complete dictionary of slang and other vocab that defied scrutiny. The imaginary place was called 'Leylanarck', and among the characters were Stackaxe, McGheeta, Mrs. Castembryce, Sleth and a mysterious entity known as the 'Cotsitlot'. He provided no end of entertainment with his fascinating blend of imaginary characters and the endless quotes they were purported to have uttered. He was a Salford legend. The Warbler would approach you while you were carrying something heavy and whisper a volley of urgent nonsense, guaranteed to make you nearly drop your cargo:

'Stethlets!'

'Steth what?'

'He ate six!'

'What?'

'Stackaxe! He ate six meat 'n' potato pies! Six bunyats! All the lot . . .'

'*Eh*?'

'McGheeta had tracksuit hair. He stayed late 'n' all. And the back of his neck was one mass of mistletoe. Did *you* 'ear it?'

The Warbler asked this question obsessively to all and sundry. I always thought, 'Did you hear it?' was a reference to the Big Bang, mainly due to the high concentrations of LSD I was subjecting myself to on a weekly basis, but he was actually referring to the amazingly long and loud farts he liked to produce. The man was a fart factory and could deliver the goods as well as any I've ever met. Even my dad looked up to him on that score, himself a champion farter. The Warbler's patter never ceased, and he'd tell you about men and women from Leylanarck who had 'five legs dangling like Milligan', or 'dog feet and a basket o' whelks'. None of it made sense to normal people, but the whole crew was fluent in *Warblerspeak*, often incorporating the more famous expressions to camouflage discussions about skulduggery when in earshot of the office workers.

On one occasion we were doing a move in a south Manchester dole office, and as we were carrying a desk down a corridor the Warbler said, ''Ang on, put it down 'ere . . .' I let the desk down, thinking he wanted a rest, before I noticed the microphone nestling in an alcove. It was used for calling the dole claimants through to the inner sanctum of the interview room. The Warbler took the mic, which was apparently switched on, and began his tender assault on the unsuspecting ears beyond the glass, out in the public waiting room:

'And now . . . the end is near . . . and so I face . . . the final curtain . . . my friend . . . I'll say it clear . . . I'll state my case . . . of which I'm certain . . .'

The entire building was suddenly alive with the man's mellifluous tones. People waiting in the main lobby were stunned, trying to work out what was going on, and the staff looked utterly bewildered. Sinatra couldn't have managed it any better and this old Salfordian was doing it for free, for the Rastas and the winos and the wannabe gangsters. He replaced the mic with lightning speed when he realised someone had tumbled him. We continued to carry the desk down the corridor, just two menial knobheads in a world full of them. Or so it seemed.

There was a period when I stopped going in the pubs with all the local heads, as my amphetamine fuck-ups had raised a hermit-like aspect of my personality to the surface. The herd was a thing to avoid at all costs. The night I finally recovered, and went straight into the heart of a crowd of grafters and heads in the Red Lion, Kezz pulled me to one side and forcefully said, 'Let's see the *real* you tonight, Ian. Don't take any shit off these wankers, and if you're outnumbered don't worry. I'm here and I've got your back.'

The lad who'd known me since I was five years old was still my surrogate older brother at age 20, and it was good to know his tough love was still available. It set me back on the road to sanity. Whenever I started to feel the paranoid demons encroaching, it was a relief to know that Kezz, with his catlike gait and shaved jet-black hair, was lurking there to stave them off like a lion with a pack of hyenas, if I needed him.

But arrangements had been made. Grafting and boozing with the crew all over town enabled me to save a modicum of money for my Israeli voyage. With a scant $200 I went through yet another door in the wall. This time there was no coming back.

* * *

On December 10, 1985, I flew to Israel to begin my life on the road. My mam and dad and my girlfriend, Carol, came to the airport to wave me off. The Israelis were carrying machine-pistols, keeping guard on our little flock as if they expected a PLO onslaught any moment. I was fascinated and pissed off in equal measure at the thought of all that firepower, and the fact that it was actually foreigners wielding it on our turf. An announcement declared it too cloudy for take-off and we were bussed to Bradford unexpectedly. As I climbed onto the bus, having hugged and kissed my dear mother and Carol, my old feller gave me a hard pat on the back and a firm handshake, followed by his finger in my face.

'Keep yer nose, clean, Ian.'

He tapped his own nose after he said it, and the message was received and understood. I had to keep my nose clean.

It was the first time I'd ever been on a plane, and I was already 20. I was glued to the window throughout most of the flight. The yellow lights of England's eastern seaboard gave way to a brief blackness, followed by an endless changing configuration of white lights – Europe. Yes, I'd been to France before (and Wales), but this was the first time I ever felt like I was actually *going* somewhere.

I'd arranged the placement on Kibbutz Sde Boker a few weeks earlier at the kibbutz office in Broughton Park, an affluent Jewish section of Salford. The interviewer was a gorgeous Israeli girl, a soldier. I eagerly signed up for the expedition; anything that could put a few thousand miles between me, the drugs and the crews of nutters I'd grown up with was worth a shot, I reasoned. Especially if it was full of raven-haired beauties like this one. About two or three weeks after the interview, a letter from the kibbutz office came through the door, informing me exactly where I was being sent. I was excited as I eyed the map of Israel and ecstatic upon realising I was going to the south of the country, into the heart of the desert.

It was the first and last time I ever went somewhere knowing beforehand where I was going to sleep that night, or even in possession of a return ticket. People talk about the thrill of gambling or shoplifting, but once you've been bitten by the travel bug all else pales into insignificance.

The flight took four and a half hours. When we landed in Tel-Aviv a hot wind was causing the palm trees to wave about crazily. It was a different latitude, subject to different eco-chemistry. It brushed the senses with a much warmer hand. We were met at the airport and driven for three hours south into the alien clutches of the Negev desert. The hot night bristled with antennae, festooned with blinking red warning lights. Occasionally we streaked through a lonely desert town and brief glimpses of Middle-Eastern architecture exploded dramatically into view before the minibus was swallowed by the emptiness of the open sands.

The kibbutz, when we finally reached it, was entered by a half-mile-long driveway lined with olive trees. We were deposited in the dining hall and assigned three-to-a-bungalow by an American wearing army pants and a check shirt. The spacious dining hall was part of a small cluster of modern structures, one of which was the tiny post office, the other the shop. This centre enjoyed deep shade from the looming trees all around it, a cool oasis for meeting and swapping gossip. The dining hall was at the top of some open-plan stairs, which allowed the fresh breezes to sweep through the covered square between it and a small bank of PO boxes, one of which said 'Volunteers' on it; they never let you forget you *volunteered* to do what they made you do on the kibbutz, whether you were enjoying it or not. The shop was quite small, with a couple of aisles dividing four sets of shelves crammed with condiments, vodka, beer, bread and assorted trivial hardware.

There were several free-standing walls around this focal point. They featured little stained-glass windows bearing that distinctive Hebrew hallmark of coloured geometric rectangles, representing the triumph of civilisation in a hostile universe. Right off this strange little centre were the footpaths that led to the kibbutzniks' homes. The paths had recesses containing benches and soft orange lighting at intervals, for night-time socialising. The attractive stucco bungalows, often in clusters at the ends of cul-de-sacs, emitted hoarse, raucous Hebrew epithets from their ever-open windows. The voices and the accents were dry, like the desert itself, conjuring childhood images of the exotic East: Athens, the blue Mediterranean, Arabia, Sinbad and crumbling biblical towns baking in a golden ocean of mineralised powder.

But the kibbutz was a miracle. An isolated freshwater spring teeming with orchards and greenery, thanks to the computerised irrigation systems the Israelis had invented and the genetically modified strains of fruit and vegetables, designed to give higher yield under harsh conditions. Sde Boker reminded me of a holiday village, one whose residents were on a weird permanent vacation. Everyone rode bicycles everywhere, except when they headed out to the distant fields and chicken houses, then it was jeeps, pickups or tractors with trailers in tow, containing volunteers.

Our bungalows were down a path across the large lawn adjacent to the centre. Past the swimming pool and along a sandy track where the hot wind blew ferociously and you learned to slit your eyes as you approached. We lived at the interface between the kibbutz and the surrounding desert. Out on the edge. Volunteer bungalows had slat windows (if they faced out) which were kept open at all times, and tiled floors. They were basically a room with three beds, a small kitchen and a tiny bathroom. The view from our front door was a vast expanse of golden dunes, with a bizarre, pyramid-shaped mountain way off in the distance. Every day we swept the sand from the tiled floor and every day it blew back in, but we were happy. There were cacti and the odd tumbleweed dotted here and there. The stucco bungalows were distributed about a small network of sandy paths, with barbeques for our use. Some of them were occupied by Israeli soldiers, the kibbutz security. The soldiers held excellent barbeques, bringing live chickens from the chicken-houses and waiting till the very last minute to slaughter them. As they mixed their sauces and lit the kindling, the birds would be clucking about on the ground, unsuspectingly pecking at whatever took their interest. The soldiers were quite evil in the way they relished beheading the birds with their daggers and bayonets, each man making a grand show of his viciousness. The chickens were lobbed into large containers full of a heavenly marinade. It was the juiciest, most tender meat I've ever eaten.

I had a large number of psychedelic tapes with me, and the scouser I shared a room with had plenty more. He was there to escape the evils of drugs, he told me, and I nodded understandingly. By the third night we'd had a good drink and swapped some stories about going to the footy with the boys. We'd totally alienated our third roommate, a university-educated Bradford lad who seemed to think he was a member of the aristocracy. His U2 and Marillion tapes were mercilessly ridiculed and pretty soon it was all Talking Heads, Seeds, 13th Floor Elevators, Robyn Hitchcock, Squeeze, Coltrane, Ivor Biggun and the Red Nosed Burglars, Ian Dury, Magazine, Lou Reed and Muddy Waters. The scouser played a sax, so he knew his stuff. He took a job in the kitchens and quickly began dropping off cases of Maccabi lager in the bungalow during his lunchtime, fresh from the walk-in fridge.

We woke at 4:30 every day and went to the canteen for a collective breakfast. Then we worked until eleven, converging on the canteen again for lunch. The food was always fresh vegetables, meat, herbs and grains. It was nice to spend an hour in the company of others, letting the sweat cool off as the bright sunshine washed through the dining hall. I worked way out in the olive orchards in sun and shade, enjoying the sensation of my mind slowly shedding the tremors of yesteryear. I worked with a small group of Yemenite Jews who would give me drinks of sweet cold coffee from a flask. They looked like living hieroglyphics. Their big white eyes, hook noses and jet-black ringlets reminded me of an ancient eastern fable.

One of the resident soldiers had gone to my school and he recognised me; I'd grown up in Britain's second-largest Jewish neighbourhood and the laws of probability dictated such an encounter might occur. He was a few years older but he was alright, a major stoner. I spent a lot of time in his bungalow with other soldiers, smoking herb and listening to music. While discovering the gentle sounds of Neil Young with that mad Jewish moon shining through the glassless window, I began to meet my first Yanks. One was an American-Israeli soldier, a cool kid who told a lot of stories about parachuting into Gaza and Lebanon. It was magical to be in a tropical desert, stoned, talking to Americans whose music, literature and films I'd admired my entire life. I remember, when I asked one of them where he was from, he replied, 'Kansas,' in a low, almost moody voice. I didn't realise at the time, but the rest of them mocked him for being from the Midwest, but all I could say was, 'Wow, fuckin' Kansas! It must be brilliant there!' It's analogous to the Yanks who, upon hearing that I'm from Manchester, reply, 'Nice!' while professional arseholes from the English southeast giggle vacuously.

At that point there were only about four western birds on the kibbutz. We'd all flown in on the same flight but I had spied many darkly gorgeous *kife* (women) among the native population. The kibbutz was highly conducive to sexual activity, with its romantic backdrops, compact living and scantily-clad demeanour. I often heard it said that a couple arriving on a kibbutz stood a very slim chance of remaining a couple once they were enveloped by the communal mindset and the willing spirit of adventure.

Right before Christmas more volunteers arrived, including a lively southern group who'd flown out of London. Our northern group had arrived a few weeks in advance of them. The volunteer population swelled as some Canadians and an American lad arrived. The nights and days were filled with eager chatter, drinking, sex and fascination with the stars and the Negev. The desert was full of antelopes, porcupines, giant spiders, snakes and wolves. There was a wooden hut on a dirt track, way out beyond the fringe, where we went to party and where we ate our Christmas dinner at a long table full of traditional English food. The English girls all worked together and made a fantastic spread. The hut had a kitchen, as well as a 'disco room' with mirror-balls and a DJ booth. On New Year's Eve, walking out to the hut alone, I stumbled upon the silent silhouette of a large wolf ahead on the trail. We remained still for about five minutes, the suspense killing me. Eventually, as I considered turning and pissing off back to the bungalows (the sounds of rampantly drunk volunteers' music barely audible in the distance), the wolf turned and loped soundlessly into engulfing blackness as I continued to my goal.

It was always hot, day and night. My bones became relaxed to the marrow, something I'd struggled to achieve in the amphetamine craziness of Manchester. I'd been swimming into ever more alarming waters for a long time and was here escaping them, like the scouser. The kibbutz was a desert fantasy come true, but after a few months the lure of the real world called like a siren from the ancient rocks of the cities: Tel-Aviv, Jerusalem, Haifa and a crazy place called Eilat that was Israel's most southern point, right on the Red Sea at the top of the gulf.

We'd run amok on the kibbutz and got away with it. People had been caught shagging the wives of the kibbutzniks (not recommended, as everyone carried handguns and kept M16s in their closets in case of a terrorist attack), as well as burglarising booze from the large fridges in the kitchens. There was even one utter weirdo from London who was exposed as a peeping Tom and thrown off. I felt sorry for him, to be honest; he was obviously not for public consumption. Every Friday was Shabbat, and we enjoyed a sumptuous feast with lashings of kosher wine pilfered from surrounding tables or donated by kibbutzniks who enjoyed watching the crazy English make dicks of themselves. One Saturday morning I got smashed on vodka with the Bradford aristocracy. I went to visit a girl I'd been going with, a Canadian called Jane who was rooming with a couple of nutcase birds from Cumbria in a nearby bungalow. They were still sleeping their hangovers off in bed and their door was locked. I literally dived right through the window into the room, landing in a heap, surrounded by shards of flying glass. I only copped for a few scratches, but the girls were not amused. The aristocracy later informed me that I'd 'become emotional' over all the trouble I'd caused my mam and dad in recent years, before I'd set off to see Jane after the vodka brekky. The elders of the tribe considered throwing me off the kibbutz but we made it easy for them by jumping a bus to Tel-Aviv.

Tel-Aviv was an eclectic tangle of ancient and modern: prehistoric backstreet caves that sold amazing falafel and hummus, cheek by jowl with sleek and flamboyant architecture designed by the talented Jewish craftsmen and architects who'd returned to the old country in the late 20th century. The ancient bus station area was always crammed with massive crowds. Its rotting covered terminal featured a couple of counters set in the crumbling turquoise-green walls. Outside, a series of parallel bays bounded by sickly-green metal barriers signified the different stops for various locations, north into the green hills and south into the sands. Across the street, in the scorching sunshine, traffic and endless babble, there were several large falafel places, old glassy cafés with mirrored walls and long bars which sold beer, wine and spirits, with gigantic arrays of spices, sauces, vegetables and peppers in bowls at tables on the pavement out front. One in particular became my home base when I went to Tel-Aviv, very conveniently located directly across from the station. The place had a big, horseshoe-shaped bar with plenty of stools, and the food was sound. The guy who owned it was a big, rum cunt, always wearing a white shirt and a navy yarmulke, and he would give me a smile and a wink if I brought a girl in, knowing a long session was on the cards.

John from London made the rounds of the hostels packed with Brits in the cities, and remembers the scams and schemes of the time:

'We devised a clever little earner while staying in Tel-Aviv. It was a break from the hot work out in the fields. We'd remove our clothes apart from our shorts, and walk barefoot along the boulevards, stopping people and explaining that we'd slept on the beach the previous night and woke up to find all our clothes and possessions stolen. Could they possibly spare a few shekels for us to obtain lunch? The Israelis are generous people and they'd toss you a nice wedge without question. Don't ever let anyone tell you the Jews are tight. It's a myth. Others would take you round the nearest market and sort you out with a bag of fresh food. One bloke took me to his flat, above the main street where I'd accosted him. He gave me a load of new t-shirts and shorts, all designer gear. When we were leaving town on a trip, we'd coach a couple of the other English from the home hostel to keep it going and pay it forward in time. Man United fans would team up with Millwall lads. Bristol boys would be at it with Geordies. We called it "begging" and it worked a treat if you were good at lying and acting. I always felt guilty doing this, but it was a great way to learn how wonderful and giving strangers can be. And, of course, sometimes things went pear-shaped.

'One evening, on an expedition from a kibbutz up on the Lebanon border, I got talking to an old Russian Jew sat on a bench at the beach. He was watching someone doing Tai-Chi just as the Tel-Aviv "green flash" sunset occurred. The flash happens just as the sun disappears behind the Mediterranean horizon, and they say it's amazing. I'd been tripping on acid for months so it was fuck-all to write home about from my corner.

'"You look hungry," the old geezer said in a Russian accent, smiling. "If you like I can make you some dinner."

'He invited me back to his flat. I explained I hadn't eaten in days and had all my possessions stolen. I was fully-clothed but had stashed my bag.

'In the flat, he made me steak and eggs and produced a bottle of vodka. Back at the kibbutz I'd been polishing off a bottle of vodka a day (at 90 pence apiece who wouldn't?) so I made a big dent in it pretty quickly. Another bottle came out and I ploughed into that, too. Every time we did a shot, we'd shout "L'chaim!", Hebrew for cheers. I vaguely remember him offering me the freedom to take a bath. I did, having been travelling constantly for a few days on Egged buses in 100-degree heat. My nuts were reeking. While I was in the bath he came in the bathroom to bring a towel or some nonsense. I stumbled out of the bathroom but my clothes had mysteriously disappeared. I crashed out on a bed, pissed drunk. When I woke up the old boy was trying to suck my cock! I launched him off and he went sprawling across the floor. He started weeping and offering me money. Money to suck my noodle or as an alternative to getting pasted further, I wasn't sure. I'd kicked the old boy off me, hard enough to give him the message but soft enough not to kill him. I didn't wish him any harm. I got dressed and jogged through the deserted streets, paranoid that he'd phoned the police and reported it as a burglary or assault. I went back to the beach, where my holdall was stashed deep under a boardwalk. It was the wee hours, and I was sick at not having a place to kip. Everywhere was closed. I tried to sleep under the pier, but the drunks and the giant ants kept me awake. I wandered onto the beach and climbed up the ladder into a lifeguard lodge. As I scrambled inside I realised the lodge contained several shadowy figures – homeless Israeli kids. They lit a candle while we discussed my evening and they laughed at my bad fortune. We discovered we had a friend in common, a vagabond kid called Tal from my kibbutz who used to live on the streets of Tel-Aviv. He was seeing some mad Cumbrian bird.

'The silhouette to my right goes, "Here, Englishman, your fortunes have just changed." He passed me a joint. A quick smoke and it was lights out as I drifted off in this little nest of vipers. Bob's yer uncle.'

This was a typical nightly predicament for scores of British lads out there. They occupied different areas of the city and even had local pubs they favoured. It wasn't unusual for a crew from one pub or hostel to kick off with another; the lads who hung out down Ben Yehuda and Allenby Streets might turn up at the Blue Angel pub in the northern beach area. A little mob staying at the Home Hostel could wash up in swanky Dizengoff, sometimes with violent consequences. It was very odd how some lads from across Britain would act like tribal brothers on the strength of a fortnight on the ale. But on the occasions when I was forced to quickly relocate from one hostel to another (following skulduggery of some kind), I would receive a suspicious and hostile welcome from the Brits there. We were all up to no good and territory had to be guarded.

6

THE GOLDEN EAST

What am I doing here?
— Arthur Rimbaud, writing home from Ethiopia

In mid-1986, Israel's blazing cities contained youth hostels packed with British and European youngsters. Our average age was around 22, with some as young as 18 and others as old as 26. I was 20. Their walls were covered in graffiti from all over the world, scrawled or patiently applied by vandals and artists in numerous languages. The drinking and smoking were rampant, as well as experimentation with a hallucinogenic, apple-like fruit which grew on the trees lining the streets of Tel-Aviv. After witnessing one English lad stupefied on it, performing a weird involuntary puppet dance with sightless eyes and an expression of total vacancy, I decided I didn't want to poison myself to that extent. A mate of mine, Doug from Surrey, put it quite succinctly:

'I've seen grown men runnin' up and down the street, cryin' like babies, an' spilling their life stories to any cunt who'll listen. They can't stop cryin' or dancing about. If you want to do that to yourself get on with it, but don't fuckin' ask me to do it.'

Doug had served two years for manslaughter back home after smacking someone whose head hit the deck a bit too hard. He had a faultless record with the birds but he was shit-scared of the apples. The entire region was full of strange fruit, and as you went south you encountered intense clusters of it.

Down south in the Eilat bars favoured by the Brits, lads would come in with wild eyes and dark tans, relating their recent odysseys across Egypt on land and water. The Egyptian border came right into Eilat, so it was a cheap returning point for those who'd gone on one-way tickets to sample the relics of an ancient vanished civilisation. But you had to go to Tel-Aviv for a stamp in your passport, as you needed a visa if you entered Egypt from Israel. A lot of traipsing between the Egyptian embassy and Israeli customs was involved, but Egypt sounded most alarming and it had to be done. Normal people didn't go to Egypt for their holidays back then, especially if they had Israeli stamps in their passports. I bought a one-way bus ticket from Tel-Aviv to Cairo and joined two lads from Yorkshire on the quest for magic. When I cashed my last paycheque from the Eilat hotel I'd been working at, the cashier had given me a hundred shekels too much. I took it as a good sign. I checked into Tel-Aviv's Home Hostel and went on the ale with some of the lads I'd met over the past several months. There was a top crew of Brits who used the Home as a base when in Tel-Aviv. They were all proper party animals who didn't give a shite about anything. Sleeping rough became commonplace. To sleep by the side of the road was always an option taken after long drinking sessions, with few bad results. Guys would stand up in pubs and sing their teams' footy songs all the way through, then someone else would get up and outdo them. Everyone followed their teams via games on telly and it was a blast discussing matches we'd been at as opposing supporters. A good few of them were serving apprenticeships on the begging. It was a good earner, as long as an old bloke didn't try to suck your cock.

A scouser called Russell was working at the Home as chief cook and bottle-washer and he was a proper nobble. He introduced me to 'buckets' – smoking hash by using the vacuum created by pulling air into a plastic two-litre bottle through a bucket of water. The plastic bottles had their bottoms cut off and submerged in the water. The hash was packed in an inverted glass bottleneck with a perforated top and placed against the open mouth of the plastic bottle. When you raised the bottle and the water level dropped, the hash smoke was pulled through the system and filled it. You then placed your mouth over the top of the two-litre, as if taking a drink, and pushed it back down into the water. The water forced the smoke into your lungs and sent you to the moon. Russell had a special room set up in the hostel dedicated to doing buckets. There were plenty of European and Israeli girls happy to sample it. This led to some very romantic evenings for those of us in on the scene.

The night I met Russell we did some buckets and went to a nearby café for a drink. He told me his entire life story; how he got picked on at school but ended up being the toughest kid there out of sheer determination. He had the gift, and it was a pleasure just to sit in my cosmic head and listen and laugh at his scouse tales. Then he went serious.

'You've got very old eyes, man,' he told me. 'I know I can trust yer. I'm gonna tell you somethin' now, right. Every fourth Thursday, Avi, the owner of Home, has me run the monthly takings to the bank in his jeep. It's always guarded at the hostel, and that's the only time I ever get outside the watchful gaze of Avi with it in me hands. One of these months I'm gonna just drive the jeep onto a boat bound for Cyprus or Greece, and do one. There's fuckin' *thousands* of dollars in that kitty every month!' (The next time I returned to Tel-Aviv, Russ was gone and so was the jeep convertible. Avi didn't want to discuss it.)

It took a day to arrange visas. Then we set off for Cairo.

The bus ride was a gruelling several hours. I almost didn't make it after leaving my wallet in a sandwich shop near the bus stop and having to leg it round the corner to retrieve it just as the bus arrived. The Yorkshire lads never seemed to stop arguing with each other in those broad accents, a patient debate in which each tried to outthink the other in an endless verbal chess-game. I lay on the seat behind them and surveyed the landscapes. We drove through the Sinai desert, passing the burnt-out tanks and bombed buildings which the Israelis had blown up before handing Sinai back to the Egyptians six years earlier. There were spent tank shells by the side of the road and in the distance flapped the incongruous parasols and hotels of Mediterranean holiday resorts.

We checked into a hotel in the heart of Cairo, the biggest city in Africa. After some brief haggling we secured a grand room. The suite was massive, and the three of us shared with a Belgian lawyer who never removed his leather jacket, trousers, boots or sweater the whole time he was there. It was significantly warmer there than in Tel-Aviv.

'I am doing it to lose weight for my girlfriend,' he said.

Someone should have told him you sweat salts, not fat, and he could have been a lot more comfortable. A lawyer should know that oil and water don't mix, surely.

I slept on a big antique settee, Mick was on another. Pete and the

Belgian bagged the two single beds. The room had grand doors and an ornate balcony with fabulous wrought-iron decorations, from which we could survey the insane panorama of the city. The skyline defined the geographic location, African-style dwellings interlocked with eastern minarets and mosques. Huge ornate western façades and modern concrete hotels. Neon advertisements in Arabic reflected off the slow Nile as it cleaved the madness like an endless, mythic snake. The constant sound of car horns and wailing music assailed us from all directions. The aroma of cooking meat and spices wafted upwards with some frequency. The hotel's fixtures and fittings were like something out of Agatha Christie. Large, robust rubber plants were situated about the room in big pots. Once we'd found our bearings, Yorkshire Mick had an idea.

'A bloke on our kibbutz told me about a market 'ere where you can score hash dead easy. Let's get some and then get summat to eat.'

We plunged into the streets, taking this backstreet, then that main drag, transfixed by the sheer age of the place and the sound of the crowd. The odoriferous mayhem of the boulevards occasionally opened out into a timeless square with a statue at its centre. These statues were no Queen doo-dah from a few hundred years ago. They were massive likenesses of the Pharaohs who lived in Ancient Egypt, *five-thousand-year-old granite hunks of stylised monumental art*, supreme under a reddening, dusky sky. The looming, age-blackened buildings had alien designs and features built or carved into them from a bygone era. The shops were open-fronted affairs with no windows. There were cave-like openings, inside which men were selling carpets, oil, spice, shoes and gold, or else up to their eyeballs in dirt and grease, dismantling machinery and motorcycles under the harsh gleam of naked bulbs. After a few inquiries we were directed to the market where we literally scored hash in two seconds. We had barely set foot in the place and were already hoofing it to some immense palatial structure to roll a joint on the front steps, and watch the olive river of twisted Arabs flowing past.

Suitably ill, we bought some shawarma from a street vendor, succulent lamb, goat and chicken chopped with tomatoes and onions, roasted on a vertical spit. The vendor gave us salad, too. I was shocked to discover half a locust mashed up among the lettuce and onions. Its beady red eyes and twitching antennae testified that it was still alive.

When I pointed it out, the vendor shrugged and peered at me as if I was an idiot. It was only later that I realised the big insects were an important source of protein in Egypt.

We were wearing shorts and sandals, nothing more. The air was hot and wet, strange for a desert location. It complemented the tiled façades, the constant African drum music and smooth stone statues from the ancient world reminding us that we were someplace truly exotic.

That night in the room we made a bong from a plastic bottle, a pen, foil and wax. We smoked the hash till we were frightened. Mick and Pete played cards and argued in their Yorkshire lingo about the logistical difficulties of bringing turquoise and gold up to the surface 5,000 years ago. I lay on the settee and dreamed of ancient civilisations, pyramids, sphinxes, Stonehenge, magic mushrooms and more besides. It was like those years of drugging and being a latter-day hippie back home had culminated in this visit to the centre of the mystic world.

One favourite route taken by the British was the felucca trip down the Nile to Aswan. You would have to go to Luxor, a city 450 miles south of Cairo, and hang around till you found a captain of a felucca willing to give you a ride. After a brief haggle, you jumped in and set off on the epic cruise. Gary from Oxfordshire remembers his trip down the world's longest river:

'We found a captain and his son who agreed on a price for a French couple, a lad from New Zealand and me. I think it was a four-day trip to Aswan. The felucca was surprisingly small, but still roomy, and we all stashed our bags in the hold. There were mosquito nets we could pull around at night. We all slept in the same little space, except the captain and his son, who slept down below in a chamber. After a couple of hours sailing on the first day, they took us round an old market in the middle of nowhere to buy food. We sailed another day and stopped at a few ancient temples, one of which was for the crocodile god at Crocodilopolis. I scored a piece of hash before we set sail. I would sit right at the bow of the boat, smoking joints, watching the world go by. The others had herb as well. There was always one going around, which even the old bloke had a puff of. There were water buffalos wallowing in the reeds. Local kids from every village would come out and wave to us as we went past. The sky was pure blue, not a cloud anywhere. The land all around was baking, man. There were abandoned temples carved into the rocks at the riverbank, with hieroglyphs and columns in relief, half-submerged in the water. It was unreal, totally chilled, just coasting through a foreign world of wonder.'

A trip to Egypt wasn't complete without going to Dahab in the Sinai. Dahab was a dream come true in 1986, a totally isolated marine oasis on the Red Sea, cut off from the rest of the world except for a rickety old bus that made the trek from Cairo a couple of times a week. The sand and sea provided a very fitting Egyptian colour scheme of turquoise and gold. The place was a cluster of small huts and open-air cafés with music systems and a steady supply of powerful African bush. Everything was run on generator power. The only accommodation at the time was a few little structures made from palm fronds, strung along the southern end of the tiny colony at the end of the world. It cost about a pound a week to stay there and the only security was a little round dustbin lid laid against a hole in the palm fronds. Amazingly, the Belgian lawyer left after one day, saying he'd been there nine years earlier and it had become too commercialised! He'd probably have a heart attack if he went back today and saw the hotels and supermarkets hulking on the beach.

People travelled to Dahab to see the coral reef at the northern end of the cluster of huts and cafés. The reef composed a huge underwater cliff, stuck with innumerable technicoloured growths, housing and supporting a vastly bio-diverse array of exotic fish and other creatures. One day some Americans arrived in an open-topped rented jeep, brandishing scuba gear and spear-guns. They steamed into the water and immediately began shooting the beautiful fish, whooping with abandon when they bagged a particularly colourful specimen. The tranquil community tried to ignore this intrusion by the global brats and there were discussions about giving them a kicking. They left after one day, having received the message. A little way around from the main reef was a dark, snaking gash, perpendicular through the continental shelf, lined with more coral. It opened out to the sea in a vast, warm, shallow expanse forested by lush seaweed in crystal-clear water. I preferred to get heavily stoned and snorkel this silent sunlit world alone for hours, thinking my private thoughts and feeling 100 percent contented.

Back in Israel it was business as usual. The north of the country was a startling contrast to the south, with its temperate climate and high-rise enclaves. Weird apartment blocks and houses on stilts were distributed among a hilly green landscape. Insecurity and suspicion were a way of life. The Israelis were rapidly colonising every workable inch of the north, taking advantage of lessened irrigation pressure due to increased rainfall. The character of the northern kibbutzim was totally different from the paradisiacal wilderness of Sde Boker; fish farms and factories abounded. Periodic showers of *katyusha* rockets didn't dissuade the Israelis from expanding into the undeveloped valleys of northern Israel. They were determined to build a functioning economy in their Promised Land. The port of Haifa was a major recipient of British travellers who arrived on ferries from Greece, having partied their summer away on the islands. Many British had made their way to Greece on the legendary Magic Bus from London to Athens. It took several days but it was cheap. Every stoner and scallywag knew about the Magic Bus and flyers advertising it were posted at the hippest spots in Britain's major cities. The lot from Greece were welcomed by the Brits already in Israel at the end of each summer. But the Israelis were growing tired of their shenanigans, and made life hard for those seeking a farm to work on.

A lot of British were sent to total hell-holes on the Jordan border, down in the desert. They were barely settlements, just a small group of caravans and huts at the top of a hill that was a hundred degrees in the shade. There would be groups of lads wearing Adidas shorts and sandals, drinking beer and vodka in the noonday sun, discussing hooligan exploits at the football back home or chilling out listening to music. The Israelis were in possession of an amazing bag of tricks when it came to making the desert bloom. They used specially hybridised seeds, designed to survive in the hostile climate and be cultivated in a more concentrated manner than nature would allow. Normally, desert plants have extremely long roots with which they pull the maximum amount of moisture from the soil. They're forced to live a fixed distance from each other as a result. Patches of perfectly-spaced cacti and succulents bristled all around like futuristic, crowded desktop icons. All the action took place beneath the surface. The Israelis had overcome the spacing and yield issue with genetic engineering. Their irrigation systems were computer-regulated and you needed a degree in hardware design just to operate them. The shovels we used were bizarre little things, with a small jutting blade protruding backwards at an angle, but they were perfect for manipulating the giant sand on a human scale.

One job that even the hard workers tried to avoid was the plastic on the melon fields. They covered fresh-planted melon seeds with a special plastic strip, about three-feet-wide and a few hundred long. The plastic contained photoactive pigments to optimise the power of the sunlight. The strips were ploughed into the ground at the edges with a specially-shaped plough blade attached to the back of the tractor, which laid out the plastic from a roll, covering and sealing in the seeds. When you reached the end of the row, you would cut the plastic with a Stanley knife and quickly shovel sand over it to seal it in. The computers pumped nitrogen gas through the system at set intervals, providing much-needed nutrition to the developing seedlings. The farmer had you chase him along in his tractor, making sure the plastic he laid down was all sealed in by the sand. You had to run along with a shovel and quickly dig any plastic in that had worked itself free of the earth. The farmers weren't exactly team players. You'd be gasping for water on many occasions as they raced along on their hobby horses. Carrying a Stanley knife and a shovel while dressed in shorts with bare feet didn't help, but it was too hot for anything else.

The giant ants, bees and wasps were a curse, but the horseflies were feared the most. Large and grey with black markings, they would dart in from nowhere and bite you painfully many times, dive-bombing with horrific precision. Every bite drew blood, and you literally had to stop working until you managed to kill it. The melon fields I worked on occupied a vast expanse, with only the Jordanian border checking their growth. As the weeks wore on, I admired the endless sandy plain with its plastic strips glimmering naked in the setting sun, all my own work. They were long days but someone had to do it, and it was a great way to lose weight and tone up. When that phase of operations was completed the bastard would simply sack you, as he could do the rest by himself. All that for ten quid a day.

Brian from Eire was one who drifted in, having spent some time in Greece first:

'It was a wild place; I was woken up one night by a livid white lizard about a foot long, under my pillow. I chased the thing around the room and eventually managed to stuff it through a hole in the window-screen, getting a few nips in the process. There were scorpions everywhere. You had to check your shoes every time. When I got laid off there was a neighbouring *moshav* [cooperative farm] about a mile away. I walked there with my backpack, hoping someone needed a worker. Anything rather than spend more time in that fucking office in Tel-Aviv. As luck would have it, a farmer there needed help. I started immediately. I was given a horrible little caravan to live in, with a stove and fridge. It was quite a large *moshav*, with a lot of English mobs on it, all partying and living it up every night. One night myself and a South African guy made the trek to the neighbouring farm for a party. During the walk, we encountered a huge and vicious wild boar on the trail. We shit ourselves, but fortunately it didn't attack us. It just snorted and growled a lot and finally disappeared into the foliage. Definitely a change-of-underwear job. I tried to pick up a snake that I later found out was extremely poisonous. Clueless, I truly was! I must have had a guardian angel watching over me through all my travels. The night we trekked to the party, the party was interrupted by Israeli army soldiers who came into the room pointing machineguns at us and giving it the big 'un, for some reason. It was a hell of a way to complain about the noise.'

Many young men made the decision to go on the road quite spontaneously:

'In August 1986 I went to the Greek island Ios on a fortnight's holiday with my mates, and had the time of my life,' says John from London. 'The night before I was due to go home, we were sat in a bar, talking about how great it would be to just stay there, and not have to go home to our boring lives. There were quite a few backpackers and others working in the tavernas, and I just had this sudden thought: *Fuck it, why not stay here?*

'I told my mates I wasn't going home, and they left the next day. I think they expected to see me at the football with my tail between my legs the week after, but that's not what happened at all. I got a job working in a bar, and spent a couple of months enjoying the best summer of my life on what people call the Island of Sex. We were inventing new cocktails daily and all the Brits were piling into the bars, drinking them. We had some outrageous names for these drinks and they were potent as fuck. As the time went on, I started meeting lads who were treating Ios as just one link in a chain. A lot of them had travelled to Greece on the Magic Bus, and they had all sorts of stories to tell of thieving in the service stations from London to Athens. It took them days to get to Greece but a good few of them had done it a few times 'cos it was so cheap – about 30 quid. They were going on to Israel to work the winter on a kibbutz or building site. I jumped on a ferry myself and soon found myself even deeper in this Mediterranean culture. I spent eight months in Israel, on kibbutzim and working behind bars in Eilat. The British I met there were mental, just on the piss permanently and up to all sorts. I saw lads get locked up for fighting and drugs and shoplifting. Jim from Brighton got stabbed in a fight with some Israeli dealers one night. He was in hospital for a couple of weeks, laying in bed spitting blood into a plastic cup. As soon as he was out he was back on the piss again, supping pints in the Tropicana bar. A couple of dozen lads were sleeping on the beach, and we all looked out for each other. We'd go to the Peace Café every morning and wait for the Israelis to drive by and pick out the ones they wanted to work. You had to haggle with some of the piss-takers. We'd established a going rate for labour, and sometimes you'd score a cushy number. Every day, lads would meet in the pubs and talk about what they'd done that day, how much the pay was per hour, etc. It was a like a little culture within a culture. Everyone kept track of the footy back home, and we'd get to see it on telly sometimes. But we mainly worked and drank. We built houses and apartments from mud bricks. Some lads worked behind bars and in hotels.

'My mates didn't see me for a year. They were still doing their shitty jobs when I got back to London. I knew then that I could never settle for that. Once you've sampled the travel bug you never get it out of your system, and your bitter mates just seem like a bunch of saps, moaning about the weather and trying to label you a lying cunt 'cos you've done what they dream of doing but haven't got the bottle to do themselves.'

I shared a room on a *moshav* near Gaza with John for a while. On a *moshav* several (sometimes dozens) of farmers lived together, each owning a large plot of land. They split the cost of the computerised irrigation systems, nutrients, hybrid seeds, etc by joining up with the farmer who owned adjacent fields. The volunteers lived in trailers or snake-infested huts, cooked their own meals and paid for their own food rather than eat collectively, as in the dining halls of the kibbutzim. As volunteers we earned around $15 a day, and the farmers had us by the town halls until we'd earned enough to escape. It was like a hard labour camp. John well remembers a special kind of visitor we would receive in our huts:

'There were these spiders living in the desert that the Israelis called yo-yo spiders. These things were huge. They ate scorpions, for fuck's sake. They would catch them in their long front legs and devour them alive. Israeli soldiers told us they'd seen hard men cry like babies after yo-yos had punctured their trainers and big toe nails with their massive jaws. Yo-yo's bodies were about nine inches long full-grown. When you tipped them over with a long stick their fat, pink legs met in the middle like a crab's. They were covered in a hard, shell-like material, pink and stippled. Their jaws actually looked like crabs' claws. I swear I still have nightmares about stumbling to the toilet in the dark, shitting myself the whole way there and back.

'My first night on a *moshav* in Gaza, the farmer had set a few traps around my hut to catch what he referred to as mice. The traps were like chip-shop trays full of a kind of glue, which the rodents would stick to. Then you disposed of them. He invited me to his home for a meal. At the end of the night he said, "If there are any mice, just throw them in the trash with the tray." I got back to my hut and turned on the light. In several traps were these giant rats, which started jumping about and squeaking hysterically at the sight of me, dragging the trays all over the floor. I had to shove each one out using a broom handle. I left them outside on the sand. The following morning all the trays had disappeared. The farmer told me that the desert has many predators. They had simply taken the lot, lock, stock and barrel. And then there were the giant lizards . . .'

The farmers knew the Brits were the hardest workers but we pushed our luck every day. One farmer I slaved for was a decent guy, but he had his limits. He and another farmer shared me and a black South African lad called Rob. We worked both their plots, planting onions, melons and other stuff. Rob was a good laugh; he would whine to the girls all about the prejudice and fear he suffered in the shanty town he came from outside Durban. In truth he was a bank clerk and came from quite a comfortable family, but it got him laid. Every Thursday the volunteers would all meet for a giant piss-up at a bar in the middle of the date palm orchard. Some of the younger Israeli Rasta types ran it. The bar was next to a small zoo which contained a giraffe and some wild boars, as well as a couple of exotic cats. There would be music and girls and plenty of herbals. Once or twice we got a bit too close to the animals after a skinful, and almost suffered a gouging. On another occasion, a Hearts lad from Edinburgh stamped his boot on the wall right next to my head in the middle of a conversation. I was sat on the floor drinking a beer. I wondered what he was doing until I turned and saw a splattered scorpion on the wall next to my face.

A stay of six months on a *moshav* was considered a long time. Lads and girls would use them as a place to bask in the sun, save a little and run wild on a nightly basis. When Rob and I discovered some people on our *moshav* who'd been there several years we pissed ourselves laughing. As we drank beers in his trailer that night and Rob cooked a wokful of gossamer egg-pasta and garlic, he joked, 'Yeah, mate, I think I'll probably do about 17 years and then try and work out what to do next.' I laughed and told him I was considering 20. Within 48 hours we were physically thrown off the *moshav* by the Israelis for being persistent offenders in the mayhem department.

After that week's Thursday gathering, we decided not to go to work. I'd been woken up at 5:00 am by Dodi, my Moroccan farmer. The pasta and garlic was a disgusting mulched mass all over my pillow. Dodi took me to work but brought me back to my trailer when he realised I was still as pissed as a fart. Not going to work was a big no-no, making us liable for an instant sacking. Rob had been so fucked up he'd not even bothered driving his tractor out to the fields. The Australian and English girls we'd been with were nowhere to be seen, having fled the previous night when I'd climbed on the roof of Rob's trailer and delivered a sermon of some kind upside down through the window.

The primitive *moshav* store was manned by an eagle-eyed geezer. He had everyone's name in a ledger, which they would sign whenever they bought anything. This was subtracted from our monthly wages. Most of the food was out of our financial reach, as the wages were pitiful. Nobody on the *moshavim* ever bought meat at the little store, as it was prohibitively expensive. Rice, beans and pasta was the staple. That day we went into the store and started ordering all the choicest cuts of steak and lamb, etc. He knew something had snapped; this was Israeli food, not volunteer food. The place was run like a hard labour camp and we'd just lost the plot, totally sick of it. I remember surreptitiously gouging a piece out of a freshly-baked loaf, and stuffing it in my mouth without paying even though I wasn't even hungry. It was one of those silly moments when you're still pissed from the night before and you're giggling like a child and begging to be thrown in jail, always a possibility in Israel. I encouraged Rob to do the same, and he did, very obviously. The shopkeeper went mental. He took note of our names while we hefted our load of meat and went for an all-day barbeque. He reported us to our farmer, who was out searching for us. We were utterly legless by late afternoon and the farmers had cut off all our electricity. I crashed, then woke up, brain-dead, wandering naked through the *moshav*, visiting all the English in their rooms. Hardly anyone batted an eyelid, including the women. The following morning, with the contents of our fridges and freezers dripping all over the floors of our respective hovels, they took Rob south and me north of the *moshav*. They dropped us at bus stops in the middle of the desert. They tried to avoid paying us the paltry month's wage they owed us, but we managed to get it out of them. Once again, I was near-destitute, in the middle of nowhere without a roof over my head, and without a single person in the world who knew who or where I was. A typical day in that period of my life, really.

*　　*　　*

Among the characters making the trek across Channel and Med back then was a young man from Oldham called Ged. Ged was a particularly adventurous soul, even by the standards of the reckless English travellers. He was a glutton for total risk. In the mid-80s he had settled into a rhythm of migration like many others, but he bit off more than he could chew on one trip. His story is a testament to his roving spirit:

'It was 1986, I had lived in Newquay, Cornwall, on and off for eight years/seasons. Every winter me and a few others would go on our travels: Greece, Israel, Turkey, Morocco and other places, just dossing about, living off our wits and doing odd jobs. We worked the kibbutz and bar and restaurant jobs, but we religiously came back to our "safe jobs" in Newquay, which was our little bit of heaven. This particular September I stayed on at Newquay, in my cosy little job at Ron's fish and chip shop, for an extra fortnight. I told my half-dozen fellow travellers I would catch them up in Israel.

'As things turned out, the trip turned into a nightmare; I flew into Cairo and stayed there for a couple of days, but got all my money and clothes nicked. I took the decision to hitch to Israel. I had hitchhiked many times in my life and many miles throughout Europe, so it held no fears for me. My first lift came after about six hours on a red-hot, sweaty, clammy day. I had just enough cash for two big bottles of water. I desperately tried not to gush them down, but even before the first lift I had only half a bottle left. The first lift I got was an Arab with full headdress who did not speak a word of English. He just grunted at me to get in the cab, an old 1940s truck with a few sheets of metal tied up on the back. I was knackered, and tried getting some sleep, but the Arab insisted on playing the radio as loud as possible and humming along and tapping the dashboard. Four hours later he ordered me out of the truck. I asked him the way to Israel, and he told me I was in Israel, but I was in the middle of nowhere with not a soul in sight.

'It was now about six o'clock, and all I could see was a dusty track ahead of me. I assumed that this must take me onto a proper road. I set off walking, singing favourite songs to myself. It went dark about ten-ish and the weather suddenly changed from very hot to very cold. All I had was my t-shirt, Levi's and desert boots (very apt). It was fucking freezing, man, and there was no shelter or anything for me. I walked briskly to keep warm; it was very eerie, not a cloud in the ink-blue sky, no birds, no noise apart from the odd distant aeroplane many miles above me. I walked all through the night. I must have sung every song they played at Live Aid the previous summer, just to keep me awake and sane.

'Morning came, and still nothing in view. All was still deathly quiet. I trudged on and on. I must have covered over 30 miles during my 12-hour romp, this being on the basis that the average human being can walk three miles a hour. By 9 am I was seriously flagging and I spotted a big rock and crashed out behind it. I was half worried that the plentiful lizards would eat me while I was asleep, but I was past caring. Of course I had drunk my last drop of water hours ago, and had not eaten for almost 24 hours. I wasn't hungry yet, just dying of thirst; I kept trying to make saliva but it was not forthcoming.

'After a few hours' kip, I awoke in the blazing midday sun. This was the hottest day I'd ever experienced, and I really thought I was going to die in that Middle Eastern desert. I got emotional and began to cry. I thought of all my loved ones and the fantastic memories I had. I yearned to be home in England, either in Newquay or back in Oldham, Lancashire where I was brought up on a rough old council estate; no matter how rough it was, I wanted to be back on it amongst family and friends.

'Meanwhile, I was still on this very remote and lonely dust track, with no vehicles in sight. My biggest concern was not about dying; I'd got to the stage of accepting that. The thing haunting me was that nobody would ever find me out here, all alone. By the time anybody discovered me I would be a bundle of bones, picked to bits by vultures, but there weren't even vultures 'cos there was no life whatsoever out there. It was a total fucking death trap. I did lose my mind a bit. I screamed out, I lashed out; I shouted up at the skies to God, "How could you leave me here all alone?"

'It became dark, which meant it must have been ten o'clock at night, and the temperature dropped again. I had been walking now for almost 30 hours, which equalled 90 miles. *Surely I must be near some village or town,* I convinced myself. Once more the freezing night kept me awake and my senses sharp. I thrilled at the remote noise of an aeroplane. I think four passed high above throughout the night; amazingly, it gave me hope.

'Early morning, the blazing sun rises. I once again find shelter, only this time it's the remnants of an old wooden shack. This gave me some comfort and hope. I slept for a few hours, but was so thirsty I could produce no saliva whatsoever. I reckoned I was going to die of thirst; I was fit enough and mentally tough enough to accept the harsh conditions, and even the hunger, but what I was going through was defeating me with dryness, and I had accepted my fate; life cannot continue without water. I was doomed.

'Nevertheless I marched on and on, and a few hours down the road I heard the most wonderful noise imaginable; the sound of an engine! It was a few miles behind me, and I looked for what seemed an eternity. Was I dreaming, hallucinating? Eventually, I could see this wagon coming up the road towards me. I cried unashamedly; I knew I'd survived a near-death experience, maybe one of the worst deaths possible, and this was my salvation.

'As the wagon drove towards me, I prayed it would stop and not just drive by; that would have killed me. But the wagon stopped for me, and I was very relieved that the driver was an American. He was a big, powerfully-built man in his late 50s, who looked like an ex-Marine. He had an air about him; clean-shaven, well-made and confident.

'"Jeez, buddy, what the hell you doing out here?" he asked, in what I reckoned was a Texan drawl. I explained the whole story to him about being robbed and trying to get to Tel-Aviv. He told me I was on a very remote road and in another day I would have died. He reckoned only half a dozen vehicles used that route a month! Luckily for me his was one of them. He delivered components to Israel from Egypt. He gave me a bottle of water, some fruit and sandwiches, he was well stocked-up. The journey took him three days, he told me; I was only a third of the way and the next village was 50 miles away! He let me sleep in the cab and when I awoke we were on the outskirts of Tel-Aviv. His name was Vernon and he was a great man. When we stopped, he took me for a meal at an American diner. We had the full Monty: steak, egg, chops, chips and two pints of lager. Then he gave me $50 and we hugged each other. He was my guardian angel. Within a couple of hours I'd found my mates and was so relieved to be with them once again. I would never recommend hitchhiking through a desert to anybody.'

Ged's story continues later in this book, and unfortunately becomes very tragic. But it serves as a warning to anyone who believes that lads' travel antics have no serious consequences. The whole Israel-Greece connection was a world unto itself, and those who frequented it were cracking lads, ragamuffins and vagabonds. It felt like an indelible urge was being stamped on one's spirit with each passing day; could we ever go back to the daily grind in Britain after living like this? Some could and some couldn't, and those that couldn't were to become the victims of their own adventuresome genes. Ged is perhaps an extreme example of how these lads sometimes ventured out a little too far in the noonday sun. To hear his story is to admire his honesty and his complete trust in the alien world around him. Like many of us, Ged lived like he had an angel on his shoulder. Or in Ged's case, maybe a whole choir of them.

The business of travelling for work and play became concentrated in specific regions: the Israel-Greece dynamic, the building sites of Germany, Spanish coastal resorts and, in time, Australia. Germany became a target for tradesmen who, upon qualifying in the British construction game, discovered there was no work or decent wages there – so they went to Hamburg, Hanover, Berlin, Stuttgart and Düsseldorf. The German culture was a shock to some and a curse to others; the practice of drinking a beer for breakfast could make or break a man, and plenty were mangled irreversibly while others used the experience as a springboard to further pastures. Some of my mates went to Germany and had quite a time of it there. We'll hear of their adventures later.

7

QUALITY STREET

There's no bread. You'll have to have toast.
– the Whit Lane Warbler

Engand in late '86, was quite a contrast to the Negev; sun-blasted stucco, giant insects, wild cacti and babbling people were replaced by quietly-cultivated hedgerows and the twittering of sparrows. A visiting foreigner could never suspect the calamity lurking beneath the civilised exterior. The train from Gatwick into London was wood-panelled. The women wore tights and exuded aromas of lavender or jasmine. I'd jibbed the train on my return, as I was utterly skint upon exiting the plane laid on for us by the Israelis. The previous few months had slowly become more insane, with the British lads being arrested, stabbed, deported or simply disappearing, and the Israelis organised a special flight for which they sold cheap tickets and tried to force as many of us to leave as possible. With Mick and Pete from Yorkshire and a lad from Sunderland I'd walked the London streets all night, feeling the biting cold of late autumn and inhaling the misty southern air under the amber halo of the English streetlights.

Alex Ferguson came to manage Manchester United a week or two after my return, and everyone was discussing what this driven Scottish manager – who'd led Aberdeen to European Cup Winners' Cup glory – might do for the Red Devils. Manchester seemed permanently pinned beneath a great pall of grey smog at the time and one day, while working in one of the office blocks, I asked one of the Irish lads, 'How long has it been all gloomy like this?'

He just stared at me with a puzzled look on his face, and then I realised: it was *always* gloomy like this. The contrast with the bright desert had just heightened the effect for me. People arriving in England from sunny climates are not exaggerating when they describe its depressing effect. But it was still home, and I threw myself into pubbing and clubbing with my mates, walking the stoned drizzling roads in that sacred amber midnight, scoffing chips and singing football songs. It felt great to be back, but less than two months later I was in a travel agent's, buying a cheap consolidator ticket to Toronto on an ancient DC10.

For a while, a good few of the boys had been travelling down to London to sign on the dole in between trips abroad. London was a big place, and back then there weren't the same computer networks as today. They would sign on at multiple dole offices all over the capital and rake in several simultaneous giro cheques. They were earning more money than most blokes who were time-served tradesmen, but that's the way the barrels work when you give 'em a hard enough spin and hold them against your temple with an adrenalin-shaky hand.

As one character put it, 'Because people were supposed to be there looking for work, they were assigned a dole-funded hotel room, plus brekkie, while they went about trying to find a job. One lad could "own" up to eight or nine hotel rooms. He might rent it out to others, or stage wild parties on a nightly basis, funded by multiple dole cheques. I heard plenty moaning about how it could take two days across the capital, on bus, tube and taxi, to collect all your giros and cash 'em. A right pain in the arse, it was. You could be eligible for this red carpet piss-take for up to a year, if you played your cards right. London was full of fuck-ups, birds who let loads of lads shag them at the same time, or total pill-heads and alkies who'd lost the plot beyond recognition.'

The lads had a whale of a time pillaging London, like a swarm of slimy peacocks in a barnyard full of drugged foxes. The crafty cockneys were not prepared for the many-pronged assault on their dole-cheque Fort Knox. Within a couple of years the Mancs and other northerners had emptied the coffers, good style. The London hotel scheme was quietly killed in an embarrassed ceremony enacted somewhere in the Houses of Parliament.

One of the personages involved in a major aspect of the scam had this to say about it:

'I went down to sign on in London, and had a bit of cash, so I wasn't in any hurry to find a job. It quickly became obvious that these cunts didn't have a clue how to manage their system, so me and a mate decided to do a day's travelling 'round London, claiming dole at different offices. We thought we'd get caught and just plead insanity, but no one tumbled us so we just signed on everywhere, getting all this money and these hotel rooms. I couldn't believe it. I had hundreds of pounds coming in weekly. We'd be wandering 'round the tourist areas looking at daft souvenirs, supping beer and doing whiz, the lot. At night we started jumping the rent boys, nicking their money off them and pretending we were queer-bashing idiots but just into it for an earner, really. The rent boys were loaded with cash and we taxed 'em to fuck. We also knew some cockney blokes down there who did mock auctions – video recorders that didn't work or didn't exist and just fucked off with all the money off the people who'd bid on them, leaving them with nothing. Some of the lads specialised in doing handbags in the pubs and clubs, and we had credit cards and cash out of those places, week in week out. London was backward as fuck for clubbing though, and we often went back up to Manchester for a weekend of proper acid house-style mayhem.'

Acid house was a supposedly new thing that had been invented from scratch, and it was fast becoming the recreational mode of the masses. It sounded like someone repeatedly hitting a steel tray with a hammer, but thankfully that improved. In late 1985 it had been quite rare to meet 'straights' who took LSD, but that was about to change, big time. Spain was a focus for the electronica permeating the clubs and a new enthusiasm was born for the fortnight in the sun, marking one of the major milestones for the latest generation of lads abroad. They fanned out from their homes on that tiny blob of pagan rock called Britain, hungry to sample the rest of the world.

*   *   *

Back in Manchester it was business as usual, with our crew quietly dismantling the city centre and flogging it to the highest bidder. It was a while later, after Paddy had sadly died of a stroke and a couple of the other lads had sloped off to their various fates, that PG took control. PG had grown up in a neighbourhood of five-storey tenements, grim hulking fortresses of the dark Caledonian north. I visited Glasgow with him and found it to be an awesome place, including the food. The square sausages and black puddings were outlandishly good, as well as the large rounds of bread you could perfectly fit them onto. We made sure to gather plenty to take back south with us. The butcher we bought them off had the singularly most intricate and colourful tattoo on his arm I'd ever seen in my life: a near-neon array of tropical birds fluttering around and above a Celtic sword, its blade wrapped in the fluorescent coils of a divine serpent, deeply embedded among a mass of bioluminescent flora.

The streets of Possilpark where PG had grown up resembled the classic image of the Gorbals, rows and rows of tenement blocks running parallel down hills with a flourishing main street dissecting the area. Every shop was somehow different and the crowds were alive with chatter. The main street was a brown-brick canyon with vertical sides, the lively glass windows of the stores along the ground floor with several storeys of flats above them. This wall of colour was broken up along one side of the street by the perpendicular junctions at the bottom of the slope, where the tenements loomed like the barracks of a great stone regiment. It was like stepping back in time, as even then England's ambitions to be the 51st state of the USA had begun stirring. The area had as much character as anywhere I'd ever seen, and PG casually informed me that Possil made the Gorbals look like Milton Keynes. I had no reason to disbelieve the man, as we stood in the Possil Bar downing measures of whiskey that were 30-odd percent stronger than the ones we were allowed in England. Funnily enough, on my first visit to the place I'd unconsciously worn a green and white hooped sweatshirt, which was just as fucking well; these people were *not* Rangers supporters. PG was an intense bloke, with jet-black hair and a touch of the superstar about him. A few of Manchester's main faces happened to have been his lifelong friends since infancy, hardened men who'd relocated from Glasgow to Manchester and bestowed a unique gangster flavour on our city.

PG himself never made reference to his mates' distinctions; he was himself an accomplished blagger and wasn't about to advertise the fact by blabbing like a rank amateur. It was the other lads on the crew who would nudge me, and say, "You know who that is, don'tcha?", whenever a major face came in the pub, or stopped to talk to PG through the window of the cab, as we endlessly cruised Manchester city centre. The QS were known and feared throughout the Manchester underworld, and it seemed that everyone knew someone who knew someone who was part of it. Their tentacles were tangled and vast.

For the past several years we'd been pilfering filing cabinets, shelves, chairs and desks as a matter of course, but in PG we experienced a quantum leap up the ladder of skulduggery. Various types of electrical office equipment and their accessories were now the target, and lots of 'em. Fortunately we held innumerable codes and secrets, and we regularly cracked combination locks on corridors across Manchester, swiftly and silently disappearing with our state-of-the-art booty. (The expression 'state-of-the-art' became a standing joke with the crew.)

Between '85 and '87 our office swag visits to Paddy's gypsy gave way to myriad pubs, shops and warehouses in the Red Bank, Cheetham, Harpurhey, Moston, Collyhurst and Ancoats areas of north Manchester. Here, generations of barrow-boys and boxers had meshed with wide-boys and gangsters. One day, PG took me in a very tiny pub on a backstreet right outside town, where his mates from Glasgow liked to drink. The pub was a deafening cacophony of crazed Celtic-Mancunian expletives, a loud and fantastic jukebox, the surge of beer-pumps and the crack of pool balls. His mates were like the cast of *GoodFellas*, only bigger, harder and much more interesting. The first time I ever went in there I was 19 years old. The landlord was a big United fan, an immense, heavy-set chap who kept a picture of the team up on the wall.

'D'yae wanna game o' pool?' PG asked me (he knew I didn't play it and was therefore useless) and I proceeded to set them up.

As his lifelong pals watched, I systematically demolished him. PG grew angrier as his grizzly mates chuckled. I didn't want to make him look shite, but it was like I was possessed of some magic eye, some United-born crosshairs that acted as the keys to victory. Even when I tried to miss, the ball would shoot straight into the pocket or hit every cushion and then disappear obediently. They were all smiling and winking at me at PG's expense, but it was a fluke, and only I knew it. It was a cosy baptism compared to how I'd have looked if I'd played my usual game.

The little boozer was always open whether we went there at 8 o' clock in the morning or midnight, and you couldn't go in there without having a pint. Creature comforts were not a priority. The bar ran down one side and a few small tables ran down the other. There was barely room for two people to pass in between. Miraculously, a fruit machine was crammed into a corner. The pool room was through a door in another room. Everyone drank bitter or Guinness and if you ordered lager it was flat and stale. The floor was unvarnished and worn, the tables and chairs were ancient (PG constantly promised to kit the place out in new gear, but somehow he always forgot to) and the windows were dingy and opaque. There was barely room to swing a bat. At night the pub was almost invisible, just a few muted amber halos hovering outside the window or front door.

From this minute and unassuming chamber I was to learn that a significant fraction of the grafting world had been conceived: tickets, t-shirts, snide perfume, sunglasses, concert and sporting programmes. It was also the GCHQ at the heart of a Greater Manchester rumour mill, some of which was real, much of which was pure bollocks. In time, the notion of forging any and all commodities which could be thus duplicated would find its way out of the area to the furthest expanses of the globe, much of it outsourced from East Asia. Manchester lads from all over the city were travelling to knock out their gear from Stockholm to Sydney.

It was around the time PG became skipper that I decided permanent travel was the antidote to dreary England. It was a straightforward drill – graft for a few weeks, save a wedge and steam off through the clouds strapped inside a large aluminium tube with fins on. I taped all my albums and intended to spread the psychedelic word to everyone I met on my travels. Anywhere would do, but preferably somewhere with sunshine and/or women, who we called *kifes*. Sex we called *yensing* or *nemming*. It was a streamlined hybrid slang that had been around forever, but which the boys from the football and the grafters had taken up wholesale and added a few words of their own. The timely collision of fashion-crazed teenagers with old-school grafters had revealed many shining new aspects of Mancunian slang. Everyone relished the usage of terms designed to convey illicit information in the presence of those about to be conned, or battered, or sexually propositioned. The grafters who pitched market stalls up and down the land, kids, jibbing trains for football, and the 70s-style Perries haunting Manchester's clubs all freely utilised it; it was a way of letting people know you were 'in'.

But those foreign climes continued to pull like a magnet. A warm sun on your back and a *kife* to *yense* was just the script. It seemed like everyone had the same idea simultaneously to explore unknown lands. The world came to represent an endless stretch of virgin soil. The air and seas above and around it were the channels through which we motored to our goals.

Each time I returned to Manchester I'd be back on the crew the next day, patrolling the city in our trusty Salford Van Hire truck which was in our possession for years at a stretch. The crew had been downsized by now. An old bloke from Ancoats had arrived on the scene who we called the Travelling Man, after he was knocked back from a boozer one day having been mistaken for a gypsy. The trousers he wore were stiff enough to stand up on their own. Bruiser often speculated that it was solely this support that enabled him to remain vertical after three o' clock in the afternoon.

More and more lads were grafting around town. People started wearing a lot of paisley while listening to psychedelic sounds. The 'Bands and Musicians' section of the *Manchester Evening News* classifieds grew exponentially. I had toyed with the notion of forming a band in late-'83, early-'84, but people told me my 60s-style sounds were too old fashioned. I grew out of it and moved on. I couldn't play an instrument but I could sing and the singer was usually the famous one, which suited me. I kept one eye on that scene, but the earners had become majestic. Money was flowing like daylight from PG's doorstep wallet, keeping me firmly under the wing of the old school.

Between '83 and '85, LSD and amphetamine sulphate had been a natural extension of my adolescent experimentation with magic mushrooms, harvested from the lush plains of Heaton Park in north Manchester. Going to Israel had taken away the thirst for tripping, but when you're surrounded by an ocean it's easily re-established. I'd felt 'unhuman' and very different from people my whole life, and in acid I had come home, as it were. The strange inner landscapes and visual effects, the cataclysmic psychological upheavals, explosions of laser-like insight and intense euphoric backdrops felt very *me*. I loved it, and so I'd become attached to the social scene associated with these illicit substances. Their purveyors and consumers appeared to be immensely in-the-know as regards physical reality, political conspiracies and, best of all, music. Indeed, music was among our most important nutrients, providing a vast number of sources for inspiration. Bands were rapidly crystallising around Manchester as those graduating from Scally University earned recognition from an increasingly sympathetic media. The Prestwich lads were slowly evolving into two arms of a semi-organised underworld, some were dealing drugs, some were into fraud and thieving, others were grafting on markets. Plenty worked honest jobs but were psychopathic maniacs, just waiting for an excuse to drop out of civilised society and resort to a life of violence and crime. I slipped through all the cracks and enjoyed the cosy sensation of being buoyed in an ocean of skulduggery and mirth. My talents as a shoplifter and opportunist tea-leaf kept me in booze, books and even the occasional article of clothing – but decent clothing was restricted to necessities like M&S crew necks, Levi's from Affleck's Palace or rampant smash 'n' grab fiascos conducted while drunk, the fruits of which were invariably exchanged for contraband alcohol and cigarettes.

8

GREAT WHITE NORTH

Ice-cream is exquisite – what a pity it isn't illegal.
– Voltaire

I'd missed going to the match and the pub while I was away in Israel. Back in England, the mid-80s youngsters were adopting those hooligan designer fashions from five years previous. In Manchester the 'dressed-down' look was morphing up a queerly hippie slope. Flares and baggy shirts were in. The fact of our being there amidst its earliest manifestation meant we still dictated a lot of the next styles, but I wasn't sure about this one. The few who'd made it to Egypt were inclined to sing Madness' 'Night Boat to Cairo' to rub it in to those who'd stayed behind and adopted the beanie hat and the Housemartins' 'Caravan of Love'; we preferred fezzes and to boast of our adventures. As for music, it was psychedelic all the way, but few clubs existed to cater to us at the time. Along with the blooming numbers of British cottoning on to the casual styles, many in Manchester were making music and drugs part of the trip. The mid-80s saw strange rivers coalesce, with narrow jeans becoming flares and smart haircuts growing out into hippie-length acid-dos.

Within a year or so football and clublife would remarry, but the dealers were still on the brink of hatching their real plans. Football hooliganism wasn't dead yet, though. Pete, an Ancoats Red, remembers how, while still he was quite green in the insane world of the travelling football fan, he and his mates took a nonchalant trip to Nottingham to watch Manchester United play:

'Around 1986, we went to see United play Forest away. A group of six set off on the short walk from Ancoats to Chorlton Street bus station that morning. Can't remember why we got a coach, because I always hated coach travel, so there must have been a valid reason. Maybe a problem with the trains or something. Anyway, you couldn't miss our coach. I can remember it as though it was yesterday. It was fully painted with a countryside-style mural. Trees and hills all over the fucking thing. It had the words "The Countryside Rambler" or something very similar wrote right down the side of it. Quite ridiculous looking, yet just a standard National Express bus under all the bullshit. We got to Nottingham nice and early, despite it being an everlasting journey. The coach station was built into the bottom of a shopping centre. I go straight to the toilet in this shopping centre while my mates are fucking about in a shop somewhere. A lad comes in who sounds like a cockney or at least a southerner to me (inexperience on my part at the time), so I make an assumption that he is United. He asked, "What score do you think the game will be?" I replied something like "three-nil United." He then says something like, "If you wasn't a kid I would fucking drop you where you stand," and walks out. I'm stood there drying my hands, thinking, "What the fuck?" I find my mates and tell them about this cockney that has just threatened me in the toilet and off we go looking for pubs, pretty much unconcerned. We go in a few pubs and I'm hearing more and more people speaking with this "cockney" accent. Young as we were, we were good dressers and, for young lads, game as fuck. We stood out a million miles amongst these Nottingham lads, as back then the differences in fashions between the bigger cities was much greater than it is now. I suppose we had been well clocked by now and probably everyone in Nottingham city centre was aware of our presence. It got to about one o'clock and we'd had a few by then and were giddy as fuck.

'We found this pub with a dinnertime karaoke session. One of our lads gets up and the bird that is hosting it asks, "What's your name?" He says, "Tony." "Where you from, Tony?" "Manchester," says he, at which point every fucking eye in the pub turns to look at us. For the first time I realise that everything is probably not as it should be. He starts off with his fucking "Monster Mash" and the other lads are giggling away 'cos they're sniffing poppers, but I was now paranoid as fuck. Everyone was whispering in everyone else's ear, lots of pointing our way, lots of dirty looks, and I'm trying to convey this to the rest of the lads without looking like I give two fucks. The trouble is, we had a very,

"Fuck them, we're Mancs and they're backwards," kind of attitude, and my drunk and poppered-up mates thought it was a piece of piss. Meanwhile, "The Monster Mash" has finished and that daft cunt is on a roll and now banging out some Elvis song or another. I'm thinking that we need to get out of this pub but know that I'm in a minority of one. I'm bursting for a piss, so I steam to the bogs, whip my dick out and I'm pissing in a hurry when a big half-caste scouser comes in and asks me right out, "Are you a Manc?" I say, "Yes." He tells me, "Look at the exit when you go out of here. It's completely blocked. I can have a word if you want. My bird's from Swinton, but you'll probably still get a slap." Suddenly, the toilet door flies open and in come the rest of my mates and, without me having a chance to say anything to them, I hear, "Fucking come on then you black cunt!" and a flying head-butt lands on the nose of our only chance of walking out of the pub alive, as everyone piles into him. He is down and I'm like, "For fuck's sake, you stupid twats!"

'Tony is still singing away outside and we can hear him, but at least now the other lads were focused. I tell them we're in the shit and the only thing to do is pile out of the toilet and run for our lives. I swear it was like a scene from *The Benny Hill Show* but it's the God's honest truth. We took a deep breath and then we ran out of the toilet in single file as that's all there was room for.

'We're heading for the door shouting at Tony to run like fuck. That daft cunt is waving at us from the stage and we're snaking round the pub looking for an exit. Amazingly, we all get out of there completely unscathed and we're off across town, laughing our bollocks off. We're now all agreed that our luck can't last, and it's time to head for the ground and find some other Reds.

'We knew we would find all the Miles Platting lads somewhere near the ground in a boozer, Brian Gaffney, Marshy and all the Grey Mare lot. We were just about to jump a taxi when I saw this big cunt outside a shop. He had "cut here" and a series of dotted lines tattooed right across his throat (classy stuff), but he was fucking massive. He must have been 18 stone and pure muscle, with a couple of big meat-heads. I just glanced at his tattoo and he says, "What the fuck are you looking at?" I think I just said, "Nothing," but he said it again, "What are you looking at, you little cunt?" I knew he was not going to leave it, so I picked up the sandwich board from outside the shop and ran at him with it. I launched it at him, but it just bounced off him. He took hold of me with these big fucking shovel hands and threw me against the shop window, then threw me to the floor then up in the air. Basically he just threw me about all over the place like a little rag doll. To be fair he never once actually punched me. This man would have done major damage to me if he had. When he had enough of throwing me around they just fucked off and left us.

'We went to the ground and we were in the side section, the overspill from behind the net. We're sat right at the segregation with the Forest fans. Who is there, on the other side of the mesh netting that separated us, but the first guy I saw that morning who said he would drop me! I told Brian Gaffney, like the big girl I am, and Gaffney is keeping an eye on the cunt. Remarkably, at the back of the stands we were all sharing toilets, no segregation at all, which is something I came across quite a few times, years ago. Just before halftime this big lump gets up and goes down into the stands. Gaffney says to me, "Right, come on," so I follow him down to the toilets. There are just us three in there. Gaffney says to the lad, "What score do you reckon it will be, mate?" Knobhead says, "Forest will win," and with that Gaffney chins the cunt and his head bounces off the urinal wall. The bloke was out cold. Result.

'I'm not certain, but I think the game finished one-all. The final sting in the tale of the trip was that, after the game, all the United lads were fucking off one way and we had to go the other. This was not a good feeling, but we made our way unscathed into the town centre. We knew our coach was due out at six, so we had plenty of time, arriving back at the bus station at about 5:20 pm, or so we thought. It turned out that Nottingham back then had two bus stations that were almost identical.

'So we're looking around for our stupid Country Rover coach home, which should stand out like a sore thumb, but we can't see it anywhere. At ten to six I find a member of staff and ask, "Where's the coach back to Manchester?" He replies, "You're at the wrong station, mate. You want the other coach station."

'So we're running like fuck through Nottingham town centre, trying to find this other coach station, and just as it comes into view the most ridiculous-looking coach in town is pulling out and heading away from us. We ran and fucking ran after that coach. It was getting stopped at lights just long enough for us to get within 100 feet or so, then they would turn green and off it went again, until finally it reached the open road and disappeared into the distance. We trudged back to the coach station only to find that was the last coach to anywhere that was any fucking use to us. No Liverpool, no Preston, no nothing. Just London, Derby, Birmingham and places we'd never heard of. We ended up getting the coach to Birmingham and picking up the train from New Street. No fucking way was I hanging around in Nottingham. What a day that was. It's hard to convey everything that happened in that one day, and the tension and excitement it caused, using mere words. I miss those days badly, and I wish I could have fully understood then that when they have gone they have gone. Being young is so much better than being old and having responsibilities.'

Pete was to go on to many more football adventures (some of which are covered later). From his experience, it is obvious football hooligans were both predator and prey in turn. Going into other cities in a small group took bottle, as there were many local animals waiting to have a pop. Pete laments the passing of his youth, and, like many of us of this persuasion, recoils from responsibilities as the chains they truly are. This attitude seems to pervade many of our generation; we are more suited to life as it was in 10,000 BC than how it is today, but we cope. Just.

1987 was the year Rick Astley sang 'Never Gonna Give You Up', causing many in Manchester to wince at his association with the Northwest. It was symptomatic of Britain's domestic cultural stagnation; the parrotheads of yore had hijacked the charts, while those in the know were going loco down in Acapulco. For a while it looked like the parrotheads would win the war. Fortunately, a few saw what was coming.

Bands in California and Europe had been exploring the 60s retro-trip for several years, and had recorded albums reflecting a trend towards three-minute singles that were poppy, harmonious and intelligent. Needless to say, if you took your influences from the British music charts, you wouldn't know about this scene, which became known as the Paisley Underground. In response to a growing demand for a place to celebrate it, Manchester's Electric Banana club opened. The Banana quickly became the Asylum, a psychedelic second-floor haunt above George Best's old boutique, Edwardia. The Asylum was owned by a very liberal chap, who permitted wacky-baccy consumption and even provided rolling papers in bowls on the bar. It was a small space that was optimised brilliantly. The bar ran along the right-hand wall. A raised 60s-style dance-floor occupied a compact illuminated alcove to the left. Slide projectors threw bizarre images onto the walls – laboratory scenes, fluorescent undulating bacteria and mesmerising kaleidoscopic patterns – while regulars posed in psychedelic shirts and danced to music by bands like the Creeps, Rain Parade, Plasticland, Green on Red and the Dream Syndicate.

It wasn't much, but it was something. The self-same group who'd adapted the Bowie influence into the Perry thing were at the heart of this scene. This wasn't a coincidence. Nor was the fact that Thursday night was *the* night the Asylum was open; the same night Britain would be sitting at home, bored shitless by *Top of the Pops*. Today, Rick Astley's tune enjoys immortality; it's been described as 'the stupidest prank on the internet' by unsuspecting web surfers who, upon clicking a link, find it jumping from one corner of their screen to the other in the form of an annoying YouTube video known as a 'Rick Roll'.

The Asylum was destroyed by a fire after an all-too-short spell as the coolest club in Britain. Clubs in Manchester tend to lead very short lives, and fire is usually the means by which they die. It's simply the endless gear-wheels of Mancunian ecology doing their job.

*   *   *

So my next stop was Canada. Despite droves of people having settled there, Canada was a kind of non-country, occupying very little space in the British imagination. I was to discover that, in geographical reality, it occupied as much space as virtually any country on earth. The plan was to meet a girl I'd had some great times with at Kibbutz Sde Boker, and take a trip across Canada on a train. When I received the letter from Jane, suggesting I go west and we continue our little fling, I was only too glad to oblige. It was February 1987, not the most favoured time of year for a Canadian odyssey, but that never occurred to me. Jane met me at Toronto Airport. Toronto was a big city, with clusters of high-rise apartments and skyscrapers sprawling away from the centre. Every day felt like a Friday; people were relaxed and brimming with pragmatic optimism. This was where Martha and the Muffins were from, and the city landscape resonated with imagery from 'Echo Beach'. The architecture was space-age, the coniferous foliage plentiful and the snowflakes tumbled out of the turquoise sky like glittering fragments from an exploded UFO. The snow, the pine trees and the blue skies reminded me of old Talking Heads tunes, songs about the American government and its great cities, listened to while surveying the prairie of someone's bed-sit back in Manchester. I'd be surveying the real prairie once the train made it to Manitoba.

There was no end to the Ontario forests and weird lagoons draped in frozen white. The sight of snowmobiles, or 'skidoos' as Canadians call them, was commonplace. The trains contained upper-decks composed of a glass dome to view the expansive countryside. The odd hippie or weirdo would sometimes join us in a couple of beers up there in the dome car, including one who recited Gordon Lightfoot's 'Wreck of the Edmund Fitzgerald' in its entirety. The landscape stretched to the North Pole in one direction and down to the Gulf of Mexico in the other. Romantic images filled my head when I saw names like Canadian Pacific on the sides of boxcars in isolated eastern towns. The topography changed as we headed west. Ontario's crystalline forests became a great white desert of unending snow. We raced along the shores of great lakes. The glancing northern light was surreal in winter at this latitude; the sky was sometimes an eerie orange colour and the water looked pea-green, spangling and dancing as far as the eye could see.

One of Jane's brothers was in the army and living in a trailer on the vast prairie around Brandon, Manitoba. We'd come through an expanse of white to be met at the station by this guy driving a station wagon with a big grin on his face. In the car he asked if we had any music. I passed him Lou Reed's *Rock 'n' Roll Animal*. He smiled and reached for the volume dial.

'I love to fuckin' crank this shit!' he whooped. Excellent.

In the trailer he sparked up a joint of Mexican weed that sent me into a hallucinogenic orbit. We reminisced on the times we'd had on Kibbutz Sde Boker, playing Talking Heads and Soft Boys, blasting off each others' memories. We boarded the bubble train once more. Banff, Alberta was a swish ski resort. We phoned ahead to reserve a room from a railway platform several hours east. Upon entering the hotel foyer they told us, 'Nope, we don't have you down here.' We remonstrated mildly and suddenly the desk clerk found the note from the phone call.

'I'm very sorry,' he told us. 'You're in luck.'

We were sent to a massive suite at their other hotel, the Ptarmigan Inn, overlooking a snowy vista where cable-cars and distant skiers negotiated slopes in a cascade of white flakes. There were posh motels, contemporary chalets, fancy restaurants and skiing shops packed with top jackets, hats and gloves, precisely the type of clobber targeted seven years earlier in Switzerland and Germany. The Banff ski-bum community was a hotbed of scallies and rich folk from Vancouver and other cities in the region, as well as the rest of the world. The ski-bums wore sports gear worth thousands of dollars, carried impressive weights of weed, went skiing every day and were paid for it. And they all had university degrees! It was a new world in every sense. The Rockies' rugged heights took my breath away. We reluctantly climbed on the train to Vancouver, having smoked a final joint on a nearby summit while admiring the spectacular views.

We spent some time in Vancouver before heading back east. After eight weeks in transit across one of the world's biggest countries, I went to stay with my dad's cousin and her family in Windsor. The awesome Ambassador Bridge led to Michigan, USA across the Detroit River. Detroit resembled a 1970s *Spiderman* cartoon, a bristling cluster of gun-metal skyscrapers silhouetted against a purple sunset. The Ambassador was a massive suspension bridge like the Golden Gate. My dad's cousin's sons took me to see boxing matches. On Fridays they smuggled each other across the bridge in the large trunks of cars, so they could go and run amok in the mad canyons of Detroit. It was a total trip.

Returning to England after three months in Canada I was even more alienated than before; instead of returning from a tropical desert I had now lived in a temperate, technologically-advanced region. People spoke English as a first language and sanitation reigned supreme. Canada was no longer a gap in my imagination. Men Without Hats, Neil Young and Martha's Muffins now had a place in my swede to call home. Some of my mates, including Dave-D-, one of the lads who'd done the graft and acid of the early 80s, also began to put out their tendrils. Our cellular network of friends was about to explode, carrying individuals in all directions around the globe, like seeds bursting from a plant at a special time in its life cycle.

'Round about 1987 I was living in Crumpsall, North Manchester, in what Marc Almond described as bedsit land,' Dave remembers. 'I'd done some proper travelling in Europe by now, but was at that funny age where you feel like you've really arrived as an adult and are almost ready to settle down. All the mad robbing and posing with our imported continental booty was a distant memory. I was like, "Fuckin' gimme a flat an' some tidy herb and I'll be a model citizen!" Little did I know how my life would change. Me and my girlfriend at the time, J, were knocking out about a nine-bar of sputnik a week in eighths and sixteenths. We knew loads of skulls from all over the area and our flat was a cracking hub for people wanting to exchange music, score herb or just hang out and get baked. We'd all grown up together or met through the pub network as we got older, and most were ex-football types who'd chilled their brains off with the gear. Everyone was dressed down, with only the divvies still worrying about spending a ton on tracksuits that had all turned to shite once the big designers had migrated to the Far East. People had started coming and going to points distant and we always had a good knees-up whenever one of the boys came back from abroad. People would return to Manchester and just rejoin the party while others jetted into the blue. It was a comfortable existence; the distributors we were scoring off were mainly hippies or pseudo-Hare Krishnas and, looking back, it was a very gentle scene. Don't get me wrong, I'd done some travelling, slept rough and gone on some proper jollies with Man United. But it was time to get lush and have some comfort in my life. You could conduct all your business stoned off your box with the drugs crowd. It was always a smile and a handshake and Bob's yer uncle. At this time you could rent a bed-sit (which they now call studios) for around 40 quid a week. Most of the people we came into contact with were pretty mellow cats, into their LP collections, hi-fi and smoke. The likes of Bob Marley, Talking Heads, Floyd and underground stuff from California were the stoners' soundtrack. Despite having to live with the spectre of Thatcher, Greater Manchester Police's Special Patrol Groups and the Mickies winning the league every year, life was good. Then one day it all changed . . . for the worse.

'Another dope dealer in the flats, a harmless soul who lived with his bird, had his door kicked in and three bandits waltzed in. They whacked the bird round the head with a bat and stole the poor guy's weed and money. They called it "taxing" and probably thought it was dead clever. I call it scumbag rats thieving off the good guys. In my mind it was the start of an era that saw the degeneration of any sort of code of conduct amongst those living on the wrong side of the law. It made my blood boil and it escalated to protection rackets, turf wars, club closures and the end of just being able to get on with it without any mither. It caused a split in our community, with some lads just wanting some peace and quiet, and others talking bollocks about how they were gonna get a gun to protect themselves.

'That chain of events, coupled to the fact that even if you wanted work there was none worth talking about, prompted me and the missus to reply to an ad in the *Manchester Evening News*. It read, "Fun in the Sun and a Grand a Week." I'm not usually one to fall for that type of bullshit in the paper, but the fact that it was in the sun got me thinking. The location for the seminar was the Britannia Hotel in Piccadilly. We got straight down there for a blimp [look] at the proceedings. The main guy holding court was in his 40s, about five-foot-four with a massive hooter, a pony tail and a floral shirt. I nearly walked straight back out but was collared by an Amazonian beauty with a clipboard. Cindy was tall, tanned and slim, with the most beautiful blue eyes. Back in '87 you didn't see many midriffs but this one, Jesus, it was nut brown, flat and truly washboard-splendid. Most of the birds round north Manchester already had three kids by the time they were Cindy's age and the only washboards they saw were the ones they cleaned shitty nappies on.

'"Hiya, have you come about the job?" she asked us. Even my girlfriend was a bit taken aback by how fit this girl was, and it was her who replied, "Yeah, we just want to know a little bit more about it." Back then timeshare was relatively unknown and certainly didn't carry the dodgy rep it has now. Cindy explained that, basically, the job involved inviting (dragging) holidaymakers to take a look at a five-star resort in Tenerife, and in return the tourists would get a free meal or some duty-frees as a thank-you. It sounded like a doddle to me, so I collared Mr. Pony Tail to get the full SP and to establish whether he was full of shit or not. We left the venue with Joe's phone number, a brochure of the resort and all the info about the job.

'Ten days later we'd sold most of our stuff from the flat, given our budgie to Billy Coy's mam, had a leaving party and were at Manchester airport with another couple we'd met at the seminar. I'll always remember that first morning, waking up 2,000 miles away in the Canaries. I gazed at the sun rising over the Atlantic from the window of the apartment they'd put us in, and thought, "Fuckin' hell, Dave, you've *got* to make this work," 'cos by comparison, waking up on a wet Wednesday in Crumpsall . . . well, think about it!'

Tenerife was waking up to an invasion of English who seemed to be landing there by the day – especially the droves of football supporters from the east London area, including members of West Ham's notorious ICF. Dave Dolan rubbed shoulders with many of these characters and others from other parts of Britain. Others headed for points east, such as Greece, on the famed Magic Bus. Ged, the unfortunate guy from Oldham who lost himself in the Israeli desert, went to Greece in the late 80s, but this time he lost himself in a more difficult place to define: inner space. The following is taken from Ged's writings concerning his misadventure in Athens, provided kindly by Carl Spiers:

'At the end of the summer season in 1987, I left Newquay and went back up to my hometown Oldham in Lancashire to see my folks and mates. I only lasted a few weeks before boredom sunk in and the need to travel. I met a lad called Alan who was a couple of years older than me, around 27. Alan was quite a character; he had been in the army for a few years, in 2 Para, and had done the whole Northern Ireland trip several times. He'd seen mates killed and blown to bits, and this left him mentally scarred. Many times, very depressed, his behaviour would deteriorate. He eventually got discharged from the Paras and joined the French Foreign Legion. Even they kicked him out after six months for being too disruptive!

'Alan, in his defence, was supremely fit; he ran for miles every day and I hooked up with him on some runs. He was relentless in his quest for fitness, and one day he told me he had a mate living in the mountains in Greece high above Athens. He asked would I like to join him over there? I told him yes right away; another adventure for me.

'We got the Magic Bus from Victoria station in London a few days later and that was an experience in itself. Everyone on it seemed to be a druggie or a lunatic. I had smoked dope for years but Alan was very anti-drug and would lecture me about the perils of drug abuse. But I am one of those – when in Rome – and I spent most of the three-day trip with fellow dope smokers, which pissed Alan off, and we hardly spoke (I was to pay for this later).

'When we finally hit Athens, we all went in different directions and me and Alan booked into a shabby hotel room for the night. He was still sulking and hardly spoke a word to me, even though I tried to make conversation. Next day we got a bus high into the mountains, some 35 miles away from Athens. We ended up in this very remote village with only about ten houses, all single-storey whitewashed stone cottages. I asked Alan where his mate lived, and he told me to be patient. We then walked for a couple of hours higher into the mountains. I was knackered and it was red hot. I was carrying a big rucksack, but so was Alan to be fair and he seemed to thrive on pushing himself to the limit. I lagged 30 yards behind him for most of the arduous journey.

'Eventually we found his mate stood outside his pad, which was a fucking cave! Him and Alan hugged each other and started whooping with delight. Then, they began some kind of Paras ritual, funny handshakes and shouting some kind of slogans and stuff. Very weird.

'Alan introduced us by saying, "This is my mate Ged from Oldham. He'll be staying with us for a couple of days, then he's off to find some work."

Fuck me, I'd thought I was here for the duration; Alan had really stitched me up big time. His mate was called Scully and he was OK with me. Scully fed me up and we all got pissed on raki; he had bottles of the stuff. Scully was a recluse up there, and only went into Athens every few weeks for groceries and necessities. He had no cooker or electric, but loved the whole survival routine, as did Alan.

'Alan did not lighten up and more or less ignored me most of the time as they reminisced about their Para exploits in Ulster; some of the things they reckoned they got up to would have brought the British government down, and I didn't know whether to believe them or not. Alan had this annoying habit of mentioning the fact I was Irish every half-hour, but thankfully Scully was not biting, thank fuck. He looked a right nutter.

'On day three up in the mountains, Alan suggested it was time I left to find some work. He said Scully could no longer carry me, so I left, half-relieved because Alan was being a right cunt with me, and Scully could get very emotional when he had flashbacks from Ulster. His memories of losing good mates to what he described as "Dirty Fenian cunts" were jarring my nerves no end.

'So I bade farewell and headed back into Athens. I had a few bob, perhaps 300 quid, so I was alright for cash for a few weeks. I booked into a shabby hotel room right in the centre of Athens, but rather than look for graft I ended up on the piss. I met a Dutch feller called Frank and an Irish bloke called Macca who came from Cork. We went on the lash every day and night, drinking bottles of raki. Raki was so fucking cheap and we never ate fuck-all apart from the odd bag of crisps. We would more often than not end up crashing at my humble abode, all three of us pissing our pants and wetting the bed and settee; we were sinking fast into oblivion,

'The hotel room stunk of piss and spew, and after a couple of weeks I awoke to find both Frank and Macca had fucked off and taken a few items of clothes of mine. They did not rob my cash, which I stuffed in my undies every night, but I missed them. They were my drinking buddies even though I knew they were no good for me nor themselves. I carried on pissing up my money, and one day I collapsed outside this bar I had been using. The owner was a top fellow called Markos, and he got me to hospital. Apparently I was in there for four days, unconscious. They did all kinds of tests on me and some doctor came to the conclusion that I was mentally ill. He informed me of such, and I challenged the decision, but they forced me into a straitjacket and the next thing I knew I was entering an asylum!

'I was shitting myself; I had flashbacks of the film *Midnight Express*, Billy Hayes and his time in the loony bin. I was sweating profusely and screaming for help. Some big Greek orderly who looked like Demis Roussos injected me up the arse and that was it. I blacked out within five seconds.

'I awoke a few days later in a dormitory. I saw a date on a clock on the wall, and I worked out the dates; I thought I was in hospital, but soon realised that I was in a loony bin. When I looked around at my fellow patients, many with long unkempt beards and long shoulder-length hair, incoherent and sobbing, I discovered I was living in a fucking nightmare. I summoned a nurse who spoke broken English. She told me as best as she could that I had had a nervous breakdown and would be treated and out in a few days, which gave some relief. But the noises and sobbing of the lunatics was awful. I would scream at them to shut the fuck up, all to no avail. On and on they mumbled, sobbing and sometimes letting out horrendous screams.

'I tried to sleep as much as possible to shut this lot out. A couple of days later I was up and out of bed and walking about. I was given access to the library and found some books in English, mostly old crappy cowboy adventures. At least they took me away from this god-awful nightmare.

'One night I was in the showers and I heard this awful noise from the next cubicle. There were really heavy sobs, pleading for mercy; I peered over the top to see what was going on and saw two orderlies raping a young lad who was only about 16. He looked up and saw me. His eyes were pleading for help, but I couldn't help him. I felt helpless, but I could not get away and back to my bed fast enough. I carried the guilt for years after that.

'Another time, I walked into the wrong room down a long corridor and I witnessed a horrendous scene. Half a dozen lunatics were stabbing another inmate in his legs and arse. There was blood spurting everywhere. They each stabbed him relentlessly for at least 30 seconds, before leaving him a crumpled heap in a pool of blood on the floor. Once again I felt helpless and disgusted with myself for not being able to help this desperate man. Fortunately, he didn't die, but I had nightmares for years about both of those horrific incidents.

'I could hardly sleep at night, for fear of being raped or stabbed. I was always being winked at by grubby Greek loonies who would rub their balls and lick their lips at me. I demanded to see the head doctor and pleaded with him to release me. A week later I got a visit from the British Embassy. He got me out that afternoon and gave me £100 for a flight home. I was back in England the very next day, a broken man. I had lost three stones from my normal 11 stones. I went back to my mam and dad's and didn't come out of the house for six weeks.'

Obviously this was no run-of-the-mill lad's tale of mischief abroad. The mad abandon where drinking is concerned was certainly common, but the kidnapping and admission to a psychiatric hospital were definitely not. The episode left a scar on Ged which, tragically, was never erased. Something had been irreversibly set off by the horror of what he had witnessed in that medieval place. Ged never recovered, and spent a lot of time in various institutions. Eventually, he took his own life in 1999. He is sadly missed by friends and family alike. When I received Ged's tale from Carl Spiers, I was shocked. Ged's sense of timing and his degree of observation, coupled with the respect he had for others, make it all the harder to accept that such a person was forced to suffer as he did. Ged's extremism functions as a warning to others, to those who throw caution to the winds and dive in too deep.

Chris from Guildford put it like this:

'Sometimes you've walked 20 miles in 100-degree heat. Parched, aching, feeling like you're dying. Why? It just seems like outside

England all the rules break down and you get lost off the beaten track. I've met many who bear the scars of recklessness from their travels; the lads with the craters in their flesh from the Jericho fly that lays its eggs inside you, which erupt and fly out weeks later. It's a terrifying thing to happen. There are other scars, like the one I have on my leg, after a bus crash in Turkey; going down a mountainside, the brakes failed. The driver tried to drive the bus into the wall of the mountain, but it started rolling over. We rolled several times and my knee smashed right through a window. It was badly gashed and needed dozens of stitches to hold it together. I've met a lot of lads with scars from their travels. When you're out on the road, it's like you just don't care. Some lads go completely mental, with too much drink and not enough sanity anywhere to keep them in check. And worse dramas than that have happened to people. Some people didn't make it at all. When I hear of those who've died I always know it could easily have been me or one of my mates.'

Ged's was one such tale, a real tragedy that surely couldn't have happened to a nicer guy. May his memory live on in those who knew him or are touched by his story.

PART 3
THE NEW WORLD

9

BERMUDA TRIANGLE

An asylum for the sane would be empty in America.
— George Bernard Shaw

History is a patchwork quilt; every civilisation has made contributions to the jigsaw of what it means to be human. We have customs and manners in common, but there is a discontinuity in human culture called the New World. Until recently football, decent beer and travel had little to do with the USA, but today we see a merging of old and new as never before. For many, America represents the New World above all else (despite countries like Canada, Australia and New Zealand also staking a claim). The stereotype is defined as follows:

Once upon a time, a chunk of molten minerals spinning in space cooled down and congealed. Within several epochs, people evolved from monkeys who'd evolved from worms who'd evolved from dirt. They built shelters for themselves out of rock, slate, plaster and other earth materials. They organised themselves into communities, and made sure to set aside some common ground for socialising and games. The village green or town square was always built from attractive, durable materials, remnants of mountains and soil. There was a clear line dividing 'public' and 'private', and people were intellectually curious about other cultures.

The world's civilisations developed like a street; the earliest established communities represent the oldest houses. Younger civilisations represent newer homes, built along the street over time. It's an extremely sociable place. To be branded rude or difficult is a universal stigma that nobody wants. People play games like football, cricket and rugby to create a sense of continuity and sanity.

One day a new family moves into the street from a new place, a place where natural resources are imagined to be superabundant. They are very wasteful but, inexplicably, they consider the treasured public square itself to be a waste. They say the pavements are also a waste of taxpayers' money (they detest taxes); people can easily drive instead of walking, even when the distance is negligible. They buy the public square (they're in with the mayor, who they mistake for Jesus) and build a stand serving rapidly-prepared food that contains huge amounts of fats and sugars. A gigantic illuminated sign atop this fast-food outlet carries greater importance than the village itself; visibility from the nearby motorway massively increases its profitability. The sign is constructed from much higher-quality material than the establishment and the food it serves. A side window enables drivers to pull up and be served without ever leaving their cars. In fact, labour-saving devices powered by fossil fuels appear to be sacred to the family. They're embarrassed to be seen walking unless as an end in itself, for exercise. They salute a flag which resembles the costume of a Marvel comic superhero rather than a simple statement about who they are. They declare it a crime to deface this flag anywhere in the world.

The new family's house is hurriedly knocked together from chipboard, plastic and waterproof paper and set at the end of an insanely long driveway. It's most important to them that the house be bigger than their neighbours' homes. The back garden is surrounded by a high fence and they make it very clear that anybody found wandering inside this fence will be shot to death. It is their right to bear arms, they say.

The family's obese child is different from other children. He is depressed and preoccupied with money in ways that only much older people should be. He plays a peculiar game he has invented, alone in his well-secured garden, a strange kind of football which requires an array of expensive protective equipment. He's as preoccupied with self-protection as he is with harming others. Often, he sits silently thinking about Jesus and waiting for the Prozac to kick in; indeed, a supplementary arsenal of chemicals – like Viagra for Daddy and Botox for Mommy – solves all the problems that Jesus can't, but they don't discuss that. They believe these chemicals will help them control the world.

Fossil-fuelled labour-saving devices, weapons, pharmaceuticals and Jesus; the family insists these four articles of faith are connected in some mystical way. When pressed to explain exactly why that is, they stare blankly, bearing a lifeless and evasive expression called the thousand-yard stare. The Prozac has kicked in.

* * *

America is bigger than all that, of course. It's the nation of religio-capitalist freaks that landed on their feet and exploited everything; no end to the lumber, the oil, the ore and the cereal crops, supposedly. They smashed through the eastern forests and mountains and onto the plains. The invention of the Colt six-shooter enabled them to defeat the mighty plains Indians – who adopted wild horses long before civilisation hit them – and barbed-wire territory soon followed. Americans can almost be forgiven for believing they can control nature. Six-shooters vaporised the acrobatics of the Sioux and led to the Golden West. The Great Plains – the 'breadbasket of the world' – provided entire countries with food and America with cash. The drunken wild men who formed the Gold Rush were among the first to inhabit the West Coast. The succession of wooden shacks and wagon-trains they'd long called home established nomadic frontier-dwelling as an end in itself. Restless bastards that they were, Americans soon felt the grass growing under their feet. No surprise, then, that it was they who were first to the moon. They ran out of places to go, so they blasted off a futuristic shack known as a lunar module. Gorra love 'em.

When I passed through US Customs in early 1988, I was broke but planned to stay in the States for a while. I never travelled with more than a couple of hundred on me in cash because I didn't have it. Plain and simple.

You may recall John Allen's hapless false start back in 1977, when he was hosted by an eccentric clergyman in the heart of Manhattan? Allen returned to England, not quite deported, with renewed intent to enter the USA and stay there. Let's refresh our memories with a quick trip back to 1977, where Allen remembers his plot to bounce right back at the Yanks, refusing to be beaten:

'Two months after being sent home I was back in the States, wiser and ready to embark on a proper trip. I'd got a free flight out of the church crowd, as they felt guilty about what happened last time. I flew to Washington DC, which was the closest airport to where they lived in Maryland. The Chesapeake Bay was gorgeous, a vast waterway with luxury homes and loads of Yanks in boats riding about. I stayed with yet another preacher and his wife. She was quite an interesting old bird in a wheelchair from having polio as a kid. I got to meet the movers and shakers of their village and then planned to fuck right off on my voyage across America.

'I bought a Greyhound bus ticket to Houston. On the way to Texas I met these two super-posh English girls on the bus, from Surrey and Hertfordshire. They were going to New Orleans, to meet some guy down there. Their parents were apparently connected to the petrol company Burma. They were nervous as fuck about meeting this bloke, as they were only young girls away from home for the first time. I was only 19 and they were younger than me. The funny thing is, they'd never have looked at me in England 'cos of my accent, but the shoe was on the other foot over in the States. The bloke came to pick them up in a convertible Mustang. He was a bit put out at the sight of this unexpected limey geezer, but we ended up hitting it off really well. He was from old money stock and we had a whale of a time down in New Orleans. My trip had finally begun and it was the start of many great adventures across the USA. I sometimes laugh about that plaque I drew on that shithouse wall in Liverpool, as my California dreamin' in that smelly bog has come true in more ways than I could begin to describe.'

Allen also travelled through South America and began to write a series of hilarious memoirs. He is now a personal friend of mine in New England and has spent the past couple of decades touring with his band, the Big Bad Bollocks. They are a favourite on rowdy Saint Patrick's Day evenings, when the beer is flying and the music is cranked up to the max.

Mid-to-late 80s America was still as distant as it had been in 1977 for most people in Britain. All we knew of it was what we saw on television, an often video-quality representation due to pixilation conversion on TV shows like *Different Strokes* and *Soap*. Back in '77, I'd believed that when you went to the USA the world actually appeared that way and the States was subject to different laws of physics. To actually *be there* was difficult to imagine. It seemed everything in America was built to be watched on TV, or at least through a window, even if it was a 'dirty old window', as Kim Wilde had sung on 'Kids in America'. Actually walking down a street in New York City was something I'd dreamed about all my life. While I'd been travelling across Canada, my mate Dave Leckie had spent three months in Miami. He had much to say:

'It's fuckin' brilliant, Ian, just like on the telly. Palm trees an' posh high-rise flats an' nice big boats everywhere. Even fuckin' Disneyworld was good!'

Dave brought some photos of his trip round to our house as proof.

'This is just a normal street, mate!' he'd declare, shoving a photo of what appeared to be a cluster of palaces interspaced with incredibly green lawns and ornate streetlights in my face.

'There's birds like this all over the gaff, seriously!' he'd guffaw, holding up a picture of semi-naked, athletic blondes. A sea-green fluid lapped onto a white talcum-powder beach stuck with spangled palms and basketball hoops behind them.

The aquamarine Atlantic, the healthy-looking foliage, the bikini-clad females and turquoise sky sucked me in like a goose to a jet engine. I signed up for the mission forthwith.

*   *   *

In February 1988 we flew from Gatwick to Newark, and were secreted deep among the concrete canyons of Manhattan. We trammelled the sidewalks like freaks, bedazzled and hypnotised by what we found there. The people looked like muppets, Goliaths and werewolves, eating gyros and 12-inch sub sandwiches as they moved along in expensive suits. Stretch limos lined up outside amazingly compact carwashes. Suited-up chauffeurs leaned against black bonnets smoking cigars and talking in gestures like gangsters. I was propelled by nervousness as I was penniless and had no job or means of finding one.

In the bars people called for Harvey Wallbangers, Screwdrivers and Waldorf Salads in proper accents. They read the *New York Times Magazine* and busily discussed the Yankees, the Giants and the Mets. Rap music played on radios, interrupted by the Four Seasons or Odyssey. This in turn was replaced by white noise and reports of pneumatic drills and cement mixers, incessant chatter and cappuccino machines. Manhattan's foreign influences oozed from every pore of the place, then blended, repelled and settled into an exhilarating urban emulsion; neon shamrocks glowed green in the windows of Irish pubs. Awnings decked out like Italian flags fluttered above crowded delis, containing immense glass cases loaded with pink meats. The Jews of the diamond district shuffled along in guarded debate, their ringlets trailing in the steely wind. African traders sold every possible manner of goods along the edge of the pavement. The scale of the buildings was beyond every other continent of the time, even the lowest structures completely dwarfed Manchester's CIS Building, then the tallest in the city.

There was no evidence whatsoever of the rave culture that was starting to engulf us back home, but the Yanks had their own version of 'raving' in early 1988, as we would discover.

After a couple of days among the compressed neon craziness we flew on to Miami. The 1988 spring break party was gathering steam nicely. I prayed I would find a job, any job, to keep me there awhile. Southern Florida was a dazzling profusion of yellow-green tropical foliage and backyard kidney pools arranged like beads beside the blue Atlantic. We took a taxi to the hostel where Dave had stayed the previous year. The Sol-y-Mar was an interesting place. One half of its occupants were apparently American or continental *Mafiosi* of one kind or another; guys from Sicily, Corsica, New York and Boston sat around the pool, reading newspapers, as if waiting for a signal of some kind. They were actually pretty handy, knew loads of the local Italian restaurant owners and could sort people out with jobs here and there. But they were a grim lot – cards very close to chests, penetrating eyes, like reptiles lounging in the sun all day. Grey-haired older guys would enter into business deals with the younger element, dealing weed or other substances. Many were on the lam, hunted by the police forces of the northeast. Elder statesmen used their position as established wiseguys to lure younger associates into dirty work. A promise of a boost into the books was a huge incentive for young soldiers from the cities of the East Coast.

The other half of the Sol-y-Mar's inhabitants composed wayward Yanks, lunatics who'd fled the normalcy of the big cities and decided to hide out. They lived like overgrown teenagers in the tropical playground of Fort Lauderdale, supping beers constantly and swapping mad stories of riding the rails and Greyhound buses. They were the drifters and hobos of American legend. A good few of them accompanied us on our boozing sessions. The thin smattering of English was supplemented by a few Aussies and Europeans. Overall, the mood was one of mad abandon; sea-dogs would turn up off boats from the Caribbean, while the Aussies frequently jetted off to South America, returning weeks later with amazing stories from the Andes or the wild cities of Brazil. We never saw the Southern Cross, being utterly skint. But through it all the sun kept shining and the view, at least, was free. There were even parrots and monkeys living in the area, which pretty much sent me over the edge. Like most British people, anywhere with nice weather and exotic beasts resembles a perfect dreamworld to my jaded, pissed-in eye.

The Fort Lauderdale Strip was a gleaming testament to American decadence; spotless and wide, it ran parallel to the spangling blue shoreline loaded with glassy lounges and cafés. Every place was committed to the science of hedonism, drunkenness and general mayhem. The bars had an open-air quality, with numerous televisions situated on wall brackets. Each one broadcast a sporting fixture, at least half of which were live: football, basketball, hockey, baseball. Everybody watched in a frenzy of chopped attention spans.

The razzmatazz of American football had me entranced from the start. The players looked like astronauts and the pitch was Astro*turf*. The 80,000-strong crowds appeared bizarrely indifferent to the magnitude of the event in which they were participating. Perhaps it was me that didn't take it seriously, as it wasn't 'real' football. Fort Lauderdale was a tourist destination for folks across the US. The bars overlooking the ocean had walls festooned with pennants, helmets, towels and flags from every football team in the country. There were turquoise Miami Dolphins towels next to black and gold Pittsburgh Steelers pennants. Deep-green Philadelphia Eagles t-shirts hung near silver Dallas Cowboys helmets. At the time I failed to understand that teams from both the AFC and NFC were represented; Miami frequently hosted the Super Bowl, the decider between teams from both conferences. The area was host to *all* American football fans. The bars had open fronts or plate-glass windows. Pitchers of ice-cold lager were dirt cheap, if not free. The sunshine and bikini-clad roller-bladers, architecture and palm trees mesmerised the English mind. It definitely wasn't Salford.

Fort Lauderdale had several large yachting basins and marinas, each of which contained hundreds of undulating multimillion-dollar boats. There were sailboats, power yachts, speedboats and even amphibious vessels moored and docked everywhere. An extensive network of canals, called the Intracoastal Waterway, formed a labyrinthine maze of marine 'streets' extending several blocks back from the beach. Access to the Intracoastal was gained through the many drawbridges that interrupted the main drags running perpendicular to the strip. The whole place was full of poisonous sea-snakes, manatees, large fish populations and colourful aquatic birds and reptiles. The streets which backed onto the Intracoastal were some of the most opulent and lavish in the entire USA. Countless white mansions with fanciful columns and balustrades divided America's prime real-estate between gleaming fresh lawns and exotic contemporary condos, moulded from smooth concrete in wildly sexy geometric forms. All along the ends of the backyards ran several miles of well-kept boardwalk. Every ten feet there was a thick wooden pole or a sturdy metal cleat to tie off your yacht for the night, like it was only a fucking car parked outside your house.

Dave found a job working in the kitchens of one of the hotel restaurants along the strip. He found his American workmates obsessed with material possessions and customers preoccupied with social status – an odd twist for a country supposedly free of the constraints of the class system:

'I was a dish-washer and bus-boy, and the Yanks were unbelievably arrogant and disdainful towards us when we were collecting their dirty plates. It was like, if you had a job like that in a country with so much opportunity, you had to be either genetically inferior or else a convicted felon who couldn't get anything better, so they treated you like shit. Americans have no discretion and their rudeness is in a class of its own. I worked with a few young lads and women of various ages in the kitchens of a big hotel. One of the lads used to come in stoned off his box every day, and a middle-aged woman would always suss him and start bollocking him, telling him he'd never have the nice cars and the boats he wanted. He looked at her with his bloodshot eyes and grinned, saying, "Yeah, but it helps me to dream about it."'

I was fortunate enough to land a job on the yachts, working for different people who waxed and varnished the fibreglass and wooden beauties. The yachts came in many shapes and sizes and the larger ones were like buoyant palaces, with numerous spacey berths secreted away beneath decks, big TVs and plush, king-size beds. The bathrooms (or 'heads', as the sailors call them) often contained Jacuzzis, and for some reason the showers always felt nicer than the landlubber variety. The swish, air-conditioned salons (lounges) had graceful sofas, excellent stereos and thick carpets. The drinks cabinets were well-stocked. Sometimes the captains would take us out for a day's sailing. We'd drift aimlessly around the Bermuda Triangle, barbequing freshly-caught fish and drinking cold beers in a warm wind, watching the sun go down over Miami. The air was alive with private jets, coming and going from the Keys and the Caribbean, or simply planes from Lauderdale trailing their 'FREE BEER ALL DAY' banners, advertising the clubs on the strip. The sterns of the yachts had swim platforms, beyond the transom. The sport-fishing rods would strain and lurch in the cockpit at the hands of the Yanks in their Quint-style fighting chairs, reeling in monster marlin or mako sharks. There were huge refrigerator chests loaded with cold lager, and bait-prep areas. It was arguably the nicest lifestyle anyone could ever have. The sensation of diving off the swim platform into the cold blue Atlantic, knowing that beneath me hundreds of feet of water contained all manner of streamlined carnivorous beasts, is one I'll never forget. That mythic patch of water will remain in my heart till I die.

Back on the strip, the students had arrived in force for spring break, and the plush hotels and clubs were swarming with young people hell-bent on finding satisfaction. There were clubs that opened right onto the Intracoastal. All day long yachts full of beautiful people would roll up and disgorge their lusty, drunken cargo. Masses of half-naked women flowed into the crowd like a spreading honey slick in a sea of testosterone hornets. The hostel we stayed at was packed with lads and girls all up for it day and night, and little posses headed out to the strip on the hour every hour. Inevitably, we had a crazed session there one day and wrecked the place.

It all started when a lush from Georgia, who we'd christened Chevy because he looked like Chevy Chase, introduced us to a wine called Wild Irish Rose.

He walked up to us and asked, 'Are you guys partying today?'

'Partying? What, is it someone's fucking birthday or something?' That was just the way we lived. There was no fucking party, I can assure you. It was all in the name of anthropological research.

This mental wine was 18 percent alcohol by volume. All the English and Aussies went to the store around the corner and bought themselves a couple of bottles. Some people may have even had drugs, but I'm sure it was all sanctioned by a qualified doctor. Back at the ranch, we started lounging by the pool and getting generally baked and pissed as farts. When we ran out of fuel, I volunteered to ride back round to the store on a bicycle for more. It was a twisted mission. I should have died a number of times, weaving about in the roaring traffic on A1A, the main coastal route into Miami. Dave remembers it well:

'Back at poolside, things had progressed to a frenzied degree in the noonday sun,' he laughs. 'A scouser came running out of our room, carrying one of the Aussies' bags. He emptied the entire thing into the pool: clothes, traveller's cheques, shaving gear, the full Montezuma. The Aussie went ballistic and went and grabbed the English lad's bag. Into the pool it went. Then someone launched a sun-lounger in, followed by some other cunt's bag full of clothes. Within minutes, people were leaping from the top balcony into the pool with other people on their shoulders, throwing bags, seats, plants, sunglasses, shoes, money, lizards, dogs and monkeys into the pool. It was a mini-riot!'

I remember talking to a Swedish girl who suddenly disappeared. I looked down and she was sprawled on the deck, looking dazed. Across the pool, one of the Stoke lads was laughing his bollocks off; he'd thrown a balled-up, saturated towel, aiming for me, but missed and nearly knocked her out. By late afternoon the place looked like a bomb had hit it. Even the *Mafiosi* had beaten a retreat in the face of the carnage. Unfortunately, as a result of this outbreak alcohol was banned from the hostel. We had no choice but to booze in the bars and clubs. Fortunately, they were literally giving it away.

One day, I was working on a yacht with a couple of Aussies. A gorgeous blonde in a bikini was sign-painting a nearby yacht with the name *Wild Goose*. One of the Aussies was also a signwriter and they discussed the gold-leaf she was using. It gave me the idea to learn the trade myself. There were so many boats there that a signwriter would never run out of work.

The canals and the ocean weren't the only way in and out of Lauderdale; the extensive Interstate system of America was an efficient and convenient way to steam across the continent. I regularly surveyed maps in gas stations and wondered what it felt like to just head west in a car. I'd heard about Auto Driveaway – a system where you delivered a car across the country, leaving a deposit to be collected upon delivery of said car in good time. I wanted to try it for myself. Unfortunately, I had to return to England for personal reasons. If that hadn't been the case I highly doubt I'd ever have gone back. But that was that. Auto-Driveaway would have to wait for later.

10

THE BACHELOR HERD

It should be possible to explain the laws of physics to a barmaid.
— Albert Einstein

By mid-1988, a sense that the world was catching up with us gripped hard. More and more were discovering the acid house scene. Returning from Florida, I went to London, working on the roads with a pneumatic drill and a load of Tottenham and Arsenal lads. One morning the newspaper headline read, 'THOUSANDS OF EURO '88 RAIL TICKETS STOLEN BY LIVERPOOL AND MANCHESTER GANGS!' The tickets had apparently been knocked off by a mob of grafters. My cockney mates on the roads were offering me loads of money for the tickets but I knew absolutely nothing about it.

I spent some grim times boozing in a big pub in Ruislip Manor, opposite a kebab house where I tasted my first ever doner. It was identical to the gyros we'd eaten in Manhattan (but different from Cairo's shawarma). I became a kebab addict for life. The boozer was always packed with Arsenal fans, and they weren't the friendliest people. It was a stark contrast to the motley heads encamped in the various bed and breakfasts I was living in, career criminals, sex maniacs, prostitutes, Americans and suicidal, suited-up geezers who'd fucked-up big on the stock exchange. But most were lads and lasses from up north, in search of work and adventure. They were all over London.

At one place in Crystal Palace, the lunatics had clearly taken over the asylum; the landlord had arranged it so that residents' dole cheques included the rent money instead of it being mailed separately to him. Predictably, everyone signed on and just pissed all their rent away. In response the landlord installed two heavies, a scouser and a Glaswegian, to enforce the law. The day they arrived, they went door to door in the big house demanding rent from the occupants. The lads living there mobbed up and proceeded to dish out a serious slapping to the gruesome twosome. They ended up locked in their room for a couple of days, pissing in the sink and having food delivered through a window by a local girl who hung around the place. Inevitably, those of us involved were ejected by the police.

I ended up on the ale with a psychopath from Sunderland, who knew a lad I'd grafted with in Israel. He was plotting many evil crimes and trying to rope me in. In a rotting boozer overlooking the Crystal Palace radio transmitter, I did a body manoeuvre when he went for a piss. I ended up crashing in Ruislip Manor on a mate's floor, before finding yet another room in Paddington. The routine at the time was work in the Smoke all week and hoof it back to Manchester at the weekend. I always seemed to bump into mates waiting for the National Express at Victoria on a Friday afternoon, many of them fresh back from Europe having been on a mission of some kind. One night I was woken up in my Paddington pad when a bloke was almost murdered against my door. The police were asking lots of questions the next day, but I couldn't help; I'd just flown in from Cairo and I was knackered. I only vaguely remembered hearing the horrific volley of shouts, screams and kicks launched against the door, but I felt guilty for not snapping to my senses and helping the guy – assuming I could have done.

I was travelling to Manchester to watch United and it was clear things had changed. Everyone was busy, especially the grafters. Whether it was stealing paving stones, selling snide clothing or flogging counterfeit passes for sporting and concert events, there was money to be made. The gangs of the 70s and early 80s had dissolved amid the plastic hordes that began to trickle into football. But the so-called casuals continued to ply their trade – their hooliganism and territoriality were ages old.

Pete from Ancoats already had his eyes opened by a wild day out in Nottingham, among others, but there were other cities and other mobs yet to be encountered. Pete was a graduate of the United school of grafting excellence, living on his wits in the late 80s. He and his mates took regular detours into strange waters just for the hell of it. They loved to chance their arm, but on one occasion they bit off more than they could chew:

'Back in the late 80s there was a Barnsley-Sheffield United FA Cup replay at Oakwell. It was a midweek game, and me and six of my mates – all Reds – had gone to the races at either Doncaster or York. I'm not sure which, because we went virtually every week to the races somewhere. There was good money to be made at the racecourses during that time – not from gambling, just a lot of drunken, clueless people with too much money. We had a very good day financially, so I said, "Should we go to Barnsley versus Sheff United on the way home?"

'We were playing the winners in the next round so it made it a bit more interesting for us, and at age 17-20 everything is an adventure. We took the train over to Barnsley and went in a town centre pub/club-type place. It was a really odd place, this, I'll never forget it. They had bicycles hanging off the ceiling, and these mannequin things randomly hanging out of the wall. It was a bit weird, to be honest. We were sat having a drink when this big lump walks in and asks, "Are you United?" We say, "Yeah, why?" Not even clicking on he means *Sheff* United. Two minutes later there's about 20 of them piling through the door and straight into us! I'm under tables, over the bar, even trying to climb up the wall on one of these weird dummies to escape. It was like *Tom and Jerry* in there.

'Eventually I got collared and the next thing I remember is being brought round by a copper. We all got a good hiding and one of the lads had a broken arm, although we didn't realise at the time.

'After we get cleaned up we say, "Shall we go home or what?" But we all agree, fuck it, we'll go to the match and in with the Sheffield lot. Fuck these Barnsley cunts! It's pay on the gate and I can't remember much about the match, other than we're stood behind the goal down at the bottom right. I've had a look around where we are and it seems safe enough. We're having a bit of a laugh, and my mate with the arm is (understandably) whining on about the pain. It's just after halftime when I start to notice a definite shifting in the crowd behind us. I half-glance around and can see that the family types that had been there have all disappeared and been replaced by lads. Before I can say anything to our lot, I get a tap on the shoulder and this lad asks me, "Where you from?" I say, "Manchester," because there's no point lying – I can't carry a Sheffield accent off – and he says, "You think you can come in here and take the piss?" I say, "We're from Manchester but we're Sheffield United fans."

'I've barely got the words out when he nuts me squarely across the bridge of my nose, then they all pile into us and there is nowhere to go because we're at the bottom and there's railings to keep people off the pitch.

'When we eventually got rescued by the police there was no sympathy there. It was, "You shouldn't be here, you Manc bastards. Fuck off before we nick you." We were turfed out of the ground into loads of little smelly Barnsley bastards, waiting to try it on. By this point we'd had enough, and we fucked them right off. The train bringing us home must have looked like a hospital train; we were bruised and battered to fuck, with blood everywhere. It was straight to the hospital for me and my broken-armed mate. The lot of us have since followed United all over the place, sometimes with the main firm and sometimes on our own, but it never got as bad as that for us again.'

This grim brush with Yorkshire's casuals wasn't the best of results for Pete and Co, but it served to illustrate how every team in the league had organised themselves into some kind of casual firm. Even the towns who fell into Pete's mates' "we're Mancs and they're backwards" category. But in the late-80s it was Manchester who led the way in the art of clubbing and music. We'd been doing psychedelics for years and were right into the sounds and the dancing. The art of steeping one's brain in alarming chemicals was commonplace, along with the music accompanying these experiences. Things were seeping into mainstream media in ways we'd never before seen. All of Greater Manchester County, from Stockport to Wigan to Rochdale, avidly jumped into the retro-hippie experience with both feet. The same thing was happening in other regions, too. It wasn't long before the scene settled out into a lawless bedlam, peppered with violence, fashion and football. Slowly, each major city's football crew worked their way into the drugs supply end of the rave scene in their area. As with the continental designer explosion a decade earlier, the face of British football hooliganism was radically changed. In Manchester, home of football's largest firm, there were other agencies to consider who wanted a slice of the action. A heavy-duty overlap between football, street gangs, Salford families and other organised groups created a precarious equilibrium; it often threatened to go up like a volcano, similar to the fragile balance of peace in the grafting world. The major players involved in drugs distribution and retail were surrounded by a tie-dyed cloud of groovers who loved to take acid as much as deal it. Their customers grew exponentially, pumped up by the media frenzy over the phenomenon of acid-house parties, held in warehouses off rural motorway junctions. Dominic Lavin, author of the sex- and drugs-charged *Last Seen in Bangkok*, was one such chap. He remembers the way tastes altered and evolved over time, as the stroboscopic rave era slowly reared its dilated head. Neither was he a stranger to the idea of travel.

'My background's a bit of a weird one,' the well-travelled Lavin will tell you. 'I was actually born in Finland to an English dad and Finnish mam. At the age of two I decided to move my parents back over to Wigan where my dad was from, after hearing about Wigan Athletic. Wigan is a great place honestly and even though I haven't lived there for nearly 20 years now I won't have a bad word said against it. Although, when I arrived in 1972, having a mam with a foreign accent made us something of an oddity. I'm not saying we suffered racism, it wasn't like that, but because of my mam's strange Nordic ways and the fact I was a short arse I did have to fight my corner a few times. If we'd lived in parts of Manchester or Liverpool our uniqueness would have gone unnoticed, but Wigan isn't known generally for its cultural diversity.

'I grew up on a terraced street near the rugby ground and my mam and dad were churchgoers. They were both teachers (my dad at the school I went to) and they had great ambitions for me and my sisters to become lawyers or doctors. But at the age of 13, instead of doing extra homework I was more interested in cutting the bottom off my Lee flared jeans, sewing the "Lee" belt badge to the front hem and hanging about at the top of Wigan with a can of butane under my Benetton rugby shirt. Solvent abuse doesn't get the credit it deserves, and it was all the rage in the 80s. Despite receiving bad press from ambulance drivers, doctors, coroners and other pious killjoys, it proved to be for me a very liberating pastime. I can't actually remember the first time I sniffed glue, but I've a feeling it was during the teachers' strike, where all at once whole fleets of kids would get ejected from afternoon school to go dipping the pick and mix at Woolworth's or send fire engines to their mate's houses from a call box.

'I suppose that phase was like the 60s, "If you can remember it you weren't there, man." But in all honesty there was nowt better than sitting in one of your dens with a tube of glue and a few sandwich bags, then enjoying a more solitary pleasure at home with that copy of

Penthouse that was hidden under your bed. It wasn't long before I became a connoisseur of the wealth of readily-available solvents and flammable liquids. Evostik was good for a couple of sessions, but regular users complained of a loss of potency and headaches after a couple of good excursions. There were two types of lighter gas, the yellow and red can or the red, white and black can, both of which were great but with the latter the cold had an anaesthetising effect and you could actually pull your own teeth out after a few toots. These days it's that Swan Vesta shite with loads of special nozzles for different types of lighters. My personal favourite was a stain-removal solution called Dab It Off that you could get from the local car spares shop which, mixed with a couple of dabs of trainer glue on the back of your ruler, gave a pleasant mix of delirium and euphoria. Liquid paper eventually got banned from our school because of the recreational possibilities it offered pupils. I heard rumours that there was a gang in Kirkby who used to ignite the lining of their Israeli parkas and get off on the smoke from it, yet these days cokeheads think they're onto something good!

'Around 1984-85 I started going to the match rather than just going to watch sport, if you get my drift. It was about a year or so after I'd started taking an interest in the fashions. Up to the age of 12 or 13 you just wore what you were told, and it was about that time that your outgoings started to exceed your pocket money, so shoplifting and other petty forms of pilfering helped pay for the Wrangler flared cords and the coach ticket to Darlington, or for the hire of the van going to Warrington. I suppose a lot of the stuff about football hooliganism is very hackneyed. I'm not running down people like Cass Pennant or Tony Rivers because I love reading their stuff. My point is that there are people much better placed to write about hooliganism, the genesis of Stone Island, and how it all changed at raves, than I am. I was never Wigan's top lad, I've never organised a rave or been to prison, but I have steamed across the odd pitch with my mates. I've been chased by angry hordes from Burnden Park to Bolton railway station, and sat in the back of one too many ten-year old Ford Fiestas on motorway service stations at 4:00 am on bleak Sundays, where my four friends have three Berghaus coats, 11 grams of amphetamine and 14 functioning brain cells between them, waiting to get moved on by the police.'

Lavin went off the edge, to be swallowed by the strange gurgling weir of rave-era clubland. He saw numerous friends and interlopers dive in alongside him, but he got away, and the years he spent among the paradise beaches and sweatshops of the Far East shaped his outlook and expectations in ways he didn't foresee. The rave scene worked its magic on the underground economy, sweeping the Dambusters and other little firms into a supply-and-demand maelstrom they completely failed to anticipate. Anybody with half an inkling developed a curiosity about this 'new' stuff called acid that the middle-class media drips were salivating over in the tabloids. Mellow, a Dambuster, was shocked at the demand for acid by what had been until then straight-headed members of society:

'When we first made the trips to the 'Dam we were doing it for no one else. A little earner for the few local heads we knew, and ourselves. The heads were all footy lads and grafters who just wanted a nobble at the weekend. Then it was for the heads, ourselves, and a bit extra for people who were approaching us in pubs knowing we had it. Within two years, between the end of '85 and the end of '87, it was like all the straights had latched onto it. People I'd never have dreamed would even smoke pot were going to clubs tripping and going berserk. We doubled, and then tripled, our trips to Holland, and it still wasn't enough, in fact it was a joke. We couldn't cover it to save our lives, and we'd started meeting more and more lads from Manchester who were doing the same as us. In 1984, you were lucky if you bumped into anyone looking to schlep acid back to England to deal. It was unfashionable and no one saw it as something to do. It was considered loopy shit that did yer 'ead in and they weren't interested, not including the football lads we knew at United and City. But in '86, all these new characters were coming out of the woodwork, getting a clue and wanting it.

'I'm not even sure if it started in the clubs or whether they were just doing it and going in pubs and that. You was lucky to see one other firm in '86 even, but by '87 every fucking ferry had three or four little firms who you'd see at the regular places in Amsterdam. Then the funny music started, the divvy acid house shit that sounded crap, and loads of bollocks on Radio One. Some of that wasn't even club-based. It was just knobhead musicians who were out of touch but who'd started doing acid. It was like a load of hippies and hooligans had given the straights ideas, and they'd started liking it. It was dead weird, but the main thing was we couldn't bring enough of the stuff back with us! The football crowd took to it dead quick 'cos they weren't frightened of it. When the

Manchester scally bands came in we were satisfied that our heads had done the business and spread the word. But, that said, I went to Ibiza a good few times then and there were some right clueless cunts getting into it.'

Aye, Mellow lad. That's very true. Some of the clowns will linger in my memory like a bad fart in a stalled elevator. But let's stick to the good stuff. It was all about forks in the road. In the early days outfits like the Wide Awake Firm and the Huyton Baddies had split off from the domestic mod revival. During the psychedelic genesis of 1983 the Dambusters split off from the Club Tropicana crowd. The cool kids had always gone off abroad, leaving the stiffs marooned on Blighty Island to be dictated to by the piss-poor media. Thanks to Madchester, that same media was about to improve massively.

From 1988 to 1990 the world seemed to shrink. The international borders within Europe came to mean less and less, and the long weekend in Amsterdam, Ibiza or Stockholm grew in popularity. Young people embraced foreign cultures selectively and, being British, the party aspect was the one they all wanted to learn about. One small group of musicians had now peeled away from the clowns in the mainstream media, to make great music with drums and guitars for the first time in over a decade. They were called the Stone Roses, Happy Mondays, the Charlatans and a few others. I remember the first time I ever heard the Stone Roses, lying in bed one morning in my tiny Salford bed-sit. Dissatisfied by the music scene (a la John Allen), I was reading *Psychotic Reactions and Carburetor Dung*, a compilation of American rock critic Lester Bangs' writings. I had my headphones on and, for some inexplicable reason, was listening to the radio. The first few guitar clucks of 'Made of Stone' began to infiltrate my consciousness as I relished the book. I stopped to listen, preparing to be disappointed. The song gathered pace and the vocals kicked in. I began to seriously wonder who it was. This had a modern edge to it, and the mood said it was current. As the song bloomed into its chorus, I lay there knowing it had to be a new band but I was confused. I hadn't realised bands made such interesting music anymore. I listened for the DJ to announce the name but none was forthcoming. I asked my mates had they heard this song and sang what I remembered of the chorus to them, like you do. They shook their heads and toked on the sputnik. It became a bee in my psychedelic bonnet.

One thing was for sure, Rob W's Mandean prophecy had come to pass and the Exodus was underway; as droves flocked to Madchester to sample the delights, many peeled off in aeroplanes to faraway adventures. The media was on the case and about to finally catch us up.

* * *

My long-time friend Kezz had enjoyed his foreign holidays but he'd never been one to live abroad. Instead, he settled into a mad pub life, along with many others. Attending United matches never went out of style for some, and the tales continue. 'We went to St. James's Park last week,' Kezz told me one day. 'We ended up in a boozer with all their lads. I was that pissed I lost my fuckin' ticket. I was crawlin' round on me hands an' knees lookin' for the bastard! Their lads ended up getting down there and lookin' for it with me! I'll never hear a word said against them Geordies. They could have filled us in royal, but they never.'

Occasionally Kezz and Co would broaden their horizons without the excuse of a football match to go to. One night in summer '87, I was in Manchester with a cockney mate and we dropped some acid. We bumped into Kezz and he told us his recent past:

'One of the lads, Tez, was working in a pub in Preston so a few of us went up to see him. I borrowed my brother's mate's car for the trip. We went in the pub and were getting evils off the locals straight away. As time went on it was obviously gonna be on top for us. More and more of 'em getting bolder and braver. There was only, like, five of us. I ended up just losing it. I told the lads, "Right, on the count of three." I counted to three and the lot of us just give it, "*Aaarrrggghhhh!!!!*" and we launched our tables right across the pub at 'em. They shit themselves and scattered, and we were giving plenty out to them that didn't. We smashed the pub to fuck. We were behind the bar just helping ourselves. Pint pots on the optics an' everythin'!'

Kezz made several violent movements, mimicking himself pumping whisky into a 20-ounce glass in the air between us. My cockney mate Dave's eyes were like saucers.

'After a bit someone shouts that the Old Bill are coming so we leg it out to the car. Everyone's in the car an' the fucker won't start! I jumped out, going mental. They were doing roadwork there and I just picked up a paving stone. I lobbed it right through the car windscreen. Then I picked another up. The lads are bolting now. I fuckin' smashed that car to fuck with paving stones, I was so pissed off. Then we had to hide from the police. Somehow I made it home. The next day I took a Matchbox model of that car and a hammer into the pub. I walked up to my brother's mate and put the Matchbox model on the table in front of him. Then I smashed it to fuck. "Your car's in Preston," I told him. "An' it looks like that."

'That Monday I was at my probation officer's. He asks me, "So what kind of a weekend did you have, Mark?" "Aw, nothing too rowdy," I told the cunt. "I just went out an' had a pint of orange and that." If only he coulda seen me trashing this fuckin' boozer in Preston!'

To say we laughed (given our condition) was an understatement. Needless to say, the concept of love 'n' peace never completely made it through Kezz's forcefield. There are enough stories about Kezz to fill a book of their own. Another mate, who'd been at Preston, once found himself smack in the middle of Kezzworld:

'He suggested we retire to his flat for tea after a session. Debbie, his missus, wasn't happy with us coming home pissed and wanting scran and all that. They were rowing while I kept my head down. Finally a meal arrived with some cups of Rosy Lee and beer. I was just settling down to it when the entire meal was chopped in half by a massive knife. Straight through the food and plate and into the tabletop. Kezz lifted the entire table up and launched the lot, three meals, drinks and all, right through the fucking window! We ended up having to phone a glazier and go to the chippy.'

They were mad, mad, mad times, a flight into the unknown. As more people experimented with acid, the music played in clubs began to change. Stuff that sounded commercial and talentless was a lot better when you were out of your mind. By comparison, music like the Stone Roses was almost too good to be true.

Dominic Lavin was beginning his own flight into the unknown around this time, starting at quite an unlikely location.

'By 1988 I'd somehow managed to wangle myself onto a degree course at the University of Leeds,' says Lavin. 'It was during those three years that the hooligan/house-music transition took place. I entered with a rolled-up newspaper looking for a scrap and exited with some rolled-up Moroccan looking for an all-nighter. Oh, and with an honours degree in geography.

'By about 1991 the herbal life had opened up for me, and rather than have a job I was making ends meet buying hashish and skunk at a couple of ounces a time and selling what I didn't smoke. I spent a very carefree 12 or 18 months rolling up at people's houses, to spread a little happiness while potmarking settees as I went. I did get into the E's and clubbing but found the comedowns made me very depressed.

'Around 1992 a fork in the path appeared for myself and the gang of mates I had. We'd all been into clubbing and were all well sorted for E's and speed, but a small faction split off (a bit like the Judean People's Front) and started smoking heroin. The "Foily Boys" or the "Tooting Popular Front" (in deference to *Citizen Smith*) congregated in Cockney Paul's house and the rest of us dispersed around the local pubs.

'I was to some degree a sort of pseudo-hippie; I couldn't be arsed with aggro really and sought answers, wisdom and true enlightenment with herbal-assisted meditation, whilst wearing Stone Island jeans, Chipie shirts and Best Company sweatshirts. This quest for knowledge, karmic peace and balanced chakra led me to take a job as a telesales "executive", selling advertising in *Exchange and Mart*. To be honest, the fact that I'd actually got a job proved to be something of a surprise to most of my friends and family, although the true logic behind my switching to Babylon was that it would fund a trip to Thailand. Meanwhile the Tooting Popular Front had become engrossed in the Dark Side of the Spoon and spent their evenings doing the nod. The heroin issues among my mates had also made me take a few healthy options as a knee-jerk reaction and I started Thai boxing to keep fit. I actually wasn't bad at it and fought a few times, but after a good hiding from a bloke who went on to become European Champion I eased off on the competitive side of things.'

Heroin had insidiously crept into the biochemistry of the scallywags; whether it was common-or-garden 'brown', the luxuriant 'China white' or some mix of the two, it was consumed via several channels. Most people favoured 'chasing the dragon', as opposed to snorting (which was popular in America). Chasing the dragon entailed tapping out a small amount of powder onto a square of foil, before holding a lighter flame under it for a second to burn off the more volatile toxins. The consumer will have constructed a 'tooter', also from foil, which was a tube placed in the mouth, the approximate length of a cigarette. Next, the flame would be placed beneath the foil again and the powder would liquefy. The foil was then tilted at an angle and the liquid 'chased' by the consumer and inhaled via the tooter, making sure not to waste a molecule of the precious opiate. A seasoned smackhead can chase the heroin around the very edge of a sheet of foil, describing a concentric square, wasting not a centimetre. I've seen them zigzag with unsurpassed precision back and forth across a piece of foil just a few inches wide. Extreme needs can create amazing feats of craftsmanship. Unfortunately, it also creates a crime economy all of its own.

I well remember heading down to Moss Side in Mojo's car – which had a removable gear stick for security purposes – to score high-grade brown. It was always a rapid interchange of evasive code (via payphone) designed to ensure that the punter was kosher and identified. Scores of machine-pistols and other automatic weapons were lurking in the event of a mistake and adrenalin was high on the menu. The habits of addicts are well-documented, so I won't repeat them here except to note two immediate responses I observed; upon scoring, desperate addicts would scamper into the toilets of nearby Rusholme's Indian restaurants with a double Kit-Kat, anxious to use the foil. Seasoned pros, on the other hand, would wait to pull in at the shops along Bury New Road or in the bases of the high-rises in Greengate on the way home, and pick up a roll of real foil, pull into a quiet factory street and get the ball rolling. Sometimes, the dealer in question would be in the act of running from the drug squad as he actually organised the deal over his mobile phone. This was the case one time when we scored off a guy near the BMW shop on Oxford Road. One punter once remarked, 'The strangest thing about heroin is that even when it's complete shite and you're laying in the gutter vomiting while people walk on you, you're still relatively content.'

But it was a sad gig. A girl I knew who was hooked told me, 'I hang out down Moss Side with this same crew of smackheads. They spend all their time and energy shoplifting batteries from every shop between Longsight and the city centre. All day every day, anxious as anything. Then they weigh the batteries in for gear off the dealers. They immediately head to someone's flat to shoot up. Then they sit around talking about all the things they're gonna do when they get *off* the stuff! One night, in exchange for some gear, I deliberately led a guy into a trap where he was attacked by some of the Moss Side dealers. I still regret it. It was one of the shittiest things I've ever done.'

It was an alternative world to that unfolding in the psychedelic clubs, and, like the heroin itself, was delicious and dark. Unless it was white.

While ecstasy took over the minds of the masses, alternative and re-released music flooded the charts. Bryan Ferry's 'Let's Stick Together', Tom Jones' version of Prince's 'Kiss', U2 and B.B. King's 'When Love Comes to Town' and Yazz and the Plastic Population's 'The Only Way Is Up' were all constantly played on jukeboxes. But, with the exception of Ferry, the music was dull and overly commercial; the proper heads stuck to old Perry-boy soul favourites or else embraced the new Madchester bands as a fitting complement to their inner excursions. By now I'd been enlightened as to who that amazing band had been; the possibilities of what their imaginary album might sound like had become a reality, living up to my expectations for a change. I was agog at the Stone Roses, couldn't believe someone had come along with this kind of sound. Happy Mondays were even more alarming, both original and twisted in equal measure. The fact that they were all from Manchester was no surprise; we'd been suspended in an innovative broth for a few years now, waiting for the rest of the country to catch up. I had no idea that so many more bands were about to explode, but I did wonder if any of them knew about Robyn Hitchcock or the American Paisley Underground bands we'd been listening to in Prestwich for the past six years.

The pubs of north Manchester and Salford were alive with opportunity during this period and many characters hit the tops of their games. I became closely acquainted with Andy, a professional grafter, and along with Dave-B- the three of us embarked on an era of wanton recklessness. Andy was already something of a legend in the area; he'd run away with the funfair as a young teen, and spent years travelling Britain, setting up waltzers, sideshows, big wheels and shady deals. He was a big lad, built like a rugby player, with homemade tattoos across his throat, arms and hands. His ability to covertly roll massive joints was well demonstrated. Our HQ was the Ostrich pub on Bury Old Road in Prestwich. We spent most afternoons in there, stealing the cling-wrapped butties off the bar (made by Margaret, the bang-on barmaid) and forcing pool cues through a seam under the Perspex jukebox cover for free credits. We were always careful that Kev the landlord didn't spot our tricks; he was an ex-rugby player among other things, and handy as fuck.

The Prestwich lads had split into two distinct factions demarked by two pubs, the Ostrich and the Foresters. The Ostrich lot were involved in everything from drug dealing and flagging to construction and theft of anything that wasn't nailed down. One mob used to come in on Friday afternoons wearing black ski masks, as they'd been working on some project that involved toxic dust. Us and them shared beers, joints and conversations until one week they weren't there anymore. It transpired that the ski masks had been used for more than dust. They'd carried out a string of bank robberies and had all been arrested. One of our mates had actually been asked if he wanted in on that ill-fated last job, and sensibly declined. The Foresters lot were pure grafters who worked markets with snide gear. They all loved to gamble, and tales of their immense bets at one-card turnovers were legend. These were lads who owed each other thousands. They played a bizarre game of reversal of fortune on the turnovers, the debt moving back and forth and all over the place. Once in a while someone would decide to call in a bet and his counterpart would refuse to pay, insisting on double or quits. This sometimes led to lifelong mates knocking seven shades of shit out of each other.

Andy had many irons in the Madchester fire, and among them was flagging. Flagging entailed stealing Yorkshire stone flags from the streets of the inner city, or from outlying towns. The Yorkie was sold to builders, who paid handsomely for the prized stone. It was dirty, hard work, and the proceeds almost always went immediately on booze and cannabis. Andy wasn't shy about lifting stone from anywhere in Greater Manchester but he had his limits. One night, we'd gone in the Kings pub off Whit Lane in Salford and he'd amazingly rolled a 13-skinner, a gigantic joint, with neither myself or Dave-B- noticing.

'Why don't we do a few streets down here in Salford?' I asked him, sarcastically. He took an extremely long pull on his supersized joint, dragging an inhuman quantity of tetrahydrocannibinol into his lungs, before shooting two intoxicating jets into my face that totally enveloped my head. His red eyes floated in their sockets like jelloid diamonds as he stared into another dimension in disgust, a veteran cobra in a world gone mad. My eyes stung me into wakefulness; getting battered was preferable to being murdered. Salford was not an option, but the city centre was.

By the late 80s the lads involved in the travel and fashion explosion had reached marrying age, but somehow most had declined to take that option; marriage was for tossers and no-marks, for those who had no imagination or balls. The turn-out in local pubs reached a peak. Our generation enjoyed a second wind, a scene bereft of the restraints of children and mortgages, but we weren't getting any younger. United hit a bad patch, and attendances dropped precipitously as drunkenness rose. City enjoyed a brief spell as an average football club, which was much cause for celebration among the blue men. When United won the FA Cup in 1990 it was a portent of silverware to come.

The continental second wave was about to hit, transforming everyone into ecstatic groovers, clubbers and pill-heads. A strange new sun shone on Manchester during this time and those not 'on tour' mobbed the boozers and made nuisances of themselves daily. A huge population of 20- to 30-year old singles (and not-so-singles) assailed the clubs every night, looking for drugs and sex in a feeding frenzy. Subconsciously, the pressure to settle down and buy a house terrified us, so we plied ourselves with powerful cocktails and danced among space-age laser lights in the hope we'd be teleported to another place, where all was paradise. No such place exists, of course. We merely contributed to the growing civil unrest in society, slowly enlightening the mainstream media via a lager, ecstasy and pot-fuelled tornado. Best of all, the women were just as eager to have fun as we were.

The children of the time have their own tales to tell, too. Too young for the clubs and the drugs, they found their own distractions. Johnno was a young kid with a mixed background in 1989. His dad was Australian and his mum came from the very streets where grafter Colin Blaney had been raised. Johnno was a United supporter and a typical scallywag of the time. He recalls childhood experiences with his cousins in Collyhurst:

'My mam's from Collyhurst,' explains Johnno proudly. 'My two cousins, Kevin and Lee, lived down there with my auntie and uncle. Kev was four or five years older so I'd hang about with Lee who was nearer my age. When my mam and dad went to Spain for a week I went and stayed with them. That weekend was one of the funniest I've ever had. Lee was a little scally, like most kids down that way. They were living in a close built around a big playground, a wasteland really. This was where the Collyhurst Flats used to be as described in *Grafters* by Blaney. A decade after they were demolished the "new" estate was already in decline. There was a network of little mazy streets off Rochdale Road; people, especially kids, strolling about everywhere, plus plenty of stray dogs, some vicious and some mangy little mongrels.

'I didn't live in the area so everyone wanted to know who I was. These Collyhurst kids were non-stop, back and forth doing this, that and the other. There was a shop at the playground we went in at least once an hour, money or not. Two kids came legging it out of the shop and a massive bang and smoke bellowed from within. The startled owner emerged puffing and panting. They'd let a Roman candle off inside and it was firing like a bastard. The owner's face was a picture. It was around bonfire night so everyone was building bonfires. We went down to the railway for stuff to throw on our bonfire. It was some sort of junkyard with all sorts of discarded odds and ends. One lad with us had been expelled from school and was giving tips on how to get kicked out. His advice was to pick up a chair and just start twatting your teacher with it. I can honestly say I never took his advice.

'After tea northeast Manchester was under cover of darkness with the constant sound of fireworks and bangers near and far. We sat on the swings and a bloke and a younger lad approached. 11-year-old Lee dived off the swing and shouted, "Hey, you're that cunt who grassed on our Kev! C'mon Johnno, let's get our knives out!"

'This muppet with a shaved head and jam-jar National Health specs nearly jumped out of his skin. He booted his younger companion up the arse and screamed, "Fucking run!" and they legged it. I instinctively chased them with Lee, wondering why we were chasing a grown man. The bloke and the kid were actually screaming in terror. Lee just stopped. He was pissing himself, the mad cunt. Apparently, our Kevin had been arrested nicking stuff from JD Sports on his work experience and this lad had grassed on him. That lad's face when Lee said, "let's get our knives out" was pure terror. I should feel guilty, but I still end up laughing at it after two decades. This was just one weekend I had in the unique entity that is Collyhurst.'

I well remember Salford with my own cousins in the mid-70s at bonfire night. Kids firing air-bombs from Chimney Pot Park at the pigeons on the roof of St Ambrose's church across Liverpool Street. Building bonfires in Kersal, using a telegraph pole for a centre-pole. My uncles lobbing next door's shed roof onto the fire when it threatened to die an early death. The chaos and lawlessness inherent in the inner city is eternal. It never tires and its children are wild and free. In the 70s they were asking a 'penny for the Guy' outside the busy supermarkets and bus stations of the city. They later became the single men and women, the companionless maniacs, who created Madchester; its one-night stands, its jealous territoriality and its fireworks. More than mere pennies were earned. People like Mellow with nothing to lose and everything to gain were among the profiteers:

'I was knockin' out acid for a few years, but the E was too bulky to smuggle. I got rid of a few inside England, but it was mostly moody pills I banged out at that point. I'd done a few E's but it was fuck-all to write home about. I was more into the general lifestyle. The beauty for me was, all's yer needed was a scruffy pair of faded Levi's and a plain t-shirt and you were cool. The summer of 1990 was the peak for the masses, I reckon. We were in them clubs nightly. And raves were the big thing. One night we drove down to the middle of nowhere for a warehouse do. I had 80 E's on me and I got rid within 20 minutes. These were the real McCoy but I didn't realise it. Some punter walked up to me, beaming about my gear. I thought, "Fuck me, if I'd won a million pounds I wouldn't be walking round like that!" The lads I was with dropped some and started dancing when the DJ's lights kicked off. Strobes and colours and all that lark. I thought, "What a pair of knobheads," and dropped one myself. 20 minutes later I was flopping about like a fucking loon. Arms going, hugging punters, shakin' me 'ead with creased eyes like George Michael or something. This DJ put a tune on. Blue lights in tubes were coming down all around me. I could feel this little black hole in me belly growing massive and the whole building was falling into it like a roller-coaster ride. All the smiling faces and the throbbing beat. All the smells of sweat and tinkling laughter from these hippies. It all collapsed into this black hole of goodness inside me. Everything was falling down these tubes of blue light and I was terrified but overjoyed at the same time. I was shitting meself 'cos I thought I'd caused the rave to get swallowed up by my buzz. It was as if the rave and the countryside outside were me and me alone. Then I realised I was off my swede. I was wandering between all the dancers, laughing and kissing people. One of me mates slaps me round the neck and says, "Fuckin' gerra load o' you, you soft cunt!" I didn't come properly to me senses for hours. The music and lights just threw me for a loop. I've never been the same since! The funny thing was, I wasn't even looking to cop off. I just wanted to feel another mad rush with that same buzz, the music and lights all coming together again. I chased that feeling for years. I went all over the world in search of a chemical sensation in my blood. People called me stupid but it didn't stop me.'

Ecologists have an interesting expression they use to describe the animals in a population that fail to find permanent mates, and who consequently become a source of aggravation to those that have. They call these animals the 'bachelor herd'. The bachelor herd is composed of free-ranging males who frequently encroach on the territories of mating couples, having none of their own. It may assume the form of an actual herd, or else is a catch-all term for a loosely-associated population of males in search of ever-scarcer females. The mating couples in a population reproduce and establish territory amazingly consistent in size to that of other 'married' couples. It's a sad grid. The bachelor herd have no compunction about raiding this territory for food, or even trying to mate with the resident female. They definitely like to party. Territory, of course, means property, and most of those on the lag in the late 80s and early 90s were in no condition to buy a house. They were constantly on the move, working and grafting and travelling. But as they voyaged and poisoned themselves, did many of life's later-cherished luxuries evade them? Did the lads who settled at home know something we didn't? Bachelor-herd membership provides protection against aggressive males in the fight for resources, but among the ravers of late-80s Britain we were our own worst enemy.

*　*　*

After an ill-fated engagement to a very intelligent barmaid with real drug problems, I headed back out to the Middle East in July '91 for rest and relaxation. Egypt and Israel, the usual merry-go-round of hard work and uncontrolled partying. Israel was a tense place in mid-'91. Just a few months after the scud missile attacks by Iraq during the Gulf War, everybody carried guns everywhere you went. The Palestinian *Intifada* had also gathered full steam by then. Incidents of murder and bombing were common, ramping up the air of general distrust directed by Israelis against the outside world. I lost a significant amount of weight working on a building site in Tel-Aviv.

The night before I flew home I bumped into Dougie from Surrey, the guy who'd served two years for accidentally killing someone back in

Guildford. Unfortunately, a mate from Manchester had broken Doug's jaw on a kibbutz a while earlier. It was great to see him though. He even offered to reimburse me my flight if I stayed there on tour with him, but I'd had enough. I wanted to go home to see my sister Jane, whose first child Amy was due any day. As ever, Doug had a gorgeous bird with him, a German blonde who was also flying home the next day. Dougie recalled his nights bouncing on a pub door while scuds rained down and the windows were waving like water. We went to a well-known Tel-Aviv bar and got pissed while we watched the movie *Arachnophobia*. Given the yo-yo spiders, it was most appropriate.

I flew into Gatwick, jibbed to Victoria and took a National Express to Madchester on a return ticket crumpled for months in my wallet. I borrowed a pound coin off a woman from Didsbury and took a bus home. I was straight back on the grafting crew. The day after I flew in I went to the pub in town where I knew PG would be. He signed me right up for that afternoon, moving a load of computers. PG had recently split up from his wife and his lifestyle had changed accordingly. We ended up in that tiny hidden HQ in Ancoats, where they were having a serious drink. A well-respected chap had just been released from prison and everyone wanted to buy him a sherbet. A giant Glaswegian from the Collyhurst Flats told us how he'd done a hit of acid the other night and a TAG team had burst through his door in a mistaken raid. Wrong flat. They'd apologised to him and timidly retreated, but his head was in bits. He was six-four, built like a brick shithouse with a voice to match. I swear he could have taken on a bear and stood a decent chance. The notion of him tripping was a difficult one to embrace.

The big United landlord had gone by now, replaced by a smiling, humorous bloke who PG knew well. My return from Israel coincided with a new chapter in the grafting game around town, with PG putting some very productive months in as crew boss. One day a weirdo wandered into the pub, clearly a gangland tourist wanting to catch a glimpse of these legendary characters. They sat him down and started filling his head with all kinds of shite. The landlord introduced PG as 'Mister Apple-Macintosh', and the bloke's eyes were bulging with possibilities and madness. Fuck knows how he interpreted that one. Mister *Rowntree*-Macintosh would have finished the guy off completely, I reckon.

I shared a flat on Salford Precinct with a mate for a while. I spent my first night there hanging from the 15th floor window of Ruthin Court, tripping my brains out on acid. The Salford Lads were swarming all over the precinct. The Brass Handles pub hosted intense techno nights several times a week. The strobes slashed the darkness and the natives danced impeccably. African students from the university sat among it all in silence, impenetrable silhouettes amid mayhem, smoking herb and relishing the wildness of the sounds. Exotica and electronica, gang war and One Love, all coalesced in Manchester at the time. I felt divided as to whether I wished to leave at all anymore, it was so exciting just to be at home. The 1992 European Championships were significant in that Peter Schmeichel saved a crucial penalty in Denmark's semi-final against Holland. We were proud that a United player had been in the spotlight. These days Schmeichel isn't spoken of very highly due to his defection to Manchester City, especially after he wore a blue sweater on derby day. I've always believed Schmeichel such an important component of United's best-ever era that he could do whatever he liked. After all, Eric Cantona does.

11
AMERICAN ROAD FEVER

The road to truth is long, and lined the entire way with annoying bastards.
— Alexander Jablokov

1992 was clubs galore. Music was great but my hunger for the road overrode post-Madchester's attractions. I flew to Orlando in late summer, this time determined to make it to the West Coast. The night before I left I was so nervous I was shaking. Standing in the Red King in Whitefield with Dave-B-, MC Hammer's ridiculous 'U Can't Touch This' pounding from the plastic DJ's deck. At one point the screech of tyres came through the open window and Dave said, 'You'll be hearin' plenty o' that tomorrow night.'

I had little money and no idea what I would do when I got there. I just had to give it a go. I flew, I landed. Met an Australian girl who was lovely, but work was hard to find. I was broke and panicking within days, despite the tropical splendour. Traipsing along huge commercial boulevards full of raging traffic like a demented vagrant bloated on all-you-can-eat buffets. I met a lad in the Orlando hostel one day and he seemed a cheerful type. He noticed the Salford devil tattooed on my arm.

'Alright mate? Where you from? I'm from Stockport,' he said by way of introduction.

He was leaving the next day and had been travelling America on a 30-day anywhere-in-the-USA air pass. He had three days left on it, and held it out nonchalantly.

''Ave it, mate. Just be careful when they ask you your name at the gate. That's the only security they have in place for inner flights, believe it or not!'

This was pre 9/11, and I believed it thoroughly. I tried to go stand-by to Los Angeles, but didn't make it. I had about $20 to my name at that point, and ended up on a puddle-jumper to Key West, more from impatience than anything; I couldn't be bothered waiting for tomorrow. I found a couple of jobs in Key West, but didn't fancy it. Despite its idyllic location on the planet, Florida was subject to annual battering from the forces of nature. Hurricane Andrew hit the pastel peninsula in 1992. The Orlando hostel was packed with refugees from South Florida, sleeping in the hallways. I flew back to Orlando the night the hurricane hit. A small crowd were hunkered in the Key West airport bar, boozing and waiting, watching the news on the big-screen TV. The flight was a nightmare; even the stewardesses were shitting themselves at the massive sheets of lightning blasting through the clouds to our right. The plane was bucking about like a harpooned fish.

The situation on the ground in Orlando was pure chaos. I searched for work as my cash dwindled, and was lucky to find a last-minute job driving a bus for the hostel. I'd been literally walking out the door to return to Manchester when I was called back by an English lad who worked there. He told me they were looking for someone, as the usual driver had left for England. This meant I could have a bed rather than a berth on the floor with the refugees.

When the hurricane arrived, everything went insane. Andrew was the costliest storm in US history until Katrina in 2005. Florida was devastated. The volume of evacuees meant skulduggery was rampant. Robbers, up from Miami to escape the storm, were selling 'magic numbers' and all manner of stolen goods. The south Florida hurricanes were notorious for attracting a convoy of rip-off merchants, cowboy contractors who'd come and take untold fortunes off people as deposits toward rebuilding their homes, only to disappear forever. (I met some lads from Britain who ended up grafting for these cowboys; their stories will be told in due course.) Magic numbers were credit-card numbers people used to make long-distance phone calls. One way to obtain them was to watch over somebody's shoulder while they dialled their personal number. Some even resorted to using binoculars from rooftops in locales with lots of business types. There were networks of criminals all over the country, exchanging the numbers by phone across the USA to keep the authorities off the scent and the numbers active for longer. In this way it was possible to build up a stockpile of the desired digits. It was an industry all of its own.

It seemed like every hustler and scam artist in Miami was sleeping there that week, and it made for some wild nights out. All holidaymakers and residents in southern Florida had been emergency-evacuated to Orlando. Magic numbers were fetching a fortune.

I drove the bus to the Epcot Centre and back twice every day. They gave me a free room and a couple of hundred dollars a week. The pubs all had happy hours with free food, so I ate there. Not the healthiest of diets. The hostel was packed with European girls vacationing after spending the summer working on Camp America. It was easy to become acquainted and I enjoyed a purple patch, women-wise.

It felt great driving down Interstate-4, Orlando's busy main artery, especially at night. The masses of Technicolor neon signs blinking and glowing in the heart of the tropical darkness made it seem like a wonderland. I rarely had more than $50 to my name and was running on sheer adrenalin. I sold my return ticket to a kid from London for $100. I ran into him on the front porch of the hostel eating a whole cooked chicken, gabbing about how amazingly cheap chickens were in America. He'd been working concerts up and down the East Coast, an Anglo-Asian cockney. At the airport I checked myself in and accompanied him to the gate, where we did a little swap and he disappeared through the portal. That night I went out with a cockney girl who knew the lad. 'His parents are multimillionaires. Richard Attenborough attends parties at their home,' she told me. I realised I should have charged him a lot more than $100!

Everyone at the hostel was dealing in second-hand tickets because the security at the airport was so bad. Some lads had been in and out on so many different tickets (including their own) that when they left the States they had no idea whether their visa was 'in' or 'out'.

Inevitably, with all the Yank grafters and lads up from Miami, a mob of English and Americans went out every night on a major piss-up, and it was a rampage; lads walking around in a drunken daze, spunk stains on their jeans from lap dances in the strip clubs. They stuffed themselves silly in all-you-can-eat buffets, which we didn't see in England back then. Some were becoming a nuisance in the pubs on Church Street, Orlando's booming tourist centre. Rodger, an Aston Villa football casual, was well at it:

'There was this big group of us, from England and America, and it seemed we were all a bit reckless and full of brainstorms. One night we went to a club, and onstage was a band performing Village People songs, dressed in the outfits and everything. I thought, "Wow, they sound just like Village People." When I turned around, there was a poster on the wall, advertising for a Village People gig that night. It actually was them. We were tickled pink. There were soccer coaches, football hooligans, globetrotters and general wide-boys, all together on the ale. The lads were selling magic numbers and buying airline tickets. They'd sell them on to other people then shoot off into the wild blue yonder. The hostel in Orlando was a major message centre for the English lads in America, who were steaming all over the gaff. People would be sending clothes, money and contraband to others across the country by other lads who were going that way by Driveaway.'

The route west led to unknown mountains and the Pacific Ocean. Rodger continues:

'We drove from Orlando to New Orleans, 650 miles. 100 miles an hour through a cyclone followed by beaming sunshine. It rained so hard we had to pull over and get the canvas roof up, good style. An hour later, we were rolling it back off again and it was giving off masses of steam. The Interstate ran through the bayou on stilts with massive trees looming on all sides. It was reptile country. If you broke down somewhere in the middle of the night you were alligator food. Remain in the vehicle was the drill. We couldn't believe it was a Saturday afternoon back home. All the lads would've been just sat in the pub. Watching the horse-racing, playing cards and talking shit. Meanwhile, we were flying through a big jungle in Louisiana on a bridge that was a hundred miles long. Well after dark, skyscrapers appeared in the distance. We slipped off the Interstate into New Orleans.

'We went exploring, but it was commercial as fuck. Bourbon Street was hammered with tourists, but every place was a rip-off, and over-the-top. There was no soul there whatsoever, which surprised us. We knew some other groups of lads going cross-country at the same time as us, but it was so packed there was no chance of meeting up with some heads and having a mad sesh. It all looked totally staged and the street buskers sounded like studio-quality musicians. Birmingham was better, I swear. The streets outside the tourist zone were full of litter and rubbish. The place was a right shithole. We didn't even bother getting drunk, but returned to our hotel room instead and had a good kip.

'Next stop was Dallas. If you travelled west to Dallas at the wrong time of year, you might hit a "storm", as they called them on the TV weather in New Orleans. We set off in ignorance, and all day tornadoes and thunderstorms raged out to the northeast, always to the right, and in retrospect that was quite an experience. We did 850 miles that day, and got into Dallas well after dark.'

When those funnel-shaped clouds rips across the landscape in the flashing lightning, all day and night, you wait for the Tin Man to appear on the Yellow Brick Road, believe me. Dallas stands in contrast to New Orleans with its giant glass towers and sleekly configured freeways. There is plenty of oil money there. But in the darkened tangle of motels and highways to the east of town, it has its underbelly.

When we stopped for food at a diner, some blokes told us to stay away from East Dallas; it was a dangerous place. As soon as we arrived in the city we headed straight for it to see what the fuss was about. It was a hot night with a mad stormy sunset. We dropped the Cardiff girl travelling with us off at the motel and set off for a club. The storms we'd been racing all day and night had us awestruck. The club's car park was full of African-Americans and puddles reflecting the dusky red sky. Our white faces must have stood out a mile. A hooker in a mini-skirt approached the jeep convertible, casually giving my bollocks a feel through the window. She spoke to us in a mad drawl. 'Blowjobs $15.' She had a pretty masterful grip. While my attention was distracted she skilfully dipped my wallet, then dissolved into the crowd.

When I realised, the shit hit the fan; we spent several minutes careening around the huge car park looking for her. Gang-bangers from the East Dallas ghetto were jumping out of the way as Rodger zigzagged angrily. I did a quick mental calculation of the probable number of guns there and calmed down dramatically. The wallet wasn't important, money-wise. I was down to just $40 anyway. But contact addresses were in there, too. Contacts are good to have on a continent of endless highways, extensive ghettoes, neon liquor stores, several time-zones, massive, spiritless suburban hinterlands and millions of crazy people. In fact, to an intercontinental jibber, contact numbers are priceless – they are the skeleton that holds together the dynamic web of survival. Crazy Villa boys couldn't be allowed to get you killed for the sake of $40; even if he *had* loaned me that money, it was *my* wallet (and my bollocks).

*   *   *

We headed west the next day. The great state of Texas unrolled at excessive speeds and seemed to last forever. Steaming into the unknown with Nishman's in the sky rocket is an exhilarating sensation. An ability to siphon petrol on the fly comes in very handy. We hit little towns surrounded by sagebrush and open plains. A bald eagle on a fencepost by the road held us in its inhuman gaze.

If you're on Interstate 70 you'll eventually hit Denver, Colorado, at the top of a big hill called the Continental Divide. The geology of the Rockies is distinctively American. American artists reflect the accumulation of fractals in their paint colours, using pigment ground from those very rocks. We were delivering the jeep to Denver and arrived with a week to spare. This meant we could use it to explore the place before handing it back. We unwisely phoned the jeep's owner to tell her we were in town. She became so aggressively insistent that we return it to her immediately that we said no; we'd delivered it in excellent time, and we were perfectly entitled to keep it for a few days. Every day we called to inform her of its continuing good condition, to be met with a shower of abuse and threats. We kept the vehicle until the very last day, despite her saying she'd given the licence number to the police; she didn't have a leg to stand on.

Denver was settled by an itinerant mob of cattle-shaggers and alcoholic gold-miners. They lived in log cabins and spent most of the time talking shite about how they were gonna strike it rich one day – kind of like Rodger and me. Denver was once the second-largest city west of Omaha, Nebraska. The sprawl of that megalopolis Los Angeles put an end to this status. Once a frontier outpost, the 'Mile-High City' was home to a lot of gambling and other activity due to the presence of organised gangs. In time it assumed a more respectable position, perched there on the Rocky Mountains. The cool climate and limited opportunities ensure that it's a tough nut for those in search of work without a visa. Denver is smaller up close than it looks from afar. A cluster of thin skyscrapers melts into residential areas, strip malls and queer little office blocks; I wondered, does having sex in Denver qualify you for membership in the Mile High Club?

The nearby ski resorts provide work according to the season. By now our money was gone and the Lacoste t-shirts were starting to moulder in the holdall. Rodger seemed a bit more concerned about this than me, being a football casual of the 90s. We arrived in early September, so skiing was knackered. Denver once housed the busiest rail-hub in the

United States. Today it's home to the largest airport in America, another throughput centre. People stop off for a shit and a shave before jetting onward to less remote locations. The only jobs freely available were delivering local newspapers. We turned up one morning at the assigned meeting place and were promptly offered a crushed tin-can for a toke. They were smoking rocks in the Rockies. It was seven in the morning and these blokes looked like total wrecks. There were several cans on the go, presumably to fuel some enthusiasm for delivering papers in the mile-high chill of early fall. Middle-aged men smoking crack through perforated tin cans, delivering newspapers for a living. That was our Denver. Not that there's anything wrong with it, mind, if you're a complete twat.

'We found work one day,' remembers Rodger. 'Helping some blokes fit a massive plate-glass slab into a drive-through window at a new bank out in the sticks. It was bang in the middle of a man-made desert. Red sand imported for construction of the sprawl around Denver. The Manc I was with thought it was a real desert! We barely did anything all day. They took us to an all-you-can-eat Mexican buffet afterwards and we all got pissed. One of the blokes let us stay at his house for a few days while we looked for work. It's like that in Colorado. People are very accommodating and will really open their doors to you if they think you're there to be productive.'

It's easy to obtain free gifts in Denver and you don't go hungry. But you must leave after a while, as countless others have done before: west, west, west. The trek across the high, cold deserts is jarring and dreamlike; the blue mountains, lunar landscapes, cliffs and canyons of Utah can be gruelling in a modern car, so the pioneers of old must have been dropping like flies. All the while, California beckons and you press on. After we dropped the Driveaway off in Denver we were hitch-hiking, almost completely broke. A couple of frantic days came to nothing. Food was scrounged or nicked. We chased ghost rumours of Driveaways heading west. We were desperate. Previous attempts to find a pub that screened English football were forgotten; we were beggars, not choosers now. We finally copped a ride off an Aussie and were California-bound. He told us to call him 'CJ' but we couldn't do it. We camped in the Utah desert the first night. Me and the Villa villain, listening to the coyotes howl and the wind sing its alien tunes while Crocodile Dundee slept in his cushy motor.

Once we hit the California border things became cosmetic again. The Aussie tried to kick us out at Sacramento after dusk. We insisted the deal was all the way to San Francisco. He gave in, sullenly pressing on in bare feet and shorts with a bandana around his head, freewheeling down mountain curves on the wrong side of the road. We said nowt. We were English and we didn't give a fuck if we died right there on that picturesque crag. Maybe it was psychological, but when we stretched our legs in Sacramento all the women seemed unusually beautiful. The air tasted different. Even the fast food was better than that encountered in America's neon interior. Interstate-80 delivered us into a different country. The buildings grew progressively larger and swankier. Even the foliage looked high class. We swooped over the Oakland Bay Bridge; there was an initial burst of excitement when we believed it was the Golden Gate – we didn't have an atlas – dying at the sight of the metal trusses rather than suspension cables. Suddenly we were flying down Market Street, a main drag which diagonally dissects downtown San Francisco. It was late and dark, but the neon lights were many.

Using Rodger's last remaining dollars, we checked straight into a low-rent shithole with rats running down the corridors. (I saw them with my own eyes.) We shared a bathroom with everyone else on that floor. The enormous hotel betrayed clues as to its once-grand status, but had slid from being an elegant early 20th-century gem to latter-day seediness and ruin. The foyer was large, dirty, and soulless. We met a black guy from Dallas who said, 'Hey, my buddy's living out here, and earning a living by stripping at a gay club. I'm actually thinking about doing it myself, whaddaya think?' Some good banter went back and forth. Market Street and the surrounding area was a lot older, filthier and more eastern-looking than I expected. It felt more like 1970s Ohio than modern California, like a Tom Waits album cover. There were supermarkets, bars, government buildings, confectioners, gay clubs and arcades full of flashing lights. The general appearance was of a rundown urban core shrouded in neglect and sleaze, especially the Tenderloin neighbourhood.

Rodger eventually had his brother wire him a few hundred dollars from Brum. He moved round the corner to an international hostel where only non-Americans could stay, for some strange reason. Completely broke, I discovered a back staircase and adopted a tiny landing between floors as a bedroom. A quick mooch through the rooms earned me a free sleeping bag which I stashed on the roof under a concrete table. The hostel had a biker bar under it that stayed open till four every morning and the pounding music resounded through the entire structure. It was right off Castro, the gayest street in America.

San Francisco's Chinatown is something else. 100 percent Chinese people everywhere. Every kind of market stall selling weird and exotic foodstuffs. Blokes push handcarts full of laundry up impossibly steep hills. The complex aromas of Oriental food engulf the sinuses. San Francisco also has a quite extensive sex industry. Dozens of peepshows and strip clubs wink and entice. Arrays of neon lights surround graphic descriptions of what awaits the lucky voyeur who ventures inside. And, of course, there is the psychedelic thing.

As world leader in the hippie years, the city still maintains a fair few head shops and other assorted remnants of the drug culture. The colourful houses lining the 11 steep hills upon which San Francisco is built look pretty and quaint. The Haight-Ashbury area still retains an aura of consciousness-expansion and possibility. It's easy to imagine the Grateful Dead, Jefferson Airplane and Janis Joplin enveloped by a purple clockwork fog, talking hippie talk and playing acid-inspired tunes.

Not a single toilet cubicle in Golden Gate Park had a door on it. Whether this was a deterrent to drug users or cottaging homosexuals, I couldn't tell. The city has more than its share of both. The compact, highly-functional neighbourhoods immediately outside the centre are some of the most beautiful and charming in America. The rich blend of residential and commercial is like a neighbourhood dream come true. They sit washed by that gorgeous Mediterranean-like sun.

I often went hungry in San Francisco, sleeping on the back stairs in my stolen sleeping bag, wondering what would become of me. Thankfully, I met a bloke from Bristol who'd just divorced his wife and done a runner with a few grand from the pub he was managing. He sorted me out with some meals and beers while he was in town. Between him and an Anglo-Indian lad called Chris from Eccles, I managed to survive. One night, on a drunken tour of the Tenderloin, we played pool and swapped punches with the locals. We were ejected from several bars on the bounce and finally stumbled into one packed with beautiful women dancing amid smoke and strobes. Unfortunately, they were all transsexuals, proper ones – blokes with threepenny bits. Fortunately, none of us had to find out the hard way, but one Yank bloke did. After wowing a 'girl' all night, drinking cocktails simultaneously with their arms entwined, as lovers do, he left with his prize. A half-hour later he was back, looking visibly shaken. I asked him what had happened but he refused to discuss it. He'd been blinded by the light. My advice to anyone bar-hopping in San Francisco is to make sure that beautiful woman is a beautiful *woman*. And avoid a bar called the Motherlode unless you like she-males.

Fisherman's Wharf was home to a large sea lion population, laying around at the edge of the water like giant leeches. Alcatraz was shimmering in the bay. Farther away, often bathed in thick fog, stood the magnificent form of the Golden Gate Bridge. Chris from Eccles lived in the Mission District, which was largely Puerto Rican and Mexican, and had a reputation as being pretty rough:

'The first night I stayed there, there was a body, taped off on the ground, a gang shooting outside a liquor store,' he remembers. 'Nobody really gave me any bother, as they assumed I was Latino. I was just glad to find a roof over my head. It was always good to bump into a Manc or another English lad out on the West Coast. They were all trying to stay there. These lads weren't tourists like the knobheads with the posh accents, on college-leave doing Camp America. They were working-class blokes who just lived for the minute. It was a bit dodgy at times, but the memories are worth every second. I found some work making cabinets and chilled for a while. I had a great Californian bird who loved me and I just wanted to stay in America.'

The Mission District is unrecognisable these days. Its gentrification has brought numerous trendy ethnic restaurants and galleries, plus urban yuppies eager to make a fast buck, occupy a renovated loft and sample the bohemian delights of hipsterism. It can only be a good thing but, like Times Square, such transformations always leave me feeling that an authentic aspect of the human soul has been quashed forever. A bit like the plastic football grounds in England and the plastic 'fans' who pack into them. Sometimes we need a little nibble at life's underbelly. It's the fat on the pork chop of existence, a treat for being a good little doggy and towing the line. Call it what you want. It smells like blood and it tastes like satisfaction.

* * *

As you pass from northern into southern California you feel the earth settle beneath you. The air-mass undergoes a subtle change and the rocks upon which you ride seem suffused with a more relaxed and glamorous spirit. Things feel fluid and malleable, as if from an earlier volcanic epoch. Monsters and monster-egos roam the earth in search of great adventures. Wannabe film stars, rock singers and models flit around the canyons and beaches. The Pacific manifests as a gorgeous blue curtain off to one side. This entire corner of the continent is hanging off, connected by a supersized crack in the earth's crust called the San Andreas Fault. Earthquakes are never far from one's mind, or a potential tsunami in the vastness of the world's largest ocean.

LA is immense. There are so many identical boulevards intersecting each other that you suffer *déjà vu* on a minute-to-minute basis. This effect isn't helped by the fact that every film you ever saw was filmed in Hollywood. The America trip was always different from those other, more travelled roads; while lads hit Spain, Amsterdam or Germany in droves, there were few English in the States even as late as '92. (Not including Orlando holidaymakers, that is.)

My first morning in LA, an Aussie bodybuilder ripped my sleeping bag to shreds while I was out. He occupied the bunk underneath mine, and the night before I'd kept him awake by singing Doors songs till I was hoarse. It was a late night, spent boozing with a Glaswegian grafter I'd hitched a ride from San Francisco with. He was working concerts across the USA and was loaded. I had 25 cents to my name, literally.

'You fucker!' Aussie Arnie said when he saw me the next day. 'I heard your accent and knew you were from Manchester. I was at the Hacienda the night they sent a bunch of bouncers up from London and they stabbed the lot of them. They didn't just stab one or two . . . they stabbed the facking *lot*!'

It was the Salford Lads he was talking about. Some of the bouncers were his mates. In response to the sleeping bag incident I pissed on his mattress. Twice. One time it wasn't even an accident. He came back to me for advice weeks later when he decided to go cross-country himself. He was loaded up with flyers advertising raves organised by the English in Venice Beach, planning to offload them at the youth hostels he hit along the way. He was quaking that morning, just as I had been in Manchester the night before I set off. It's a fantastic feeling and I envied him; once you've suffered American road fever you never have it again. Some kind of immunity occurs.

I met guys in LA who were totally spent; empty shells where human spirits once dwelled. One German bloke spoke nonsense continually. As a form of self-protection he claimed to be HIV positive. A Colombian called Oscar lived behind a secret partition in the Venice Beach Hostel. The night I met him, he was suffering from the flu:

'Man, you gotta go score some rock for me. I'm sick but I can phone my guy and he can meet you down the block.'

I ventured out to meet a spindly little black guy outside a liquor store. Unfortunately, one of the English football lads had punched him a week or so previous. He recognised me as one of their friends. (I'd been there.) An English guy had been murdered in that neighbourhood just a couple of weeks earlier while scoring at a crackhouse. There was a lot of tension between the two groups. Ignoring his proclamations of my doom, I grabbed the gear and scampered back along the boulevard to where Oscar was pacing his secret apartment. When the chance to leave LA and visit Vegas presented itself, I took it with both hands.

I was to sign-write a motel acquired by a guy from LA. I hitched a ride with a bald-headed gambling fiend from Chicago. He was to be the motel's manager.

'I really shouldn't be goin' to Vegas,' he told me. 'Last time I went there I blew 15 grand in two days.'

He blew five grand in one day and was gone. I spent my nights wandering the vast casinos, those twilit grottos of sin. Back then the strip was already an abomination in neon, with a profusion of gimmicks constantly impinging from all sides. They were building a tower right across the strip from where I lived, destined to be the world's highest. In 1992 it was a huge concrete pole protruding from the earth, just a precursor of things to come.

Vegas was pure casinos, each very different from the rest. The Silver City was probably my favourite. The complimentary drinks seemed to flow that bit more readily there. It felt like the Wild West with its wooden décor, bright lights and friendly waitresses. They sailed about in sexy dresses, carrying trays full of drink orders. They never complained if you snagged a Heineken or a Martini on the sly, as it was all free anyway. The Stardust was another. Its metallic blackness studded with rhinestone and neon stars reminded me of the Octopus ride on Blackpool Pleasure Beach. The Stardust was massive. Dozens of tables sprawled across its main room. It was always packed and the stage was right there. You could watch a singer while you slurped freebies or had the odd dabble at blackjack or craps.

One day I built a giant sign with an Israeli carpenter, a guy with dreads and a mad sense of humour. I was to paint it once it was erected. It was in front of a motel owned by an Iranian guy, right next door to a motel said to be owned by the Mafia. The guys working the desk next door were also Iranian. They watched us work all day with concern. As we pulled the sign into position they informed us their boss wouldn't allow it, as it blocked their own sign. Our Iranian dragged us into their lobby and began pleading.

'*Pleeeaase*, you have to let me make sign!'

The neighbour had a phone to his ear with his boss on the end of it. He wagged his finger comically. No.

'Come on! I have to have sign for customer!'

Words were quietly exchanged down the line. Finger coolly wagged again. They made him pay us for our day's work and we left him literally sobbing on a couch in the Mafia's foyer.

I met a bloke from Manchester there who sold snide passes to the VIP rooms in the casinos. 'Anything you want,' he told me. 'I'll have you playin' cards with movie stars for the right price. I also sell American IDs.' The only other English in Vegas back in '92 were the straight-heads staying up the strip in the youth hostel, and most were backpackers just passing through. I was living at the sole remaining sleaze joint on the entire Las Vegas Strip, a run-down motel called the Casablanca. Eric, who owned the hostel in Venice, had bought the place and intended to bring it up in the world, with my sign-writing skills featuring heavily in the equation.

I ate my evening meal every night at the Circus Circus, diagonally across the street from the Casablanca. The world's biggest all-you-can-eat-buffet made sure I never went hungry. The constant explosion of regurgitated change clattering into chrome winnings trays reminded me that some punters did win in Vegas. The Circus Circus was a gigantic, wooden youth club with a thousand rooms, each more novel than the previous. An American Indian woman called Jo became the Casablanca's manager. She knew how to talk to the gang-bangers. She knew how to do a lot of things, and I ended up spending many a night with her. Her husband was serving 11 years for armed robbery. I figured I'd be long gone when he came out.

One night I was talking to a lad from Macclesfield outside the Casablanca when two Yanks approached us, a black guy and a white guy wearing gang colours.

'Hey Homes, how about doin' some partyin' tonight, huh?' They were staying at the Casablanca and their faces were vaguely familiar.

'We're in town from LA and gonna score some crack. You guys in or what?' We assured them we certainly were and we set off for a crackhouse in north Vegas. In a dim, ransacked neighbourhood we made our way to a bungalow at the end of a cul-de-sac. All the streetlights were broken. The black guy gave a secret knock and hissed, 'Hey, it's me!'

A shadowy figure let us in and we walked cautiously down a long hallway into a room completely shrouded in darkness. The most alarming part was when I heard the click of an automatic. The guy dropped his pistol to his side once he'd established we were safe. My previous research scoring heroin in Moss Side ensured I wasn't totally freaked out, but this was America and life was somewhat cheaper. We were the only white people in the building and the scene was utterly bizarre; little groups in the darkness passed glass pipes about. The place carried the stench of desperation. The black guy turned and said, 'Nigger, let's get the fuck outta here.'

We went back to the Casablanca but returned to the crackhouse numerous times that night. It was the first time I'd been called 'Nigger' or 'Homes' by an African-American, but not the last. Once I established a relationship with those at the crackhouse they told me their tales. One guy said he was on the run from the LAPD for murder. He'd been staying at the Casablanca weeks earlier and one day threatened to throw a TV through a window. He said he was completely innocent. Another had shot a guy in Hollywood and done a runner to Vegas. If my new friends made a decent score they sometimes rented a room at the Casablanca. Their motel room was a sordid nest. Between them they consumed thousands of dollars of rock each week. They smoked it through a short section of car aerial stuffed with gauze. An elastic band was wrapped around the end to prevent burnt fingers. Like the complete twats in Denver, they also used a squashed beer can, perforated in the cradle of the squashed part. The morning after that first encounter was my 27th birthday. I tried, and failed, to sign-write the front window of the Casablanca. I was a complete wreck. All in the name of research.

12

THE SHITE AT THE END OF THE CHUNNEL

The man who has no problems is out of the game.
– Elbert Hubbard

The mid-80s television comedy-drama, *Auf Wiedersehen, Pet*, was about a gang of English bricklayers, electricians, plasterers and carpenters working on a building site in Düsseldorf. It served as a timely illustration of where the British economy was heading. Money and employment were scarce in the UK, and the lure of foreign cash was impossible to resist. Germany was a vigorous place, offering endless possibilities for tradesmen, and a whole subculture evolved. Men would leave for months to work construction as migrants. The break-up of families would, in time, be compensated by relief at the increased earning power of those who took the plunge.

For many, this served as all the proof they needed that Britain was no longer a desirable place to eke out an existence. The utter failure of the Conservative government to provide their people with any kind of trade or manufacturing work caused yet more to head for the UK's exit door. Evermore dissatisfied tradesmen and businessmen were abandoning ship. Young single men who had nothing to lose travelled in droves to Germany and Spain. Many of them had wrought havoc on shoplifting trips back at the turn of the decade, but they were older now, and more sensible – sort of.

For bricklayers, Germany was easy money; everything was automated and the English once more found themselves trailing the continentals in the way they lived. Even the time-honoured business of carrying a hod of bricks up a ladder had been replaced by motorised conveyors, promoting bricklaying to the status of craft rather than penance. Some of my mates were inevitably in on it. Kenny Lewis travelled to Germany with another friend, Paul 'Bucky' Buxton, and a lad called JB, one of the old -school heads from the neighbourhood. The lads went to Germany several times, and several times they had fun and games while trying to be upstanding citizens of the Fatherland.

Germany was a magnet for British and Irish builders, many of whom had good reason not to want to hang around their homeland. It attracted men who were newly divorced, bail-jumpers, chancers, boozers and drunken hooligans. The building projects in Germany's cities afforded easy anonymity, and the inevitable *émigré* subculture emerged:

'One of the first sites I ever worked on in Germany was a massive project involving new apartments and a massive bank in Berlin,' Kenny remembers. 'The site was actually run by an English firm. I couldn't believe the sheer numbers of blokes from all over Britain and Ireland, packed in the cabins in the mornings, all chattering and having a laugh. There was Dublin, Glasgow, London, Leeds, Coventry, Edinburgh, Cork, Manchester, Liverpool, you name it. It was like fucking Vietnam, with every cunt having a nickname depending on where he was from, like Carlisle Col, Guildford Greg or Dundee Dickie. A load of them had a con on; they'd come in for the roll call and then just fuck off to this mad pub all day. The foremen were splitting the wages with them. One day, we decided to do it ourselves. When we got to the pub it was unbelievable. There were hundreds of blokes on the piss, blokes in their 40s and 50s who'd left their wives and done one to Germany. The amazing thing was that at nine in the morning these cunts were dropping E's and dancing about all over the fucking place. Blokes in their 50s! The first day, a lad from Glasgow took us for breakfast to this place on the site. The woman asked us what we wanted to drink, and we got orange each. The others asked for something in German and the woman came back with a case of lagers. JB nudged me and said, "I know what I'll be having for my breakfast tomorrow!" Lads would set up their line and start laying bricks. Every time they returned to the start of the line they'd chug a beer. They'd be on it all day.

'All you needed as a brickie in Germany was a trowel, pins and a level. Some just turned up with a trowel and jumped on someone else's line, throwing bricks down. The funniest thing was the hotel scams. You'd land somewhere and bung them a fortnight's room rent straight away. Then when the third week started you'd tell the hotel owner that you'd have to wait till Friday when you got paid to pay your rent. Come Friday, it'd be bag packed and brought to work and fuck right off with all your gear to another hotel. In Wesel, we stayed in one place that was dead nice. The manager was a right proper sort. But out of our window I could see a red flashing light in a window next door, and I asked JB, "What the fuck's going on in there?"

'"It's a fucking knocking shop innit, you cunt!"

'We went round there, and this posh manager was sat on a big red couch with all these prozzies, saying, "Alright lads?" as we walked in. It'd be beers in the morning, a bit of graft and round to the knocking shop for a blowjob in the afternoon. I was 30 at the time. No spring chicken, but these massive sites were full of British and Irish blokes in their 50s, rolling joints, music playing, lying around on the rooftops stoned. And all getting paid for it.

'The first time we went, in 1993, we'd bought a Manchester Council van that still had its lettering on the side,' laughs Kenny. 'Back home, we'd be driving down the street and blokes would go past in real council vans and beep and wave at us. Their faces would change, mid-wave, as they asked themselves, "Who the fuck are they?" In the end we took the signs off 'cos it was too strange. It was just me and JB that first time. JB was driving and we made good time to Germany. But he lost the plot totally once we got there and decided to go home. He was mental on the piss and he needed to get away from that culture. I wanted to go to Oldenburg to meet a girl I knew. On the way there we stopped at a petrol station. Luckily we did, because the wheel-nuts had come loose on the van and had ground right into the wheel-rims. It was only a matter of time till they just fell off, and the wheel with 'em. We had to get the wheel fixed so we went to a bar to have a drink. We'd been drinking Bitburger beer all the time, as that was the local brew, and we ordered a couple. We ended up chatting to this bloke, who took a right shine to JB's blond hair and blue eyes. He told him he was a brother to him and that he was part of the master race and all that. He even let him stay at his house until the car was fixed. He turned out to be an ex-SS bloke who had memorabilia from the war and everything, a proper mental case.

'JB had let his beard grow into a right Catweazle state by then, with all the boozing. I didn't see him for a few days. We'd been staying in the same room in the hotel and every night it was the same thing; in the dead silence in the middle of the night, you'd hear a cap unscrewing, and then, "glug, glug, glug . . .", as he downed his fix of schnapps. Then he'd be talking gibberish to me in the middle of the fucking night like it was 12 noon or something. Next I heard from him he phoned me at this bird's house and left a message saying, "The van's fixed, phone me at the hotel." I assumed that was it, he'd just shoot off home. It took him seven days to get home. He'd been hanging around in a park with all the drunkards and tramps in Oldenburg, living on the streets! Anyway, he picks the van up and drives directly to the ferry terminal, steaming off his head, and sails to Hull. Once in Hull, still on the piss, he drove back to Manchester. On the way home, he saw a billboard advertising Bitburger beer and nearly shit himself – he thought he was back in Germany!

'When I went with JB and Bucky in '94, we headed for Dippoldiswalde, near Dresden. We started working, me and JB on the bricklaying and Bucky doing carpentry. We went to the baths one day for a swim. On the way home JB announces, "I'm having a shite in these bushes," and he runs off towards these trees like he's gonna shit his pants any second. A few weeks later we're invited to this party by some Germans, but JB won't wear it. He says, "No one's taking me anywhere, I'll drive myself." We go to this bar and JB turns up later, totally smashed, singing United songs. So we all have a good booze and all the old footy songs are coming out. We're fucking arseholed after a couple of hours. He's off his trolley, wasted, and we bump into him again at this party. We get a lift home to the room, which all three of us share. When we wake up the next morning, JB's nowhere to be found. Bucky looks out of the window and says, "Where's his car?" This hotel was in the middle of nowhere and so was the party, so Christ only knows where he's ended up.

'The next minute the phone rings and it's the bloke in the bar downstairs, asking for JB. "Look outside, the police are here," he tells us.

'The cop van was outside, and it looked grim. "I bet he's fuckin' dead," Bucky says. We were well shitting it.

'The police come into our room and tell us he's alive but he's in the nick. Then one of the coppers asks me, "Are you Kenneth Lewis, the driver?" I have no idea what he was talking about. Driver? I still can't drive to this day. We have to go to Freiburg police station, wondering what the fuck he's done now. When we get there, we see him walking past in handcuffs.

'They had to get an interpreter for the interview and they interviewed me. They kept asking, "Who was driving the car? How many drinks did the driver have?"

'After a grilling in the station we went back to the room, asking ourselves how the hell he was gonna get out of there. We looked through his stuff to see if he had any money floating around, but not a carrot. We looked in his bag. Those shitty undies that he'd wiped his arse with on the way home from the baths were still in there, the dirty cunt! Unbelievable. We went to the pub, and wondered how to get JB out of nick. Then all of a sudden he comes strolling in, large as life.

'"Alright lads? Get the fuckin' beer in," he says.

'"Get it in yourself."

'"I can't," he says, "I gave all my savings to the coppers."

'He'd bailed himself out with all his savings, everything he'd earned in Germany. The three of us had a big row that night, and Bucky fucked off to Dresden. Me and JB were left, and the car was a write-off. He'd smashed it into a tree while being chased by cop-cars and helicopters. They'd been after two blokes who'd escaped from prison and, because he was driving all over the road, the helicopter cops thought it was him. When they saw he was pissed out of his mind, they wanted to know where the other guy was. He told them it was me, the daft cunt. We had to go and get all our tools from the site the next day and I had to pay for everything. JB was brassic lint. We went to Dresden, then Dortmund. We took a train from Dortmund to Amsterdam, where we would fly to Manchester. At least that was the plan. We booked a flight from the 'Dam to Manchester in Dresden and right away he opens a bottle of schnapps and throws caution to the winds. I thought, "If you can't beat 'em, join 'em," and got on it myself. We had our bags and tools and everything, so we went and stashed everything in lockers, levels, trowels, the Monty, while we waited for our flight. We bumped into some Aussies and had a bit of a smoke in a few cafés. I ended up losing JB. There were no mobile phones then, really, so we were separated. I went and got my bags and took the train to Amsterdam airport. While I was waiting at the bar for my flight, I actually heard them calling for him over the tannoy. I couldn't believe it. I flew back to Manchester, and that was that.

'A couple of days after I got home, he phoned me. He'd had to ask his missus to send money over so he could book another flight but now he was back, safe and sound.

'"Where's all the tools and presents for the kids?" he asks me. I tell him they're in a locker in Amsterdam fucking train station. He was so bladdered he couldn't even remember that part of it. He'd missed his flight and everything. Now he was back in Manchester and all his gear was in Holland. He decides he's gonna fly back the following day to get everything. He asks me, "D'you fancy coming with me tomorrow to get the tools?"

'"No, not really," I answer.' He'd been banned from Germany for three years after waking up with his head cabbaged, helicopters shining beams on him and German coppers pointing guns at him. Despite that, we went back again the following year, but that went *proper* pear-shaped . . .'

As time lurched forward into the 90s, the British people were forced to ask themselves how they felt about being part of Europe. Many said, 'No thanks!' but most had no problem with the cheap booze and cigarettes available on the continent. Plenty risked covert voyages across the English Channel to return with their duty-free cargo. As firms of smugglers made the precarious journey over water, deep below them the Channel Tunnel was being constructed, another symptom of a shrinking world. Not since the Ice Age had the island of Britain been physically joined to the continent. Modern engineering was sticking the two back together like geological jigsaw pieces with its mighty tunnel-boring machines.

The British government claims it is losing £2-3 billion per year in excise duty to tobacco smugglers. Almost one in five cigarettes smoked in Britain has been smuggled into the country by criminal organisations or small firms of grafters. Criminal gangs fight a daily battle with British Customs as they attempt to improve on this number, while the authorities seek to reverse the trend. Counterfeit cigarettes are big business, too. The well-known brands are generally targeted for consumer faith, and many cigarettes smoked by Brits today are not what they seem. Cardiff boy Jeff Marsh became involved in tobacco smuggling around this time, and remembers how things were:

'It was the early 90s, and suddenly everyone was going across to France to buy the cheap beer, wine and tobacco, which was cheap as chips over there,' Marsh fondly recalls. 'Me and my mate were students, so one of the local gangsters asked us to drive trips for him, and he'd pay us £50 a trip. We were over the moon with this and started going twice a week, but before long we would be going every other day as greed kicked in. We would leave about 4:00 pm from Barry, and when we got to the services at Reading we would have a burger meal, then dump a shedload of base [speed] into our coffee to keep us up for the long night ahead. We'd be flying as we wellied it down the M25, talking 100 miles an hour about all sorts of shit. On the ferry we'd be sat in the bar, whizzing our boxes off, drinking coffee and eyeing up all the continental birds. We'd arrive at Eastenders [beer warehouse in Calais] in the early hours and load up with hundreds of cases of lager and wine, then we had to drive for another 45 minutes to just across the Belgian border to load up with tobacco, which is dirt cheap there. We used to pull out several cases of beer from the middle of the van, then shape the small bundles of tobacco to roughly the same size as the crates, then put the beer back on top. To the untrained eye, it looked like we only had beer and wine on board. The biggest problem was the tobacco used to stink to high heaven, so we used to tip diesel in the back of the van to disguise the smell.'

The Chunnel was the latest in mankind's line of larger-than-life engineering megaprojects that stretched back millennia, from the Great Pyramid to the Apollo missions of the late 60s and early 70s to this gigantic hole in the ground. Its construction would open the door to European holidays that no longer required sailing or flying. It was a new variable in the equation that was grinding up human experience into a homogenous mass of cultural sameness. But the lads didn't care about that, they just wanted to score some speed for the long haul, grab some contraband and bring it back to Blighty so they could earn a butty. As ever, various agents of law and order sought to obstruct them. The British lads' attempts at overcoming these barriers proved both nerve-wracking and hilarious in equal measure. Appointed protectors of decency were rarely decent, and often grabbed the opportunity to scoop free swag for themselves. Marsh and his mates were afforded a novel glimpse of foreign policing in this moonlit world:

'Going through the Belgian border they usually didn't stop us, but coming back was a different story. All these army steroided-up types, armed to the teeth, used to take your passport off you. They'd argue with each other in a foreign language, open the van and say, "You are overloaded, please leave ten crates here," and make you take off ten crates. Another time, we had a bottle of Southern Comfort in the front of the van we had bought on the ferry and one of them reaches in and says, "For me? You shouldn't have bothered," and took it. We weren't about to argue with them, and they knew it. Some other boys I know were stopped there, strip-searched and a small amount of weed was found on one of them. They were taken to a police station, stripped naked, hosed down with freezing water and in the morning fined £50 each. We were getting a bit fed up of the hassle at the Belgian checkpoints. Then, one night, we noticed another van, containing guys we had seen on the ferry lots of times, leave the tobacco warehouse in front of us and pull off the main road down a dirt track. We followed them and it turned out it took you through some tiny villages and then back onto the motorway on the other side of the checkpoint. Happy days. That was the last time we were robbed by Belgians anyway.'

'Spanish Dave' was another character who took advantage of the smuggling situation to bring vast quantities of alcohol and tobacco into northern England. He describes how entire networks of smugglers would form and disperse with their booty once back in the UK, to offload it and then hotfoot it back across the Channel for more:

'They called me "Spanish Dave", but there were about five or six "Spanish Daves", as well as "Turkish Tommies", "Greek Gerries", "Portuguese Petes" and "French Franks" on every ferry and train that went across or under that Channel. Once people knew about the opportunities over there they flocked, man. Like a swarm of locusts. Every ferry had at least one little mob on its way to do the business. Some of them went all the way to Turkey or down to the south of Spain. They knew other English lads who made a living off the ciggies. If there was a drought or a sting on somewhere, the lads would always let you know. If some dealer called open season on for a week or two, then the word went out and it was chaos. Everyone bang at it, going for loads of baccy like there was no tomorrow. I was getting on a bit, I looked more like a worker or a holidaymaker and that made it easier. A couple of younger lads who went with me sometimes even took off on a coach and we'd meet up on the ferry to do the final leg in the van. We called it "the acid test". I knew a few younger lads from United, and through relatives and friends could get lads from other teams to come over with us. When we got back up north with the gear, everyone in every pub in north Manchester or Sheffield or Preston was waiting for cigs. I'd barely get chance to order a pint before they'd mob me, saying, "C'mon Spanish, get yer fuckin' fags out. I'll have five 'undred off yer!" We did a bit of booze as well, but there wasn't much point, as everyone wanted the toe-rags [fags] off us, and it was lucrative times, no question.

'A few years ago the Spanish cracked right down on the cigs going from Spain to England. All the big-time stuff got snuffed out, so that was limited to Spain. No more containers or anything like that. There's a huge market in Spain though, so the grafters started knocking the fags out over there. Some have been nicked and that puts people off. I kept it small and crossed the Channel I don't know how many times. I lost count long ago.'

Spanish Dave was never arrested during his smuggling career in the early 90s. It was during the 1980s where he earned his stripes, smuggling Levi's into Russia, which he would sell for a small fortune. But the Russians caught him:

'To be honest, the thought of getting nicked in France or Spain never bothered me one bit. When I got lifted in Moscow in the 80s, I absolutely shit me britches. Thought to meself, "This is it, cunty, now you've got yerself into a proper mess and these boys don't piss about." I'd read a good few books about people arrested in Russia on trumped-up charges, never to be seen again, or held in tiny, chimney-shaped cells, forced to stand in their own excrement and tortured daily for months to admit to "spying". I'm not ashamed to admit that I was sobbing like a babe and utterly terrified, the first night in that cold stone cell in Moscow. As it turned out, my abject fear and the obvious nature of my crime – two large suitcases packed with pairs of Levi's and nothing else, intended for sale over 48 hours and a quick exit as usual – convinced the Ruskies that I was no spy. They gave me a severe dressing down and deported me, telling me that if I ever returned I'd disappear into a black hole in Siberia. I stuck to playing the stock exchange for a few years after that, but I went back on the road when the cigs and beer thing started up a few years later. It was just too good to turn down.'

Mad Welshman Marsh and Co were seasoned bad lads by this time, and they shared Spanish Dave's lack of trepidation when it came to avoiding the European police. But Marsh recalls that it wasn't always plain sailing; even on your own doorstep, the shit can hit the fan:

'We never had any hassle from the French police at all, but coming back into the UK was where the real hassle started. As you drive out through the tunnels, there are two lanes, with a customs point in the middle. Loads of guys in yellow jackets are stood around, who seem to have lists of number plates. Every so often they wave certain vehicles into hangars on either side [the search areas]. Many a time we sailed straight through in our Transit, only to see poor bastards we had been at the tobacco warehouses with being tugged.

'We would try to drive out and position ourselves behind one of the many vans full of Asians, who we thought would be more likely to be pulled, as it's obvious the booze will end up being sold on in their shops. This usually worked, but one night we were behind a van of Asians who had a van full of Stella, and we were so sure they would be pulled. As it happened, they sailed straight through and we were stopped. The customs weren't that bothered about the booze, although we knew plenty of boys who had had their whole load confiscated. What they really wanted was tobacco, as they know that's where the big earner is and the biggest loss of revenue to the UK.

'We were sat on a bench, whizzing our nuts off, and customs were climbing all over the van. Our advantage was we didn't look worried, because if they confiscated the load, it wasn't our money; the gangster behind it fully expected to lose the odd load, so our only problem would have been how to get home from Dover. Customs guys kept coming over saying things like, "What's the booze for, boys?" We'd say, "Engagement party," but all the time they are staring into your eyes, trying to see signs of fear. If you had drugs on there you wouldn't be able to stay calm, you'd be crapping. They let a drug dog loose on the van and we sat watching as he sniffed around the boxes. The tobacco was hidden right there. They even lifted the dog onto the roof to sniff about. Obviously the dog is not trained to sniff out tobacco or we would have been fucked. He was only there for drugs.

'A customs official then said that they felt the dog's senses were being baffled by the strong smell of diesel we had tipped in the van. They were sending for a bag of heroin to plant on the van, to see if the dog could find it. Our bottle started to go now, as we thought they were gonna plant smack on us and stitch us up. They came back with a leather bum-bag which they said contained ten grand's worth of smack. One of them lifted some random crates and hid the smack under it. A few crates to the left and he would have found the tobacco. Phew! They let the dog back on, and he found the smack straight away.

'They told us we were free to go and lifted up the massive roller shutters, so off we went. A few minutes up the road and a traffic cop pulls us over. He says, "I think this van is overweight, follow me to a weighbridge." We followed him onto Dover docks to a weighbridge. He checked the chassis-weight capacity and told us we were over the limit. He had the power to seize the van. We said, "How many crates over are we?" He said, "Five or six." We said, "If we leave six crates on the roadside, can we go if we promise it won't happen again?" He agreed and we left, six crates lighter, having donated the booze to the coppers' Christmas bash, no doubt.'

As expected, the frequent travellers involved in tobacco smuggling became known faces among the customs officers and police working the main ferry terminals, and soon their names became known to patrolling officers. Typically, the authorities engaged the smugglers, addressing them frequently by their names – just as the Football Intelligence spotters did with known hooligans at football games – as a way to demonstrate their proficiency and ensure their subjects didn't become emboldened through anonymity. Marsh, of course, was no stranger to football violence, having served a two-year sentence for the stabbing of two Manchester United supporters, as well as being involved in the smuggling of illegal weapons like CS gas from France. Slowly, he and his mates' faces became known by those policing the border at the point used most frequently by the Cardiff. Marsh sensed it was time for a change:

'After this time, we started to get pulled and harassed a lot. They started calling us by our names, saying, "You throw a lot of parties." One of our mates who also went regularly had his van taken from him and kept by customs. They had brought in a law that, if you were smuggling, they could seize the van you were driving. If it was a hire van they would make the hire company come and get it, so you would lose your deposit and the hire company would chase you for all the costs involved in recovering the van. I picked up the local paper one day and saw that some guys we knew who did regular trips had been busted and jailed for nine months. Even though the court accepted that they were only driving for a Mr Big, who they had refused to name. That was the end of it for me and my mate. It just wasn't worth it any more. We had been getting £50 a trip but had made more profit by buying duty-free fags, spirits, etc, to sell. After the first few times of having crates "stolen" from us, we sometimes used to tell Mr Big that we'd had ten crates taken off us and would keep them for ourselves. We worked out that, even after he paid for the van, our wages, diesel, ferry fare, etc, he was making £700 profit a trip. He had a lot of vans going every week. The guy's in jail now, doing a ten-stretch for a drugs conspiracy after moving up the ladder to the big time and coming unstuck.

'I reckon we were one or two trips away from being nicked, so we got out at the right time. We had a top laugh doing it. It's mad to think that now you can go over to Europe and bring back as much as you like with no hassle, unless they catch you reselling it. My days as a smuggler are good memories, but it was a time and a place that came along for me when I was young enough to want it. I wouldn't change my life one bit, but you've got to stay paranoid if you want to get away with a lot of this stuff and them that forget that are the ones who relax and end up behind bars.'

This happened to a lad from our neighbourhood, but he was smuggling amphetamines, not tobacco. Steve was apprehended at English customs driving a vehicle which he believed contained a fair-sized lump of speed. A customs search revealed an amount ten times larger than Steve believed was actually there. It turned out he was being used as a decoy by a gang using the same ferry. He was sentenced to a decade in Canterbury prison. When he came out, I bumped into him at the dole office one day.

'What did it feel like when you got pulled over, Steve?' I asked him. He shook his head and gave me a wide-eyed smile.

'I fuckin' *shit* meself, mate.'

It was symptomatic; people were either running away abroad or taking ever-greater risks back home. Either way, it led to trouble. Mellow was glad to be out of it, for the most part:

'I was doing a regular burner to foreign climes as me mates were getting deeper into shit in Manchester. One time a little syndicate got together to do a deal, a lad whose cousins ran snide shops and another bloke whose brother-in-law grafted with us sometimes. A third party brokered it with the Cheetham Hill mob for a weight of sputnik. They turned up at McDonald's car park and did the deal. Halfway home they rolled a joint with the gear and it was total snide shit. A lot of money was at stake. They went back to the pub in Cheetham Hill. It kicked off, and the lad whose money it was got fucked-up bad. They shot him, stabbed him, poured petrol on him and set him on fire. He ended up with a round-the-clock police guard in hospital. The main lad who'd stepped up against the Hillbillies was now a wanted man. They were cruising his street in a brand new Merc, sending out the message big time. He had to fuck off away for a while till the heat died down. I thought, "Thank fuck I'm out of it all!"'

Indeed.

13

MARRAKECH EXPRESS

The most hazardous part of our expedition to Africa was crossing Piccadilly Circus.
– Joseph Thomson

Large numbers of individuals hitting Spain, Israel and Egypt led to a taste for things North African. Morocco offered some seriously exotic adventures to those prepared to run the gauntlet of millions of beggars, thieves and conmen. There weren't many of the usual nutters around, so the endless boozing sessions were not going to happen. Just as well in a Muslim country. It was all about exploring, and in Morocco there was much to explore. Relatively close to England, the country held much which could put a lad in serious trouble if he failed to keep his wits about him. Keeping your wits about you in a country responsible for producing over 40 percent of the world's hashish was not an easy thing to do, though.

When I bought a cheap ticket in early 1993, everything in Morocco looked timeless, quintessential African or *Arabian Nights*. The tiny towns in the High Atlas Mountains resembled something from prehistory; stark cafés with hanging carpets, holes in the wall selling myriad spices and condiments, women working in the fields with buckets hung on their backs, picking leaves and buds. Bound for Marrakech by bus, I took a short break in a tiny town. I was stood in an alcove containing a wild-looking Berber man selling mint tea and wafers. As I sipped my refreshing beverage, another white person came from nowhere and bought a drink. He looked like he might be Italian, or maybe even Native American. He was wearing a strange silver suit that resembled sharkskin. His top button was undone and a black tie hung loosely from his button-down collars. His hair was straight, dark and shiny, worn in a longish 70s style, and his features were streamlined and quite gleaming. I was shocked when he opened his mouth to order, and a thick northern English accent flowed from his cakehole.

'Eh oop, lad, ah'll 'ave some o' that tea thou's servin' thur,' he chortled sarcastically to the vendor, cocking an inquisitive glance in my direction. I asked him where he was from, but really wanted to blurt out, 'What the fuck are you wearing a suit and tie for here?'

'Ah'm from near Rotherham,' he told me, expertly pouring a second cup of tea from the ornate silver teapot from a considerable height, Moroccan-style, without asking the vendor, who was now sat on a low stool and virtually invisible. The mysterious Yorkshireman flicked his hair back from out of his eyes, and hissed.

'What yer after?'

'Eh? Oh . . . no, I'm just travelling round, having a laugh,' I told him, but he looked unconvinced.

'What yer *after*?'

'Whatta yer got?' I enquired, absently. He feigned outrage at my unintended sleight.

'Wha-?! Wh-! You fuckin' name it, lad, I've got eet!'

A long list of hash products was trotted out; names, number, hybrids, pedigrees, all champion tackle. He was a seasoned campaigner in the cannabis trenches, throwing out the various geographic locations like a wine connoisseur discussing vineyards and their myriad beneficent qualities. This place had good soil, that one had decent sun, the other was fed by an underground stream and caught the wind at the right time of year – excellent for transplanting such-and-such a bush from Asia. He talked at length like a salesman who doesn't even care if you buy – so long as you allow him to at least demonstrate his extensive knowledge of the trade, along with a few statistical analyses of why he was so great at what he did. I listened, rapt, and walked away with a lump of hash whose colouring and aroma were otherworldly. As I clambered aboard an ancient bus, I was still wondering where the guy lived, slept, ate, etc. Rotherham has fascinated me ever since.

The road to Marrakech terminated in labyrinthine streets whose red stucco buildings were coated with tiles inlaid with dizzying geometric designs. The psychedelic grid opened out into the insane Jemaa l-Fna (pronounced 'jar-il-afna') Square, the focus of the madness. I checked into a hotel in a corner of the square. My room was a grand affair, large brass cauldrons and huge plant pots with small palm trees in. There was a covered courtyard in the centre of the building, with a high stained-glass roof, which I could see through a big open window in my room. There were louver shutters on the exterior window, overlooking the square and its ocean of babbling calamity. The people teemed like hungry ants and smoke rose from numerous tents. There were groups of people trickling into and out of the square via a series of small portals arranged about its edge.

Jemaa l-Fna Square houses innumerable entrances into a mazelike arrangement of roofed corridors, composing the largest covered bazaar in the Islamic world. The covered bazaar, the suuqs, is a dream come true for those who seek exotic and somewhat stereotypic intensity in foreign corners of the globe. There were merchants selling fabrics, leathers, handicrafts, perfume, gold, spices, carpets and animals. Once in a while you'd pass a lad in a Fila t-shirt and a pair of decent hiking shoes, but there was no time for fucking around; there was too much to see.

One day, I wandered through the suuqs for over two hours and at one point was very definitely exploring a non-commercial avenue. It was all ramshackle apartments and caves, and I was getting some funny looks. I had to turn back and re-enter the dark tunnels, following my instincts for long periods, eventually emerging into the square at an entrance completely opposite from where I'd gone in. It was a mesmerising place.

The square itself was packed with boxing matches, snake charmers, fire eaters, magicians and scores of food vendors, with tables and chairs in tents lit by strings of naked bulbs. I stumbled upon a little fox cub tied to a stake driven into the hard-packed red earth of that red city. It looked terrified, bewildered by the activity and the Arabic music. Pickpockets, drug dealers, prostitutes and tricksters were everywhere, doing their thing and trying to get by. Anything you wanted, you could have: a pink elephant, a young girl, a gold bar, a game of high-stakes cards. It was one of the first places I'd been where I was wary of them robbing from me. It was usually the other way around.

The few English I spoke to were interesting sorts. The usual discussions of traveller's cheque fraud, counterfeit foreign money, snide train passes and drug smuggling were always conversation starters. I filed all information away in my growing anthropological dossier for future reference.

There was a lot of hash about; chunks as big as small cars, to be exact. I travelled by bus from Marrakech to Agadir, a smaller city in the south, and met some Moroccans whose father owned a plantation in the Rif Mountains. Along with a couple of girls, we went on a walkabout. We saw some truly awe-inspiring vistas, overlooking an entire continent. I chilled out for a while, enjoying the company, the ancient minarets, the ragged squares and the other attractions. The dusty streets were bright, sandy and sun-blasted. But this appearance masked what went on inside the multi-storey stone apartment blocks. Malcolm, a well-spoken Londoner, describes a visit to a local party:

'Late one night in Agadir, the Moroccans led me through a maze of crumbling apartments that looked as if they were constructed from dried mud, about five floors in height. There was no asphalt on the roads, just dust that had been there for thousands of years. Arabic prayers were wailing from speakers on nearby minarets, and all along the bottoms of the buildings there were old men and women, just hanging out on chairs, staring into the night. Inside this apartment block we went into a room on the second floor. Instantaneously, I was transported back to the twentieth century. It was like a bucket of cold water in the face. There were some other English in there. The place was thick with smoke from scores of pipes, bongs and joints. But the most alarming aspect of it all was the music. It was pure techno, and the stereo was a state-of-the-art thing. Everyone was dancing like mad. The locals were pushing their product on us, and weren't taking no for an answer. They had girls there, and they were also for sale. They could get you anything you wanted, they said. It was incredible, this full-on rave taking place inside a building that appeared to be prehistoric!'

I met a Yorkshire lad there who had an expression of pure terror etched in his face. He was the utter antithesis of the stranger encountered in the Atlas Mountains. A Leeds fan who had never been a hooligan, but had somehow been caught up in hippiedom. As we shared a pot of mint tea at a pavement café, he explained why he looked so doomstruck:

'I come 'ere with three grand cash with the intention o' buyin' up a pile of hash,' he drawled. 'The first night I went to meet these Moroccans, and they told me they had to make sure me money was genuine an' not forged. They took it away, an' only brought half of it back, sayin' the cops had nicked t'other 'alf an' there was nowt they could do about it!'

I nodded sympathetically; from what I'd seen it could happen to anyone. He was big lad and could obviously look after himself. Unfortunately they had him in the grip of fear.

'Anyway, I bought a massive brick of hash and they delivered it to me room,' he continued. 'I'd already had to move to a cheaper room 'cos me money was nearly gone, and they brought me a right lump. Then they took me to a party, and there were girls there and music and everythin'. I went wi' one o't' girls, and the next day the dealers were back, tellin' me the same coppers were after me for child molestation! They threatened to grass me up to the coppers if I didn't give them back their big lump of hash. I told them to fuck right off, and went and locked meself in me room. Every noise I heard, I thought it were the police comin' to lock me up for the rest o' me life. By the end of the afternoon I was shaking like a leaf! I ended up lobbin' the chunk out of the window and being relieved I'd got rid of it. Fuck knows how I'd have got it out of the country anyroad.'

I spoke to other lads there, and a surprisingly large fraction of them had similar tales to tell. The Moroccans were very adept at lulling foreign visitors into a false sense of security, and then pulling the magic carpet from under them in a trice. They would offer to change money at higher rates, to find you a girl or drugs. Basically they just took your cash and gave nothing in return. They always used the police as a shield to hide behind. Victims who'd smoked hash, been with or at least given alcohol to a girl (who was in on it) were terrified into not going to the police once they realised they'd been ripped off.

The security technology at Agadir airport far exceeded anything I'd seen anywhere else in the world; three-dimensional X-ray images in full colour of each person's bag on a television screen, moving in real time. It wasn't a place you'd want to smuggle drugs through. You should probably only do it if you *really* want to get nicked. And so, back to England I went.

*　　*　　*

I hadn't been home long, painting signs for clubs and pubs around town, when I saw an advert in the *Manchester Evening News*. The position asked young people to interview for a job travelling in Italy, selling oil paintings to corporations in the major cities. I phoned the number and arranged an interview in the Portland Hotel, one of

Piccadilly's biggest and poshest. When I arrived at the Portland, I was directed up to a room where an office suite had been set up for interviews conducted by a bloke in an unbelievably expensive-looking Italian suit, with an inner-city Manc accent. A woman who spoke in a similar tongue was present. They made it very clear they were looking for beautiful young girls who were fluent in Italian. The bloke looked hard as nails and not to be fucked with. Whoever they were they were organised, no doubt about that. I toddled off, and thought, 'You win some, you lose some.'

A few weeks later there was another advert in the paper, for selling oil paintings on the beaches of Spain. I called and was told to report to the Mitre pub near the cathedral. Not quite the Portland but a nice little boozer nonetheless. A weird interviewer called Dave with a half-arsed Australian accent saw potential in me. He told me to be outside the Mitre on an afternoon the following week. I turned up and there were more people waiting there, a girl from Walkden, a Kiwi bird, a lad from south Manchester, a Geordie and an Irish lad. I had about 25 quid to my name – after all, it was only Spain, 'round the fucking corner really. As we were about to take off, a lad from Swinton called Marcus ran up and jumped aboard. One of the boys.

'Fuckin' graftin'?' he shouted over his shoulder from the front seat. 'Me and me mates 'ave bin at it for years. Spain'll be a doddle, no problem!'

We made our way down the motorway towards London, where we were due to pick up a cockney. Marcus provided a non-stop barrage of information about grafting in the Mediterranean, Manchester United and world travel as we went. Dave looked sheepish in the face of Marcus's enthusiasm and encyclopaedic avalanche of street slang. We stopped at a pub for a piss, so we retired to the lounge for a quick couple of jars and a discussion about Spain. Dave looked annoyed but resigned when we emerged, and off we set. My money was almost halved before we left northern England. I helped myself to a few decent books and sandwiches from the service stations as we hurtled south. The cockney clambered aboard right at Piccadilly Circus and we parked up at Dover ferry terminal. We crossed the next day. The fact that Dave arranged to pick the Londoner up at one of Europe's busiest junctions should have told us he was a complete dildo, but we didn't notice at the time.

'That Walkden piece has got a right set of bladders on her,' Marcus muttered to me in the van. He was so love-struck he felt obliged to use a Manchester steak pudding as a simile.

'You've got a chest like a chippy, darlin'!' he enthused drunkenly, falling about laughing as the others tutted. On the ferry, the Geordie tried to caution us about our language and drinking, but in the middle of his sermon the boat lurched violently. He was flung down a flight of stairs, landing in a heap at the bottom. We were in stitches.

The journey through France was fabulous, stopping off in tiny cobblestone hamlets with stylish brassieres and cafés. We spent the night in one bar with a jukebox loaded with English punk rock. Some gorgeous French birds got pissed with us and we pogo'd round the bar until the early hours. It was brilliant, and the only downer was the fact that miserable Dave refused to wait for us the next morning if we went home with the French girls. I was down to my last pound at this point.

We rammed it through France and the twisting roads of the Pyrenees. It nearly killed me, hungover as I was. Dave was getting far too Man United (excited) for his own good on the hairpin bends. At the Spanish border we all walked across while Dave drove the van. The paintings were hidden in panels under the floor and he didn't have a permit.

'We'd better be on the look-out for cockney twats once we get to Spain,' Marcus told me. 'The ICF are running the place. Where's Salford when yer need 'em?'

Spain was hammered with cockneys. While Dave tried to obtain a permit in Barcelona we hit the promenades, knocking out the paintings. The paintings were manufactured in the Far East by schools of artistic grafters. The canvasses came on a huge long roll, played out along a succession of painters on a conveyor belt. They each applied their assigned colours to the allotted areas, like a human screen-printing train. Once the pictures were finished the roll was cut into individual paintings.

Each different picture was produced by the hundreds. They were the business. It was piss-easy to sell them, as they looked like originals. We had about 20 different pictures and could easily display each as a one-off. Once or twice the cockneys came over to investigate but we blanked them. As we progressed into Spain, from Tossa to Llorett to Blanes, the character of the towns changed, as did the numbers of cockneys. Beautiful towns were completely overrun by hordes of British bulldogs who acted like they owned the place. Listening to Cass Pennant, it seems that they did. They were working the doors, dishing out flyers, serving in cafés and hanging out on the beach smoking herb. And that was just the tame ones. The big boys were buying the deeds to bars and clubs and sticking their fingers into cigarette-smuggling operations. It's the way of the world that all great adventures eventually become businesses, be they smuggling runs, grafting souvenirs or even English football clubs.

According to Pennant, Tenerife was certainly locked down by this time. The numbers of cockneys there had reached saturation point. The club culture was well-known to Spanish authorities and was on its downward arc. Whether Marcus of Salford's ambitions could have dented it was superfluous to the point.

'The next stage Playa de las Americas moved into was the rave era that started late 80s and moved into the 90s,' Pennant remembers. 'It was the Lineker's Bar celebs' haunt/thrill-seekers scene. This followed about the time of the Old Bill clampdown of the known football faces on the island, which cut the violence and returned the Americas to a safe holiday resort once again. Which, it could be said, in a ironic twist allowed and made way for even more serious business-type characters to buy in and do what they do; the timeshare sharks and the rest of it. If I look back upon as it was in the 80s, Americas was a young person's resort inhabited by the English that was, at times, pretty much lawless. For Chrissakes, they only ever deported you if you were nicked and that had to be for something more serious than fighting. They had seen enough of the English ways to assume we just loved to fight, even if we were on holiday. And who could complain when we are first-class in stereotyping all foreigners ourselves?'

The English menace was being repelled and we arrived just as the operation was underway. Marcus was a joiner by trade but he had the travel bug, big time:

'I went down to London to work on that Barbican Centre,' he said. 'I made more money under Maggie than I knew what to do with, so I'll never slag her off to anyone. If you've got the sense to learn a trade the Tories will reward you. It's only the knobheads who complain 'cos they've got no ideas. After that I fucked off to Crete for a few months, working at anything I could. I worked in this gorgeous restaurant and put loads of weight on, the food was so good. The Greeks are fuckin' mental. They just come out with totally out-of-order insults to each other. Scream in each others' faces! Like, *I will fuck your mother* and things like that. I thought, *Fucking hell, if you said that round Swinton they'd break yer legs!*

One evening I went out and soon had a massive crowd around me, right on the seafront. They were biting big-time and the money rolled in. All of a sudden the punters were distracted and silenced. I turned to see two Spanish policemen standing to my left.

'You do not have permit,' one grimly informed me. 'I have to close your shop now.'

A quick glance at the peeping local proprietors of knickknack shops told me everything. Our paintings were vastly superior to their bric-a-brac and they wanted to be rid of us. The copper tried to seize my swag. I swept it up and legged it round the corner, into a burger joint. I scoffed a cheeseburger, listening to the Thompson Twins' 'We Are Detectives' playing on the jukebox. I'd never realised it was such a good song. Fortunately, I'd organised to meet a few vacationing couples at the same spot the following morning, to sell them certain paintings they'd fallen in love with. This came in handy, as I was utterly potless and living on Marcus's considerable generosity. I flogged a load of paintings and told Dave I'd sold none. Then we threatened to launch his head into orbit unless he produced the money to get us home to Manchester and gave us a lift into the centre of Barcelona. Dave forked out the cash but dropped us outside the wrong train station. Typical.

'Bollocks!' Marcus spat. 'Let's go and see the Nou Camp.' We did just that and enjoyed a great day in that Mediterranean city. We ended up on a London Victoria-bound bus, pissed as farts. Nobody had knobbed Chippy-Chest, but it was irrelevant. We thieved our way home and disgraced the name of Manchester on the coach by holding loud and obscene discussions on many taboo topics. It sounds great, but standing around in French coach parks waiting to have your collar felt over a packet of crisps isn't as glamorous as it seems, believe me. Back in Manchester, Marcus gave me a quid for a tram back to Prestwich at midnight on Market Street. Barring a piss-up in Swinton a few weeks later, I never saw him again.

PART 4

INTERCONTINENTAL JIBBING

14

THE GOLDEN WEST

Crime is a product of social excess.
–Vladimir Lenin

Colin Blaney's crew claim to have invented many of the slang words associated with late-20th century 'lad' culture. Perhaps the best-known and most enduring is the expression 'jib'. Jibbing means getting something for nothing, jumping a train, or a coach, or even a plane, to a football match without paying the fare. It means jumping over the turnstile at the stadium, or accessing a private section inside that stadium. Beyond football there was a whole world of things to jib.

'I remember once in the late 80s, three of us jumped off this ferry in Greece,' Mellow says. 'We'd come from Cyprus. The guard was chasing us 'cos we had no tickets and we leaped over the side, just launched ourselves onto the dock. One of the lads fell in the water and we thought he was gonna get crushed by the ferry! Not long after that we were off to pastures new. Jibbing round the States in 1989. It was still a piece of piss back in the early 90s. You could pick a rental car up and just drive it forever without getting caught. Total cluelessness. It seemed outside Europe was the place to go if you wanted a proper free ride. You could do an entire continent without paying a penny.'

(Younger lads like Johnno these days use 'jibbing' to describe just about any movement, paid or not. It could be a lad sneaking aboard a ferry or a lizard scampering up a wall.)

Things were changing by 1993. Manchester United had begun their monumental assault on Liverpool's League Championship honours. I was emigrating right at the start (though that wasn't my conscious intention), after years following the Reds with little to show for it. In

October I bought a ticket to Orlando and began saving avidly. By the launch date in December I had a fair wedge set by. My mate Dave-B-decided to accompany me for a couple of weeks. It was good to travel with money for a change, but I knew it wouldn't last long. Too many nights out to be had. We took a rental car from Orlando to Fort Lauderdale. In Lauderdale we quickly established which pubs were showing live football and wallowed among the large British population of south Florida. Predictably, we checked into the Sol-y-Mar. The place was architecturally unchanged but had a population of more gangsters and weirdoes than ever before. I had to find work if I was to stay. To add to the pressure, Dave was on holiday so he wanted to be on the piss all day, every day.

One day I noticed a lad in an adjacent room folding a pile of t-shirts and jeans with incredible meticulousness. I concluded that he'd spent a good fraction of his life either in prison or the army. I socialised with the Yanks, knowing Dave was leaving after a fortnight, and made the lad's acquaintance. He told me his name was John. After a few nights out, boozing and having a laugh with the locals in the bars, he told me his name was really Joey and that he was from Boston. He was on the run from the police up there. One day he told me, 'You know what? I'm 24 and I've spent nearly nine years of my life behind bars. I ain't never goin' back up to New England until they fuckin' drag me there.'

There was a cowboy from Texas, also called John, who had apparently just been released from prison and was under some form of judicial order. Another guy from Quebec and one from New Jersey, both musicians and dope fiends, also told me their names were John. It turned out there were a lot of Johns knocking about South Florida, all up to no good. By some miracle I bumped into Gavin right outside the Sol-y-Mar, an Aussie writer and boozer I'd known since the '88 trip with Leckie. The day we encountered each other it was like we'd each seen a ghost. It had been six years. What were the odds of just bumping into each other like that?

As ever, he was criss-crossing the USA and making plenty of friends, usually gorgeous girls and fellow pissheads. We began doing the rounds of the bars and pubs in search of decent women. We romped in yuppie clubs like spoiled children, telling them we were with the RAF investigating UFO sightings. The Johns sometimes came with us and a great time was had by all.

One afternoon, Joey asked, 'I'm gonna go score and sell it to the Europeans at the International Hostel down the strip. Wanna tag along?'

I decided it was in my best interests not to. I had a sign to paint. A couple of hours later, Joey returned empty-handed and calmly told me what had happened:

'I went to a ghetto called Plantation and headed straight for a house I know. It was a low-rise neighbourhood with palm trees bustin' through the sidewalks. Everyone was black and the area had a ton of crackhouses. I had a particular one in mind. I went down a narrow alley lined with wooden fences and garages, then turned again, then again. I needed a freakin' ball of string to remember the directions. I had hundreds of dollars on me and I was the only white guy in town.'

I listened to his tale as I painted, wondering if he'd met the Minotaur. He had.

'From out of nowhere a guy was in my face with a gun,' he continued. 'He pointed it at right at me. He knew I had the money and where I was going.

'He says, "Fuckin' give, Homes! Gimme the money!"

'I gave him the cash and walked back down the main road. Then I got a bus back here to the beach. Fuckin' punk!'

I was amazed at Joey's composure; he was acting like he'd just experienced some very minor distraction, not a serious threat to his life. The fact that he was stoned probably had something to do with it. I was aware that Joey was a Mafia associate in Boston and guns were a part of his daily existence.

'See me, I'm a soldier,' he told me. 'I give my life to my lifestyle and I don't whine or bitch about shit when it happens. In Boston I'm answerin' to an old timer and he makes me run errands and collect money every minute of every day. I can't complain and if I ever do I'm out of the running forever. What the fuck would I do then, huh? My father, he came to Boston from Sicily. Guys like me are born into this thing and we run errands and do the spadework for the older guys until we get a break. It's fuckin' hard but what else am I gonna do, seriously? I can make a grand or two every week if I'm a hard worker. So a guy threatens to kill me, so what? It's the life. And there ain't no other life here for me. That guy who just robbed me, I know who he is, but there's nothin' anyone can do down here.'

He was also answering to an old timer right there in Fort Lauderdale, a grizzled, grey-haired bloke from New York City who called himself 'John', which was still Joey's moniker to people he didn't know or trust. John worked in an Italian pastry shop by day, and was funding half of their enterprise. The loss of the money caused a big row back at poolside in the Golden West, the motel where they were staying. John was a big, rugged motherfucker who told me he drank the cheapest beer and smoked the cheapest cigarettes. Such things weren't important to him at that time. 'See these,' he said, pointing at his can of Bud Light and pack of Player's Lights, 'they're shit.' He made it clear he was used to the finer things in life, and as soon as he was able to return to the Big Apple he'd be tucking into the best the city had to offer. He was a rum cunt with a murderer's gleam in his eye.

These are the people occupying the motel rooms of South Florida. Solo flyers and barracudas attracted by the pastel apartment blocks, the climate and the glamour. Many are there to perform specific errands and many are on the run. It was inevitable I'd be rubbing shoulders with this crowd. Aussies or British backpackers sometimes discovered the Sol-y-Mar when the International Hostel was full. There was a home for runaway kids called the Covenant House on the corner of Miramar and Vistamar Streets. The kids used to hang around outside. They were missing persons from all over America. Absconded from Nowhere to this tropical wonderland. Joey was often to be found dealing crack, or buying crack with them. Sometimes I'd spy him with one of the lads, taking hits off a glass pipe between parked cars, one eye out for the police cruisers that patrolled the strip and adjacent neighbourhoods.

One day, a one-armed guy turned up in a sports car from California. He was a proper nobble. One-armed Gary was probably the most honest and decent of all the lads I grafted with in South Florida. He jumped from his car, having literally just driven from LA, carrying a six-pack in a most unorthodox manner. One beer was in his hand; he'd forcefully inserted his stump through the hole made by the plastic ring of the six-pack. Guzzling and talking a mile-a-minute about his trip, he held the remaining portion of his arm at an angle so the beers didn't slip off.

'Here you go!' he shouted. 'Help yourselves. I can't hold these fuckin' things like this forever!'

The car was a beauty, a DeLorean with gull-wing doors. Identical to the model used as a time machine in *Back to the Future*. DeLoreans are manufactured with a silver stainless-steel exterior, but Gary's was re-sprayed maroon. Most of all I admired the California licence plate. They were rare on the East Coast. The sunset emblem with the word 'California' in typeface evoked romantic notions of the West. American licence plates immediately become a huge fetish item to British men visiting the States. They quickly compile a mental catalogue of the various colours and designs associated with each state, which they recite to other Brits as proof of their credibility. Anyone trying to pass themselves off as a seasoned head over there was instantly rumbled as a bullshitter if they betrayed this tendency. Such attention to detail was lost on American men, who considered this English trait effeminate.

The wonderland offered numerous opportunities to make easy money, one of which involved the black stuff. We'd scout the streets in the DeLorean and sell recoating jobs on driveways and private cul-de-sacs. We crammed squeegees, brushes and rollers into the car and towed a little trailer containing brimming tubs of sealant behind us. We knew some mad gypsies from a motel buffet-bar who sold us pavement sealant dirt-cheap. I'd go back a few days later and paint white lines on the surfaces and it looked great. We did driveways and parking lots in posh developments around Miami and Fort Lauderdale, putting a fair few quid away during the first months of 1994.

I was living on a big luxury yacht which I looked after at the time, and my expenses were minimal. We'd hit the clubs once we'd washed the tar off ourselves, telling the girls that I owned the yacht. It was a necessary tool in the UFO investigation. The engineer on the boat was a guy from London called Roy who'd been the British saloon-racing champion back in the 70s. He had a James Hunt playboy boat-race and a permanent grin. The guy I worked for on the boat was called Rick and he was a bull of a man. He took me to topless bikini bars and challenged me to drinking contests while the dolly-birds cheered us on. Roy had to come and literally carry us home on a few occasions. A lad from Glasgow put me onto Rick one day when I was walking around the marina with Dave-B-.

'The guy's name is Rick, man. But watch out, he can really . . .' As he said this he made several violent drinking motions with his hand. I was soon to learn that Rick was a major boozer who could put it away like it was going out of fashion. The company we worked for were something of a legend in the area. They specialised in buying DEA 'snatchbacks' – vehicles seized by the coast guard and drug enforcement agencies in Miami. We often joked about finding a bag of coke down in the hold or stashed in a cooler. The company sold sports cars and even small planes. Their brochure looked like a series of stills from a James Bond movie. One day I met one of their top employees. He rolled up in a Mercedes, looking very *Miami Vice*, walked up to me and shook my hand.

'Alright mate? How you doin'?' He had a broad cockney accent, and explained that he'd left England years earlier and made big bucks in Florida. He was a Tottenham boy and a bit of a rum lad, as were most of the Brits I met down there.

Being recognised around Marina Bahia Mar, where the yachts I worked on were harboured, meant invitations to parties with the super-rich yachting crowd. The boats – ships, really – would be full of socialites boozing and eating food from lavish buffets. I would ask Gary to explain to people how a shark had bitten his arm off. It made for some excellent cocktail-party conversation. He had 20 stories that described in intricate detail the circumstances of his misfortune, one for every occasion. There was the Gulf War, the water-skiing accident, the saltwater croc and the time he trapped his arm while diving and was running out of air. I never did properly find out how Gary lost his arm but I suspect he blew it off making a pipe bomb.

We had contests to see who could last longest without smiling. We'd bear incredibly serious expressions while discussing airspace security and White Pointer sharks with half-drunk, gullible, rich folk. We treated Miami like a carousel, jumping on and off as we saw fit. The yacht, the sports car, the money and the one arm conspired to convince people we really were international men of mystery. It provided yet another purple patch with the ladies and a lesson for life; many people are gold-digging parasites and you shouldn't trust them. They will eat your turds if they think it will make them rich. But true love conquers all and it never dies. Just remember that, you sucker.

My bus-driving days in Orlando had seen a fair few European *kife* come and go, but these girls were mainly American. They were mesmerised by the possibility of knowing someone with real money. You could literally see the dollar signs in their ghoulish eyes. Beautiful, horrible fuckers.

A mixed bag of English arrived at the Sol-y-Mar sometime around

February 1994. I had moved off the yacht and was now living in the Golden West. The place was a honey-coloured stucco madhouse. Aussie Gavin, Joey, 'John' and a few others lived there, including a private eye from Boston who was the image of Humphrey Bogart. He would nod quietly toward Joey and mumble, 'That guy's goin' to jail *real* fast.' He and Joey knew a few hoods in common back in Beantown and they regularly swapped news. It was like living a movie. We had some great nights by the pool, singing and telling stories. We'd nip to the Sol-y-Mar with Joey to do business with the New Age English colonising the place before hitting Banana Joe's for a drink. Aussie Gavin was also a signwriter and we helped each other find work on the yachts and shop-fronts in the area. In fact, I'd been with Gavin the day I saw that bikini-clad girl sign-writing a yacht called *Wild Goose* back in early '88. It led to my attending Central Manchester College until 1990, and kept me in town through the height of Madchester.

The Golden West's balconies stretched along its L-shaped length, overlooking the pool and the street. I'd often walk out in the dead of night to find one of the lads drinking a cold beer in the tropical starlight, just meditating on the expanse of dark ocean. The jagged palms and blinking neon along the coastal curve felt like they were a million miles from Manchester.

Bobby was another acquaintance made during my anthropological studies in Lauderdale. He'd just been released from prison for killing a DEA agent. I regularly bumped into Bobby in the bars on the strip. He'd been a coke dealer in Miami. The DEA agent had tried to kill him one night during a mock deal. As the agent was taking the drugs, Bobby realised he was drawing his gun not to arrest but to shoot him in the head; it was more than just a set-up, it was a planned murder. He drew at the same time and shot the agent between the eyes, killing him instantly. Bobby had a wide track-mark scar running up the middle of his forehead, the legacy of the high-calibre bullet from the agent's gun.

'I knew he was gonna kill me, and I knew it was me or him. When it went to court it was obvious what he tried to do, so they gave me a sentence of nine years and later reduced it to five,' he told me. He was a bearded, wiry little fucker, ex-Special Forces from Vietnam. He looked ten years younger than he actually was, like a miniature version of Chuck Norris. Dave-B- and I met him in the Days Inn Lounge on the strip during the first week there. He'd been out of prison a month and come to Fort Lauderdale with a new attitude. He lived at a halfway house for newly-released cons, an utter bedlam full of heavy-duty characters. When the English lads from Spain started turning up a few weeks later with pockets full of ecstasy, the whole scene became completely insane. When worlds collide it really does go pear-shaped. I could only stand so much of that.

It began when I bumped into a lad from Oxfordshire called Rob, who I knew from assorted places. He knew some Dambusters as well as a few scousers. Rob was a football supporter but not necessarily a hooligan. He was a ponytail-sporting New Age thug, game for anything. The kind of kid who'd developed late and decided he wanted a slice of the pie. I walked right into him one day on the Lauderdale Strip.

'Alright mate! What the fuck you doin' 'ere?' I asked him, already knowing the answer.

'Waiting on the Manc and the scouser to come through with the gear,' he told me.

The Manc and the scouser appeared on a flight from Spain a few days later. They'd stumbled through customs at Miami wearing lightweight Lacoste and Fjällräven sports jackets whose zipped pockets were laden with ecstasy pills. Fjällräven was one of the big labels introduced to the UK by football travel, but I wasn't familiar with it. I just remember the logo with a curled-up fox and 'Manc' going on about how good it was. These three hit the bars, clubs and hostels, offloading a bang-on pill that fucked you up royal.

'Then we went back to Spain and returned a week later,' remembers Rob, 'with a couple of thousand Dennis the Menaces. We went back to Spain again and then back to Miami with a thousand Rhubarb and Custards right in time for Super Bowl weekend. We went to every party in town and knocked the pills out to anyone who wanted them. It was fucking mental. We just didn't care about getting pulled and so obviously we never got pulled.'

It seemed everyone in the Greater Miami area had been hit by the love bomb during that period. The happy threesome joined forces with the local lunatics, including Bobby Track-Mark and a couple of other halfway-sane halfway-housers. I would bump into them in the bars once in a while. They'd all be whispering intensely, a pack of teeth-grinding, bulging-eyed mental cases. After a while Rob and his buddies went off and enjoyed months of adventure in the southeastern states:

'When we'd got rid of all the gear, we started working for these mad Scotch-Irish gypsies, or whatever they were. We met them through the people who owned the motel we were staying at. Our landlords were from Haiti and they spoke Creole. It was a bloke, his wife and her sister. The women were stunning. They'd be outside sunning themselves every day in bikinis, giving us the big smile. He was a sound guy so his missus was off-limits. Her sister was a beauty queen; I swear she could have been Miss Haiti, no problem. We chilled with them for a while, smoking the ganj and just hanging out, making very nice spicy shrimp stews and listening to mellow tunes. They were good people. The only ripples ever made were those northern dicks arguing about football. They never stopped having a go. Fort Lauderdale has a few English bars so you can watch live soccer every week. Matt Busby died right before we started our runs into Florida, and I remember the tension between them. It was tribal.

'One day these blokes came to stay at the motel and we got talking to them. They were part of a crew doing tarmac and asphalt; a big family with a Scottish name from Carolina. These mad cunts had been on local news shows up north for ripping people off after the big hurricane two years before, offering to surface driveways but not using aggregate, just lobbing a load of tar right onto soil and pissing off with the cash. A few in-and-outs with a motor and the whole thing would be falling apart 'cos it wasn't anchored to anything. I didn't fancy it, but the money from the E wasn't gonna last forever. We went off with them on a tour of the southeast and every day was a nerve-stretcher. We were already out on our visas and these gypsies considered getting nicked an occupational hazard. One night in Georgia, we were just finishing a job on the massive driveway of this big mansion. The owner came home from work. He was a big noise in town and it seemed that everybody knew him. He was saying how good it looked and getting his wallet out when his neighbour moseyed out and called him over. There was a lot of whispering and the guy darts into his house. He only comes out with a fucking shotgun and starts pointing it at us and the tyres on the vehicles! Tells us he's calling the cops 'cos his neighbour saw what we did and it was a rip-off! I'm terrified and Manc and Scouse are straight over the back of the truck into a pile of steaming tarmac. I jumped in the cab with Alex, one of the family, and we screamed out of there, tyres spinning and everything. Alex was fuming that we never got paid but I was just relieved we didn't get killed. I just wanted to get home and spend some Saturdays watching footy after that, but we worked for them for a few months. Manc and Scouse were introduced to more of the same. They ended up working out in Texas on some huge road project. They lived in an adobe hut in a baking desert, guzzling themselves into oblivion. I'd get letters off them back in England, saying they'd just spent twelve hours working in 100-degree heat and now they were loaded and ready to party. Brilliant lads. They ended up back in Fort Lauderdale months later, chilling with the Haitians and enjoying the ocean. Me, I straightened out and got married.'

Gary returned home one day to discover that Joey had borrowed his car without asking. As the hours wore on, it became obvious that he hadn't actually borrowed it. Joey must have decided to return to Boston and figured, *Why pay for a Greyhound bus when you can just steal your buddy's DeLorean?* We never saw the car, or Joey, again. Gary flew back to California in disgust at the episode, vowing never to return to the East Coast as long as he lived.

With Rob in Oxfordshire and the crazies temporarily in Texas, building roads, it was just me, Aussie Gavin and the Yank misfits again. In time, more British bled out from the Sol-y-Mar into the neighbourhood motels. We welcomed a few to the Golden West. A sizeable pack of cohorts began to patrol the strip. Little groups of us sometimes took off up and down the eastern seaboard for one reason or another. Three guys in particular emerged as major heads among the Brits at that time; I've been asked not to use their real names, so I'll use their nicknames instead: Scotch Jock (so named because it drove him absolutely livid, for obvious reasons), Bungle Bear and the Killer. These three were (roughly) from Glasgow, East Anglia and Lancashire, respectively. They were without doubt seriously disturbed individuals. They'd just missed Rob, Manc and Scouse's little era, thank fuck, because even southern Florida wasn't ready for six of them simultaneously.

Scotch and Killer were a proper pair of pissheads, but Bungle didn't drink as much. Their room in the Golden West was something to behold: giant, life-sized photographs taken from porn magazines and blown up at a local printers on glossy paper; at least two or three bongs or joints going round the clock, plus a coffee table loaded with open bottles of Scotch, gin, tequila and rum. There were cases of beers stacked next to the fridge, ensuring they never ran out of supplies for the hard days they spent sitting on the long balcony, watching the world go by. Their fondest wish was to try and lure one of the monkeys from the jungle behind the Sol-y-Mar into their room for a party. Fortunately, the jungle was a couple of blocks north of the Golden West, so it never happened. It was common to be heading out to work varnishing yachts in the morning and to hear a raucous shout from the balcony.

'Alright mate? D'you fancy a fuck before you go to work? We've got some right sorts in 'ere!'

The shouter would stand back to reveal an orgy taking place through the open door to their room. Puerto Rican hookers and white-trash crack whores on the run from trailer-park existences up north jumping about, stoned, on the beds. They trawled their women from a strip-club called the Pink Pussycat, as well as the topless donut and booze joints.

The three had taken time out to come to the Miami area to scope out possibilities. I didn't ask for the details. Their usual schedule was to stay on the move, from one end of the country to the other. They were all three experts on cannabis cultivation and its corresponding economics. It was an education just to spend time with them. One time, the Killer disappeared for a couple of weeks. When he came back we went for a drink at Banana Joe's, a bar on the strip overlooking the turquoise Atlantic. As distant cruise ships crept along the horizon and we tucked into some red-hot chicken wings, he told me where he'd been.

'This past couple of weeks I've been in Manhattan, mate,' he said, taking a long pull on his Budweiser. 'We know some Japs up there who grow weed in the high-rise apartments. They're fuckin' wizards, chemistry students. They rent a little apartment, pay about three grand a month for it and they fuckin' hammer the place with grow-tanks. It's wall-to-wall light closets and hydroponics. How the neighbours don't smell it I do not know. They bang out a couple of good harvests, feed the plants the best shit, nutrients, molasses, the works. Generate a pile of sweet-as-fuck weed. Then they take it all apart and fuck off to another apartment a few blocks away to start all over again.'

'Sounds mental,' was all I could manage in response.

'It *is* mental,' the Killer spat, incredulously. He'd acquired the nickname due to his ability to always kill a bong or a joint. His appetite for THC was enormous and nobody in their right mind would ever challenge him to a smoking competition. 'These Japanese make 30 grand every three months,' he continued. 'That's well out of our league. We've been thinking about getting into it ourselves but we don't like the thought of being that close to people while we're growing plants. And getting all the gear up to the floor you're on is a nightmare! I went and helped the Japs build a grow-factory and it was fuckin' nerve-wrackin'. Stood in a big lift with half a dozen other cunts who might realise what you're up to any second. They were on the 35th floor!'

They made me nervous when they talked business, so I changed the subject to hitching across the States. It was a subject we all had some experience of. In the time since Dave-B- had left Lauderdale I'd gone on some excellent hitching jollies. Plenty of lads and lasses in our crazy Golden West neighbourhood were up for it. The three of them amazed me, the way they would spend piles of money on certain luxuries but somehow never lost their taste for hitching and doing Driveaways. They periodically owned cars but usually sold them after a few months. This was the main reason we were mates. I went on a hitching trip with them to Louisiana and it was one to remember. We drew straws to split into two groups of two. The idea was to make it a race to New Orleans. The losers had to buy drinks the entire time we were there. They all had credit lines, but I was skint. To be honest, I didn't care who won the race; it was just a nobble, as we say in Manchester.

I was drawn with the Killer. Scotch Jock and Bungle were together. Me and Killer fancied our chances big-time. We were both from the Northwest and felt that we wouldn't fall out as much as the other two. Scotch and Bungle rarely agreed on anything. It was hilarious to see them traipsing off to a truck stop on the edge of Fort Lauderdale early in the morning, already arguing. Me and Killer were still nursing our hangovers from the night before. We went straight to the International Hostel to check if any Europeans were taking Driveaways west, and ran right into two German blokes who had a brand-new Lincoln Continental bound for Los Angeles. Just the ticket. I'd recently had a thing with a girl from Hamburg, so I dropped a few place names and German curiosities she'd taught me and we were in like Flynn. Even better, the Germans were happy to let us drive while they consulted their guide books. We gunned the sleek American monster up to a ton and steamed towards Louisiana for our just desserts.

We were making great time. Within a few hours we'd blasted through the Florida panhandle. The Alabama sky was a great southern blue and the cool air (relative to our tropical HQ at the Golden West) was a comfortable temperature. When we stopped at a tiny gas station in the middle of nowhere, Killer suddenly cocked his head up and started looking around like an excited meerkat.

''Ang on! I *know* this area! We stayed 'ere for a few weeks last year. There's some fuckin' *sound* lads livin' round 'ere, mate. You've got to meet 'em . . .'

The Germans caught the gist immediately and began to object, saying they were on a schedule and they couldn't possibly stop here. Killer was fervent in his conviction that this was an experience I had to have. He persuaded me to drive almost 30 miles off course down sandy back-roads. A weird little Mississippi town was his target. We stopped next to a small shack that bulged multitudes of coloured neon beer lights and satellite dishes.

'Get in 'ere, mate, they've got it goin' on, I swear!'

We left the Germans fuming in the back of the now dusty motor and went inside. It was a crazy bar full of rednecks, many of whom were dressed head to toe in camouflaged militia gear. One of the pick-up trucks in the parking lot actually contained a deer carcass. Another had a shotgun clearly exhibited on a rack in the cab. The jukebox was blasting out Creedence Clearwater Revival's 'Fortunate Son'. Killer definitely knew a few of the guys in there, which frankly amazed me. It was one of those moments; in a Mississippi bar with a beer in hand, savouring the cigarette smoke and loud banter and neon lights. Not caring about anything whatsoever. So what if we had to buy Bungle and Jock drinks all weekend? Within minutes the song 'Dreamweaver' had replaced CCR. The bar was bustling with characters. Killer told me a few of the usual tales of growing weed out in the hills. Then he grabbed my arm, nodded for me to take my beer and dragged me down a corridor to a small door. We went into a room with several bearded rednecks from the bar. At that point, I noticed several of them had bows and arrows or shotguns. Most of them were drunk.

'Get this down you,' Killer ordered, handing me a glass of JD. I partook of that, and then some other things. The blokes explained to us that they were going on a hunting trip.

'We need a couple of chefs to cook the hot dogs and burgers,' one guy told us. 'Y'all can handle a butane barbeque, I believe.'

'We're the men fer the fuckin' job!' Killer announced, before singing a song about Blackpool and the Red Rose to the room. Nobody could understand what he was saying, including me. They offered us a tent to stay in for the night, which Killer refused. He explained that we were involved in a race (and had obviously realised that an overnight trek through the woods with a load of drunken rednecks carrying guns was not the way to go).

We slept in a bus shelter that night, freezing our bollocks off and feeling like we were dead. It was tropically pissing down but those few degrees of latitude made a huge difference. Our blood was thinned out from living in the banana belt a while. It was hell.

The next morning we managed to find a coffee shop and ply ourselves with caffeine. We fell into a diner some miles further and ravenously devoured a full fried breakfast. We were now properly hitching, thanks to that cunt, and it was two hours before we got our first ride. It was totally out of our way but at least we were going somewhere; a 40-minute hop to a local town that reeked of old times and solitude. We knew there couldn't possibly be hostels in this part of the world (where evolution was considered a make-believe fantasy propagated by weirdoes known as 'scientists'). We made do with a large truck stop where a gaggle of fat blokes were eating donuts. We negotiated the large, oily puddles in the pock-marked cinder ground and asked for a ride. We snagged a lift to New Orleans within an hour and were once more on course. The guy was delivering a load of window frames from Memphis to various locations around the southeast. He had a big box of coffee and donuts which we destroyed in record time, despite our earlier feast. Killer quickly established that the guy was a speed freak. The two engaged in a happy conversation about the wonders of amphetamine. He turned to me.

'Them cunts are probably suckin' lorry drivers' cocks in Florida, tryin' to get a lift,' he said with a satisfied grin on his kite, folding his arms.

Right as he uttered those words, we passed them on the hard shoulder. Bungle Bear caught a glimpse of us and attempted a desperate, frantic wave, while Jock glared in resigned horror. Killer burst into uncontrolled laughter and I thought he was genuinely going to piss himself. It was one of those moments when probabilistic mathematics is defeated. The game of life had us both shrieking with joy. Even the driver joined in and he had no idea what the fuck we were laughing at.

By the time they caught up with us in the heart of the Big Easy, we'd blown $200 on one of Jock's credit cards. The Killer had it and had been practising Jock's signature the entire trip. As they exchanged credit cards (Jock also had one of the Killer's) they talked me through every single bar in the city. The music in the bars was great, but the bars themselves weren't as genuine as the shit-kicker hut Killer had shown me in Mississippi. Many of the jazz joints were plastic and overly self-aware. Even one-off places resembled chain restaurants. For the second time, New Orleans was too commercial for my liking. We had a couple of nights there, mooching about among the tourist throngs of Bourbon Street, before hiring a car and hoofing it back to our tropical wonderland. Thankfully, they paid; I was still skint.

15

THAI'D UP

*Writing is like prostitution. First you do it for love, and then for a few
close friends, and then for money.*
– Moliere

Many Manchester bands have been associated with Manchester
United – New Order, the Stone Roses, Happy Mondays, even
Simply Red – but one of Manchester's biggest musical success stories
weren't Reds at all. They were City fans and also Britain's biggest band,
at their peak. Johnno, a United supporter from north Manchester, has
no problem tipping his hat, in his own self-tortured way:

'I was 14 when the Oasis single "Live Forever" broke into the top
three on the singles chart. I remember seeing the video and I couldn't
understand why the singer was dressed like a 60s throwback. Like most
of my mates, I had no particular style; I'd wear simple sporting t-shirts
like Reebok, Nike, Russell Athletic, etc, with a pair of jeans or trackie
bottoms. No originality whatsoever. I sported the must-have hair of that
summer amongst the lads in north Manchester, the under-shave. My
hair was pretty longish as I had let it grow and the barber shaved
underneath it. We all looked right stupid cunts and the style faded
quickly, reverting to a simpler straight-cut.

'*Definitely Maybe* became one of the biggest albums in British
history. More and more lads chose the "Liam look", the hair combed
forward with sharp sides and a fringe. This style hadn't simply appeared
in Greater Manchester overnight. I remember seeing the remnants of the
Madchester era a few years earlier and it was identical. It's said Liam
Gallagher is merely a carbon copy of Ian Brown but this isn't accurate;
after everyone got over Happy Mondays' *Thrills, Pills 'n' Bellyaches* the
style evolved and adapted into what became the Oasis style. 1993-94

had been dominated musically in the UK by utter shite such as 2Unlimited and Capella. My own personal tastes had been gangsta rap like Snoop Doggy Dogg, Cypress Hill and Warren G. In retrospect there's nothing worse than a skinny blond white kid rapping along like a sad twat, but I wasn't alone in that one.'

They were part of the post-Madchester story, this ragtag gang of Blues from some council estate south of town. The mid-90s offered some promise and organic excitement in music, and Oasis were at the head of that wave. It signalled a new dawn in chart music. If Oasis copied earlier musical templates they did it with tremendous energy, and they were never properly credited for their songwriting – more Glimmer Twins than Lennon-McCartney, ironically.

Behind all this, the travelling circus continued. People still wanted to get away, even though the charts had apparently come to their senses via old-fashioned guitar bands with soul.

Most Brits who relocate go to English-speaking countries like Australia and Canada. But there are always people who prefer to remain out of the loop and do their own thing. Wherever you go in the world you'll meet British people, be it South America, Africa or Outer Mongolia. Dominic Lavin was one who relocated in an easterly direction. His baptism in East Asia was a prerequisite to writing the depraved but honest novel *Last Seen in Bangkok*. Lavin's book studies the recent phenomenon of British men of a certain age travelling to the Asian sex capital in search of pleasures unavailable in the UK, due to beer bellies, ugly faces, shit weather and an altogether different culture. *Last Seen in Bangkok* furnishes the reader with a detailed tour of the alcohol-sodden grottoes of Nana Plaza and Pattaya, where beautiful young Thai girls lure their drunken, bloated prey inside for a blowjob or a quickie. Many middle-aged Brits fall in love with the bargirls, and this is an undesirable side-effect, as they are only after one thing.

'For a lot of reasons, I'd always felt a bit of an outsider,' Lavin explains. 'Growing up I had a Finnish mam, so that marked me as different from day one. I built up a load of friends in Wigan but my family went and moved me to Bolton. At university I was a casual when everyone else was an indie kid. When everyone was raving I was right into the herb. I'd never quite been in step with anyone, but the first time I got to Thailand it just felt right. That was about 1994, and landing at Bangkok airport was a massive culture shock. I got off the plane and walked into a wall of humidity, then walked into the arrivals hall which was swarming with a mass of humanity. Growing up in the North of England you don't realise it until you go somewhere like Thailand, but most people in the Northwest are in some part for a lot of the time depressed. (I'm sorry if that offends anyone.) When you arrive in Bangkok every cunt's smiling and it really gives you a lift. Me and my mate Tommy got off this 14-hour flight via Frankfurt. I remember it well; I was wearing Timberland boots, Replay Jeans and a blue and salmon pink-striped Henry Lloyd polo shirt with a pot burn in it. I was carrying my sports bag through the mass of people when these two very pretty girls in traditional Thai dress accosted me and Tommy with their enchanting smiles.

'"Hello sir, nice English man, can I talk to you please?"

'Who was I to object?

'"We think you nice man and want you to be our boyfriend."

'"Uh, I'm not sure about that, I've just got off the plane." I was a bit bowled over by it all.

'"But sir, if you not our boyfriend we have to work in bar and go with big fat German pervert!"

'In time-honoured *News of the World* tradition, I made my excuses and left, to spend two weeks spread across Bangkok, Pattaya and Samui. It was fantastic. I was really taken with the laidback attitude of the Thais. They've got this saying, "Mai pehn rai." It means, "It doesn't matter." Thailand at the time was very much a developing country, and the gap that I perceived between Thailand and the West was huge. It was great. People say the weed there is the strongest they've ever chonged on. They touch down and score a furtive ounce for four quid off a Thai gangster who probably has a massive pig tattooed across his chest. Roll a joint in their hotel room. English people aren't used to seeing the aurora borealis on their hotel room wall but they soon get used to it. They get their first taste of Thai corruption when smoking a herbal Woodbine on the porch of their beach hut and the local copper demands 20 baht (about 40 pence at the time) to avoid arrest for possession of a controlled drug. It's a different world.'

* * *

An alternative existence outside the English-speaking world was one way to go, but the Anglophone sphere was usually too tempting for most. 1994 was a time that seemed to revisit the heady trivialities of 1983 and its assorted temptations, minus the plastic effervescence and yuppie tedium. Manchester had come out of the 80s and into the 90s, gleaming like a weird dream machine. Its continental bent and reputation for serious shopping, pubbing and clubbing sent people silly; the sidewalk cafés that had first sprung up (to be mocked) around 1986 had slowly proliferated and established themselves as a distinct characteristic of the city centre. Except among the fetishist collectors and football hooligans, the old casual fashions were almost forgotten; people were allegedly growing up.

But things were about to start changing. The evils of chav culture were brewing underground. There were decent young people alive and kicking in our country, but they would be faced by choices: should I stay or should I go? In time, many would indeed go. Johnno, born in Australia, had adopted England as his native country and grew up in Manchester. Inevitably, he was an avid football supporter and United were his team. Johnno's heroes weren't the Pearsons, Macaris, Robsons and Coppells of the 70s and 80s, but Cantona, Neville and Giggs. Johnno was still a kid, albeit one who wanted to sample life's little treasures. That England had its shadow world – a kind of parallel universe that evolved along with the sunnier aspect – was made very clear to him when he came face to face with a product of this dysfunctional dark side.

As the momentum from the Cup Winners' Cup pushed the city through its golden decade via architect Ferguson's mastery, the gargoyles and the ghouls of a new era were putting down roots. A bizarre and wolfish ingredient in modern British society began to thrive, suckled and enabled in turn by the swollen breasts of political correctness and denial. A generation was coming of age that had failed to be enticed by the deteriorating atmosphere of once-great football grounds. They were now busily going off their trolleys in a vacuous culture, devoid of outlets and focuses for their youthful energy.

'What a year 1994 was. This was the year United won the double for the first time with Eric the King, and they were unstoppable,' Johnno remembers. 'The World Cup was on in America and Romario and Baggio were the stars of the tournament. I was 14 that year, and my voice had broken not long before. I had been nicking the beer my dad had bought on trips to French *hypermarches* in Calais. He also bought back loads of tequila and Bacardi. The tequila was obviously going to be missed so we topped this up with water after we'd had our swigs and burned our throats. I remember months later him saying the French bastards had sold him some snide, watered-down spirits.

'The country was starting to change, according to a lot of the older people. My old feller, an Aussie, kept saying it was for the worse. I could sense change was coming, and with a parent from the other side of the planet you never know what that could mean. England had seen its youngsters transform from casual culture to a land of freaks, and I can't blame my dad for seeing it for what it was. I lived near Prestwich Mental Hospital in north Manchester and often used their extensive footy pitches to have a kickabout with my mates. One night we had a right shit-up. While we were booting the ball around this girl came up to me. She had loads of earrings in both ears. I remember a stud in her tongue and one in her nose. She had a fair few scars on her face. She kept walking towards me whilst I jogged backwards, egging her on to chase me. She tied her dyed-purple hair back with a bobble off her wrist. I was horrified to see her hair completely shaved at the sides, previously hidden when she had it down. I realised this bird with murder in her eyes was an actual mental patient! The next minute hell broke loose and a load more crazies appeared. This weird lad came up in a red Chicago Bulls t-shirt, a snide bum-fluff 'tache and yellow teeth. He said to us, in a southern accent, "It's okay, guys, I'm not gonna hurt you. I just want to let you know that she will kill you, and if she kills you, then we all have to kill you." We fucking legged it, looking over our shoulders as we made it home by tram and foot.

'This girl and her little mental mob started patrolling the area, trying to find out where I lived. Some tit gave her my name and approximate address. A girl who lived round the corner from the hospital told us she'd even broke into a house screaming that she was looking for me! After telling everyone at school about our adventures into nutcase land (leaving out the cowardice on our behalves, of course), we decided we mustn't let one psycho chav ruin our football matches and arranged to play again that night. When my mates Ste and Phil came to call for me, I got up and let them in. Ste was white as a ghost and looked like he was ready to throw up at any second. Phil told me that the nutter from the night before had found out where Ste lived and grabbed them on the way to my house. This mob of mentals forced them to show where the elusive Johnno lived. They marched them all the way in broad daylight holding a piece of glass to Ste's throat. Talking about how they were going to slit my throat and watch me die. They were coming out with weird shit like how they'd love to ride their bikes off Mount Everest to commit suicide. Ste then told my dad they were there and he walked round the corner to speak with them, ordering us to stay inside. Ste visibly had the shit freaked out of him; he'd had a piece of a broken bottle digging into him for a few miles. Phil was just being Phil with a daft grin on his face; he seemed to be enjoying it. Suddenly, my dad ran round the corner holding his wrist like he was hurt. He ran inside and shouted to call an ambulance. My sister was shouting at my dad, asking if he was okay. He turned round and told us he was holding his arm back because he wanted to hit the bitch. My mates cracked up laughing because of his Aussie accent. He rang an ambulance and said a young girl had slit her wrists and to hurry up. The ambulance took her off with her sobbing friends in tow. My dad told us she had rolled up her sleeves to reveal a load of stitches where she had slashed herself in the past. She then bit open the wound so the stitches came loose, and pulled the thread out like an old pair of laces from a shoe. This resulted in her wrists flopping open in front of my dad and horrifying nosy residents of my street. The dibble were called but didn't turn up for nearly an hour. Typical of the local coppers at the time. They weren't on the ball at all.'

Johnno is interesting because he has a historical connection to the casual era of yore. But England was changing around him by then. The mental cases were taking over the asylum. A red Chicago Bulls shirt? In our day that was deserving of serious pain, if only psychological (until we grew out of pretty clothes). The way was being paved for the emboldening of England's worst young thugs, the bullies and cowards. The age-old tendency of British youth to use knives was massively exacerbated. Football grounds were no longer a refuge for those who needed to vent their spleen. The troubled youth of the mid-90s were forced to take their fury into civilian life. The 70s terraces and the 80s train stations had given way to CCTV and all-seater stadiums, and that fraction of the youth that will always tend to mob up and fight was removed from football from the bottom up. Only the older set remained, puzzled at first by the lack of new blood trickling through. This sanitisation meant that the thugs and knife merchants grew in number away from football.

But there really is no 'away', as environmentalists say. They are referring to toxic waste, but the same principle applies to human behaviour; when you interfere with the energy in a system, you are asking for it to surface elsewhere.

The new-style casuals were also feeling the pinch, as others around the country began to sniff the air and wonder. Tough, working-class kids were slowly being usurped by middle-class sissies, drawn to the grounds by the seating and the megastores. Johnno is neither a sissy nor a person who uses knives on innocents, but he rapidly began to feel out of place and he wasn't alone.

Meanwhile, the old-school crowd were growing older. Colin Blaney embarked on a photographic quest for inner peace while Scouse Robin Peters became increasingly involved in sourcing vintage sports and fashion wear for his growing business. It's ironic, but his early excursions to Europe, grafting at concerts and shoplifting designer gear, had taught him much about the fashion world and the demand curves associated with it. Peters isn't alone; today in Liverpool, one entrepreneur has actually named a clothes shop after that student rail-card company that propelled lads into Europe all those years ago. Transalpino in Liverpool centre is one of the hippest casual shops, where collectors can find rare footwear and clothing from that golden age of fashion.

*   *   *

Meanwhile in early 1994, I was working Florida's Intracoastal canal network in various luxury boats, pleased to be away from the grey existence in England. I had a vague awareness that things in Britain were changing, but I was too immersed in my own explorations to believe it was anything worth worrying about. My involvement with the characters living in south Florida had revealed to me a vast underworld populated by American grafters. I eventually took a Driveaway to Utah and flew on to California, but I was distracted by several strange avenues en route and beyond.

Possibly the strangest was a guy I met working in a shop where I sign-painted the windows. He was a southerner, from Tennessee, and he took me into his confidence for some reason, possibly because his father had been a signwriter. I was painting the window of the shop one night and he said to me, 'You know, I really shouldn't be here.'

I shrugged, and he continued.

'Let me tell you something. The FBI and the Medellín cartel are both looking for me and I'm not sure what to do next.' He then embarked on a long and detailed account of how he was a big noise in the recording industry in New York, and had negotiated the surrender of Colombian drug lord Pablo Escobar to the authorities. My initial scepticism slowly dissolved, as I studied his obviously expensive attire and well-manicured appearance – quite incongruous, given that we were in a relative backwater – but then he showed me where he lived.

'It's right through here,' he mumbled, taking me outside to a darkened recess doorway adjacent to the shop. We went inside. There was a secret apartment in there, but no windows. The walls were covered with photographs of this guy with very major stars from the music business. He even had autographed gold and platinum discs from heavyweight music stars affixed on the walls of his secret abode. I was amazed.

'If you don't believe me, look at this,' he said, holding out a Spanish-language newspaper from New York City which contained an article about him. I couldn't understand a word of it, other than the double photo of him and Escobar with both their names in a Spanish caption beneath. The newspaper was dated the previous week and New York was thousands of miles away. Was this proof? Fuck knows. I completed the painting of that window, expecting a Colombian hit squad to open up on me any second. The guy was working behind me in full view of the street outside. It wasn't the best sign-writing I ever did.

I spent several weeks doing odd jobs, sampling the weird life in that balmy desert climate. Money was tight and I lived hand to mouth. I slept rough, lived with English nutters in swanky apartments and saw Kiwi coke dealers living the life of Riley. I ended up with a California girl in a tri-level condo with a pool and Jacuzzi. An insane Mexican bar provided me with live English football. Manchester United were making a bid for the double that year and, via my dad on the phone and the bars in the area, I followed their amazing fortunes. For money I painted signs and did day-work with the Mexicans. We'd stand on a street corner and wait to be picked up. The Mexicans were very accommodating to this strange gringo. They taught me some words in Spanish and often stood aside to let me have a job before them. Their leader was a short guy who wore a ten-gallon hat and smoked enormous cigars. His face bore many scars, but he was a gentleman.

One day in LA I met a complete wreck of a person from London, a Chelsea fan. The guy was several years younger than me but he looked 20 years older. Upon further inspection it was determined that he was a methamphetamine addict.

'I'm a fuckin' wreck, matey,' he told me. 'But I can tell you things from the speed scene that no human man could ever appreciate.'

His name was Larry and he had been through the mill, as we say in Manchester. His skin was crinkled and aged, with the translucent, fragile cast one associates with old-age pensioners. He was only 25. His teeth were all destroyed or decayed and his hair hung limp like dead hay. Much of what he said was very intelligent, creating a bizarre contrast to his appearance. His story was utterly shocking and I relate it here to the best of my memory:

'I was just a traveller, making my way across America. But when I went to Colorado I found work very hard to come by. Some guys I met in Denver said there was a place in Arizona where you could deliver ice [methamphetamine] and get paid good money. I decided to go for it, as there was nothing else going on. I didn't want to go back to England. My nice Irish girlfriend disowned me because she didn't want to get involved. I ended up meeting these bikers and being recruited as a mule carrying meth on Greyhound buses away to Chicago, Minneapolis and Seattle. The bus trips were fucking murder, but they let me have some meth for myself and that's where the trouble started.

'At first I just met them in bus stations and got sent on my way, but in time I became more involved. The base ingredients are tightly controlled by the government, and they eventually had me buying at chemists all over Arizona and surrounding states. It was travel sickness pills and antihistamines they were after, ephedrine, the more the merrier. Once I got to dropping them off at lock-ups they started to show me how to do some of the basics. They took me out to a little trailer in a box-canyon in the Arizona desert. It was like a cartoon, tumbleweeds and cactus and little sandstone cliffs. There were these tall pine trees round us, but they looked diseased. The trailer was a meth lab, and they had a generator and a small creek nearby for water. They showed me a process called the "red, white and blue", which was a three-step thing and it fucked me up, good-style. The fumes were terrible and I didn't have the sense to realise how much harm it was doing to me. After a while they put me on a different production method, and I made loads of the shit. We had loads of chemicals left over after we made the meth and they just emptied it into the creek or the soil. I slept in a nearby trailer and you could taste the meth all around. I was completely destitute by now, so I couldn't get away. When I call them bikers that's not properly true; they were meth cooks who just happened to have bought Harley Davidsons, but I don't think they were part of a biker gang. I was virtually a captive of these blokes for a few months.'

Larry became hooked on meth and smoked his way into limbo. When I met him he was little more than a human skeleton and he could have been imprisoned for his part in the production of methamphetamine. Larry escaped his captors when they asked him to go on a shopping mission to a nearby town.

'My teeth were falling out and my skin was grey and wrinkled, full of horrible sores and weeping zits. I knew I was totally screwed and had to get away at any cost. One day they sent me into town to get petrol and some travel sickness pills from a chemist. I just drove right out of town and kept going until I was well away. I hadn't looked in a mirror for months and when I did I nearly died! The waste from the trailer was always bad, and they gave me a few bags to secrete in parking lots and stuff. It was glass jars full of chemicals and they stunk like fuck. I didn't drop it anywhere where I should. The thought of those poor fucking pine trees and animals and plants will haunt me forever. It reminds me of me – a burnt-out shell. I just abandoned the vehicle – a station wagon – and caught a bus to California. I had a bit of speed to get me through, but other than that I was screwed. I went to LA and felt like I'd been freed from prison, even though I was a horrible wreck compared to how I was before I got into meth.'

The last I knew, Larry was stuck in LA with no money and no friends or family back home to bail him out. This once smartly-dressed young cockney had been put on the skids by meth. He wasn't the only one. Methamphetamine production is a blight on the American West. Countless tons of soil and water are contaminated every year, particularly in Arizona and Missouri, where privacy and open spaces are easy to find. Trees are poisoned and creeks are engorged with toxins, which kill cattle and sheep. The small trailer-labs belch toxic smoke and emit by-products which kill virtually every living thing in a considerable radius.

From Los Angeles, I drove to Illinois, and made a brief stop in

Chicago to watch United demolish Chelsea in the 1994 FA Cup Final. I thought of Larry and how he was oblivious to his team playing in an important match. I met a Chelsea bloke in the pub who said he'd been deported from the States once before. He'd served time in a Maine holding facility for counterfeit notes, but now he was back.

'I spent most of my time singing football songs and acting like I was off it, just to deter would-be attackers,' he explained. 'Thankfully, I was labelled a right nutter and it kept the predators away from me.'

He had a convincing demeanour and wild blond hair. I could see how his plan had worked. From there I ventured to the northeast, where the weather (and the people) are colder than most.

16

MEGALOPOLIS

It is not down in any map; true places never are.
— Herman Melville

They say Irishmen can identify 40 shades of green and Eskimos 50 types of snow. Yankees, on the other hand, are especially adept at cataloguing the myriad insanities afflicting humankind. They are as completely surrounded by madness as Irishmen and Eskimos are by chlorophyll and crystal. People organise into cliques and safety in numbers equals common sense in the northeast. Meekness is despised. They see British politeness as cowardly behaviour and aren't shy about letting you know it. Most strangely, almost none of them have ever been in a physical fight with another full-grown male. That would simply not be on. What the northeast of the USA reveres the world reviles, and vice versa. It is a very rum and contradictory do.

New England landscapes are truly beautiful, but the citizens are disjointed and horror-struck. Bostonians are largely of Irish and Italian descent and this odd blend lends a despondent air to the place. Evolved for tens of thousands of years in Mediterranean or Celtic mildness, they suddenly find themselves on the eastern edge of a continent. Their genetic confusion in the face of battering nor'easters is clearly evident. For relief, many travel down to the Cape and the islands, Martha's Vineyard and Nantucket, where lonesome dunes and attractive beach homes overlook the sapphire Atlantic. Summers are tropical, but in winter the sea roils like an enraged walrus. The silver sky spits ice into its grey, lurching depths. Wintertime is the acid test for those who fancy they can outwit the cabin fever.

Martha's Vineyard has top bars on balconies that overlook white yachts bobbing in blue harbours, their sails, antennae and ropes awash in sunshine and white-caps. Deserted beaches branch into forested coves with trees looming over the ocean's edge. The Vineyard had a dropout quality and many inhabitants were once hippies. Drugs were rampant, with the locals, the British and Irish scallies and vacationers from the mainland running amok. Edgartown centre, an orderly grid of immaculate white clapboard houses with dark green shutters, covers about eight square blocks. Many Edgartown homesteads date back to the 1600s, much earlier than most Europeans imagine. The windows are often multi-panelled and of the original glass, easily identified by its many imperfections. High privets cast shade on boathouses and resplendent white-painted sheds. Night-time windows glow with well-stocked bookcases, liquor cabinets and hand-carved hunting decoys. That square mile houses the highest concentration of beautiful, tall, blonde-haired, blue-eyed women in the United States of America during summer. It says as much about gold-diggers as it does about wealthy America's flagrant admiration for virtual Nazism and social Darwinism. The artificially-selected offspring of these elite unions are often athletic and intelligent, but sometimes fat and ugly. Such is the molecule they call DNA.

You meet interesting people on the Vineyard; fishermen, sailors, lobstermen, hoteliers, realtors and scallywags from Europe. It is the waterfront, after all. Back in the summer of '94, the going rate for house-painting was $30 an hour and times were good. We were abuzz with the World Cup and the island was packed with lads and lasses, partying and spunking their beads like drunken pirates.

'I arrived on a ferry fresh from Ireland in May 1994. Lookin' for cheap laughs an' following Ireland in the World Cup,' explains Mike from Cork. 'The Vineyard was full of lads from back home and, to be honest, I avoided a lot of them 'cos they were out of control. Boys who'd never been cokeheads had their noses buried in a mountain o' the sniff throughout the tournament. At it from the minute they knocked off to the boss pickin' 'em up the next mornin' at six for work. You can do that when you're in your 20s. We drove to New Jersey in a van for the Italy game and it was complete madness. All our lot really believed we were gonna win the competition 'cos we beat Italy. A little firm of us went from Boston. Cork lads and some plastic Irish Yanks. We were all on the building game, either on the Vineyard or in Boston, and loaded up with marching powder. I don't even remember the fuckin' goal, one of the most famous Ireland ever scored in the competition. Ask me if I gave a shite, like.

'I met a mad Yank in New Jersey who had the same name as me and he was working on the Vineyard. He ended up coming back in our van and he found me tons of work. Every night we were watching games on the telly, eyeballs burstin' with the hokey-cokey. We were raking it in and flew to Orlando for the Mexico game. Fuckin' disappointment that was. We took a van down to Jersey again for the Norway match but it was shite. Ireland's group all ended up on the same points. We got in a battle with some local wannabe gang-bangers from Newark and had to bail when they squealed to the cops. Irish lads never look for it at the match but we can only take so much shit off idiots. Without guns they're not so clever. I missed us getting beat by Holland, thank fuck. I watched it on telly in Seasons bar on the Vineyard. Finally, one night I was snorting a line off the top of a toilet-paper dispenser in a cubicle in the Ritz toilets. A guy climbed up the outside wall and popped his head over. He said, "Give me a line, pal." I packed it in after that. It made me realise how easy it was to get caught. The Vineyard was the place to be in '94, no mistake about that!'

There were others, too. I'll never forget the day I met Scally Jeff and his psychedelic entourage, Acid Steve, Ron the Geordie and Stan the Man. I was in the Ritz Café with Aussie Gavin from Lauderdale. He was now working as a photojournalist for various snowboarding and surfing magazines and travelled everywhere – Sydney, Perth, Colorado and California – taking pictures, writing articles and attending parties in the mountain chalets and beach bungalows. Lucky bastard.

There was a cacophony at the door and a mob of cool cats rolled in, looking sun-dazed and totally shady. They knew Gavin. It was quickly established that they were all tripping, E'd up and generally off their tits on a frightening cocktail of incompatible drugs. They had supermodels in tow of various ethnicities, tall, coffee-coloured specimens, with coke spots around their nostrils, literally falling over tables and making a proper show of themselves. One of the lads was carrying a surfboard and wearing a crocodile-skin cowboy hat. This was Acid Steve. One was dressed in painter's whites, a tall, gangly guy with red hair, pink skin and a vulture beak of a nose. I first thought he was an Aussie, then a yank, and I finally gave up guessing. His accent was involuntarily jumping around the globe like a demented flea. It turned out that this guy's story was too complicated to tell without devoting a chapter to that alone. This was Scally Jeff, a lad who was to become a close mate and boozing partner on the island for several years.

Occasionally, when I'm introduced to someone it's the other person who is announced as the lunatic. I always sit up and take notice. In this case it was four lunatics. They had been based in Australia for years, grafting and travelling Asia. Once they tasted the easy money of America they decided to stay. We settled in for a sesh and Jeff told me about his experiences working in a pub in the Outback:

'There was this pet ostrich,' he said. 'It lived out in the backyard, with a load of other animals. Every morning I had to feed it. I'd go out the back door, all hungover to fuck, and this thing would be like . . .' He made a bird-beak shape with his crooked hand and began weaving it back and forth, millimetres from my face. 'It was as fuckin' tall as I was, mate, and evil as fuck!'

Jeff and co spent their winters in Mexico, grafting. They sold temporary tattoos and glow-sticks along Mexico's west coast. In summer they painted houses on the Vineyard. It was the perfect lifestyle, painting millionaires' homes in the sun then jetting off to enjoy the delights of the tropical Pacific. They ended up buying a villa there, overlooking the ocean from a jungle crag on a cliff-face.

'The second time we took off for Mexico, we decided to do it on motorbikes,' remembers Jeff. 'We bought them in Los Angeles and rode right down the West Coast, through the northern deserts and into the more lush rainforests of Jalisco. We took the motorcycles down from California all the way to Guatemala City. It was a buzz covering the entire Pacific Coast of Mexico. We saw the country close up, and we saw things that were crazy. Sometimes we'd get split up, due to travelling at different speeds, and we'd lose contact for a day or two and it was wild. We stayed in cheap hotels along the way, or else kipped rough in sleeping bags, which was dodgy as fuck. One time I was riding through the outskirts of some town, and there was all this grocery stuff littered along the road. Then I saw a woman sprawled out in the road, grocery bags everywhere and blood. She was dead, and cars were just driving by like she was a fucking dog or something. Another time I came across a dead guy, same deal. We sold the bikes when we got to Guatemala. The Aussie Geordies and Acid Steve went to do the tattoos in Vallarta, and I went down to Belize to look at some land we were thinking of buying.

'We got to know a few Mexicans, mad sorts. One was a drug chemist and he worked for the Mexican Mafia, cooking speed. He invited us to Guadalajara and we travelled in an open-topped jeep with his boss 'round his neighbourhood. All the locals were coming out and waving at him, throwing flowers and blowing kisses. It was like a parade, and pretty fucking scary. This guy used to go off for vacation once he'd cooked up a big batch, to spend his wedge. He paid for everything, but he wasn't a mug. As you can imagine, we incorporated some of that into our business plan.

'In the summer we schlepped back to the Vineyard to make some good old American greenbacks. There's nowhere else in the world where you can make money like America. I know, I've been everywhere. Our crew, and several more, were painting houses on the Vineyard, stopping regularly for "snow-cones" – loosely rolled joints full of moist greed buds, sprinkled with cocaine. It helped to get those extra few square feet of wall rolled out and kept the cash-flow healthy, if nothing else. You could easily save 30 grand from May to October on the Vineyard. At the end of the summer, we'd take our cash and just spunk it all up the wall.'

The Vineyard's astronomical restaurants expected $100 for two plates of food and a huge tip to boot. We managed it frequently. My own painting company was called Salamander. Every spring I went door to door, revealing my fine European sensibilities to millionaire arrivals from Boston and New York. My red Ford pickup truck had a leaking petrol tank and a broken gauge. Cost me $20. I bought it off an English scally at the Vineyard airport the day he jetted off to California. It paid for lunch, he explained. I sanded and primed that old pickup to a glasslike finish befitting a million-dollar yacht. I brushed it out in high-gloss black using paint conditioner. Then I painted fat, jagged, yellow salamander stripes all around it. I finished the job off with 'Salamander Painting', complete with phone number, on each door in yellow. A brilliant Jamaican bloke called Errol started working for me, so I painted his Dodge van the same. We were busy bees in our mad chariots. We'd race to the finish before hitting the bars for chicken wings and beers as a bonus. Errol had once escaped from prison in Jamaica and his story was a heart-wrencher. A tale of abandon and starvation, running scared in the wilds of a wild country. He met a girl who sheltered and fed him, and they eventually married and had four kids. They all grew up and made it in Jamaica and New York. The Vineyard was full of stories and the list of mad characters was endless. I met an English painter called Axe, an expert at building wooden floors. New York mobsters used to fly him and his crew out in a private jet to build illegal fighting rings in Manhattan. They always celebrated with a massive coke binge in the city, carrying it on when they fell off the plane back on the island. Axe reckoned he'd been in every jail in England and had enjoyed a career as a jewel thief back in Blighty, cracking hotel safes along the English Riviera. I painted with a professional poker player called Bill, a dead ringer for Donald Sutherland, who went to the world poker finals annually and fared pretty well. I did a job for him painting the ceiling of a posh health-club swimming pool. We worked at night with large mobile scaffolding. Bill stood watching, pretending to be dissatisfied with my workmanship with a poker face, the tight-fisted Yankee bastard.

Alan Porter was another character. A Guildford lad, he was built like a brick shithouse and grafted like a pack-horse. He spent summers on the island and wintered in Thailand. Every time he saw me he'd bellow, 'Eh oop, our Ian, lad!' from his van. A piss-taking southerner, Alan taught me how to paint professionally (i.e. very fast) and I'll always be grateful to him for that. He lived in a bungalow down a sandy path in the Chilmark woods, where we enjoyed many a beer after work, listening to loud music and laughing our bollocks off. The scally grafters like Alan and Jeff were coming and going for a decade, sampling the stroboscopic nights of the Vineyard's Oak Bluffs nightclubs in between Mexico's west coast haunts and the idyllic bay of Thailand's Phang Nga.

'We had a whole crew of Mexican birds flogging the tattoos in the clubs on the west coast,' says Jeff. 'Many a time we'd be in the clubs ourselves, and we got into some bad drugs shit, to be honest. There was too much money and too much coke and ecstasy and we totally lost the plot. We bought a villa on a cliff-face overlooking Puerto Vallarta and the parties we had were legendary. We're talking gorgeous Mexican, European, Australian and American birds in bikinis, walking about not knowing what day it was, music blasting out across the cliffs. We drove about in a rented jeep, crashing it regularly and not giving a fuck 'cos it

IAN HOUGH

was Mexico and you do whatever you want there. I lost count of the times they had to come out and tow one away from a jungle pond or the lower boughs of a large tree. The clubs were packed with gringos and they loved the tats. The money was unreal, even better than the concerts we did in Europe years earlier. I ended up marrying a Guatemalan flight attendant, and the rest of the lads got involved with Aussie birds and were spread out all over the world.'

Jeff and his crew had no regard for craftsmanship, but they blagged their way into so many cushy numbers for big money it was ridiculous. Rather than patiently brush out the large exteriors, they would climb a ladder with a five-gallon bucket loaded with paint and roll the stuff on with an 18-inch roller, leaving a stippled 'orange peel' effect. One time, Acid Steve was 30 feet up a ladder he'd unwittingly leaned against a huge window (how, I do not know) and it went right through the window, twisting around and sending the acid man flailing to the ground. 'Paint-bucket, brush, rags, all raining down and splattering across the stone entryway to this multimillion-dollar castle,' Steve explained to me. 'The owner of the newly-built home had actually flown in from California in a private jet to supervise the mixing of the mortar for the stone patio round the swimming pool. *To make sure it was the proper colour.* The stones were imported from Italy at a cost of $80,000. They were completely ruined, mate.'

He couldn't have cared less. Another time, I met Steve driving a car around Vineyard Haven, his bandaged foot sticking out of the side window. 'I placed a rotary saw on the ground that hadn't yet stopped spinning,' he told me, 'and it jumped right across my foot, severing three toes. I was airlifted to Boston for emergency surgery. The hospital on the Vineyard couldn't handle the job.'

He spent the rest of that summer waiting for his microsurgical foot to heal and changing his identity. He was very illegal and had no visa or health insurance. The lot of them had gorgeous girls who, for some reason, were always psychotic. One in particular springs to mind; Acid Steve had to literally accompany her home to Australia before he broke the news that they were splitting up. Unfortunately, she sussed out what was going on during the flight and went so completely berserk that she was clapped in irons upon touchdown in Sydney. Steve simply bought a return to New York and flew back the same day. Mission accomplished.

Back in Britain, Johnno had recovered from that first disturbing exposure to the deteriorating mental health of the English. As he entered a certain age, he began to explore the pleasures and pitfalls of alcohol. His was an introduction that countless men had undergone through the centuries. While the so-called chav culture developed around him, Johnno went through the rite of passage of a nutcase – but an old-school nutcase, nothing to do with the sinister hooded element's violent muggings and knifings of complete innocents. It's fitting that Johnno's first voyage on the Good Ship Legless occurred in a picturesque Welsh village, and even featured an old-fashioned red phone-box:

'It's a year since that nutter put the shits up me, and I'm old enough to get in pubs. My mum had gone to live in Wales, and on a weekend down there I went out with her new boyfriend, Andy. It was my first time in a pub, and the pub was in this tiny rural village. Andy's head looked like it was going to roll off with all the nodding he was doing to people when we walked in. I was chonging away on my Embassy Number Ones, drinking pints. It was mint. I lied that I was going outside to use a phone-box; I went and had a sly piss in it. The crowd inside was too thick to get to the toilets. It trickled out through the gap onto the street . . . right to the pub entrance eight or nine feet away. I'm back inside and much the worse for wear by this point. Andy's mate mentions that some dirty bastard's had a piss right outside the entrance and all eyes avert to me at this. I stand there blinking, trying to look as innocent as possible. We then had three or four more scoops in double-quick time. Another visit to the phone-box is made, this time to puke up. I'm leaning in the narrow gap between the wall and the Tardis, having a good yak. The same feller who'd clocked the river of piss outside now announces to all that somebody's eaten chips for tea and there's some regurgitated outside on the floor for whoever wants 'em. I was no better when we got home. Andy later described how, as he was watching *Match of the Day*, I stood up with my eyes closed and walked over to the television, pulled my knob out and pissed on the TV. I then gave it a good few shakes and got back in bed, while he went and got some towels and a bowl to clean and contain the mess.'

While Johnno was pissing on his chips, others were marauding unfettered. We're not just talking about flared pants and One Love here. It was about more than serious substance abuse and travelling to have a nosy all over the gaff. It was about curry too, and kebabs. Dambuster Mellow puts it this way:

'When we came home from Holland or Spain or Thailand, we'd bring bottles of sauce and interesting woks and pans. There were no decent Thai places back in the 80s, not in the beginning. This was when all the fuss about the Bangkok Hilton and heroin smuggling had been in the media for a couple of years. Some people wouldn't go to Thailand 'cos of the corruption. They were scared of catching AIDS or getting nicked or set up with bags of smack. But you've got to bring *something* back, right? The music and clubs in Manchester were untouchable, but people added to it by bringing these other aspects to the mix. Gradually, business types worked it out and started opening up sorted gaffs that gave English culture an ace twist. A bunch of lads in a pub might just look like a load of labourers having a pint, but most of them were between trips, saving up to jet off again. The same happened with Mexican food. People went to the States and then gave Mexico itself a whirl. Fucking great culture, that. The Euro footy trips taught us loads as well, once English clubs were allowed back in. After Rotterdam in the early 90s with United, it went up a gear. Food, drugs, clothes, lifestyle; everyone wanted a taste, even the straights.'

Mexico was a place I'd wanted to visit ever since reading Carlos Castaneda's trippy tales as a teenager in Manchester. I'd met and married an American girl by now and Kim was happy to embark on this mobile lifestyle, despite some early misgivings. We took Auto Driveaways from Boston all over the place. One trip in particular stands out, from January '97. We delivered a Driveaway to a Russian woman in San Diego, setting off from the suburban hinterlands of Boston, studded with McMansions, strip malls bearing plastic clapboard façades and caricatures of historical frontages. A cartoon theme-park of a world long dead.

The Blue Ridge Mountains of Tennessee were where the sun grew warmer. Arkansas was a complete dump, fields of trashy soil that resembled northern Hungary. Little Rock was a tiny, rundown shithole in the arse-end of nowhere. It was hard to believe President Bill Clinton came from there. They had snow in Southern Texas for the first time in aeons, with juggernauts overturned all along the interstate. We hit some great little Mexican cantinas, applying vast quantities of hot sauce to beef tacos. The sky was a vast blue, trailed with long, white clouds by the gulf winds. A huge ball of ice ripped half the underside of the front bumper outside Tucson, Arizona. I disguised it on delivery by tearing the tattered remainder off. Losing our deposit was not an option. Kim kept saying, 'This is exactly the kind of place you imagine a homicide will happen,' in each of the sleazy motels we stayed in. There is no need to consult *Lonely Planet* when travelling America; every town you approach on the interstate is preceded by a succession of gigantic billboards advertising gas, food, lodging and attractions, like the pages of some megalithic travel guide.

The approach to San Diego on Interstate-8, AKA the Ocean Beach Freeway, is a giant slope all the way to the shimmering Pacific. The interstate runs between steep valley sides covered in massive trees, bushes and funky buildings. Big green exit signs hang above it and cars whiz on and off in the frenetic sprawl. We checked into a hotel right on the beach and watched the sun go down through the sliding doors. Just $45 a night, a fitting end to yet another ride across America.

Two days later we walked through the battered turnstile at the Mexican border. We checked into a scruffy little room in downtown Tijuana. Mexican football was on the ancient telly but no English Premier League. The streets swarmed with people selling monkeys, parrots in wooden cages, cartons of cigarettes and lumps of dope. We spent the night in bars full of screaming, underage Americans, taking advantage of the lax Mexican licensing laws. Music blared constantly. There was an untameable sense of vulnerability I'd never known before. The sounds of trumpets, arguments and car-horns invaded our window all night long. A guy caught in a tropical downpour with no hands or feet crawled rapidly along the pavement on his elbows and knees, faster than most people were walking. How he'd lost his extremities was a complete puzzle. He wasn't even wearing pads.

We had no idea where we'd be staying each night, leaving our options wide open. We took buses down the Pacific Coast. Out in the ocean, people canoed between huge rocks that towered as a gateway to open water, like the edge of the world in *Jason and the Argonauts*. A battered bus took us from Manzanillo to Armeria, then another into Cuyutlan. The locals kept a firm eye on us and a firm grip on their goats and chickens. Cuyutlan was famous for its kilometre-long waves, sheer walls of water 20-feet high. The local kids could have been world surfing champions if they'd made it to California. One day I saw a fish, about three feet long, swimming through a wall-like wave right in front of me.

A tiny handful of gringos lived on the beach with the wintering Mexicans. We met a guy who had a mobile home and a shortwave radio. He was an avid Manchester United fan and we enjoyed a trip down Memory Lane. It seems there are United fans everywhere you go; we met another drinking in a bar on the beach. He spent his winters in Cuyutlan. Every night the crashing of the green waves took you into a dream-state, audible as they were from our hotel room. From the volcano in Colima we hit the inland road towards Mexico City.

Mexico City – or the Distrito Federale (DF), as it is known in Mexico – is one of the Americas' largest cities (two continents of megalopolis) and is too big to contemplate all in one chunk. The mind is forced to divide it into sections, each larger than most other metropolises. The Hotel Habana offered a king-sized room for about four quid a night. The Metro was notorious for pickpockets, especially on the infamous Chapultepec line to the museums. They don't use sleight of hand like European dippers, but they're more creative. They crowd you from three sides as you board the Metro and grab your wallet in the confusion. I had my phrase book pick-pocketed in this way. (My wallet was in the breast pocket of the t-shirt I wore inside-out under my jumper, tucked into my shorts.) Mobs of mariachis sometimes stream onto the buses and start belting out tunes on their accordions, guitars or various unidentifiable instruments. This can also be used as a distraction by the dippers.

Archaeological sites like Teotuhuacan slowly bake in the strange sunshine of Central Mexico. Tula was home to a band of warrior-priests who lived to take psychedelic drugs and fight with neighbouring tribes. In Cholula stands the biggest pyramid in the world, overgrown with large trees and plants. A spiral road leads to its summit, where the Spanish built a church.

We hit the Veracruz Carnival, the biggest between Rio and New Orleans, with drunken, dancing bodies everywhere. Luckily, we scored a room overlooking the central square (referred to in Mexico as the Zócalo). I drank mescal on the balcony and chewed the worm while I watched the shenanigans everywhere below. The bizarre blend of Christianity and Native American sorcery pulsated superbly.

We ventured into the State of Chiapas, recently re-opened following the Zapatista Rebellion. Indigenous Mayan Indians had fought the Mexican government toe-to-toe in shoot-outs in the cloud-forests. We visited a couple of Indian villages and saw a ceremony involving an alcoholic drink substituted for a previous psychotropic drug of old. The Zapatistas weren't having any of this Western bullshit; they wanted to be able to live as they pleased. It was an interesting illustration of how people are the same wherever you go. In one village they wore red, like United, and really had their act together; the other village wore blue, like Manchester City, and they were a sorry bunch. Their architecture was wank, like City's, and their 'parties' were shite – ditto as the above. It's a funny old world, innit?

We visited Palenque, a cluster of ancient pyramids and temples in a rainforest full of monkeys, once controlled by a Mayan prince with a club foot who shagged his own sister. Took a boat trip through a kilometre-deep canyon, along a river full of crocodiles where the Indians washed their clothes on stones along the banks. It was like *The Lost World*. On the Yucatan Peninsula we saw yet more pyramids and ruins. We snorkelled in the Caribbean and enjoyed the habanero peppers that grow plentifully. Then we headed back to the DF, via a few little towns here and there. I even found a shop in Villahermosa selling black crocodile-skin cowboy hats like Acid Steve's. (I still kick myself for not buying one.) We spent a few days at the Habana in the DF, before flying to Houston and on to Boston. It had been a good three-month trek across a large portion of the US and Mexico. It cost us what most 'normal' people spent on a fortnight in Spain.

In late '98 we took off to the southern States. A laptop served us well, both for writing and winding up people in chatrooms when we were bored. Caught in an ice storm in Virginia, we had a smash on a clover-leaf connecting interstates outside Richmond. The slip roads were coated in sleek ice. We retired to a hotel and drank. Marsha, a friend in Massachusetts whose family we'd been staying with along the way, phoned to tell us that her brother had been shot at point-blank range in the chest and was in a coma in Georgia. It wasn't a pleasant night. (Marsha's brother, Dave, later came up to the Vineyard to convalesce. We became good mates, as he was a sound bloke.)

The next day, Christmas Eve, was like Armageddon. Power lines down everywhere, including a transformer that fell right in front of the car in a shower of sparks. Clean underwear was required. We drove to

Asheville, North Carolina along Interstate 85, onto I-40. The entire interstate was deserted. We had to drive around fallen trees and mounds of debris in eerie silence. Our Christmas dinner was a Subway sandwich, after which we relocated to a bizarre motel, drinking Wild Irish Rose, while Kim settled for tea. The motel was a strange cluster of futuristic concrete buildings backed up against a weird range of foothills with parking lots and driveways intersecting it. The police never stopped coming. We watched a nightly show from our balcony: red, white and blue lights spangling, Asheville troopers steaming in to arrest crack dealers and pimps. Kim wasn't amused at being in such an environment at Christmas, but I was in my element. I enjoyed socialising with the denizens of this bizarre complex, swapping stories from our respective cultures. It was the new frontier, a mishmash of technology and lawlessness surrounded by mountainous granite, large trees, rednecks and New Age entrepreneurs drawn to the city by the 'Vortex' – an alleged field of healing energy emanating from high underground concentrations of quartz crystal. These gentle capitalist souls made a good living selling expensive holistic cosmetics and bumper stickers that read 'Keep Asheville Weird'.

We covered much of the South that winter, including Fort Lauderdale, which by then had finally lost its allure. Crashing out in orange groves full of lizards wasn't so inviting anymore. My favourite Floridian memory from that trip is of eating frogs' legs in the Everglades (which tasted more like fish than the oft-cited chicken, for the record); as we were in the South, the frogs' legs were deep-fried and tasted sensational – even if I did feel a bit sorry for the frogs.

17

1999 AND ALL THAT

The longest journey a man must take is the 18 inches from his head to his heart.
— Unknown

Any Manchester United fan will tell you that 1999 was a good year. United were scintillating on the pitch. The whole Euro atmosphere from the 1991 Cup Winners' Cup triumph was rekindled in the Nou Camp, with the greatest win in the club's history. But not everyone was cheering for United. Some were light years away from the pomp and ceremony witnessed in Manchester city centre, where an alleged million people welcomed the Reds home with the European Cup. As they did in '91 after Cup Winners' Cup glory in Rotterdam, Mancs once more sang, 'Always Look on the Bright Side of Life'. Others, meanwhile, were living in distant cities and bivouacking on star-splashed beaches. The events in Barcelona meant nothing to them, especially if they followed a different team and had had a bellyful of the Red Devils. A bellyful of red Thai curry was preferable.

The return to Britain had become something we were all familiar with by now, excitement at seeing old friends and family tinged with mild repulsion at the tame lifestyle. There were, of course, the football firms eking out an existence in tiny pockets. Some ex-hooligans and scallies really wanted to try and make it in the regular workaday world rather than by grafting snide gear. It was never gonna happen. Dominic Lavin had returned from Thailand and was once again attempting to co-exist with the straight-heads:

'I don't know what went wrong when I got back to England. I settled into a respectable job with a company BMW and Hugo Boss suit, and could be seen around town at the weekend with a large-breasted blonde on my arm and a mobile phone welded to my ear. That's where the glamorous world of IT recruitment got me. But by 1999 I'd had enough; me and the blonde split, as did me and my boss, and I was on a plane to Bangkok. Since then I've been back and forward like a pervert's arse, getting a job here or there and flitting off when the bank balance permitted until it was empty again. In the interim I've written a novel, *Last Seen in Bangkok,* based on my manoeuvres in that region. The tourist areas of the country are crammed full of fine specimens of British masculinity who will have lived the casual life. One of Pattaya's most famous bars is the Dog's Bollocks, co-owned by an ex-Chelsea Headhunter and one of Arsenal's top lads. If you believe the press, most of the patrons are pathetic, cropped-haired thugs embarking on Bacchanalian, drug-fuelled excesses with 20-year-old prostitutes. To be fair, that's a pretty honest description of the Englishman's life in Thailand; "Hurrah for them and me," is what I say. Why stand in a pub doorway smoking fags in the cold and damp of a Manchester November, paying £3 a pint, getting crippled by a mortgage, when you can sit in the Dog's watching the menagerie in glorious sunshine?'

These are valid questions. But as time goes by and the bachelor herd grows smaller, they find themselves in a cruel world. Football's cosmetic makeover means expensive tickets. Lads who spent their youths and young adulthoods roaming the nation's football grounds and the world's hot spots now have trouble rustling up the cash for match tickets, having landed back at an airport penniless with just a holdall containing their entire worldly goods.

I was fortunate that my wife, Kim, put me on the straight and narrow for my own good. New Englanders really do live through four quite distinct seasons and, even though their order never changes, the threshold from one to the next never fails to move you. It is celestial drama of a quite jolting nature, and Yankees use the seasons to orient themselves. Kim didn't drink or waste her youth hanging out with the wrong crowd – apart from the time she spent hanging out with me – but I did manage to convince her that pissing all your money away could be great fun, on occasion. For the first time in my life, with the exception of Scally Jeff and a few cockneys I worked with, I was completely surrounded by quite sensible people.

All my life growing up in Manchester, I now realised, had been spent with some warm souls, but they were only after happiness and laughter.

Couples attracted back home because they wanted to *fuck* each other and any other reason was considered daft. This lot were different; they wanted money, prestige and recognition for being experts at manipulating the game of life to their advantage. They settled down with partners chosen for their prospects rather than the way they smelled. They were the kind of people who wouldn't have lasted five minutes where I came from, for one very good reason: they took themselves far too seriously. But it was what I needed; I didn't take myself seriously enough, and never had.

New Englanders believe a long life is the greatest achievement of all. They do this by staying cleverly *within* the speed limit, or by only eating foods that are good for you. Anyone who drinks frequently to excess or eats too much fried dough is considered pathological, regardless of overall intelligence and athleticism. Anyone who swears too often is considered not a bit of a character but a person lacking in vocabulary – an opinion that found some purchase in Britain around 100 years ago. Being sensible is prized over all else. They'd rather be thrilled by following instructions than bending the rules. But they'll bend the rules if they have a lawyer's assurance that they'll get away with it. I wouldn't describe it so much as mainstream thought, more as a form of cult mentality; when 19 out of 20 people say it's Thursday, then it's Thursday – *even if it's really Saturday*. In America, they call this madness 'democracy'. Elsewhere it is called fascism, or at the very least intense bullying. But the mind-numbing minutiae of American logic needn't be discussed here.

Thankfully, not all Americans are such dry and calculating people; I have been fortunate enough to make some fantastic friends here who make all the insanity worthwhile. You have to look for them, but the good Yanks are some of the best people on the planet. Their whole crazy situation is what comes of having the biggest guns to rob everyone else of their natural resources. But I love it more than I hate it.

*   *   *

For some relief, let's return to the rest of the world. Thailand certainly isn't a place that takes itself too seriously. Dominic Lavin's exploits continued as he entered the snide goods industry, the very same one that supplies the grafters back in Britain with their wares. Lavin discovered that Thailand had no end of opportunities on that count:

'The tales of misadventure are fucking endless. I mean, where d'you start? I've got one mate, a well-known Cardiff City fan who got nicked smoking weed in a bar and was put in a cell with 20 Cambodian immigrants until two of them tried to rape him. He bit one of their ears off and stabbed the other with a plastic fork to protect his virginity (so he says). On one occasion he'd been smoking ketamine all day and drove his motorbike through the glass front of a hairdresser's shop. The same guy is the one who introduced me to the idea of selling fakes.

'The connection between Wigan and Cardiff is quite well documented and, when I heard his accent in a bar, I started chatting to him. We discussed mutual friends while he did lines of coke and things went on from there. The bar owner warned me that he was a psycho who carried an array of weapons with him. When I quizzed him he emptied his pockets, showing me his knives, CS gas, stun gun, pepper spray, you name it; we had a right good laugh. I felt like Hans Blick. He'd got a wad of cash together and disappeared to Thailand to avoid getting nicked every weekend at the match and to get away from crack cocaine. His funds had been raised by him and his mates making fake passes for things like Royal Ascot and Glastonbury and shepherding hopefuls in for a few quid. He also supplemented his wad by selling the readily available Hattie designer goods [Hattie Jacques = fakes] on a well known internet auction site. He'd apparently made £1200 on a Louis Vuitton luggage set that he'd bought for about £40. It sounds a bit low-rent, but if you get a decent price for ten Rolexes it can pay for a return flight. I remember walking through customs at Manchester Airport on my way back once with a baggy jacket on, five Rolexes on my left arm and five Breitlings on my right with the pins pulled out to stop them ticking. I felt like a World War II spiv and I was trying not to jangle as I moved, while the Customs officer looked through my suitcase and failed to notice the 20 fake Ralph Lauren polo shirts I'd crumpled and turned inside out to make them look like they were worn.'

But it wasn't just Thailand that had Brits on the graft. Australia was a hop, skip and a jump away from there, and the lads were having a royal beano in the sun. It had its own world of opportunity, from the Sydney-Hobart boat race to the Australian Open tennis tournament, and the grafters from Manchester, Liverpool and London had a corner of the market sewn-up and taken care of. But there were also good old-fashioned Man United fans there, too, like Johnno.

Johnno had finally flown the iron bird over to Sydney. The tendency to sport classic or vintage designer wear was taking hold, not just among the older crowd anxious to retain a grip on their youth, but also on younger kids in Britain. Johnno was a member of this younger element, several worlds apart from the suicidal chav trend which had replaced the casuals of old. The casuals enjoyed challenging other football mobs, but they had certain standards and codes, and tried – for the most part – to uphold them. Social commentators and academics have tried to discredit this view, but it'll be recognised in the next few years how the casuals were among the last decent nutcases to make Blighty their home before washing their hands of the place. The chav of today has made the casuals look like the fine, upstanding citizens they actually are.

Johnno's earlier brush with the mental patient was fast becoming a common experience, and he was glad to get away. Australia was a new world. But he quickly sensed a sartorial and stylistic ignorance in Oz, and a cosmetic mindlessness that irritated him. He describes how Australia's social scene is organised similarly to the old European sports clubs of the previous century – albeit with a drunken Anglo-Saxon twist – and expresses amazement at the concept of lawn-bowling clubs. This is a sad echo for those of us old enough to remember when innumerable pubs, church institutes and social clubs featured bowling greens all over Britain:

'It was 1996. Oasis ruled the airwaves and United ruled English football. Off came the dark green blazers, white shirts and charcoal pants of the school uniform. Out came the Adidas tracksuit tops worn with jeans and a white pair of classic trainers (Adidas being the choice of many). I personally invested in a navy blue Kappa tracksuit top which differed from the many Adidas wearers, but it looked mint and I hardly had it off. I was one of the first to wear a Kappa jacket round our way and it became almost my trademark clobber. Despite not wearing it for many years it's still hanging up in my wardrobe at home, complete with massive drop-out burn in the acrylic material from a disgracefully loose spliff. I'm waiting for it to become retro again so I can let my kids wear it in a few years.

'I decided do a stint in Australia. I had been born there to an Aussie dad and English mother, so I have always had the passport, therefore no visa was required. The plane made a couple of stops on its mammoth journey to Oz. We landed in Sydney and I can still remember that I had my striped-blue Fred Perry polo shirt I'd bought from a store in Affleck's Palace, a pair of blue boot-cut jeans and my Adidas classics. At this point I was totally unsure just how long I would be in Australia. I'd spent four years bragging to my mates that I would move to Oz when I was older. I sometimes wish I could go back to the very first time I got to walk the streets of Sydney as that 18-year-old kid with an Oasis haircut, only a few hundred dollars to my name, with such hopes and not knowing what was to come.

'That first day, my uncle Col asked me to meet him at the club near Botany Bay where he drank. In Australia there are clubs and bars. The culture is for the residents to become members of clubs which serve the community; there are Returned Servicemen League Clubs, better known as RSLs. There are also other league clubs, such as Professional Rugby League Clubs, etc. Effectively, there are all sorts of clubs available and the way it works is you become a member if you live within four kilometres of the club for a small fee per year, depending how ritzy the area of town is you live in. There's only one RSL per suburb, but it's not uncommon to have the main club in the suburb you live in to be a lawn bowls club. Imagine that in Manchester; the residents having a beer in a lawn bowls club! In the swanky eastern suburb town of Paddington, the locals are well-known for being extremely well-off and the area is choc-a-block full of trendy, artsy coffeehouses, bars, cocktail lounges and boutiques. The place to be seen on a Saturday afternoon is the local bowling club. The beautiful people of the 18-30 age range play barefoot bowls in their over-sized Dolce & Gabbana sunglasses, whilst sipping a cold bottle of imported European lager, or a Cosmo for the young ladies. The twats!

'I remember the first time I went to the famous King's Cross, and the King's X Hotel. The Cross is Sydney's red-light district. Although it has become a ridiculously overpriced area for yuppies, it still remains very seedy with dodgy strip clubs, brothels and scores of addicts drawn there. From that first magic moment in the cab into the city, with the twinkling lights of the skyscrapers, I was hooked. I've always been a night owl and definitely a city slicker. I will generally take a city-scene choc-full of skyscrapers, bridges and bustling streets over a pristine, pretty meadow as my ideal setting. These days it may be a nice beach with a turquoise-blue ocean, but there's nowt like a big, strange city coming into view at night-time when you're heading out on the piss.

'People I met who were my age all seemed to dress very immaturely, almost like little kids. The white Aussie lads all wore baggy shorts or jeans, generally the obligatory Rip Curl or Billabong being the main brands. It was all baggy surf t-shirts and chunky trainers like Airwalk and skateboard shoes that looked shite. The girls were similar to the English girls in the sense that the clothes they wore were to accentuate their figures, short skirts and vest-tops with their tits bulging out. This is where the comparison ended. English girls appeared to put more effort into things. I also noticed most Aussie girls didn't have any particular shape to their hair; they just grew it long in no particular style. It was like the Jennifer Aniston do that had swept England a few years earlier due to her starring in the television show *Friends*. None seemed to have any highlights even.'

It's quite comical for me to hear a typical English-raised lad discuss fashions – and women's fashions at that – in this level of detail; most American men are so utterly bereft of an incentive to *ever* mention what they wear that to do so is virtually an admission of effeminacy. Little do they know that some of the toughest nuts in Britain spent their entire formative years wallowing in a designer-label fetish, spawning extensive discussion of fabrics, hairstyles and footwear.

Those born in the 1960-1980 period are filled with psychological scars that they insist are 'normal'. The normalcy persists only if they are able to remain within their own culture, in the working-class enclaves – be they high-rise flats, council estates or transplanted suburbs swarming with nutcases – where violence, substance abuse, depression and crime are at least semi-acceptable. Once they venture outside these zones of commonality, their 'crimes' and the relative dysfunction of their general lives are thrown into sharp relief. They are products of our nation's dismal economic record dating from 30 years ago. The crater inflicted by Margaret Thatcher's Conservative government on Britain's economic landscape was a true depression – one which many of our generation still struggle to climb out of; it's hard to think (or act) 100 percent honestly when you've been forced to steal things and earn cash on the side since you were 16 years old, but we can try. In effect, we are the last of the cavemen. The last ones to remember a world lit by fire.

Mellow Yellow has an extraordinary grasp of the situation, despite being a total dropout:

'It's like a race against time; as I've aged I've become more sensible and mixed with more sensible people. But all I have to offer are memories and experiences from being a criminal, so I'm classed as an outsider even though I'm tamed right down. I can't say fuck-all about things I've done because they'll be frightened of me. The white-collar cliques think I don't notice when they talk about me, and I've become resentful of their lack of discretion. I want to say, "Fuck you!" and walk away from it all, but I can't because I'm trying to be sensible. And you know it's 'cos they weren't caned, slippered and slapped as kids, so they have no wariness in them. The younger generation in Britain, America and Australia never had corporal punishment in the education systems and it really shows. For someone like me, you can always slip back into the crime and it's surprisingly easy to do when you're older. It's corny as fuck, but all it takes is to remember living skint in a two-up, two-down and I'm ready for a mad bevy.'

No corporal punishment? Deep down you know that this is the way to go, as illustrated by the improved attitudes of kids when the constant threat of physical violence from authority figures is removed. People reaching their mid- to late-teens at the turn of the 80s inherited a legacy of territoriality and violence. As time passed they also became the first generation to experience mass vertical interaction within the British class system. Via the culture of travel, music, drugs and football, perhaps we escaped the misery of our lot. We were the ones who first woke up to the fact we could actually do something to change our lives – probably because we were the first to live in a world where change could be realistically effected.

Those original crews who got 'on their bikes' to escape recession and exploit the naiveté of continental business owners had an incentive to travel. The motivation was pure adventure, with the added bonus of an earner thrown in. As Colin Blaney explained, the Brits composed a significant fraction of the grafters working Europe's stadiums, and they refused to give up their newfound pitch in life's black market. But how well do we adapt to the culture of 'normality'?

The nine-to-five routine is extremely difficult to adhere to. Our generation has been forced to live by hook or by crook. Many of us prefer to earn money in a fluid, spontaneous environment populated by others like ourselves. The irony of this is that many of us are among the hardest workers of our age. We can literally shovel shit for hours in horrendous conditions, without food or water, in exchange for peanuts. While this marks you out as a tough customer among the young travellers, it is a trait utterly reviled by those from the middle classes. The workers populating Israel's *moshavim* and construction sites in the 80s and 90s possessed this quality. They were an unlimited supply of dispensable labour, arriving on planes and ferries all year round. They were treated like dirt by employers and rebelled by drinking, fighting and making nuisances of themselves, just as they did in Britain. These self-contradictory working-class values displaced the 'English disease' thousands of miles across the globe, where it was observed, often with repulsion, by foreigners.

The concept of the British yob is well-established. Hooligan authors now publish memoirs and make films about football hooliganism. Other youth trends – like teds, mods and punks – were rapidly paid tribute by books and movies in their likeness (or what the media thought was their likeness) very soon after their emergence. But casual culture – the continental-design mischief-makers who ran the football firms, invented rave and travelled longer and further than any of their forebears – took decades to become accepted and popularised by the media. Only now, as the bachelor herd and ex-nutters reach middle age and find openings in media and marketing outlets, do we see this happening.

Travel does fuck you up, though. There's a price to pay for putting yourself in an alien world, away from the loons and the pissheads. Like a polar bear in a zoo I miss my native landscape: alehouses, rainy streets, humour and madness. The ravaged carnival of all-weekend publife, the cackling maniacs showing off their charge sheets from Bootle Street nick in central Manchester, or some other city where they wrought havoc for a day on behalf of MUFC, their religion. When I wrote *Perry Boys* I was ignorant of the Pandora's Box I was opening in my own unconscious; for once you descend into the chaotic realms of British subculture it's difficult to emerge unscathed. Memories of thieving, kickings and mobbings assail you.

A shuddering segment of one's personal history plops onto the draining board of the mind like an unwelcome newborn relative, grinning sickly as it gurgles speech. The memories shine like vibrant hallucinations. They are diluted in the brain's timelines, but their flavours and colours never go away.

18

SMACK IN THE OUTBACK

Your theory is crazy, but it's not crazy enough to be true.
— Niels Bohr

Thailand and China are major sources of counterfeit merchandise, which grafters transport around the world to service punters at myriad sporting and concert events. Australia is closest to Thailand and, for at least a decade or two, the grafters had a field day there. Mellow, who has lived in Sydney, describes the situation in Australia:

'For years now the English have been grafting in Oz. They did it when they knew they could, coming in and doing the business before the Aussies knew the score. Recently, the Australian authorities have cottoned on and the merchandise has been severely curtailed. I've seen thousands of boxes of snide Oakley sunglasses and Armani shirts, stacked in lads' flats in Sydney, ready to go out to the punters at parades and sporting events. I remember when I first arrived in Oz. I spent time in Melbourne and out in the bush, then I went to Sydney. I was doing the rounds of the pubs with a lad I knew from Manchester, knocking out Tommy Hilfiger coats, sunglasses and snide Rolex watches, all fresh from Thailand. One lad used to go to China and order loads of televisions, and even they were snide! He had them brought over in containers, eventually he got caught and had all his tellies took off him.

'One year, I worked the Gay Pride Parade in Sydney on Mardi Gras. One of the lads bought hundreds of plastic stools and brought them in vans. There were a good few teams of grafters from Manchester working that parade. We were taking the stools and flogging them to punters to stand on so they could see over the crowd when the floats came past. Every time we sold out we'd run back to the vans and grab a load more. I was working with a backpacker from Manchester who was passing through. Some of them made $300 in a few hours, depending on which spot they had. These days it's more about tickets than anything else. The Aussies have clamped right down on the snide gear, and loads have been fined and deported and everything. It was always Mancs, scousers and cockneys doing the graft. One bloke started importing all this detergent from China. It was total bollocks and it fucking burned holes in everyone's clothes. The police ended up raiding him and they found boxes of this stuff from China that he was putting in smaller boxes and selling. There've been millions of lads over here doing the business, but it seems like it's dying off now apart from the tickets. One of the biggest tycoons is a bloke who brings snide sunglasses into Britain. He ships 'em in on containers and knocks them out all over the gaff. He's got Britain sewn up and he's not even fuckin' British!'

Thailand has other benefits than cheap counterfeit goods too, according to Mellow:

'Travel insurance is a big industry for the lads in Australia. Blokes go over to Bangkok having taken out travel insurance first. When they get there, they go to a bent dentist and say they've fell off a bike or something, and broken their teeth. There's fuck-all wrong with their Newtons [Newton Heath = teeth]. These Thai dentists give them top crowns and sort all their Newtons out for nothing. The dentists there are really good as well, but they're happy to do it on the insurance. So the lads do the ten-hour flight from Sydney, a bit of shagging on the side, and everyone's happy.'

My mate Kenny has some glowing reports from Oz of his own:

'I've met loads of people over here from all over Britain, and a lot have been everywhere before they arrived here. One day I met this lad from Bradford in a pub and he said to me, "I know you!" I asked him where from, and he said, "You were on that big job in Berlin. You were always pissed up in the pub, singing Man United songs!" It's a small world, but it never ceases to amaze me when things like that happen. The Aussies are a decent crowd, to be honest. I'd much rather be here than in the States. Australian blokes grow up with Rugby League and swimming, and they're all big lads. My local is the Coogee Bay Hotel, said to be the second most violent pub in New South Wales. Last week there was a mass brawl with all the bouncers steaming in and everything. The pub is truly massive, with a giant beer garden overlooking the beach. I like the Aussies 'cos they can have a fight but they lack the evilness of the English – they won't bully or victimise or give it the verbal abuse like you get back home. Even though they're all trained up to fuck, they're loud and leery. They're easy to talk to but they'd never involve you in a fight just for the sake of it.'

People in England think of Thailand and Australia as close neighbours, but in fact Bangkok and Sydney are farther apart than London and Chicago. The counterfeit industry serving grafters in the UK, Australia and other industrialised countries uses Thailand's prostitution and amazing beaches as sideshows to attract clients wanting to sell a few thousand replica football shirts or Oakley sunglasses. Dominic Lavin's t-shirt-smuggling adventures were inevitable, coming and going from Bangkok as he did. With the British rave scene as a backdrop, people like Lavin began to sense a profit in snide designer gear. His brushes with customs officials on his way into England were part of a largely ineffective attempt by British authorities to stem the flow of fake merchandise from the Far East, but the process was more comedic than anything. Lavin has numerous stories of his exploits and enjoys retelling them, especially the ones involving re-entry into Britain:

'There was one guy who stopped me about four times running at Heathrow on the way back. It was the same fellow every time, and I confidently let him look through my bag. I'd developed a relationship with an agent who would post the Hatties from Bangkok for me when I transferred money to her bank account (she's called Pim and works as a nude lesbian showgirl in a bar called Suzi Wong's) to save me carrying them through customs. The routine with customs is they sort of casually stand by you at the conveyer belt as you wait for your bag. Then they walk alongside you and chat as if they're your mate. Then they say, "Is it OK if we take a look in your bag, sir?"

'Obviously it isn't, but you go along with it and then, as they open up, they ask you if you know what you can and can't bring into the country. On one occasion I was reeling off the list to a fellow who'd taken a shine to me, saying, "Drugs, firearms, ammunition, livestock."

'When he dipped in my suitcase and pulled out a gecko that had somehow made it in there I was at a loss for an explanation. It had frozen solid in the hold of the aircraft so I shrugged and suggested that he put it on the radiator to thaw out.

'There was one guy who'd called in the Bollocks for a couple of beers before he got his taxi to the airport on the way home, and when he nipped for a piss somebody sneaked a bag of curry powder into his bag. When customs got him at Heathrow he shat himself, thinking he'd had a kilo of heroin planted on him.'

Of course, the business of smuggling snide clothing into Britain wouldn't be so lucrative if there weren't still some people there who placed great value on designer sportswear. Casual fashion collectors all over Britain frequent internet message boards in their pursuit of obscure labels and discontinued stock from decades past. Some of these collectors own literally dozens of pairs of Adidas vintage training shoes and deadstock tracksuits and cagoules. They barter with them to prise other, more desirable items from the clammy paws of other collectors. A network exists across Britain and across the world, wherein collectors earn their reputations via message boards according to their recent performance in shipping goods to others. When someone puts counterfeit merchandise on an internet site for sale, it is usually left to the buyer's ability to discern whether it is genuine or not.

The laws surrounding online auctions of casual sportswear are murky indeed. Counterfeits are as old as the hills, and it's been a long road from lads sewing Lacoste logos onto t-shirts and jumpers in their bedrooms to the limitless possibilities of the internet. Lavin discovered that money could be made, and if you couldn't go to the mountain then the mountain could come to you:

'When I started putting fakes on the "well-known internet auction site", I was pleasantly surprised at how much stuff sold for. A t-shirt that would go for £15 could be bought in Bangkok for £2 on a stall. If you sell 20 or so a week you've soon got a bit more holiday money. Certain brands like Diesel, Stone Island, Armani and Abercrombie & Fitch didn't seem to give a flying fuck about what was going on, while others would have your listing removed and threaten you with legal action. After a while, I got an email from a guy called Mohammed who was doing things like Stone Island and Armani sweatshirts wholesale. Fuck knows where he got them from, but by ploughing the proceeds back in I soon had in the region of 100 items on at any one time. In the run-up to Christmas that year my house was full of boxes.

A month later I boarded a flight with several thousand whiskey vouchers in the bank which I distributed generously across the length and breadth of Thailand.'

*   *   *

The Outback is not a real place. It's a concept used by Australians to denote any region that lies beyond the reach of the urban centres. The Bush is a similarly used expression, and as kids Kezz and I used to pretend we were embarking on safaris to the region in Prestwich Clough. North Manchester lad Johnno was about to become familiar with the Bush, when his Aussie dad put him in touch with a friend who agreed to take him as a worker. Johnno travelled to Moree, a town over 400 miles northwest of Sydney, to sample a life utterly different from any he'd known before:

'A few weeks after arriving in Sydney, I headed up to Moree in northern New South Wales to go and work for one of my dad's mates. My grandfather had owned a few pubs in Sydney and owned one out in Moree for a couple of years when my dad was a teenager. He'd gone to school with a feller called Doyle who I'd met once or twice when very young. Moree Shire is probably bigger than Northern England in size, yet the town itself only had around 10,000 people back then. Its main source of industry is wheat, cattle and cotton. Doyle was a contractor on one of the largest cotton farms in Australia. My dad had sorted it so I could work for Doyle and see a bit of Australia beyond the typical Bondi Beach and the inside of a pub.

'Before I left, my dad's advice and warnings about Moree were ringing in my ears – he had told me to be careful about being a smart-arse up there, something which I was and probably still am. The country folk, despite talking and acting very slow, wouldn't stand for some little pommie cunt taking the piss and were prone to belt the fuck out of you. He also gave me a few words of wisdom about the lads in the pubs to have a beer with. There was a bit of nastiness between the local Aborigines and the white population over the previous 20 or 30 years. Aboriginal rights became a focal point in the late 60s. Moree carried the burden of being Australia's equivalent of Alabama, with young black kids actually being lynched in the olden days. I was also warned about the king browns, bastard snakes that would bite you and give you a nasty dose of venom. The eastern brown snake is around the second or third most toxic snake in Australia. You heard a lot of stories about blokes having their arms or legs amputated after being bitten, some even dying.

'My dad advised me to bring a book and have a few beers, as it's a long ride up there. I set off on a Sunday morning about 9:00 am. As the train headed out through the western suburbs, I remember being in awe of how big Sydney was. We trundled out to Strathfield to collect more passengers, then threw a right up over the Parramatta River, which is a continuation of Sydney Harbour towards the northern suburbs. An hour into the trip we still weren't out of Greater Sydney. I decided to get a scran and a can of Tooheys New. I watched the world go by out the window, checking out the distinctly different countryside to that of northwest England. The scraggy trees, for one, so much different to the lush, green trees back in the UK with no leaves and stringy bark, the grass all brown and yellow from the scorching sun. Everywhere seemed incredibly flat. I had been out in the sticks on previous visits, but never this far inland and not on my own.

'The train was skipping stations every so often and not stopping. I could see their names, dead unusual gaffs like Muswellbrook, Scone, Murrurundi, Quirindi, Gunnedah, etc. The entire way, the train stopped maybe four or five times at certain towns. I used such opportunities to dive to the open doors and cane a cig down as fast as I could. The first instance, the rail guard with his flag took grave offence for some reason and told me very harshly I wasn't to smoke. He got told to fuck off before I resumed duty at my new post-in between the café-bar and the toilets, jabbering away to anyone who was daft enough to listen. I was pissed with all the Tooheys I'd necked. The same cranky rail guard from earlier told me to get back on board when I had another smoke at a rare stop. I rolled my eyes as if to say, "You can't fuck with me mate, I'm from Cheetham Hill." As if he gave a fuck where Cheetham Hill was; there were no hills anywhere in sight, with the land as flat as my first girlfriend's tits.'

When an English city-dweller first makes his way into true country, it is always an eye-opening experience. Few who haven't lived it really know what it's like; the desire on the part of urban men to wear fashionable clothing is viewed as contemptibly effeminate, as is owning a car simply for its stylish looks. Country men are raised to make money from natural resources, from scratch, as it were. An ability to fix engines and other mechanical contraptions is vital, as is an understanding of local soil chemistry, seasonal change and vegetation – particularly food crops which can be grown at a profit. Country boys wear durable boots, jeans and jackets. They drive pickup trucks, vans and quad bikes. The Adidas Vintage collection and skirted-up saloon cars with nice paintjobs are not for them; cars are generally driven by women. After a while in the country, you start to see why.

*   *   *

Around this time, 1998, I was coming to grips with the peculiarities of rural New England. (Strangely enough, Moree is also in New England – New England, New South Wales, that is.) I was preparing to attend the University of Massachusetts (UMass), where quite a few British football supporters were to be found. There were scousers, Cornishmen, Irish, Londoners and Lancastrians. There were also masses of Europeans, Africans and Asians, all well into their footy. We would regularly bump into each other in the students' canteen, where several televisions were positioned on the walls. Mike, an Evertonian, remembers the scene well.

'There were tons of lads and girls from back home attending college at UMass. We'd have major parties in the student residences, or the Harp Pub down the road, an Irish bar that had live football. ESPN beamed live UEFA Champions League games every week during the competition, and the World Cups were all covered in college. Meeting all these different people was brilliant; the Americans thought I was Irish 'cos I had red hair and a scouse accent. I met lads from the southwest who couldn't believe you had to lock your car in Liverpool when you went in to pay for petrol. It was funny, though, 'cos the Yanks who preferred American sports would go bananas when the Red Sox or the New England Patriots won. They wrecked the campus, overturning cars and setting them ablaze. Riot cops would steam them and loads would get nicked.'

Massachusetts is geographically as close to the UK as anywhere in America, but it is doubtful that sports-centred hooliganism had been transplanted onto campus by British students. The north-eastern population is also the most aware of its European roots. A larger fraction than elsewhere has visited their motherlands and love to talk about it, especially the passion of European football crowds. UMass earned a reputation as the 'most violent campus in America' while I was there, due to instances of stabbing, riots and rape. Most of it was exaggerated by the media, but the riots were real. I wondered if their preoccupation with the old country might lie at the back of it, and many involved said they loved being compared to English hooligans.

Western Massachusetts was also a hotbed of Harley Davidson-riding maniacs, and I quickly formed friendships with several bikers, eager to hear their tales as we shared a drink on winter nights. My mates in Massachusetts all owned quads, chainsaws, pickups, Harley Davidsons and guns, macho appendages vital for survival on a frontier that was supposedly closed a century previous. Most of them were carpenters, plumbers, painters, electricians and sheet-rockers. Their homes and garages were heated with woodstoves, pot-bellied iron beasts that threw off a sizeable haze from the corner of the room. A day spent chopping up dead trees with a chainsaw was ended perfectly with a roaring stove, a few drinks and a moonlit ride around the woods on a quad. There's a sense of satisfaction when you grab a log and, just as you throw it into the stove, *recognise* it from earlier in the day when the chainsaw was buzzing and the snow was falling. The feeling of self-sufficiency, the intimate contest with the natural environment, provides a strength few city-dwellers can ever know.

Country ways are close in nature to survivalism, as natural conditions and extreme climates often force people to be more cautious; supposedly vital luxuries like air-conditioning are precarious and large water reserves scarce. A normal day's work can be fraught with new challenges. I first had a taste of this as a mid-80s skinny scally, when I left Manchester and went to the kibbutz. Those first weeks in Israel, drinking cold coffee with the Yemenites and pruning desert olive trees on a motorised platform, had been lonely but thrilling.

By the late 90s, I was aware that I was still at the very bottom of the totem pole, no further along than I'd been years earlier, standing with the Mexicans on street corners in Southern California. In New England my rural awareness grew, along with that strange loneliness.

*　　*　　*

In distant Moree, Johnno was shunting toward an awakening of his own:

'Doyle was waiting on the platform in Moree as the light was fading. He was with his daughter. Having never heard a broad Mancunian dialect such as mine (and being arseholed-drunk) they didn't much understand the content flowing from my mouth. The next morning, I was woken at five by someone calling softly, "Johnno, come on mate, time for work." I groggily opened my peepers, and nearly shit myself when I realised I had no idea where I was. Then I realised the silhouette in the door was Doyle. My head was pounding and my watch said 5:00 am. My expensive sunglasses were on the floor by the car where they'd fell off my melon the night before so I picked them up and plonked them on. We drove in silence to a huge paddock full of thousands of rows of small green plants. There were several tractor-type vehicles with people scurrying around them. I got that feeling in my stomach as we drove up. Like when you start a new job or when you feel something horrible is going to happen to you. They were all Aussies but they looked a bit dodgy and scruffy. We basically went down each row of cotton (of which there were fucking millions) and sprayed the weeds with spray guns attached either side of the seat. The vehicle itself was an invention of Doyle's called a row-weeder. It was four seats suspended by a hydraulic-beam on a tri-wheeled tractor with a huge tank of weed-killer mix on the back behind the motor. Having spent my life in the urban jungles of Manchester and Sydney, I wasn't too adept at spotting a weed. At mid-morning we had a 15-minute "smoko", which is the Aussie name for a tea-break. By now it was over 35 degrees.'

* * *

Wherever you go in this world there are migrants and druggies and antisocial groups. They make life more interesting. Unlike Australia, America has a belligerent image to the rest of the world, but I've made some great friends here. They just do things a little differently in the States. Sane and balanced people sometimes have eccentric tastes. Like the woman minister whose house I painted who carried a concealed gun. Her husband had organised the permit for their winters in crime-torn South Florida and he made sure she took lessons in how to use it.

On the Vineyard, I'd actually begun to believe the association of Americans with guns was largely exaggerated; the place was populated by liberals whose obsession with being European ran from sidewalk cafés to wanting all firearms banned. Out in western Massachusetts things were very different, illustrating the discontinuity between the college towns and the 'American' towns. One night I was having a few beers with Danny, a housepainting mate. Danny always wore a bandana, shades and a bushy beard with long hair, the quintessential biker look. He was into playing Frank Zappa very loud and every night of his life was a party. He was a wild one, a Yank who lived a day at a time like a cowboy. He brought out a large steel toolbox with a padlock on.

'OK, Junior, I'm gonna show you my bits and pieces,' he said, rapidly opening and closing his eyes in cartoon fashion, letting me know I was in for a treat. He opened the box and began to pull out the pistols one by one.

'Look at this fuckin' thing,' he low-growled in mock drama, awe dripping from his voice. It was a snub-nosed revolver, made by Cortes, a Brazilian manufacturer. Most interestingly to me, the Cortes had nine chambers instead of six. It was a silver .22 with a wood-plated handle.

'Nine fuckin' barrels, baby,' Danny emphasised. 'Hair trigger, too.'

Next came a large automatic, a Smith & Wesson police-issue pistol with no safety catch. '40 calibre. 15-round clips. Illegal,' he explained. 'Only cops can carry 15-rounders. Civilians are supposed to have ten-round clips, max.' He handed me the gun, and I pointed it at a few things, enjoying its weight and size. Danny was already showing me the next one.

'Get a load of this mother. The Cannon. This is from the Wild West, man. Imagine walkin' in a fuckin' saloon with this fucker and just blastin', like Wild Bill Hickock or Jesse James!'

I took this huge gun, which was a .38, and compared it to the little Cortes. They were almost twins, apart from their sizes. Danny produced several more guns from that toolbox, and then he went and brought a plastic bait-box which contained the ammo. He had all sorts of bullets, including hollow-points. The difference in size between a .22 bullet and a .38 was shocking. Somehow, the .38s were almost bigger than the .40s; the .40s were of a larger calibre but the .38s were almost as wide and much longer. No wonder he called it the Cannon.

But having all those guns around caused problems. One night at Danny's, I noticed a hole in the exterior wall of his living room. I asked him what had caused it.

'Last week, man. Fuckin' Tommy was looking at the Cannon. He thought it wasn't loaded but it was. Pulled the trigger and shot right through a bunch of us here . . .' He described a line from where I was standing to where the hole was. 'Shit, Tommy coulda killed a couple of us!' He let out a whoop and took another drink. There was also a hole right through two six-by-six vertical support beams in his coop, where we often drank and listened to music. A friend had briefly stopped by from a hunting trip in the woods out back; his 15-year-old son had accidentally discharged his rifle, again shooting through a gaggle of revellers, and the bullet had completely passed through the two beams and away through the yard.

There are other tales too numerous to mention, like the time Danny, shitfaced, fell onto the white-hot woodstove and had to be rushed to hospital. This happened not once but twice. His girlfriend left after the second time. The parties continued indefinitely, but New Englanders also amazed me with their underlying sensibleness.

Danny kept a large vegetable garden, stocked with every juicy salad component you care to name. He knew everything about the soil chemistry, water and nutrient requirements, despite dropping out of school and never reading a book in his life. He reminded me of the mystery guy from Rotherham I met in Morocco, with his baffling array of botanical know-how. I was studying soil science at a local college back then and Dan amazed me at how much he knew simply from experience. His obligatory assortment of quad-bikes, motorcycles, chainsaws and other tools were kept in several large sheds and coops, along with a pool table, a large woodstove and a stereo. He composted all his food and regularly burned bonfires, the ash from which would fertilise his vegetables. It was all part of the country scene in New England; even semiliterate nutcases were quite well-spoken and displayed a respect for formalised education completely lacking in British culture.

*   *   *

Meanwhile, in that other New England, Johnno was making the acquaintance of his new workmates:

'Some of the cotton crew weren't my sort of people. I found out eventually that most of these were heroin users. I was a little shocked about this when it came out, as they were fairly hard grafters. My sister had been out travelling to Oz the year before and worked for Doyle for one day before calling it quits, the lazy cow. I was quite keen in staying on already. This country life was a massive novelty for me. Doyle's house was a removable home that you could stick on the back of a huge semi-trailer to transport somewhere else if need be. Inside it was very nice and cosy with all the mod cons you'd expect in a city pad. Air conditioning was a vital necessity. Occasionally you'd spot a gecko jibbing about but you had to look carefully. They were almost transparent and they scared the fuck out of you in the shower, hanging on the wall a few inches from your face.

'Doyle had a few motorbikes and quads, so we'd go for a spin out into the bush, and the scenery was incredible. Everywhere was totally flat, as far as the eye could see. The odd stringbark tree and bushes here and there was about it for vegetation. The roads were all dirt roads with bitumen roads a few miles away. Moree Town was around 40 kilometers east. This was proper bush country all right, and I fucking loved it. There were so many natural hazards about that you just didn't get in Manchester or Sydney. Aside from the snakes, there were goannas jibbing about that grew pretty long in length and, if threatened, they would have a go at you with a nasty bite. Although unlikely to attack, there were these huge eagles always flying about. One day an eagle came with its wings spread fully, screeching at us in the van. It was enormous. It was unbelievably hot during the day, and the wind was literally like having a hairdryer in your face. There were around eight days in a row when it was above 45 degrees, and the adjacent dates were not much less than 40 either. I drank water, not out of choice but out of requirement. By lunch it had always turned to warm liquid with bits of dirt and the odd insect inside, no matter how tightly the lid was on. You find these things don't matter really; it was beautiful and refreshing late in the afternoon when you'd got a mouth like Gandhi's flip-flop.'

Others from Britain came to Oz and were unable to take the plunge into honest labour. Instead, they resorted to other means of earning. Mellow arrived on his third trip to the country in 2002. Typically, he had taken the long route:

'I spent a year travelling through the Americas and Australia and had a lot of daft times,' he admits. 'I taught English in Mexico City and worked as a carpenter in Guatemala. Smacking fuck out of wood, nothing skilled. I'd always wanted to go to South America so I saved and flew to Peru. I went into the Amazon and did some mad trips on planes and boats. I worked on an eco-lodge for two months. Bang in the middle of snakes and giant trees and Indian tribes. Fucking beautiful. Then I went to Brazil and ended up working in bars, transsexual gaffs and tourist beach joints. I met other Brits there, lads who just took off from the acid-house scene and ended up going barmy on the other side of the world. I nearly got nicked in Brazil and I decided to fly to Oz. When I touched down in Oz I met these people who just drummed and gigged out in the bush. I took to it like a platypus to water and became part of the tribe. Most of them had no idea about British rave but their parties were identical to it. I went to Melbourne before Sydney and I loved it. It was like Manchester; a second city with really cool cats living there. They took me to some fucking wild places out in the bush, with lights and drugs and DJs. Best part was the birds were up for it. Not just the usual British rave shite with everyone kissing and being "friends". I thought I'd finally found my Grail. They were living in the wild, some of 'em. Feral, they called it.

'I'd been to Oz a couple of times before but never found a community like this. It was a sun-baked dream. Like a childhood vision. There were hippie chicks and dazed fuck-ups roaming free. Turkeys on acid and E. The country was parched and twisted. Some of them were on the run from rich parents and some were just junkies on smack. It made America look tame as fuck. I spent many times in drumming circles, stupefied on drugs, before I came to my senses and headed to Sydney. Thank God, 'cos I was dissolving in an alternate universe.'

It's once again about frontiers. This is the be-all and end-all. Frontiers are where laws break down and worlds collide, or at least change. But deep down we're all the same. After spending 15 years in the USA I've come to learn how the prized good manners of Brits are partly a product of having little left to do. There are no vast wildernesses to conquer, no beasts to subdue. And so the Englishman turns upon himself, glassing people in pubs, knifing people at football. A careless – nay, impolite – remark results in a smack on the nose.

In America nobody seems offended by insulting words. Superficially at least; the occasional mass-shooting is a symptom of the humanity lurking amid cold apathy. Low-level violence is unacceptable, which creates an accumulation of stress; cliques and explicit selfishness exacerbate the situation. Eventually, sub-surface forces buckle under pressure and rupture with horrific consequences.

Australia is more like England. There are more punch-ups, more boozing and more swearing. But Oz is young and as such still offers a natural wildness, like the States. Johnno finishes off his bush odyssey with a combination of American-style frontierism and British-style low-level violence:

'After a few weeks of monotony I asked Doyle to drop me off at any one of three pubs in the town centre, the Royal, the Imperial or Ned Kelly's. He told me Ned Kelly's was the only boozer with a pool table, but he wasn't too keen on dropping me off there on my own. I told him not to worry. I was from north Manchester, which of course made me invincible. He shrugged his shoulders and said he'd have a few beers with me later. I approached the pub. It had swing doors like an old Western saloon. I swung them open in time to see a chair fly past my face, skimming my nose. It was like walking into an actual Western where the whole bar was brawling. I stood at the entrance, stunned, as a group of Aborigines were smacking fuck out of each other. A huge white bloke with a big red ZZ Top beard burst from nowhere into the middle, clipping a few with the back of his hand. He screamed, "You wanna fucking blue, you black cunts?" This meant he was offering them out and they all coweringly answered, "No, no." Then he said, "Drink your fucking beer." Then they all turned and looked, surprised at me with my Oasis haircut and big sideburns. He said, "Yeah? What the fuck do you want?" I stammered, "I'm just after a beer, mate." He looked at me and smiled. "Ahhhh, you're a pommie cunt. Come to the bar, mate," he said, nice as pie. I trotted past the black lads, who were glaring at me.

'I plonked myself at the bar while this mountain of a man poured me a schooner of Toohey's. A dozen sets of aboriginal eyes watched me making small-talk with Big Ned (he was actually called Ned Kelly) and it was eerie. It became a hangout for me, on the occasions I got into town away from the endless work. Doyle would ask if I needed to go to the chemist for anything and I'd just make things up. Driving back we'd neck stubbies of beer from the case as we flew along, smacking the fuck out of dopey kangaroos along the way. Stopping for a piss in the absolute pitch black, you'd see a bit of grass or Spinifex move and you'd shit yourself, knowing a snake could bite your cock-end at any moment.'

Mellow's road was slightly different. He chanced his arm around the globe, often having to vacate a country (or even a continent) in the wake of some transgression or other:

'In Brazil I was living in this little apartment complex with some English and South American lads. The South Americans could get coke dirt cheap and they made a bomb working the tourist clubs and *Carnaval*. Europeans paid fortunes for it 'cos they daren't smuggle it in themselves. The tranny bar I worked in had beautiful blokes with tits stooging at the front to pull the punters in. I started dealing to tourists, cut to fuck. A mate from England came out to visit during *Carnaval*. He was after Lacoste t-shirts made in Peru and I had a contact there. Poor fucker had never been away before but he was a Lacoste nut. Never shut up about the proper look of the crocodile on the label and how its teeth had to be a certain colour. He was getting smashed out of his brains and pissing the bed every night, he was that nervous about blowing all his dosh on these shirts and getting them home safe. He must have been planning to flog 'em back in England.

'We went out for a meal with the South Americans and got into a row with the waiters over the bill. One of the waiters threw a little pot of chilli oil right in one of the South American's eyes and it kicked off royal. It was like Spanish against Portuguese or something. Some trannies even steamed in! My mate is handy and he knocked one waiter spark out. The bloke swallowed his tongue but he was OK. I'd smashed a vase over some other cunt's head and we were suddenly wanted men. My mate fucked off minus his prized t-shirts and I did one to Oz, leaving my coke behind. I'm still nervous going back to Brazil, but I've been to Rio twice since for *Carnaval*.

'You can get around Latin America in taxis for next to nothing. Sydney's similar, but on buses. I lived in Sydney for years and never bought a car. After four months in the States I *had* to have one. You couldn't live without one anywhere outside Manhattan. Sydney's like Salford in the sun. It's sorted. Most of my English mates there have little motors to zoom about in, down to the beach or off on a little road-trip. Now I live in the middle of nowhere. I'm just happy to walk places and appreciate the life I've had. I wouldn't change it for the world, even though I miss my family and United a lot. I spent my time hanging round in neon burger bars and clubs when I was 17 years old, but nowadays I live in a country cottage and grow my own food. I brew my own beer and talk to my dog when I get lonely.'

Hmm. Might want to go a little lighter on the homebrew, Mellow, me ol' pal.

'You can go to Thailand on your own and set up all kinds of deals,' he continues. 'Lads turn up with templates and logos and ask, "Can you copy this?" and the Thais turn round and say, "How many d'you want?" I remember once, with a gang of Mancs in Nana Plaza, we ran into some cockneys. There was a bit of eyeballing between the two groups. They started giving us gyp, telling us how they knew all these people and not to fuck with them. It goes with the territory, unfortunately. You never know what to believe. Knocking fuck out of someone for nothing's a mug's game. Most of the lads are into the earner, not the knuckle. Between the Mancs, scousers and cockneys in Oz I've never seen so many Tommy Hilfiger coats, Aussie Grand Prix jackets, Ferrari hats, snide jeans, handbags and watches. It's mental. They're limited to tickets now but they were smashing the market back in the good old days.'

The addiction to labels is global now. The scallies and Perries dictated where branded designer gear would go and the grafters have sucked the whole beast dry. Whoever had the idea first to copy popular fashions started a revolution. The original mods would turn in their graves if they could see where looking good in England eventually led to. Most ironic is that those doing the graft always made sure they looked the part themselves – wearing the genuine article as much as the snides.

Carl Spiers, an ex-skinhead mod devotee says, 'You either dress up or dress down, simple as. As a mod I always dressed up. When I stopped being a mod in the mid-1980s I dressed down. Now I'm middle-aged I dress up again and strive to wear good-quality gear. And would you believe it; all the high street shops for the past few years have been selling mod-style clothes. Paul Smith, Ted Baker, Teddy Smith, the top designers were all mods in their day and that is what they style their clothes range on. You see, mod never dies. All the big names on telly, Jonathan Ross, Jack Dee, Johnny Vaughn, etc, wear the sharp Italian mod suits we wore many years ago.'

It is true that mod never dies, but the Perry boys drove them into extinction in Manchester and Liverpool. And the Perry boys abroad sold the plastic mods of the 70s and 80s an array of third-rate clobber, just as they sold it to the punks and metalheads before them. Rob W often tells me that my generation ruined everything, that we created a counterfeit Mafia similar to those in Naples and Istanbul. We took something of quality and reduced it to shit. No wonder Carl Spiers enjoyed battering Perry boys.

19

GATHERING MOSS

*Tell me and I'll forget; show me and I may remember; involve me
and I'll understand.*
– Chinese proverb

And so we find ourselves in the Now. Some of us are far away. Some
are still entrenched in the neighbourhoods of old. Social networks
like Facebook and MySpace have re-established links between old
friends and illustrated how a native sense of humour never dies.
Technology has progressed beyond TV tennis and tennis shoes; it's not
uncommon to find yourself chatting with three different people in three
different time zones with at least two of them hooked up to webcams.
Things have changed a lot since 'Mighty Real' blasted through those
reservoirs of 70s cool.

This book's contributors were mobile jigsaw pieces that
gravitated together culturally through space and time. CCR, Colin
Blaney and Rob W were tribal elders. They saw the northern-soul
Perries become the Bowie Perries become the football Perries become
the Madchester Perries. CCR brought soul, style and Manchester
City. Blaney brought graft, designer gear and United. Rob W trawled
the depths of Manchester's hippest clubs, affecting and being
affected by their evolutionary bridges. (None attended the famous
1976 Sex Pistols gig at the Lesser Free Trade Hall. I doubt they'll be
losing any sleep over that.)

Robin Peters and Mellow Yellow were to join them in time, younger
cohorts mesmerised by the living relics of the late 70s but bored enough
to get away, along with thousands of other scallies on the graft. Others
followed, like Jeff Marsh and Dominic Lavin, products of Northwest
culture and beyond. Manchester led the country into its 'baggy' phase

while Ancoats Pete and later Johnno underwent their own journeys, within football and without.

Manchester's multi-generational Perries have kept pace with the decades, from early 70s northern soul to the football-casual era and Madchester. They've seen the introduction of railings to football grounds to prevent pitch invasions and mass fighting, while steel roll-shutters have been fixed over shop windows to stop smash and grabs. They've been thwarted by iron posts later installed in front of those same stores to guard against ram-raiders. Manchester's alleyways are now protected by remote-controlled bollards to foil getaway cars. Closed-circuit TV has cast its all-seeing eye across the city (and the rest of the UK) in a bid to put an end to serious crime.

But still it continues. Still they make music and seek rare Adidas trainers. Still they laugh. As the dust settles on a post-Madcunian culturescape, a stagnant breeze blows between past and present; we are long overdue another change.

Manchester is now a recognised force in the national consciousness. Those feverish years in the late 80s and early 90s left a succession of craters through the media as distinctive as chickenpox scars: the Smiths, James, Stone Roses, Happy Mondays, Inspiral Carpets, 808 State, Northside, and so on. Television programmes like *Cracker* and *The Royle Family* paved the way for *Queer as Folk*, *Life on Mars* and *Shameless*. In truth, many of us would have been embarrassed to own a record by those bands back then; our disrespect for the media took a while to fade, and we really were too cool for school. As we've mellowed with age we've come to appreciate it all. The musicians and DJs of Madchester were just the tip of the iceberg. Our world was the real meat of the matter, but the music has stood the test of time. I listen to the Smiths today, and can't understand why I didn't sooner. But is Greater Manchester even a real place?

Wigan native Dominic Lavin insists on beginning his emails to me with an ironic 'Hail Caesar!', possibly as a result of Manc domination of his Wigan/Bolton environment. The editor of Stockport's *Proper* fanzine recently became incensed when I described his town as being within the county's boundaries in an article I wrote for *United We Stand* fanzine. Salfordians are still insistent that they not be considered Mancunian. People from Oldham often criticise townsfolk for attending Manchester City home games instead of Oldham Athletic. The internet

IAN HOUGH

has reunited but exacerbated the fault-lines dividing us. On web forums every day, Manchester's inhabitants quarrel over whether they're Mancunian, Salfordian or something else entirely. On the other hand, many prefer to live as one. It's all in the genes.

Manchester isn't an iconic city; Old Trafford and Coronation Street aside, our various landmarks aren't nationally recognised. Other cities' postcards come readily installed with Post Office Towers, Liver Buildings, Tyne Bridges and York Minsters. Manchester has been Zen-like in its search for personality – no symbols, no forms, just an intangible sense of who we are. Fabled venues like the Factory, Pips, the Hacienda, Belle Vue Zoo and Maine Road are either gone completely or utterly transformed. It was partly this lack of visual reference points that held the city back for so long. It is extremely appropriate that its image crystallised in pictures of nightclubs shut down due to gangs and drugs, or football stadiums, or rock bands; it's what the place is all about these days. Whether that's good or bad is not for me to say.

But where are they now, those pioneers and travellers who contributed to this book? In what condition did they end up? Colin Blaney, one of the true originals, has turned his hand to photography. He lives in a privatised Salford tower block from which he enjoys unobstructed views of Manchester city centre. Blaney recently said to me, 'I'll probably die before my pictures become recognised.' He spends time wandering inner-city neighbourhoods, snapping pictures of Manchester's shrinking residential stone core, which will soon be gone forever.

Carl Spiers lives in Oldham and for years published a local fanzine called *The Royton Rag*. *The Rag* upset some people, and that's the way Carl preferred it. He continues to avidly discuss the evolution of mod to skinhead to Perry to casual, not necessarily in that order. He also hosts evenings with various luminaries of the casual era and beyond.

Dominic Lavin was driving a taxi around Manchester's farthest satellite towns recently. He had much to complain about regarding the weather, the economy and life in general. In effect he took on the taxi driver's lot, including manner of conversation. But you can't keep an old seadog down; he's taking a course in petroleum geo-science and hoping to spend much more time in Thailand very soon.

John Patrick lives in Sydney, not far from Kenny Lewis. They spend their time separately drinking Toohey's New and watching Man United

303

live at daft o'clock in the morning. I spend many hours conversing with both via internet and telephone.

Robin Peters still travels the world in search of rare sportswear, especially vintage Adidas trainers and other apparel associated with the casual culture. He runs a business, selling his finds to those who seek to keep the casual spirit alive.

Rob W still lives in the Salford council house he's lived in almost his entire life. He laughs at the inadequacy of historical records, and the arseholes like me who insist on writing books about Madchester and related topics.

Mellow has spent decades travelling Australia, Thailand, Latin America, the US and Europe. He lived with a tribe of feral people in the Aussie bush. He worked clubs in Brazil and Mexico. He dealt drugs in England and Spain. These days he engages in small horticultural projects around his home and brews his own ales. He lives a long way from Manchester.

Spanish Dave lives in a Spanish prison; he was caught and convicted as part of a cigarette-distribution ring during the writing of this book.

Jeff Marsh lives back in Cardiff. From there he assails his entire contacts list with frequent emails concerning everything from books about Welsh football hooligans to campaigns to make Britain 'British' again.

Manc, Scouse and Oxford Rob lead separate lives. Rob is, of all things, a bank manager in the South of England. Manc and Scouse continue to be the scourge of the high seas. The last I heard, they were spotted in a nightclub in Panama, drinking silly cocktails and pawing the gold-clad waitresses like drunken animals.

Scotch Jock, the Killer and Bungle have been flung to the winds. Jock drives wagons in Europe. The Killer is married to an American woman and lives in Redneckland. Bungle returned to eastern England and is apparently very normal – in which case he must have changed. A lot.

Scally Jeff, Acid Steve and Geordie Ron are all still alive, by some miracle. Jeff was selling real estate in Los Angeles when I re-established contact. He wore a suit and tie and proudly beamed at the camera from his own website. He divorced his Guatemalan wife and still likes to hang out with '22-year old Peruvian hotties', to use his words. He disappeared for a while right after I contacted him. Acid Steve is married to an American woman and has a child. He runs a legitimate business and is very comfortable, despite the maimed foot and other mishaps. Geordie Ron is a merciless bastard by all accounts. He's made some serious cash and, if I were to bump into him today, I know we'd be falling about laughing in no time at all.

I didn't see Aussie Gavin for nearly seven years. Just three days prior to writing this sentence I went on a sailing trip with some workmates to Newport, Rhode Island. Newport has a big harbour and Gavin was there, living on a luxury sailboat. It was similar to when we bumped into each other in Lauderdale, after six years roaming apart, back in late '93. We all spent the night boozing in Irish pubs and reminiscing over old times.

The lads in this book have served time in prisons abroad and at home. It's par for the course. Several say it sent them up the wall. It's the madness of animals in zoos; they become *philosophers*. Each species reacts by entering psychosis in captivity. In that altered state they unravel the secret heart of their species. This book was never about prison though; I wanted to hear about their lives of freedom. It was an honour to report their thoughts.

Many others could have contributed to this book but didn't, for all kinds of reasons. Others simply had no more room for their additional stories. John from London spent time in the States, for instance. He roomed with a couple in the South and witnessed the husband pull a gun on his wife. Then he poured petrol on her and threatened her with a lighter. It was a horrifying tale and I decided to cut it out of the story.

Another guy I spoke to became a siege negotiator; he'd worked on incidents around the world, some successfully, some not. He reckoned he could talk people out of virtually anything. It was the 'virtually' I didn't like the sound of. There were others who offered memoirs of dealing drugs with the big boys on Tenerife, debt-collecting in Los Angeles, or grafting snide goods on flea markets in California and Florida. Most developed cold feet and killed their stories. I feared the book might not happen at all, but thankfully enough of it remains to actually mean something.

When *Perry Boys* was published in 2007, I returned to Manchester. Among the old friends I met was Dave-D-. We met at a pub close to my parents' house. As we entered the pub Dave turned and said, 'Last time I was in here I had a fight.' He barged past some blokes at the bar, pointing his finger in one guy's face. 'With him,' he added. At one point during our carousing, a fight broke out between lads playing cards. Dave was straight up and into the melee with a big smile on his face. I noticed he was missing half an ear and asked him how this had happened.

'Some drug dealers and us lot kicked off in Spain,' he explained. 'It was crazy. Blokes, pit-bulls, Geordies, cockneys, the works. Some fucker bit me ear off! There were some nasty fuckers over there, mate. I went to an ICF party one night. See these tables . . .' He pointed to a row of pub tables about 25 feet long. 'They had fuckin' champagne in glasses and bottles on ice, filling about that much space. Them lads really know how to throw one, I'm tellin' yer.'

Dave told me that he still follows United at home and abroad. His time had been split between England and Portugal for a while, but now he was back in Manchester 'for good'. Dave had many stories about skulduggery in Europe but he seems reluctant to officially relate them, so I won't either. I met up with mates in Manchester that I hadn't seen in 15 years. In some ways, writing *Perry Boys* brought us all together again. It described a very special moment in fashion and football history that we were all very much part of.

Most significantly I met Kezz, one of my oldest mates. That night when I knocked on his door was eerie, like we'd just been out together the night before, not 15 years earlier. Kezz held me in a powerful bear-hug, roaring, '*Alright mate!*' and we spent a few sessions that week discussing memories each had forgotten. It was great to see him again. We'd been mates since we were two little boys, a whole world ago. A few months later, back in the US, I received some terrible news; Kezz had died of a blood clot in his heart. He was 43 years old. A character known far and wide, he perfectly embodied the streamlined blend of attitude, taste and wisdom we Mancs are now famous for. I miss him like a brother and can honestly say his death has permanently changed me.

The truth is that England itself is permanently changed; the rites of passage have been amputated from the culture. English football has improved massively thanks to the formation of the Premier League, but there are costs; the current trend of foreign ownership and rising ticket prices is alienating the average fan. Lads complain about having to sit at games rather than stand. But if you were there you'd still have your memories. We've evolved from breathless kids to drunken, jaded gorillas who have seen it all. What little remains of football's excitement has failed to draw our arses to those seats.

'I don't even care about not going to football matches anymore,' Mellow told me. 'I can watch more live games on telly in Oz than they can in England. It's shit now, football. Not like it used to be. I remember when we used to go to away games in the early 80s. We were growing out of the sportswear and into the beer and drugs. All around the streets near the grounds they'd be waiting. You'd walk through the crowds in a little firm, checking out the action. Shitebags in fashions that were years behind; some would be just knobheads, clueless. You look in their eyes and know they're no one. They'd back right off in shock when you went at them. Then you see the proper boys. They'd look at you and call it on right away and it was steamers. I outgrew that when I discovered travel. Then I discovered rave and E. Then the Premier League was created and all my mates realised how shit it had become. These days I watch live football in the wee hours and get pissed on my own beer. I can't complain.'

England is the country at the heart of the British Isles, but it has no meaning today. Even the word 'England' is a weird thing. My own relationship with it has changed. Relationships do that. They are like snowballs, growing over time, but subject to the biases caused by everything that's rolled up inside. The deterioration of football's atmosphere and improvement of the game itself disoriented me to the point where I don't know if it was right or wrong to relocate permanently abroad. But I'm happy, and that's the main thing.

The past several decades have seen a cultural legacy form, rise and finally deteriorate. Thankfully a residue remains, in the form of a preoccupation with 80s casual styles. The Perry boys abroad weren't just Mancs and scousers. They came from all over Britain and organised themselves into distant troops. But none of it would have happened without the football and music to bind us all together. That footy/music/rave lineage – 'Becks 'n' hugs 'n' northern soul', you might say – is finally in the media for its original proponents to savour.

Casual is dead. From Kick to Kickers to K-Swiss, with all that dancing in between, the lifeblood has drained off. Only reconstructions remain. Standards have gone downhill, but the hunt for vintage or reissued shoes continues. Personally, I think the greatest loss is the lack of photographic and celluloid evidence of the generation that kick-started the modern attitude. All we have are blurred and often poor pictures of the Perries and grafters who were there at the outset.

It's interesting to hear from people who joined the ranks of the football firms but later left and relocated abroad. Their personal struggles, bringing that culture with them as baggage to foreign lands, are very real. Foreigners can be difficult to deal with, especially if you've usually dealt with things by hitting people. Stereotypes often come to life all around you when you choose to make another country your home.

And yes, there's some truth to the American stereotype, but it doesn't apply to all Americans. Fossil-fuelled labour-saving devices are certainly a fixation here. Yanks love their toys: lawnmowers that resemble the moon buggy from *Diamonds Are Forever*; snow-blowers for clearing driveways in winter; log-splitters to feed the hungry woodstoves. Gender roles are also hugely exaggerated; the 'little woman' is often found baking banana bread in the kitchen while hubby works on his vintage car in the garage. While British radio and TV commercials feature fresh-voiced young guys, Americans prefer gravel-voiced, middle-aged silverbacks. They're hooked on the notion that strong, determined pioneers can methodically force nature to permanently do their bidding.

When it comes to construction, Americans have a curiously nomadic attitude; virtually no permanent structure is worthy of too much attention to quality. "Oh well, I can't see it from *my* house," is a common attitude among builders upon making a mess of something. An attachment to driftwood is the other side of the coin; window-frames constructed by pilgrim great-grandfathers frequently allow frightful drafts. The quilt your great-granny made is clutched tight against the gales blowing through the house. They'd rather freeze and feel a connection to their history than install double-glazing. It's as real a need as the British quest for sunshine.

Yanks are very positive people. We could learn a lot from them. The jealousy and envy driving Britain's gutter press is relegated to lower-class society here. There are 'tabloids', but the very word infers lies and character assassination. Morons read them. Instead, normal Americans aim to improve through a loveable, gung-ho attitude that encourages those who are talented and disciplined. Anyone prepared to have a bash is welcome. But TV commercials for Viagra, hair-restoration, Prozac, sleeping meds, health insurance, lawyers, wrinkle cream, etc, are a continual avalanche. Everyone is given the chance to feel defective. It splits the population into two groups, the psycho-fit and the massively stupid and/or obese.

The American media – be it film, radio or television – has always insisted that life be portrayed as *at least as* pleasant as it actually is. The British media prefers to rubbish and soil anything outside London, and often within it. This is partly due to cultural differences; Americans observe a sensible diet while the Brits insist on lashings of fried food, cigarettes and alcohol, six-pack stomachs and enticing skylines against chain-smoking boozers and smouldering council estates. A typical American movie 'bum' could be a British film hero. It's nice to live among the cowboys that made it to the moon.

I recently spoke with Scally Jeff on the phone. We mulled over many memories, but one conversation in particular stood out; one day, while painting an Atlantic shore mansion together, Jeff was envisioning himself as an old man in the future. He said, 'I can imagine sitting my grandkids on my knee one day and saying, "Hey kids, did I ever tell you about the time I smoked crack and fucked a transsexual?" and the grandkids go, "Aww, not *that* boring story again, Granddad!" That's how much the world will have changed by then, mate!'

Jeff disappeared briefly, and then resurfaced in Colombia. He explained by email:

'Hey, sorry for not ringing you earlier, but I had to fly the coop and escape from Alcatraz – I'm in Medellin right now and it's fucking awesome. Going to be here a while. I hate winter and decided to take a hammer to the piggy bank and flee to the Promised Land rather than opt for slow suicide by the bottle. I couldn't stand watching the second hand on the clock tick by with the same excruciatingly slow rhythm as a hibernating bear's pulse. It would bring me to my knees. Colombia is unbelievable, and the women . . . let's just say I need a special tongue sling to keep it from continually tumbling out of my mouth and landing on the dirty sidewalk. See if you can get the Korean professor to whip up something in his laboratory would ya? I'd appreciate it. It's either that or they're going to have to wheel me around like Hannibal Lecter in a muzzle with a hard-on.'

Good to see the old boy hasn't learned his lesson yet. He'll probably propel himself forever onward to new adventures. For the record, I have absolutely no idea who the Korean professor is.

I spoke to CCR on the phone several times recently. CCR – an original northern-soul Perry boy – has enjoyed looking back on his personal Manchester while contributing to this book. He told me he was on his way over to New York for one more trip. In the prologue I mentioned how travel has seeped into all walks of life, particularly weddings and stag nights. Such an occasion was the reason for CCR and his cronies descending on the Big Apple once again.

'Round the ever-tightening, over-wound carousel of Manchester and Salford,' he says with customary gravity, 'something had to give. Many good boys spun off the ride and had soft landings. Many landed on their arses, wondering what the fuck they'd been at for all these years. Me, I got off easy; kept me job and subsequent career no probs. Missed out on buying property pre-boom. Missed me fortune, didn't do huge amounts of consciousness-expanding sweeties. I supported a crap team but saw the Hac in its pomp. I was in the dry bar the night White Tony took the stage Glock-handed and announced his succession to the gangland throne . . . poor misguided fool.

'Back to that night in the ring at Rotters. One poxy, cold, sleet-driven Sunday evening, and said Derbyshire no-mark was handing me my arse in front of a paying audience. Still, I met me future wife after that show, in the Sawyer's Arms. She was working as a waitress in a cocktail bar . . . etc. Nearly a 20-stretch later she finally coaxes me down the aisle. Or down the path, as it turned out. The path was in Central Park, New York. No record buying, no gold smuggling, no fisticuffs with characters in pimpy New York clubs.

'Managed to have a good time nonetheless.'

* * *

I too have left the bachelor herd and joined the rest. Kezz is dead and it has hurt me irreparably. I'll never be the same. There's a skyscraper standing above Manchester city centre now. It looks like the mine lift-housing my dad once pointed out to me. The city has taken its 'factory' image very seriously.

Our baby is born now. My wife Kim has given birth to our daughter, conceived by candlelight during a power outage – caused not by industrial action in Britain, but by a tropical storm raging up the East

Coast of America. We have a wood stove with a glass front. I harvest trees for fuel with a chainsaw. Fortunately, there's a million acres of forest right behind our house and we have a gate opening onto it. I love to sit in front of the fire and watch the flames dance. Just like I did in Salford all those many years ago. The questions continue to surface from the bizarre clockwork of my mind.

Some things never change.